NATIONAL HUMAN RIGHTS ACTION PLANNING

National Human Rights Action Planning

AZADEH CHALABI

OXFORD
UNIVERSITY PRESS

OXFORD
UNIVERSITY PRESS

Great Clarendon Street, Oxford, OX2 6DP,
United Kingdom

Oxford University Press is a department of the University of Oxford.
It furthers the University's objective of excellence in research, scholarship,
and education by publishing worldwide. Oxford is a registered trade mark of
Oxford University Press in the UK and in certain other countries

First Edition published in 2018

Published in the United States of America by Oxford University Press
198 Madison Avenue, New York, NY 10016, United States of America

British Library Cataloguing in Publication Data
Data available

Library of Congress Control Number: 2018942241

ISBN 978–0–19–882284–4

To my father who taught me to dare to think independently

Preface

In an increasingly complex and interconnected world, with ever increasing global problems like environmental crisis, global poverty, growing inequality, modern slavery, terrorism, and different forms of violent conflicts, it has become more important than ever to recognize the universal rights of every human being. Unless human rights are respected, global security and even human survival would be at serious risk over the long term. And, in concert with the central postulate of the human rights-based approach to development, if human rights are realized, they can serve as means and ends of human well-being. Yet, despite all this, the human rights approach is faced with two sets of challenges which are causally interconnected: (1) monopoly in hard powers and (2) the lack of free flow of information, political indoctrination, and the centralization of control of collective sentiments, all as soft powers.

At the concrete level, monopoly in hard powers, political and economic, in any guise, poses an extremely dangerous threat to the realization of human rights. It can also considerably increase the likelihood of corruption that diverts resources that should be dedicated to implementing human rights.

At the conceptual level, soft power in four main guises can be a significant impediment to the realization of human rights. That is the human rights approach is seriously threatened by a quadrangle of 'particularism', 'populism', 'strong universalism', and 'strong relativism'. One side of this quadrangle, particularism, categorizes human beings based on one (or more) selected difference(s) (gender, ethnicity, colour, religion, political opinion, or other opinion, nationality, etc) and prescribes different codes of conduct for different 'social categories'. The other side of this quadrangle, populism, which has some overlaps with particularism and seems to be on the rise in different forms in different parts of the world, expresses the desire for the exclusionary negation of any difference, except one difference: between 'us' and the 'enemy'. Populism denies the pluralistic nature of society—people are treated as a unified, homogeneous body which has a common will and a single interest. Particularism and populism both have a great tendency to activate ethnocentrism, nativism, xenophobia, racism, and national chauvinism. The third side of this quadrangle, strong universalism (radical egalitarianism), places a veil over distinctions that do exist. Unlike populism, strong universalism is always of universal rather than local appeal. Although the idea behind strong universalism is to erode discrimination of any kind, in effect, it ignores differences and fails to treat different groups in a genuinely equal way. By contrast, the last side of this quadrangle, strong relativism, goes too far in the other direction. It juxtaposes different views even if they are against human rights. This side of the quadrangle can significantly weaken the ontological status of the objectivity of human rights rooted in basic human needs which are common to all human beings.

Whereas particularism and populism and even to some extent strong universalism in one way or another produce antagonistic social relationships (contradictoriness), which can result in a segmental society, and strong relativism generates agonism (contrariness) through juxtaposition of every difference in their own right and co-existence of oppositions, the human rights approach which is based on unity through diversity produces synergism (complementariness) through composition made up by all differences. As discussed in the opening chapters of this book, the human rights approach reconciles a moderate relativism with moderate universalism. It encompasses not only a set of ontologically universal values rooted in basic human needs which are desired universally at all times, but also individual and cultural differences which are bound to place, time, and circumstances. What has to be highlighted here is the fact that the idea of human rights is not Western or Eastern, but rather it is an evolutionary account which does not refute individual and cultural differences. Ontologically speaking, human beings have the same basic needs which exist in the external world independently of the knowing subject. Epistemologically, our knowledge of human needs and their corresponding rights has evolved and improved over time. There is often a broad range of items (objects or processes) to fulfil basic needs. This is where individual differences and cultural differences in the form of human interests come in. Human interests for the fulfilment of basic needs are dependent on socio-cultural context but it makes no difference to the universality of basic human rights.

Hence, in such a complex world entrenched with severe problems, it has never been so important to give effect to the human rights approach in practice. There seems to be an urgent need in advancing effective human rights action plans at different levels, from national to regional and international, for implementing human rights. However, very little work has been done on human rights action planning and it is perhaps not surprising that similar problems have crept into it as well. The model of planning predominant in international human rights law and thereby adopted by most states that have launched such plans is more like a traditional planning which is state-centric and top-down. Traditional planning, as a theory-neutral model, is like an empty box which confers power upon the states to fill it up with their own political ideologies ranging from fascism and populism to neo-liberalism. This model of planning allows the states latitude in manoeuvring for window dressing rather than the realization of human rights as set forth in international human rights law.

The main objective of this book is twofold: one, to identify various problems of human rights action planning at the theoretical, doctrinal, empirical, and practical levels, and two, to develop possible response strategies for the identified problems. As such, the present work provides one of the most comprehensive studies of human rights planning to date.

At the theoretical level, I have endeavoured to advance a novel general theory of human rights planning including four sub-theories (contextual theory, substantive theory, procedural theory, and analytical theory). This offers an alternative to the traditional state-centric model of planning which is still predominant in international human rights law. At the doctrinal level, by conducting a textual analysis of all the nine core human rights conventions, General Comments, reports, and Concluding Observations, I have striven to reveal the scope and nature of the obligation of the states to adopt a plan of action for realizing human rights and to consider how to ensure that states are in compliance with this obligation. At the empirical level, a comprehensive cross-case analysis of national human rights action plans of fifty-three countries was conducted for the first time exploring the major problems of these plans in different phases of planning and uncovering the underlying causes of these problems. At the practical level, both national and supra-national human rights governance systems are examined. At the supra-national level, a networked model of global human rights governance is suggested as a practical response strategy against the extant global governance system which is fragmented and hardly works as an integrated system. At the national level, after suggesting the establishment of a nationwide network for implementing human rights, the essential parts of human rights action planning are probed in the four phases of planning, putting forward some methodological techniques for each phase.

My aim in this book has been to speak not only to a circle of academics in the areas of law, human rights, social policy, political science, international relations, political philosophy, legal philosophy, development studies, planning studies, socio-legal studies, but also to governments, human rights practitioners, NGOs, national human rights institutions (commissions), the United Nations Development Programme (UNDP), and the United Nations human rights bodies (in particular the Office of the High Commissioner for Human Rights, the UN Working Group on Business and Human Rights, the UN Women, the UN human rights treaty committees, the UN Resident Coordinators, and the UN Country Teams).

I have incurred many debts of gratitude in the course of working on this book. Many people have offered very helpful advice or have posed insightful questions during my writing of this book. I wish to extend warm thanks to Professor William Talbott (University of Washington, Department of Philosophy) and Professor Colm O'Cinneide (University College London, Faculty of Laws) who have supplied extremely helpful comments. I owe a deep debt of gratitude to Bill Barker, the author of the UN Handbook on National Human Rights Action Plans, who generously shared his invaluable experience and for his helpful comments and encouragement.

I am especially indebted to Professor Mario Bunge (Emeritus Professor at Department of Philosophy, McGill University) for his support and his encouraging comments on the theoretical part of this book but I am even more obliged to him for the inspiration supplied by his own works as a scientist and philosopher.

I am extremely grateful to University College London (UCL), Faculty of Laws, and Ulster University, School of Law and the Transitional Justice Institute (TJI) for their generous support throughout the period of my work on this book. I owe much to Professor Alison Diduck (UCL, Faculty of Laws) and Dr Nigel Balmer (UCL, Faculty of Laws) who have won my heartfelt gratitude for their supportiveness. I am also very much thankful to Professor Rory O'Connell (Ulster University, Transitional Justice Institute) for his valuable comments and generous support.

And, my heartiest thanks, as ever, goes to my father, Massoud Chalabi, to whom this manuscript is dedicated. In his role as a Professor of Sociology, he has commented extensively and invaluably on this book as its chapters have materialized, but I am even more indebted to him for his unremitting encouragement and constant support. I am really in deficit of words to thank him enough.

Finally, I am hugely indebted to my editor, Anne-Marie Forker, at Oxford University Press, and to the anonymous readers whose helpful comments prompted numerous salutary amplifications and modifications. I am very grateful as well to Merel Alstein, Emma Endean-Mills, Kimberly Marsh, Jack McNichol, and Arokia Anthuvan Rani for handling the production of the book.

Azadeh Chalabi
Belfast, United Kingdom
January 2018

Table of Contents

Detailed Table of Contents

PART II. DOCTRINAL PERSPECTIVES

PART III. EMPIRICAL PERSPECTIVES

List of Abbreviations

CAT	Convention against Torture and Other Cruel, Inhuman, or Degrading Treatment or Punishment
CCA	Common Country Assessment
CEDAW	Convention on the Elimination of All Forms of Discrimination against Women
CRC	Convention on the Rights of the Child
CRPD	Convention on the Rights of Persons with Disabilities
GAAA	Global Alliance of Aid Agencies
GAHRA	Global Academic Human Rights Alliance
GANGO	Global Alliance of Non-Governmental Organizations
GANHRI	Global Alliance of National Human Rights Institutions
GARHRS	Global Alliance of Regional Human Rights Systems
GAUNHRB	Global Alliance of United Nations Human Rights Bodies
ICCPR	International Covenant on Civil and Political Rights
ICERD	International Convention on the Elimination of All Forms of Racial Discrimination
ICESCR	International Covenant on Economic, Social, and Cultural Rights
ICPPED	International Convention for the Protection of All Persons from Enforced Disappearance
ICRMW	International Convention on the Protection of the Rights of All Migrant Workers and Members of Their Families
IHRAP	International Human Rights Action Plan
NAP-BHR	National Action Plan on Business and Human Rights
NAP-WPS	National Action Plan on Women, Peace, and Security
NHRAP	National Human Rights Action Plan
NHRI	National Human Rights Institution
OHCHR	Office of the High Commissioner for Human Rights
OTAAM	Obligation to Take All Appropriate Measures
RHRAP	Regional Human Rights Action Plan
UNCT	United Nations Country Team
UNDAF	United Nations Development Assistance Framework
UNDG-HRWG	United Nations Development Group's Human Rights Working Group
UNDP	United Nations Development Programme
UPR	Universal Periodic Review

Introduction

The central concern of the human rights approach is to cross over from the realm of rhetoric to the realm of reality. Despite the spectacular development of international human rights instruments, there is as yet no consensus on how to put them into practice in a coherent and comprehensive way. There is indeed an urgent need for a more proactive and systemic move than merely enacting bills of rights and offering judicial remedies. This demands effective human rights action planning at different levels from the national to regional and international.

This book deals with human rights action planning, as a largely under-researched area, from theoretical, doctrinal, empirical, and practical perspectives in order to put forward a new account of such planning.

The idea of adopting a national action plan for implementing human rights dates back to Article 14 of the 1966 International Covenant on Economic, Social, and Cultural Rights (ICESCR), the right to education. The Vienna Declaration and Programme of Action adopted at the World Conference on Human Rights in 1993 also recommended each state to develop a National Human Rights Action Plan (NHRAP) for implementing human rights in general. There are likewise other human rights-related action plans, in particular the National Action Plan on Business and Human Rights (NAP-BHR) translating the UN Guiding Principles on Business and Human Rights into practice, and the National Action Plan on Women, Peace, and Security (NAP-WPS) adopted by the states to implement their commitments to the Women, Peace, and Security agenda.

After such a long time and despite a growing number of such plans, surprisingly little has been written on these plans and, thus, many aspects of human rights planning—theoretical, doctrinal, empirical, and practical—remain remarkably unknown.

At the theoretical level, it is largely unclear what type of change these plans can bring about in society and how. What is the most suitable societal context through which human rights planning can work? What is the role of each sub-system of society—economy, polity, culture, community—in providing an appropriate societal context for developing and implementing an effective NHRAP? How to inform the content and process of human rights planning? How to analyse rights in different phases of planning?

At the doctrinal level, the key question to be addressed is whether states are obliged, under international human rights law, to adopt an action plan for implementing human rights, and if so, what is the nature and the scope of this obligation, and what is needed to be met in order to ensure state compliance with this obligation?

Furthermore, it still remains unclear how to determine the degree of appropriateness of each measure taken by the states in their action plans.

At the empirical level, a number of significant questions are still unanswered: What are the main problems in the way of an effective NHRAP in different phases of planning? What are the root causes of these problems? How effective has the implementation of these plans been for realizing human rights? What are the failures and successes of current plans in practice?

At the practical level, the critical question arises as to what is the most suitable model of global governance for implementing human rights? Do we need to adopt an international or regional human rights action plan for effective global human rights governance? Moreover, there does not seem to be any objective and generally accepted set of criteria for assessing the merits and flaws of these plans. What are the integral parts of an effective human rights action plan in practice? What types of accountability mechanisms can be used in different phases of planning? How to cope with 'complex situations' when different factors external to the plan and not often under its control negatively influence its performance? How to enhance a plan's sustainability over time through a change of government?

To address these questions, this book is structured in four parts. Part I, 'Theoretical Perspectives', advances a novel general theory of human rights planning which contains four sub-theories:

1. Contextual sub-theory
2. Substantive sub-theory
3. Procedural sub-theory
4. Analytical sub-theory

The central thrust of this chapter is to proceed with proposing a new contextual sub-theory of human rights planning through which the key characteristics of the four sub-systems of society—polity, economy, culture, and community—and their impacts on the effectiveness of human rights planning are explored. Chapter 2 is dedicated to the other three sub-theories of human rights planning. Adopting a human rights-based approach to development, it first proposes the substantive and procedural sub-theories of human rights planning. Whereas the substantive theory of human rights planning provides the knowledge base to inform the content of planning, procedural theory offers procedural principles for the formation, implementation, and assessment of planning. The last section of Chapter 2 builds up a new analytical theory of human rights planning through positive critique of the three major theories of rights, namely the interest theory, the needs-based approach, and the capability approach. This analytical theory performs both heuristic and regulative roles for human rights planning. It can be a useful analytical device in diagnosing the achievements and shortcomings of human rights planning for different social categories.

Part II, 'Doctrinal Perspectives', is structured in two chapters. Chapter 3 presents the results of a textual analysis of all the nine core human rights conventions, General Comments, reports, and Concluding Observations revealing the scope and nature of the obligation of the states to adopt a plan of action for implementing human rights.

Chapter 4 is concerned with the state's compliance with the obligation to adopt a national human rights action plan while addressing two sets of questions. The first section of Chapter 4 addresses the question as to whether states are expected to adopt separate rights-specific action plans or just one global action plan covering all the rights (and rights-related topics) at once. By adopting a mixed methods approach, including a qualitative textual analysis, a quantitative content analysis, and a fuzzy-set method, the second section of this chapter attempts to clarify the obligation to take all appropriate measures (OTAAM) from which the obligation to adopt a national human rights action plan is derived. It seeks to address the questions as to what 'measure' and 'appropriateness' mean in international human rights law? How to determine the degree of appropriateness of each measure taken by the state?

Part III, 'Empirical Perspectives', contains only one chapter, Chapter 5, which presents the results of a cross-case analysis of national human rights action plans of fifty-three countries. Adopting a purposive sampling technique, these countries are selected on the basis of four main criteria, namely human rights record, geographical diversity, political regimes, and cultural diversity. This cross-case study follows two objectives. The first objective of this chapter is to unearth significant problems in the 'pre-phase' and the four phases of planning, namely 'preparatory phase', 'development phase', 'implementation phase', and 'assessment phase'. These problems are significantly detrimental to the effective implementation of human rights and their identification will substantially help generate response strategies. These are best addressed by attempting to mitigate their root causes as opposed to only correcting the immediately obvious symptoms. This brings us to the chapter's second objective, which is to explore the underlying causes of these problems.

Part IV, 'Practical Perspectives', consists of two chapters: Chapter 6 and Chapter 7. Chapter 6 examines global human rights governance architecture as it currently stands putting forward a networked model of global human rights governance as an alternative. The first section of this chapter examines the 'five-gap problem' in the UN human rights system which can have serious practical implications at the local, national, regional, and international levels. The second section explores a networked model of governance as a practical response strategy to narrow the gaps while enhancing the integration of the international human rights 'system'. This chapter also probes the practical benefits of adopting an 'International Human Rights Action Plan' (IHRAP) as a basic requisite for integrated and effective co-operation and co-ordination among various human rights related actors in a global-wide network.

Chapter 7 has a more practical orientation focusing on the four phases of national human rights action planning in practice. In the preparatory phase, it suggests the idea of establishing a national network of different stakeholders for implementing human rights and discusses the five key elements of a comprehensive baseline study before proceeding with the eleven elements of an effective action plan in the development phase. In the implementation phase, Chapter 7 addresses the questions as to how to cope with 'complex situations' when different factors external to the plan and not often under its control negatively influence its performance, and how to enhance a plan's sustainability over time. This chapter ends with a discussion of six types of accountability mechanism and a seven-feature model of assessment along with some suggestions on methodological techniques for planning.

PART I

THEORETICAL PERSPECTIVES

1

Towards a General Theory of Human Rights Planning

Part I

1. Introduction

Planning is a linkage between knowledge and action and needs to be grounded in theory. This perhaps reminds you of the line which has been arguably attributed to Kant: '[T]heory without practice is empty and practice without theory is blind.'

The current literature of planning theory is very untidy. Some have adopted a technical understanding of planning which only focuses on an analytical theory in a very broad sense such as systems theory, while neglecting the substantive and procedural elements of planning. Some other planning theories just deal with the form and substance of planning, ignoring the fact that planning does not work in a vacuum; it is shaped and worked in an economic, political, cultural, and social environment. To overcome these shortcomings, we need to develop a general theory of human rights planning, which includes four 'sub-theories':

1. Contextual sub-theory
2. Substantive sub-theory
3. Procedural sub-theory
4. Analytical sub-theory

Each of these sub-theories (hereinafter theory) has its own merits for human rights planning and cannot be traded off. A contextual theory of human rights planning explores the societal context through which planning can work. It is concerned with the general characteristics of the state, market, community, and culture as the underlying conditions of the success of planning in practice. Whereas a substantive theory of human rights planning provides the knowledge base to inform what the content of planning should be, a procedural theory of human rights planning, as its name indicates, is about procedural principles for the formation, implementation, and assessment of planning. An analytical theory of human rights planning provides a heuristic device for the analysis of rights in different phases of planning.

Note that a general theory is necessary but insufficient for human rights planning in a given society. To complement a general theory requires advancing a special theory of planning which includes spatio-temporal factors. Whereas a general theory of planning acts as a frame of reference, special theory is context-dependent and consequently is not and cannot be our concern here.[1] I will naturally concentrate my effort to develop a general theory of human rights planning through positive critique of the major relevant theories. This chapter is dedicated to the contextual theory and the next one to the substantive, procedural, and analytical theories of human rights planning.

The present chapter will first quickly review different theories of planning, and then examine the major characteristics of the four sub-systems of society—polity, economy, culture, and community—and their impacts on the effectiveness of human rights planning.

2. An Overview of Planning Theories

The planning theory literature has been widely recognized as an unstructured and cluttered landscape of ideas and theories that makes writing about planning difficult.[2] In what follows below, I will quickly review the major theories of planning and elucidate their weaknesses.

I start with the 'synoptic' or 'rational' planning theory which I would rather call instrumental planning. This state-centric theory, as the dominant theory up until the 1980s or so, posits that planning should be conceived as a technical activity of finding the best means for the 'pre-determined' ends. It is based on a nominalist concept of society which entails no substantive theory and only involves an analytical theory as a heuristic tool, such as system analysis and game theory, for finding the best means for the ends. Planners as technocrats are supposed to merely focus on procedures (the means) while politicians and others set the ends in advance.[3] This is also based on the assumption that planners 'know more about the situations on which they advise than do their clients'[4]—what can and indeed did lead to a paternalistic view of 'them' (the public) and 'us' (the planners).[5]

This traditional concept of planning was attacked by, among others, Sandercock, for being anti-democratic, race- and gender-blind, and culturally homogenizing.[6] Thomas, Paris, and Reade, among others, accused synoptic planning of describing

[1] To avoid confusion, I need to emphasize that here 'context' or 'societal context' has been employed in two senses. Where I discuss contextual theory of planning as part of a general theory, it is used at the high level of abstraction, free from any spatio-temporal factor. Where it refers to special theories of planning at the lower level of abstract, it is used as what is bounded by spatio-temporal factors and stands at the heart of a special theory of planning. Hereinafter, I name the former 'general context' and the latter 'spatio-temporal context'.

[2] Philip Allmendinger, *Planning Theory* (2nd edn, Palgrave Macmillan 2009) at 33.

[3] Azadeh Chalabi, 'The Problem-Oriented Approach to Improving National Human Rights Action Plans' (2015) 7(2) Journal of Human Rights Practice 272–98, 1 July.

[4] George F Chadwick, *A Systems View of Planning: Towards a Theory of the Urban and Regional Planning Process* (1st edn, Pergamon Press 1971) at 121.

[5] Allmendinger, note 2.

[6] Leonie Sandercock, *Towards Cosmopolis: Planning for Multicultural Cities* (1st edn, Wiley and Sons 1998) at 4.

planning as apolitical and technical while in reality it was primarily used to serve the interests of those who were in power.[7] As Philip Allmendinger argues, consequently 'the various "problems" planning set out to address were either untouched (eg, poverty and homelessness), exacerbated (eg, economic inequality) or added to by some of the solutions themselves to create new problems'.[8]

In reaction to the technocrat view of traditional planning, the critical theory of planning was developed out of Marxism. This sought to deal with capitalism and promote the idea of Marxist understanding of planning, through a central system of planning. For many years, the concept of planning was conflated with the concept of central planning used in the former Soviet Union where a life plan was imposed upon people from the top down and notably limited human freedom. This has naturally led to a general mistrust of the very nature of planning, especially any types of national planning. This mistrust was to the extent that some liberals such as Hayek strongly disagree with all kinds of social planning, describing planning as 'the road to serfdom'.[9]

The fact of the matter however is that the central planning of the former Soviet Union has nothing to do with planning per se—a point echoed by Neurath's response to Hayek that planning is 'orchestration of ways of living'.[10] As Bunge aptly says:

> Just as reflex and impulsive action are typically animal, so planned action, particularly when the plan is rational and long-sighted, is distinctively human . . . It is not just that plans are necessary to orient individual and collective action in the contemporary world. Good planning is the road to freedom from want as well as to freedom to become what one wants without trampling on the rights of others. Slaves need not plan: their masters plan their entire lives for them. Nor do derelicts: they live, or rather die slowly, from day to day. But everyone else and every social organization needs some plan of action. Improvidence is imprudent for leaving one's life, or that of one's organization, at the mercy of others. And it is morally objectionable as well for involving the neglect of duties and the relinquishing of right.[11]

Liberalism by nature is often against any central planning to the extent that it is sometimes regarded as anti-macro planning. A micro model of planning which is often placed within the boundaries of liberalism is known as 'incremental theory' which aims at making small changes from existing policies. This micro model of planning was elaborated by Charles Lindblom who describes it as 'partisan mutual adjustment' or 'disjointed incrementalism'.[12] He stresses that planners cannot and should not 'think big'. Central to his approach is the argument that 'there is no great

[7] Michael J Thomas, 'The Procedural Planning Theory of A. Faludi' in C Paris (ed), *Critical Readings in Planning Theory* (1st edn, Pergamon Press 1982); Eric Reade, *British Town and Country Planning* (Open University Press 1987); Chris Paris, 'Introduction' in C Paris (ed), *Critical Readings in Planning Theory* (Pergamon Press 1982) 13–27.

[8] Allmendinger, *Planning Theory*, note 2, at 31.

[9] Friedrich Hayek, *The Road to Serfdom* (1st edn, George Routledge & Sons 1944).

[10] Otto Neurath, 'Alternatives to Market Competition: Review of F Hayek, The Road to Serfdom' (1945) The London Quarterly of World Affairs 121–22, at 121.

[11] Mario Bunge, *Treatise on Basic Philosophy—Ethics: The Good and The Right* (1st edn, Springer 1989) at 341–43.

[12] Charles E Lindblom, 'The science of "muddling through"' (1959) 19 Public Administration Review 79–88; Charles E Lindblom, *The Intelligence of Democracy* (1st edn, Free Press 1965).

goal or vision, as much as a focus on day-to-day issues and problems'.[13] That is, ends and means are not formulated, so decision makers may not work out means to fulfil socially desirable goals. The methods employed here are only based on 'trial and error' and small-scale strategies to deal with but not necessarily to solve problems.[14]

There is another group of micro-planning theories which are often labelled under the umbrella of pragmatic planning. These include, among others, Friedmann's transactive planning,[15] Meyerson's 'middle range planning',[16] Davidoff's 'advocacy planning',[17] and Grabow and Heskin's radical planning.[18] Pragmatic models of planning stress the priority of experience and practicality over theory. For instance, transactive planning focuses on face-to-face contact with the people affected by decisions and on interpersonal dialogue in which ideas are validated through action.[19]

These theories which are merely focused on action at the micro-level may only be suitable for very small and short-term projects. It is easy enough to see that they are not adaptable to varying types of problems, social settings, and scales of action. All these theories are unable to trace long term and indirect policy consequences. It is safe to say that at least they are not suitable for human rights planning. Why? Considering the fact that basic human rights, civil and political rights, as well as economic, social, and cultural rights, are universal and inter-related and that their realization is mostly progressive, it would be impossible to move forward only by advancing micro planning. Developing a National Human Rights Action Plan (NHRAP) helps ensure that nothing falls between the cracks. Critics of macro planning have also failed to address the questions like how it would be possible to mobilize a wide range of people and organizations as well as various local, domestic, and possibly international resources in support of human rights activities only by micro level plans? How to raise public awareness of human rights issues or prioritize resources for implementing human rights only through micro planning? How to strengthen existing institutions involved in protecting human rights at different levels? And the critical point is that a multi-level, multi-agent planning for implementing human rights, which will be discussed and elaborated in the next chapters, can and indeed does protect and promote individual freedom.

[13] Allmendinger, *Planning Theory*, note 2, at 141–42.

[14] Anirban Pal, *Planning from the Bottom Up: Democratic Decentralization in Action* (1st edn, IOS Press BV 2008).

[15] John Friedmann, *Retracking America: A Theory of Transactive Planning* (1st edn, Anchor Press 1973); see John Friedmann and Margo Huxley, 'Transactive Planning and Life Space' (1985) 3(3) Urban Policy and Research.

[16] Martin Meyerson, 'Building the Middle-Range Bridge for Comprehensive Planning' (1956) 22(2) Journal of the American Institute of Planners 58.

[17] Paul Davidoff, 'Advocacy and Pluralism in Planning' (1965) 31(4) Journal of the American Institute of Planners 331–38.

[18] Stephen Grabow and Allan Heskin, 'Foundations for a Radical Concept of Planning' (1973) 39(2) Journal of the American Institute of Planners 106–14; See also, Charles J Hoch, 'Pragmatism, Planning, and Power' (1984) 4(2) Journal of Planning Education and Research 86–95.

[19] John Friedmann, *Empowerment: The Politics of Alternative Development* (1st edn, Blackwell 1992); John Friedmann, *Planning in the Public Domain: From Knowledge to Action* (1st edn, Princeton University Press 1987); John Friedmann, 'Planning Cultures in Transition' in B Sanyal (ed), *Comparative Planning Cultures* (1st edn, Routledge 2005).

With the rise of postmodernism new modes of criticism against liberal and technocratic models of planning were raised. They criticize planning as being based on positivist science, gender and race-neutral, etc. Some proponents of postmodernism demand for a more heterogeneous planning approach albeit in a very vague way.[20] Postmodernist theory of planning has been widely criticized as being anti-science, logically inconsistent, vague, and theoretically-baseless. They are against reality as it stands independently of our mind and seek to replace reality with subjective and non-commensurable social-linguistic constructs.[21] As Philip Allmendinger mentions, it is not clear 'what postmodernist planning is or should be'.[22] There is a logical contradiction in postmodernist propositions as it denies the basis for knowing anything as reality except itself. While planning requires a frame of reference against which a plan can be developed, monitored, and evaluated, the postmodernist approach contests any collectively-agreed framework. There would be then no frame of reference upon which planning can be based.

Having briefly discussed different theories of planning, a critical common problem with these theories is that most of them, in one way or another, suffer from reductionism. They are either state-centric, market-led, or culture-oriented. In terms of their social ontological assumption, these approaches are either holist or atomist, overlooking the importance of a mutual causal relationship between the whole and its parts. The next section is an attempt to go beyond them, putting forward a novel contextual theory of human rights planning as an alternative.

3. Contextual Theory of Human Rights Planning

Each of the planning theories, implicitly or explicitly, draws upon a conception of society, as an often hidden ontological assumption. These theories are either close to holism, such as those top-down approaches which are focused more on structuring forces upon individuals, eg structuralism or Marxism, or close to atomism (nominalism) such as interpretive understandings of planning, eg transactive planning. The contextual theory of human rights planning suggested here is based on 'systemism'[23]

[20] Ed Soja, 'Planning in/for Postmodernity' in G Benko and U Strohmayer (eds), *Space and Social Theory: Interpreting Modernity and Postmodernity* (1st edn, Wiley 1997).

[21] Sandercock, *Towards Cosmopolis: Planning for Multicultural Cities*, note 6.

[22] Allmendinger, *Planning Theory*, note 2, at 180–81.

[23] The systems thinking, as a meta-disciplinary approach, is a method of thinking that can be employed in any kind of problem within any discipline (see eg Azadeh Chalabi, 'Law as A System of Rights: A Critical Perspectives' (2013) 15(2) Human Rights Review 117–38; Peter Checkland, *Systems Thinking, Systems Practice* (1st edn, John Wiley & Sons 1994)). Systems thinking has improved dramatically over time. There are different approaches to systems thinking such as 'critical systems heuristics' (CSH) and 'soft systems methodology' (SSM) (see Michael Jackson, *Systems Thinking: Creative Holism for Managers* (1st edn, John Wiley & Sons 2003); Peter Checkland and John Poulter, 'Soft systems methodology' in M Reynolds and S Holwell (eds), *Systems Approaches to Managing Change: A Practical Guide* (1st edn, Springer 2010)). Traditionally, however, in planning literature, systems thinking has been conceived as a value-neutral technique used by technocrat planners to evaluate means against ends from the top-down; what was used in central planning in the Soviet Union (see eg Barclay M Hudson, Thomas D Galloway, and Jerome L Kaufman, 'Comparison of Current Planning Theories: Counterparts and Contradictions' (1979) 45(4) Journal of the American Planning Association). Moreover, as Bunge aptly

as a basic ontological assumption, and as an alternative to both nominalism and holism. Note that systemism is not to replace nominalism or holism, but instead to combine the advantages of both focusing on the whole and their interacting components at once.[24] A systemic planning is just as comprehensive as holism, but unlike that, it invites us to analyse wholes into their constituent components and the relationships among them.[25] It is therefore top-down and bottom-up.

On this view, society as a system consists of four major subsystems—polity, economy, community, and culture—each of which performs a separate function. Every social planning, in particular human rights planning, is influenced by the type of relationship among the sub-systems, the most important of which are one-sided dominance and relative autonomy.

In the dominance form of relationship, the inner logic of the dominant system is imposed, more or less, on other systems of society. While economy, polity, community, and culture all have their own role to play and should receive balanced attention in planning, in the dominant form of relation, some far outweigh the others. It means that the dominant system(s) imposes its own steering mechanism over others. This dominant sub-systemic disposition can render planning biased and unbalanced. An unbalanced planning has a tendency to underestimate the role and logic of other systems in favour of the dominant one.

Unlike the dominant form, in the relative autonomy form of relationship, neither of the sub-systems has any dominance over the other but instead they complement each other. The relative autonomy of sub-systems can provide a suitable context for planning to utilize simultaneously major steering mechanisms and products of the four sub-systems of society. Furthermore, such well-balanced context can be helpful for planning to be immune to being totally dependent on a particular sub-system. Having said that, relative autonomy is a matter of degree.

Hence, the critical question arises as to what is the role of each sub-system—economy, polity, culture, community—in providing an appropriate societal context for developing and implementing an effective NHRAP? And what role can civil society, as a mediated civil sphere between these four sub-systems, play in human rights planning? The following seeks to address these questions with respect to each of the four sub-systems and civil society respectively.

explains, a form of 'systems theory that became popular in the 1970s was another name for old holism and got discredited because it stressed stasis at the expense of change and claimed to solve all particular problems without empirical research or serious theorizing' (Mario Bunge, 'How Does It Work?: The Search for Explanatory Mechanisms' (2004) 34 Philosophy of the Social Sciences 182, 190–91). All this has caused mistrust to systems thinking among planners and human rights practitioners today. To avoid any confusion, following Mario Bunge, I employ the expression 'systemic approach' or 'systemism' instead of 'systems theory' or 'systems thinking'. Systemism, as employed here, is a social ontological assumption upon which our contextual theory of human rights planning is based.

[24] Mario Bunge, 'A Systems Concept of Society: Beyond Individualism and Holism' (1979) 10 Theory and Decision 13–30; Mario Bunge, 'Treatise on Basic Philosophy' Vol 4, *A World of Systems* (1st edn, Springer 1979); Piotr Sztompka, *Sociological Dilemmas: Toward a Dialectic Paradigm* (1st edn, Academic Press 1979).

[25] Bunge, 'How Does It Work?: The Search for Explanatory Mechanisms', note 23, 190–91.

Before proceeding further, I need to emphasize that there is a circular causality between realizing human rights and contextual development. It means the relationship between these two is not based on a sequential logic, that is, contextual development and institutional changes first and the realization of human rights through planning later. Rather, it calls our attention to interconnections between the two. Once it is said that for instance a political context with certain characteristics is suitable for implementing human rights, this implies that the higher the level of political development, the higher the possibility of the realization of human rights through planning, and once human rights are realized, this in turn can contribute to political development.

3.1. Polity

The polity is one of the four key systems of society. The state as the main agent of the political system is also the key duty bearer under all regional and international human rights documents and therefore its characteristics do matter to human rights planning.[26] The question is what kind of state is best suited for development and implementation of a NHRAP?

The state's ability to implement human rights can be differentiated into four subcomponents: (1) political power; (2) administrative power; (3) extractive power; and (4) social power. These four dimensions of state power interact with each other, although they need not always change in the same direction. Lack of any power can make the state more vulnerable to a weak and inadequate implementation of human rights.

State political power reflects the state's capacity to employ power against challenges to its authority.[27] This is sharply distinct from the distributive notion of power, known as 'regime security', which refers to the conditions where governing elites are secure from violent challenges to their rules, and also from 'despotic power' (in Michael Mann's term), which is defined as the state's coercive abilities and the exercise of the force to impose its rule on civilians.[28] The key contrast here is that of

[26] State theories vary in their assumptions as to what constructs a state. See, eg, Rebecca S K Li, 'Alternative Routes to State Breakdown: Toward an Integrated Model of Territorial Disintegration' (2002) 20(1) Sociological Theory 1–23; Timothy Besley and Torsten Persson, 'State Capacity, Conflict, and Development' (2010) 78 Econometrica 1–34 <doi:10.3982/ECTA8073> accessed 11 January 2013; Douglas North, *Structure and Change in Economic History* (1st edn, Norton 1981); Michael Mann, 'The Autonomous Power of the State: Its Origins, Mechanisms and Results' (1984) 25 Arch Eur Sociol 185–213; Michael Mann, *The Sources of Social Power: The Rise of Classes and Nation States 1760–1914*, volume 2 (1st edn, Cambridge University Press 1993); Jonathan K Hanson and Rachel Sigman, 'Leviathan's Latent Dimensions: Measuring State Capacity for Comparative Political Research' (September 2013). APSA, <https://papers.ssrn.com/sol3/papers.cfm?abstract_id=1899933> accessed 14 March 2017.

[27] Richard Jackson, 'Regime Security' in A Collins (ed), *Contemporary Security Studies* (4th edn, Oxford University Press 2016) at 203.

[28] Peer Vries, *State, Economy and the Great Divergence: Great Britain and China, 1680s–1850s* (1st edn, Bloomsbury Academic 2015); Michael Mann, 'The Autonomous Power of the State: Its Origins, Mechanisms, and Results' in J A Hall (ed), *States in History* (1st edn, Blackwell 1986).

exercising power through consensus and with the help and meaningful participation of people and civil society, rather than over them.[29]

Where state political power is weak or absent, human rights are more likely to be violated. A weak state which is unable to promote sustainable security will face numerous challenges to its authority from internal and external actors, such as violent transfer of power, insurgency, rebellion, secession, warlordism, and in very extreme cases, genocide and ultimately state collapse and anarchy.

The state's administrative power—which refers to the ability of the state to effectively enact and implement key laws and policies—is also of crucial importance to implementing human rights through a NHRAP.[30]

The economic dimension of state power which is concerned with the state's ability to extract sufficient resources, material and human, to cover its expenditures is another important element of state apparatus which influence its capacity to implement human rights.[31]

The fourth dimension is the social power of the state which refers to the degree of wideness of its social base. A state with a limited and unstable social base would be less likely to be able or even inclined to advance an effective action plan for implementing human rights. But the critical point is that there is no linear relationship between these two variables. This relationship is shaped by the third nominal variable, namely the type of political regime. For example, populist regimes through ideological indoctrination can gain mass support which may enable them to promote and fulfil human rights but quite often they are not willing to do so.

Although a satisfactory level of these four capacities is a necessary condition for the state to successfully develop, implement, and monitor a NHRAP, the extent to which a state uses its capacities to implement human rights depends on its political will which is largely affected, among others, by the state's constituents and its political ideology. Political ideology reflects the value orientation of the state. States of different political ideologies may be differentiated by their endorsement or non-endorsement of at least two key values of liberty and equality.[32] The political will of the state to implement human rights, both civil and political as well as economic, social, and cultural, depends on the extent to which its political ideology endorses the values of liberty and/or equality. For a political ideology to activate political will of the state to implement human rights, it must endorse both values equally and

[29] Linda Weiss, 'Infrastructural power, economic transformation, and globalization' in John A Hall and R Schroeder (eds), *An Anatomy of Power: The Social Theory of Michael Mann* (1st edn, Cambridge University Press 2006) at 171.

[30] For further details about the administrative power of the state, see, eg, Daron Acemoglu, Davide Ticchi, and Andrea Vindigni, 'Emergence and Persistence of Inefficient States' (2011) 9(2) Journal of the European Economic Association 177–208; Adam Przeworski, Michael E Alvarez, José Antonio Cheibub, and Fernando Limongi, *Democracy and Development: Political Institutions and Well-being in the World, 1950–1990* (1st edn, Cambridge University Press 2000); Peter Evans, *Embedded Autonomy States and Industrial Transformation* (1st edn, Princeton University Press 1995).

[31] Li, 'Alternative Routes to State Breakdown: Toward an Integrated Model of Territorial Disintegration', note 26, at 4.

[32] See, eg, Oliver H Woshinsky, *Explaining Politics Culture, Institutions, and Political Behavior* (1st edn, Routledge 2008); Daniel J Elazar, *American Federalism: A View from the States* (3rd edn, Longman Higher Education 1984).

for all. Otherwise, a political ideology which endorses neither (such as fascism) or prescribes freedom over equality (such as classical liberalism) or the reverse (such as Soviet communism) or only supports them for certain groups of people (such as most religious ideologies) will fall well short of advancing human rights as set forth in international human rights documents. Bear in mind that liberty without equality can become the privilege of the few,[33] and equality arrayed against freedom undermines human autonomy.

As mentioned at the outset, all four major systems of society have a role to play in protecting, promoting and fulfilling human rights. So far, the central role of the state, as the representative of the political system, in providing a suitable context for implementing human rights through NHRAPs has been discussed. For now, let's move to the role of societal community.

3.2. Community

Societal community is another key system of society which serves an integration function. Each community (in a non-territorial sense) as a totality entails a web of affect-laden relations among a group of individuals who are committed to a set of shared values (as the output of a cultural system). It includes a collectively recognized set of 'rights' and 'obligations' to which its members, to a greater or lesser extent, are committed. The very critical point however is that the collectively recognized set of rights and obligations which is practiced by community members does not necessarily correspond with the set of rights and obligations embodied in international human rights documents but rather this can indeed even be in sharp contrast with that. Take the practice of Female Genital Cutting (FGC) within most communities in Somalia as an example. 98% of girls in Somalia have undergone the practice.[34] Women in Somalia are highly *obliged* to undergo circumcision to the extent that they do not *deserve* to get married without undergoing the practice. The collective practice of child, early, and forced marriage, as another example, is widespread and occurs in some communities in Syria, Pakistan, Saudi Arabia, and many more countries. In some cases, the collectively accepted set of rights and obligations may not even be in tune with the political will of the state. For example, despite the presence of political will and strong laws to abandon FGC in Egypt, it is still a prevalent collective practice among a number of communities there.

Put differently, communities have the capacity to establish what Searle calls 'status functions', that is, each community can impose functions on objects and people where they cannot perform the functions solely in virtue of their physical structure.[35] For status functions to work there must be 'collective' recognition of the object or person as having that status.[36] The status functions can be very crucial

[33] Mario Bunge, *Political Philosophy: Fact, Fiction, and Vision* (1st edn, Transaction 2009).
[34] UNICEF 2016 <https://qz.com/610930/unicef-98-of-women-in-somalia-have-undergone-female-genital-mutilation/> accessed 14 September 2017.
[35] John Searle, *Making the Social World: The Structure of Human Civilization* (1st edn, Oxford University Press 2010) at 7.
[36] ibid.

within communities since they carry what is known as 'deontic power', namely a set of rights (positive deontic power) and obligations (negative deontic power).[37]

Deontic power is a matter of degree and largely depends on the strength of what I would call 'social will' which is largely overlooked in the literature and is related to communities' rights practices. What is social will? Social will is a matter of number and value, that is, social will to implement a collectively recognized set of rights, whether compatible or not with international human rights law, refers to the number of people who accept and practice the set of rights and the extent to which they value them. Like community itself, the collective set of rights is not pre-planned, but unfolded in the domain of informal interrelationships among members of the community. When community undergirds a set of rights and obligations, those who violate the set will come under some measure of community censure. Communities command affectually laden centripetal forces that seek to pull in members' commitments, energies, effort, time, and other resources for what the community collectively endorses and practices as 'rights and obligations'.

The question is when does the collectively accepted set of rights correspond with the universal set of human rights embodied in international human rights documents? What configuration of communities might at all be capable of implementing universal human rights standards? To answer these questions, I need to unpack the concept of social will in greater detail. Social will is a two-dimensional concept: 'structural dimension' and 'agential dimension'. Let me start with the structural dimension.

3.2.1. Structural dimension of social will

The first dimension of social will which has been, implicitly or explicitly, emphasized by some legal sociologists reflects the influence of pre-existing institutions internalized by individuals. The main component of this dimension, which has a stabilizing function, is shared value(s) which comes from the cultural system. As far as the community system is concerned, the degree and characteristic of commitment to the shared values and the collectively accepted set of rights and obligations depend on the relational arrangement of social networks of society. If the density and intensity of social relationships are only limited to within a community and not between social circles, what Mark Granovetter calls 'strong-ties relations',[38] then it comes as no surprise if the created commitment is characterized by a particularistic and biased orientation, and the collectively accepted set of rights and obligations promotes exclusionary practices. Such social setting can largely reinforce homogeneity of what is called 'bonding social capital' which refers to relationships amongst members of a network who are similar in some form.[39]

[37] ibid.

[38] Mark Granovetter, 'The Strength of Weak Ties' (1973) 78(6) American Journal of Sociology 1360–80.

[39] Robert Putnam, *Bowling Alone: The Collapse and Revival of American Community* (1st edn, Simon & Schuster Paperbacks 2000).

In contrast, bridging communities through less intensified relationships or what Mark Granovetter calls 'weak-ties relations'[40] can improve 'universal social integration' and build consensus, trust, and co-operation among heterogeneous groups of people who consider themselves more as a member of society (as a whole) rather than a particular community. This can be seen as a bridging exercise of social capital or what is known as 'bridging social capital'.[41] Such global integration where we can talk about a 'community of communities' can provide a suitable context for realization of human rights as enshrined in international human rights documents.[42] Needless to say that the challenge of building such community is amplified when society is economically, ethnically, and/or racially segregated. As will be discussed later, civil society and cultural value orientation can play a key role in generating weak ties and advancing universal social integration. Among other factors, it is interesting to note that some even mention the stabilizer role of women in social integration and peacemaking. As Peter Csermely argues, women-induced weak ties can be seen as important stabilizing forces in society; what was lost in a traditional society like Afghanistan where women often stay at home.[43]

Hence, we can distinguish two types of community: traditional and modern. Whereas the traditional type encompasses a particularistic biased set of rights and obligations which is at odds with the universal idea of human rights, the modern one is more prone to provide a context for the acceptance of universal human rights standards. These two types of community stand at opposite ends of a continuum. For example, the reality of the situation in most countries in the Middle East, as an instance, lies somewhere close to the traditional pole, though their degree of closeness varies. The Middle East is full of examples of traditional (pre-modern) communities based on different kinds of particularism ranging from nationalist particularism to tribal brotherhood.

Now, let me turn to the second dimension of social will which has been largely neglected in the literature.

3.2.2. Agential dimension of social will

There has always been a tension between explaining social phenomena in terms of social forces or individual ones.[44] Once significant numbers of members of a community change their behaviours with respect to a previously well-recognized set of rights and obligations, this may be subverted enough for social will to start to

[40] Granovetter, 'The Strength of Weak Ties', note 38.

[41] Bridging social capital refers to relationships amongst people who are dissimilar in a demonstrable fashion, such as age, socio-economic status, race/ethnicity, and education. Simon Szreter and Michael Woolcock, 'Health by association? Social capital, social theory, and the political economy of public health' (2004) 33(4) International Journal of Epidemiology 650–67.

[42] See Amitai Etzioni, 'The Responsive Community: A Communitarian Perspective' (1996) 61(1) American Sociological Review 1–11.

[43] Peter Csermely, *Weak Links: Stabilizers of Complex Systems from Proteins to Social Networks* (1st edn, Springer 2006) at 195.

[44] Dave Elder-Vass, *The Causal Power of Social Structures: Emergence, Structure and Agency* (1st edn, Cambridge University Press 2010) at 2.

weaken or fade away. Hence, social will can be conceived as an *oxymoronic* concept if the two dimensions are in conflict with each other.

The agential dimension of social will has a transformative or 'morphogenetic' (in Margaret Archer's term) function especially in contemporary societies where different communities as 'norm circles' intersect with one another by virtue of having some members in common.[45] Influenced by Elder-Vass, here we can talk about 'intersectionality between norm circles' and the fact that today in most societies individuals are members of a variety of cross cutting communities, each of which tends to influence their behaviour in different directions.[46] Church (religious community) may expect, for instance, Alice to do something whereas her university classmates (academic community) or her friends at sport centre may expect her to do something else which may be even opposite to what church expects her to do.[47] This 'intersectionality' can operate as a morphogenetic source to change the collectively accepted set of rights and obligations.

Where there are multiple sets of norms for the same thing and also large numbers of individuals who are subjected to pressure to conform with multiple sets of rights and obligations, then as Elder-Vass emphasizes the scope for normative change would be high.[48] Being a member of a variety of cross-cutting norm circles (communities) itself can decrease the affectually laden pressure of communities on individuals to act in compliance with their norms and can help the agential dimension of social will to start taking precedence over its structural pressure and indeed pave the way for transforming the accepted set of rights and obligations over the course of time. For example, a member of a religious or ethnic community may hold a cluster of rights and obligations that are endorsed and enforced only by that community. In such cases, Elder-Vass calls the group that endorses and enforces this cluster of norms a *norm-set circle* or more generally, *normative circle*.[49] To the extent that communities as norm circles are cross-cutting rather than congruent with each other, 'individuals become sites of normative intersectionality and society becomes a patchwork of overlapping or intersecting normative circles'.[50] In this case, individuals as active agents can help reproduce one collectively accepted set of rights and obligations while transforming another set of rights and obligations imposed by another community. This has morphogenesis potential to start weakening the social will of one community to implement a set of rights while strengthening the social will of another one; the one whose norms have been followed by individuals. In order for a new right or obligation to develop in place of an existing one, there must be sufficient practice contrary to the existing right recognized by community members collectively.

[45] Morphogenesis potential has to do with 'those processes which tend to elaborate or change a system's given form, structure, or state' in preference to morphostatic processes 'that tend to preserve or maintain a system's form, organization, or state' (Walter F Buckley, *Sociology and Modern Systems Theory* (1st edn, Prentice Hall 1967) at 58).

[46] Elder-Vass, *The Causal Power of Social Structures*, note 44 at 131. [47] ibid.

[48] ibid, at 136. [49] ibid, at 133.

[50] ibid; see also Dave Elder-Vass, 'Collective Intentionality and Causal Powers' (2015) 1(2) Journal of Social Ontology 251–69.

Alternatively, where different normative circles seem broadly in harmony with each other, they form a larger universal cluster endorsed by society as a whole and this is where we can talk about a 'community of communities' mentioned above. A society where a community of communities bonds various groups of individuals together can foster what Etzioni calls 'layered loyalties' in members of various communities and thus it is more likely to enhance a universalistic set of rights and obligations which would support universal otherhood. Otherwise, a society of fragmented and closed communities which take positions against non-members would naturally support various discriminatory sets of rights and obligations which encourage exclusivity. As Etzioni argues:

> A more realistic and normatively acceptable position lies in developing those social processes that foster what I call layered loyalties in members of various communities. As a result, members see themselves as, and act as, members of more than one community. People who have a loyalty to a region (for example, the South in the United States, or Scotland in the United Kingdom), but also to their nation, are a case in point. Attempts to develop supranational communities, for instance, in Western Europe, reflect attempts to develop new layered loyalties. To the extent that layered loyalties evolve, they discourage exclusivity and tribal wars.[51]

So far different dimensions of social will and their impacts on the realization of human rights have been explored. Now, it is time to turn to the cultural system.

3.3. Culture

Culture, as another major system of society, consists of shared values and beliefs that provide standards for, among others, evaluating, communicating, learning, teaching, and exploring. What is perhaps the most important for human rights planning is to explore what types of value-orientation pattern help provide a suitable context for the realization of human rights. Kluckhohn and Strodtbeck conceptualize cultural value orientations as 'complex but definitely patterned principles … which give order and direction to the ever-flowing stream of human acts and thoughts'.[52] As Stella Ting-Toomey says:

> Cultural value orientations form the basic lenses through which we view our own actions and the actions of others. They set the background criteria for how we should communicate appropriately with others. They also set the emotional tone for how we interpret and evaluate cultural strangers' behaviours. Value orientations influence our overall self-conception, and our self-conception, in turn, influences our behaviour.[53]

While there are many dimensions in which cultural values differ such as 'neutral vs emotional' and 'specific vs diffuse', to explicate and compare categories of culture

[51] Etzioni, 'The Responsive Community: A Communitarian Perspective', note 42 at 9–10.

[52] Florence R Kluckhohn and Fred L Strodtbeck, *Variations in Value Orientations* (1st edn, Evanston, IL: Row, Peterson 1961) at 61.

[53] Stella Ting-Toomey, *Communicating Across Cultures* (1st edn, Guilford Press 1999) at 57–58.

that affect the realization of human rights through planning, I will exclusively address two value orientations, namely:

1. Universalism vs particularism
2. Individualism vs collectivism

By providing a typology of cultures, these dimensions can help us identify distinct aspects of cultures which must be taken into account for the formation and implementation of a NHRAP. I begin with the first dimension.

3.3.1. Universalism vs particularism

An important dimension of culture that has received consistent attention from both intercultural and cross-cultural researchers and has great influence on the status of human rights in society is universalism vs particularism.

A strong particularistic culture basically puts an emphasis on one (or more) selected difference(s) which can be race, sex, ethnicity, colour, etc. The particular difference is recognized as a common identity and imposed upon all other differences.[54] This is what can be seen in, for instance, Nazism and white supremacism. Such a culture easily categorizes human beings based on the selected difference (eg gender, race, or class) and then prescribes different codes of conduct for different categories. This culture will be at the risk of 'moral imperialism' in two ways: first, a strong particularistic culture implies value infallibalism, that is, anyone who disagrees with their values must be mistaken; and second, this form of culture is also accused of value paternalism. A culture with strong particularistic value orientation may even prescribe using force to impose its value judgments on others for their own good, even if they disagree.[55] This reminds us of the 1530 judicial report to Charles V on the colonists' treatment of slaves in the Americas which stated that they treated the natives worse than their dogs. Las Casas reports some of the incidents he himself witnessed:

> [The Spaniards] made bets as to who would slit a man in two, or cut off his head at one blow; or they opened up his bowels. They tore the babies from their mother's breast by their feet, and dashed their heads against the rocks ... They spitted the bodies of other babes, together with their mothers and all who were before them, on their swords ... [They hanged Indians], and by thirteens, in honor and reverence for our Redeemer and the twelve Apostles, they put wood underneath and, with fire, they burned the Indians alive.[56]

Even a weak particularistic culture draws, implicitly or explicitly, a line between 'we' and 'them'—special rights are prescribed for 'us' and most duties are imposed on 'them'.

The second type of culture which stands in contrast with particularism is strong universalism. A universalist culture in its full-blooded form presents radical

[54] Wolfgang Hofkirchner, '"Mechanisms" at Work in Information Society' in M S Archer (ed), *Generative Mechanisms Transforming the Social Order* (1st edn, Springer 2015) at 106.

[55] See William Talbott, *Which Rights Should Be Universal?* (1st edn, Oxford University Press 2005) at 15.

[56] Sale, cited in Talbott, ibid, at 53.

egalitarianism which is in essence just formal equality. As Wolfgang Hofkirchner describes it, while particularism is the 'imposition of one selected difference', strong universalism is 'negation of any difference' and the critical point is that both in one way or another can lead to antagonism.[57]

Parenthetically, it should be noted that the claim that a culture is universal can take different forms depending upon the respect in which its value orientation is alleged to be universal namely 'universalism in structure', 'universalism in application', and 'universalism of content'.[58] The first two forms are based on the view that what is good and right, even if particularistic in content, should cover all people in all situations. Whereas universalism in structure relates to the range of cases and circumstances, universalism in application has to do with the scope of people to whom a set of values applies.[59] Universalism in these forms can cover a wide range of doctrines from religious doctrines such as Christianity and Islam to political ideologies, such as liberalism, socialism, Marxism, and anarchism. Such confusion sometimes complicates assessments concerning universalism.

What is meant here by strong universalism, however, is 'universalism of content' which relates to the status of individuals and the way in which they relate morally to one another. A strongly universal culture in this sense 'places everyone on an equal footing and in an identical moral relationship with everyone else …'[60] Although universalism in this form is normally accompanied by universalism of application and universalism of structure, the other two forms of universalism do not necessarily entail universalism of content.

Such a rule-based culture can lead to value absolutism which fails to account for variety in value systems around the world and for the changes in values over the course of time.[61] By overlooking the dynamics and specificity of circumstances, absolutism can lead to an authoritarian ethics which clearly is not in harmony with the idea of realizing human rights.[62] Strong universalism has been criticized for treating all identically by virtue of viewing populations as homogeneous such as communism which ignores individual differences.[63] It fails to take individual and cultural differences into consideration and has been accused of confusing 'impartiality' with 'uniformity' and 'equality of treatment' with 'sameness of treatment' irrespective of different specific needs and interests.[64] As Wolfgang Hofkirchner argues, this can also lead to antagonism:

> Either differences are erased and levelled down for the sake of identity under the guise of which dominion is erected. 'Communist regimes', in countries of failed 'real socialism', such

[57] Hofkirchner, '"Mechanisms" at Work in Information Society', note 54 at 105.

[58] Peter Jones and Graham Long, 'Universalism, Relativism and Difference' in D Moellendorf and H Widdows (eds), *The Routledge Handbook of Global Ethics* (1st edn, Routledge 2014) at 88.

[59] ibid. [60] ibid.

[61] Bunge, *Treatise on Basic Philosophy—Ethics: The Good and The Right*, note 11, at 65.

[62] ibid.

[63] See, eg, Iris Marion Young, *Justice and the Politics of Difference* (1st edn, Princeton University Press 1990).

[64] Gemma Carey and Pauline McLoughlin, 'The Powerful Pull of Policy Targeting: Examining Residualisation in Australia' (2016) 26(2) Critical Public Health 147–58 <http://dx.doi.org/10.1080/09581596.2014.973018> accessed 6 May 2017.

as today's Democratic People's Republic of Korea have been accused of being an instance of that variety, disregarding individuals, their search for distinction, and creativeness. Another example of egalitarianism is that form of globalisation, said to wipe out barriers to the free flow of capital and undermine higher standards for the good life.[65]

Strong universalism places a veil over distinctions that do exist in society and follows the rules. Although the idea behind strong universalism is to erode discrimination of any kind, its critics complain that ignoring differences can result in policies that are in fact biased and fail to treat different groups in a genuinely equal way.

Another value orientation, emerged historically in particular in reaction to strong particularism (moral imperialism) and exacerbated later by postmodernism, is cultural relativism, which, in its strong form (strong relativism), presents radical pluralism putting an emphasis on differences of any kind. Such value orientation fails to integrate identity and difference but rather puts what might be contrary together. As Wolfgang Hofkirchner argues, cultural relativism can lead to agonism. He goes further to say that:

> Any position is permitted. No position negates another position as there is no claim to a common identity. Each position is just different from the others, and even if it is contrary to another like black to white, it can exist alongside the other ... What you get is diversity without unity. It is postmodern pluralism with-out a universal claim but for each difference having the same right ... but such contraries can easily become contradictions.[66]

Cultural relativists deny moral absolutism which includes a claim of infallibility.[67] As will be discussed in the next chapter, strong relativism, however, accepts all views even if against human rights. The problem with such value orientation is that it goes too far in the other direction, that is, no reconciliation of differences but only the 'Juxtaposition of every difference in their own right'.[68] It is simply not true that all values are subjective or culture-dependent, and likely to change in the course of time. All normal human beings know, for example, that life is better than death and health is better than sickness. They value things like well-being, friendship, justice, fairness, co-operation, peace, leisure, and much more, and those who do not are regarded as abnormal.[69] Moreover, at the extreme, the idea of 'progress' would be nonsense to cultural relativists for whom each culture defines its own values and goals, which cannot be evaluated by any external criteria. Hence, it is no surprise that cultural practices such as FGC, foot-binding, 'Sati',[70] and even slavery are all accepted in a relativist culture (in its strong form).

The combination of a moderate relativist and moderate universalist culture would be a type of culture in which identity and difference are reconciled. This type of culture encompasses not only a set of ontologically universal values rooted in basic human needs such as health and peace which ought to be desired universally at all

[65] Hofkirchner, ' "Mechanisms" at Work in Information Society', note 54 at 106.

[66] ibid. [67] Talbott, *Which Rights Should Be Universal?*, note 55.

[68] Hofkirchner, ' "Mechanisms" at Work in Information Society', note 54 at 105.

[69] Bunge, *Treatise on Basic Philosophy—Ethics: The Good and The Right*, note 11.

[70] The Hindu practice of widows joining their dead husbands on the funeral pyre, whether they want to or not.

times but also individual and cultural differences which are bound to place, time, and circumstances (see Chapter 2). This will be 'unity through diversity', and as Wolfgang Hofkirchner says, is where:

> [a]s many differences as possible (diversity) produce as much identity as may be necessary (unity); the differences are identical in as much as they identify themselves with the identity they commonly produce, while identity, in turn, is differentiated as long as differentiation does not lead to the disintegration of identity.[71]

Whereas particularism and strong universalism produce antagonistic social relationships (contradictoriness), especially particularism can result in a segmental society, strong relativism generates agonism (contrariness) through juxtaposition of every difference in their own right and co-existence of oppositions.[72] In contrast to these three value orientations, unity through diversity produces synergism (complementariness) through composition made up by all differences.[73] As Hofkirchner holds, based on unity through diversity, we can transform social conflicts from antagonism or agonism to synergism.[74]

In a cultural context where the principle of unity through diversity prevails, destructive conflicts are replaced with constructive competitions, and such a cultural setting is more prone to satisfy people's basic human rights.

3.3.2. Individualism vs collectivism

Some cross-cultural studies have distinguished between two types of culture: individualistic and collectivistic.[75] Whereas an individualistic model of culture puts great emphasis on the importance of individual identity over group identity, a collectivist one gives attention to the importance of the 'we' identity over the 'I' identity, and group rights over individual rights.[76] For people in individualistic cultures, the personal goals prevail over common goods, whereas the opposite is the case for those in collectivist cultures.[77]

A collectivist culture in its extreme form, which is often coloured with particularism,[78] is seemingly a major barrier to effective realization of individual rights in

71 Hofkirchner, ' "Mechanisms" at Work in Information Society', note 54 at 105. 72 ibid.

73 For detailed definition of antagonism, agoism, and synergism refer to Wolfgang Hofkirchner (note 54 at 105).

74 Hofkirchner, ' "Mechanisms" at Work in Information Society', note 54.

75 See, eg, William B Gudykunst, Stella Ting-Toomey, and Elizabeth Chua, *Culture and Interpersonal Communication* (1st edn, Sage Publications 1988); Harry Triandis, 'Individualism—Collectivism and Personality' (2001) 69:6 Journal of Personality 907; Shalom H Schwartz and Wolfgang Bilsky, 'Toward a theory of the universal content and structure of values: Extensions and cross-cultural replications' (1990) 58(5) Journal of Personality and Social Psychology 878–91; John Fiske, 'For cultural interpretation: A study of the culture of homelessness' (1991) 8(4) Critical Studies in Mass Communication 455–74; Geert Hofstede, *Culture's Consequences: International Differences in Work-related Values* (1st edn, Sage 1980).

76 Harry Triandis, *Individualism and Collectivism: New Directions in Social Psychology* (Westview Press 1995); Ting-Toomey, *Communicating Across Cultures*, note 53.

77 Maureen Guirdham, *Communicating Across Cultures at Work* (3rd edn, Palgrave 2011) at 49–50.

78 Whereas collectivist orientation has to do with 'I' identity and 'We' identity, the particularistic one is concerned with 'We' and 'Them'.

particular civil and political as well as minority rights. Such cultures pull too much towards order at the expense of individual autonomy—the majority of rights belong to the community as a whole and are full of obligations on individuals. By contrast, strong individualism (ie egoistic individualism) in absence of any kind of collectivism promotes anomie (instead of autonomy) where the status of both individual and collective rights remains obscure.

An alternative to these two is where moderate collectivism (or moderate communitarianism) is conjoined with moderate individualism (ethical individualism). Moderate collectivism, combined with ethical individualism, can provide a suitable cultural milieu for promoting not only individual rights such as the right to liberty and pursuit of happiness but also collective rights such as the right to a healthy environment.

Having discussed the importance of the patterns of value orientations for human rights planning, the next section will explore the suitable economic context for action plans for implementing human rights.

3.4. Economy

The majority of human rights are resource-dependent and this makes the role of economy, as another system of society, in realizing human rights crucial. The availability and allocation of resources are influenced by the type of economic system implemented in a society. Mainstream economists particularly neoliberalists postulate that the market is the best mechanism for generating efficient economic outcomes. They are against state interventions putting emphasis on individual freedom and maximizing the output of goods and services (normally measured by GDP). They argue that the most efficient outcome will be achieved in a free competitive market.[79] The critical point is that economic efficiency is highly important for realizing human rights, yet, reliance on the market as the only steering mechanism can generate pervasive inefficiencies, which will be discussed as follows.

First, at the centre of the idea that the market alone can generate efficient allocations of resources is the problem of the 'Matthew effect' that is advantage begets more advantage. Instead of trickling down, findings have revealed that over 'the last 25 years, income and wealth are being sucked upwards as the richest 1% have gained more income than the bottom 50% put together'.[80] An Oxfam 2017 report indicates that just eight men own the same wealth as the poorest half of the world. The incomes of the poorest 10% of people increased by less than $3 a year between

[79] See, eg, Daniel Hausman, Michael McPherson, and Debra Satz, *Economic Analysis, Moral Philosophy, and Public Policy* (3rd edn, Cambridge University Press 2016); Radhika Balakrishnan, James Heintz, and Diane Elson, *Rethinking Economic Policy for Social Justice: The Radical Potential of Human Rights* (1st edn, Routledge 2016).

[80] Deborah Hardoon, Sophia Ayele, and Richardo Fuentes-Nieva, 'An Economy for the 1%: How privilege and power in the economy drive extreme inequality and how this can be stopped', Oxfam International Report, 18 January 2016 <http://policy-practice.oxfam.org.uk/publications/an-economy-for-the-1-how-privilege-and-power-in-the-economy-drive-extreme-inequ-592643> accessed 25 January 2018.

1988 and 2011, while the incomes of the top 1% increased 182 times as much.[81] Oxfam in its 2018 report also mentions that 82% of the wealth generated in 2017 went to the richest 1% of the global population, while the 3.7 billion people who make up the poorest half of the world saw no increase in their wealth.[82] Thomas Piketty who is an influential economist in the area of wealth and income inequality has compiled a large body of evidence documenting the trajectory of increasing inequality in a free market society.[83] For example, in the USA, over the last thirty years, while the incomes of the top 1% have increased 300%, the growth in the incomes of the bottom 50% has been zero.[84] As highlighted in the Statement of Philip Alston, United Nations Special Rapporteur on extreme poverty and human rights, more than one in every eight Americans are living in poverty (40 million, equal to 12.7% of the population), and almost half of those (18.5 million) are living in deep poverty, with reported family income below one-half of the poverty threshold.[85]

Moreover, as the Global Justice 2016 report has shown, the '10 biggest corporations make more money than most countries in the world combined'.[86] The question is whether in such system which is prone to monopoly and cronyism everyone has real opportunity to form his or her life, whether everyone is free from coercive restrictions (including, but not limited to, economic disadvantages) imposed by others and by circumstances in order to put his or her life plan into effect. As Claus Offe argues:

> Once markets are left to themselves, rational actors will conspire, in the interest of increasing their profits, to escape the competitive threat coming from other market participants by forming cartels or monopolies, thus subverting the ideal of 'freedom of choice' in whose name markets are often defended.[87]

[81] Oxfam 2017 report released 16 January 2017 <https://www.oxfam.org.uk/media-centre/press-releases/2017/01/eight-people-own-same-wealth-as-half-the-world> accessed 29 January 2017.

[82] Oxfam 2018 report released 22 January 2018 <https://www.oxfam.org/en/pressroom/pressreleases/2018-01-22/richest-1-percent-bagged-82-percent-wealth-created-last-year> accessed 26 January 2018.

[83] See, eg, Thomas Piketty, *Capital in the Twenty-First Century* (1st edn, Harvard University Press 2014); Thomas Piketty and Anthony B Atkinson, *Top Incomes: A Global Perspective* (1st edn, Oxford University Press 2010); Anthony B Atkinson and Thomas Piketty, *Top Incomes over the Twentieth Century: A Contrast between Europeans and English-Speaking Countries* (Oxford University Press 2007); Facundo Alvaredo, Anthony Atkinson, Thomas Piketty, and Emmanual Saez, The World Top Incomes Database <http://wid.world> accessed October 2017.

[84] Piketty, *Capital in the Twenty-First Century*, ibid.

[85] Philip Alston, United Nations Special Rapporteur on extreme poverty and human rights, Statement on Visit to the USA, release on 15 December 2017 <http://www.ohchr.org/EN/NewsEvents/Pages/DisplayNews.aspx?NewsID=22533> accessed 2 January 2018; see also, United States Census Bureau 2017 <https://www.census.gov/data/tables/time-series/demo/income-poverty/historical-poverty-thresholds.html> accessed 10 January 2018.

[86] Global Justice 2016 report <http://www.globaljustice.org.uk/news/2016/sep/12/10-biggest-corporations-make-more-money-most-countries-world-combined> accessed 21 December 2017; see also Jamie Morgan and William Sun, 'Corporations, Taxation and Responsibility: Practical and Onto-Analytical Issues for Morphogensis and Eudaimonia—*A posse ad esse*?' in M S Archer (ed), *Morphogenesis and Human Flourishing* (1st edn, Springer 2017).

[87] Claus Offe, 'Civil Society and Social Order: Demarcating and Combining Market, State and Community' (2000) 41(1) European Journal of Sociology 71–94, at 87.

The ILO estimates that 21 million people are victims of forced labour, which generates an estimated $150bn of profits every year.[88] As Hoy and Sumner indicate 'approximately three-quarters of global poverty, at least at the lower poverty lines, could now be eliminated—in principle—via redistribution of nationally available resources in terms of cash transfers funded by new taxation and the reallocation of public spending (from fossil fuel subsidies and "surplus" military spending)'.[89] A recent Oxfam report similarly shows that 'had growth been pro-poor between 1990 and 2010, 700 million more people, most of them women, would not be living in poverty today'.[90]

Second, GDP growth is not a perfect indicator of how efficient an economy is. It takes no account of other factors of a well-balanced development such as social inclusiveness, social security, housing, education, environmental protection and sustainability, level of employment, and standard of living. A country may have high GDP growth at a time when it suffers a high level of inequality.[91] In the USA, more than 20% of American children live in poverty, despite the fact that the USA has the world's highest GDP.[92] The number of infants who die in the USA before the age of one is the highest among OECD countries,[93] and more than twice as many African-American infants die compared to white infants.[94] Likewise, 15%, or 47 million people, did not have health insurance in 2007.[95] Despite the fact that the USA is the world's richest economy, it lags behind many other nations in recognizing social rights such as the right to an adequate standard of living and the right to healthcare, and has not yet ratified the ICESCR. It has also been against the right to development, and surprisingly in 2017 the USA said it would withdraw from the Paris Climate Agreement. As Balakrishnan and others argue, in such an economic system:

> [T]he question of what is a just distribution of income and wealth falls outside of the purview of economic theory. Neoclassical thinking is largely silent on questions of inequality and

[88] The ILO (2014) Brief on the Protocol to the Forced Labour Convention, 1930. <http://www.ilo.org/global/topics/forced-labour/publications/WCMS_321414/lang--en/index.htm> accessed 9 November 2016.

[89] Chris Hoy and Andy Sumner, 'Gasoline, Guns, and Giveaways: Is There New Capacity for Redistribution to End Three Quarters of Global Poverty?' (2016) Center for Global Development Working Paper 433. <https://doi.org/10.2139/ssrn.2843630> accessed 1 January 2018.

[90] Deborah Hardoon and J Slater, 'Inequality and the end to extreme poverty' (2015), Oxfam. <http://policy-practice.oxfam.org.uk/publications/inequality-and-the-end-of-extreme-poverty-577506 accessed 12 June 2017.

[91] Oxfam report, An Economy for the 99%, January 2017, at 6, <https://www.oxfam.org/sites/www.oxfam.org/files/file_attachments/bp-economy-for-99-percent-160117-en.pdf> accessed 10 February 2017.

[92] OECD (Organization for Economic Cooperation and Development). 2009a. Health data <www.oecd.org> accessed 23 March 2011.

[93] World Bank. 2010 <http://data.worldbank.org/country/united-states> accessed 15 March 2011.

[94] CDC (November 2008), 'Behind International Rankings of Infant Mortality: How the United States Compares with Europe' <http://www.cdc.gov/nchs/data/databriefs/db23.htm> accessed 22 April 2012.

[95] OECD (Organization for Economic Cooperation and Development). 2009b. OECD Factbook 2009 <www.oecd.org> accessed 23 March 2011.

instead focuses on defining the conditions under which an efficient allocation of resources emerges.[96]

No further criterion has been offered to assess the final distribution of income or guarantee the fulfilment of basic human rights. That is why the market is known as being deaf and blind. It is deaf as to any negative side effects and externalities it causes such as environmental pollutions and blind to the harmful consequences of its transactions for those who are involved.[97]

Third, another important issue with the free market is the problem of information: sellers on a market have strong interests in hiding information from buyers if it would be costly for them.[98]

Fourth, as Wright and Rogers argue, another issue with the free market is the fact that markets are not good at producing public goods whose value is diffuse to a wide variety of people, but rather it is good at producing things in which most of the benefits are captured by those who directly pay for the good or service.[99]

All these problems point to the fact that neoliberalism cannot be a suitable conceptual framework for a well-balanced development and in particular an effective realization of human rights in four domains of society. An alternative, which seems to be best suited for realizing human rights, is what is known as the human rights-based approach to development. We will discuss this approach in more detail in the next chapter, but its basic ideas will be outlined here.

The human rights-based approach to development, which is based on international human rights standards, offers a normative guidance against which economic policy options and resource allocation outcomes can be assessed.[100] Such an approach replaces a narrow concept of GDP growth as the measure of development with the idea of progressive realization of human rights. As Balakrishnan and others state 'human rights focuses on progressive improvements in a range of social outcomes, with efficiency being important only insofar as it leads to the greater enjoyment of rights'.[101] Advances in development are achieved when the enjoyment of at least basic human rights, both civil and political as well as economic, social, and cultural, improves over time. Bearing in mind that liberty without a certain level of equality becomes the privilege of the few, an important aspect of equality that must be guaranteed in a rights-based economy has to do with the minimum core content of basic human rights that no one should be denied. At the very least, full equality in the enjoyment of minimum essential levels of each of the basic rights such as the right to an adequate standard of living, education, work, and health must be

[96] Balakrishnan, Heintz, and Elson, *Rethinking Economic Policy for Social Justice: The Radical Potential of Human Rights*, note 79, at 34.

[97] Offe, 'Civil Society and Social Order: Demarcating and Combining Market, State and Community', note 87.

[98] Eric Olin Wright and Joel Rogers, *American Society: How It Really Works* (2nd edn, W W Norton & Company 2010).

[99] ibid.

[100] Margot E Salomon and Colin Arnott, 'Better Development Decision-making: Applying International Human Rights Law to Neoclassical Economics' (2014) 32(1) Nordic Journal of Human Rights 44–74, at 45.

[101] Balakrishnan, Heintz, and Elson, *Rethinking Economic Policy for Social Justice: The Radical Potential of Human Rights*, note 79 at 3.

guaranteed even in times of severe resource constraints. Boosting overall income in a society where people are deprived of a minimum level of basic rights is simply nonsense. Governments must do all they can to secure international assistance where national resources are inadequate to realize basic human rights.

Moreover, on this view, the market cannot be left unregulated. Market forces alone cannot be relied upon to generate outcomes that satisfy basic human rights and meet the minimum core contents. The market needs to be systematically regulated and monitored by the political power of the state and associational power of civil society. The human rights-based approach to development requires the state to protect against human rights abuses by business.[102] For example, the first principle (out of thirty-one) of the UN Guiding Principles on Business and Human Rights says: 'states must protect against human rights abuse within their territory and/or jurisdiction by third parties, including business enterprises. This requires taking appropriate steps to prevent, investigate, punish and redress such abuse through effective policies, legislation, regulations and adjudication'.[103]

The key premise of the human rights-based approach to development is that the realization of human rights is not only an intrinsic end of development but also a means to development. Although one can still find the view that there is a trade-off between human rights and economic efficiency,[104] research has shown that the realization of human rights can enhance economic growth.[105] By providing a body of evidence, Marslev and Sano hold that 'human rights should be seen as an active part of the growth model, rather than merely a passive outcome of it'.[106] The non-realization of, at least, a minimum essential levels of the basic human rights such as

[102] On 16 June 2011, the UN Human Rights Council unanimously endorsed the UN Guiding Principles on Business and Human Rights: Implementing the United Nations "Protect, Respect and Remedy" Framework. This guidance is based on three complementary pillars—these are: the state duty to protect against human rights abuses by business; corporate responsibility to respect human rights; and access by victims to effective remedy, both judicial and non-judicial. To put the UN Guiding Principles into practice, in 2011, the European Union requested member states to adopt a National Action Plan on Business and Human Rights (NAP-BHR) and then in 2014 the UN Human Rights Council strongly encouraged each state to develop such plans. Recently, likewise, the Human Rights Council adopted a resolution calling for the establishment of an open-ended intergovernmental working group 'to elaborate an international legally-binding instrument to regulate, in international human rights law, the activities of transnational corporations and other business enterprises'. See Human Rights Council, 'Elaboration of an International Legally Binding Instrument on Transnational Corporations and Other Business Enterprises with Respect to Human Rights', A/HRC Res 26/9 (26 June 2014).

[103] United Nations Human Rights Council, 'Guiding Principles on Business and Human Rights', 2011, at 3 <http://www.ohchr.org/Documents/Publications/GuidingPrinciplesBusinessHR_EN.pdf> accessed 2 April 2016.

[104] See Robert Archer, 'The Strengths of Difference Traditions: What Can be Gained and What Might be Lost by Combining Rights and Development?' (2006) 3(4) SUR International Journal of Human Rights 80; Dan Seymour and Jonathan Pincus, 'Human Rights and Economics: The Conceptual Basis for Their Complementarity' (2008) 26(4) Development Policy Review 387–405 <doi:10.1111/j.1467-7679.2008.00415.x> accessed 1 December 2016.

[105] Kristoffer Marslev and Hans-Otto Sano, 'The Economy of Human Rights: Exploring Potential Linkages between Human Rights and Economic Development' (2016) No 2, Matters of Concern, Human Rights Research Papers <https://www.humanrights.dk/sites/humanrights.dk/files/media/dokumenter/udgivelser/working_papers_2016/the_economics_of_human_rights_2016.pdf> accessed 23 May 2017; see also, Salomon and Arnott, 'Better Development Decision- making: Applying International Human Rights Law to Neoclassical Economics', note 100.

[106] ibid at 6.

an adequate standard of living, health, and education can reduce human capital, labour productivity, and consequently economic growth.[107] McKay and Vizard in their study by referring to different empirical findings concluded that 'policies to achieve key rights outcomes can have a positive impact on growth'.[108] Also, contrary to the assumption that redistribution (eg for the poor and vulnerable groups) can reduce growth, research has recognized that some types of redistribution can even increase economic growth, for instance, if it is spent on public goods and social services.[109] Likewise, Marslev and Sano in their research state that 'there is widespread evidence that, at least above a certain level, inequality negatively affects economic growth'.[110]

Let me recapitulate that the market mechanism alone suffers significant deficiencies and that a human rights-based economy cannot only address these deficits but also improve economic growth.

In the next section I will discuss civil society which can play a key role in an effective development, implementation, and assessment of human rights planning.

3.5. Civil society

There are different conceptions of civil society in the literature of social sciences.[111] I define civil society as a mediated civil sphere between political, cultural, economic, and societal community systems populated by different kinds of non-governmental organizations, each of which follow different specific purposes but the common tendencies among most of them are equalization or reduction of inequality, and the containment of power. This sphere is where people are seen as citizens[112] and relationships are associational. Whereas all of these four sub-systems of society are to a greater or lesser degree hierarchical based on different kinds of power (eg economic power, political power, cultural power, and social influence), civil society tends to equalize all these four kinds of hierarchies through associational power.

[107] See Gustav Ranis, Frances Stewart, and Alejandro Ramirez, 'Economic Growth and Human Development' (2000) 28(2) World Development 197–219, <http://www.econ.yale.edu/~granis/papers/cp0546.pdf> accessed 20 March 2015.

[108] Andy McKay and Polly Vizard, 'Rights and Economic Growth: Inevitable Conflict or "Common Ground"?' (2005) Overseas Development Institute, <http://www.odi.org/sites/odi.org.uk/files/odi-assets/publications-opinion- files/4353.pdf> accessed 27 June 2016.

[109] See Jonathan D Ostry, Andrew Berg, and Charalambos G Tsangarides, 'Redistribution, Inequality, and Growth' 2014, https://www.imf.org/external/pubs/ft/sdn/2014/sdn1402.pdf> accessed 14 March 2016; Nancy Birdsall, 'Income Distribution: Effects on Growth and Development', 2007, <https://www.cgdev.org/files/13505_file_Income_Distribution_Birdsall.pdf> accessed 10 May 2012; William Easterly, 'Inequality does cause underdevelopment: Insights from a new instrument' (2007) 84(2) Journal of Development Economics 755–76; Ranis, Stewart, and Ramirez, 'Economic Growth and Human Development', note 107.

[110] Marslev and Sano, 'The Economy of Human Rights: Exploring Potential Linkages between Human Rights and Economic Development', note 105 at 14.

[111] See, eg, Jeffrey C Alexander, *The Civil Sphere* (1st edn, Oxford University Press 2006); Simone Chambers and Jeffrey Kopstein, 'Civil Society and the State' in J S Dryzek, B Honig, and A Phillips (eds), *The Oxford Handbook of Political Theory* (1st edn, Oxford University Press 2008); Michael Edwards, *Civil Society* (2nd edn, Polity Press 2009); Robert Layton, *Order and Anarchy: Civil Society, Social Disorder and War* (1st edn, Cambridge University Press 2006).

[112] Note that 'citizenship' is an equalizer concept.

In the political domain, civil society tends to equalize political power (political equality). In the economic domain, the common tendency of civil society is the curtailment of unequal distribution of resources. In the cultural domain, the tendency of civil society is cultural equality via communication, dissemination of all kinds of knowledge and education, and in the communal domain, the tendency of civil society is social equality (or group equality) and recognizing all types of collective identities.

Put differently, whereas in political, economic, and cultural systems where relationships are almost formal (secondary), bureaucracy (and in fewer cases, adhocracy) is the organizing principle, in community where relationships are informal (primary), family is the organizing principle. In between, in civil society where the relationship is associational (tertiary), the organizing principle is bureaucracy but all organizations in this sphere are non-profit, membership is voluntarist, and the social network is more or less flat.

Each system of society pursues a basic goal and has its own logic. In an economic system, the basic goal is efficiency, and its logic is optimization mainly through market mechanism. In the political system, the basic goal is security (in a broad sense, including respecting and protecting human rights) and its logic is rule making and law enforcement through the mechanisms of employment of political authority and coercive force. In the cultural system, the basic goal is truth and its basic logic is 'persuasion' and logical consistency through mechanisms of argumentation, providing evidence, and information. In the community system, the basic goal is 'togetherness', and its logic is inner social conformity through the mechanisms of expressive interactions and the activation of commitment. In civil society, the implicit goal is often the diversification of any kinds of power distribution and its logic is optimization, persuasion, social conformity, advancing freedom, and challenging for human rights through mechanisms of voluntarist collaborations, mobilization of material, and non-material resources, and the employment of associational power.

Five points are worth noting here: (1) civil society can contribute to relative autonomy of each of these four systems which is crucial for the functions of each of these systems, civil society itself, and society as whole; (2) civil society can prevent cleavage between the state and societal community (national community); (3) by providing environmental immunity, civil society contributes to the prevention of corruption, crypticism, and nepotism by which political and economic systems are by nature liable to be afflicted. It is also capable to help the inflected systems to overcome such problems; (4) civil society can be seen as 'storage of weak ties' which can contribute to global integration at the societal level—what can generate synergy and efficiency in society; and, (5) more importantly, civil society can provide an associational setting for realizing human rights.

In a nutshell, strong and vibrant civil society is integral to the advancement of a NHRAP. It is a fundamental contextual means through which a genuine national human rights planning can be launched and implemented though with simultaneous inputs from the four major systems of society. Nonetheless, bear in mind that civil society which is often one of the most crucial elements of an effective anti-corruption strategy, is potentially vulnerable to corruption especially where procedures are not adequately transparent and genuinely participatory.

To sum up: in this chapter we introduced analytically five contextual factors—polity, economy, culture, community, and civil society—and pinpointed some features of these factors which can pave the road for the development and implementation of NHRAPs, and since this is a two-way road, these five contextual factors can be strengthened via realizing human rights. As a final word, let me stress again that the contextual theory of human rights planning does not assert that the relationship between the contextual development of any kind (morphogenesis changes) and the realization of human rights through planning is based on a sequential logic, but rather in most cases, there is a symbiotic relationship between these two. That is, the relationship is based on synchronic logic; each of them is the prerequisite of the other.

The next chapter will develop substantive, procedural, and analytical theories of human rights planning as other parts of the general theory of planning suggested here.

2

Towards a General Theory of Human Rights Planning

Part II

1. Introduction

The last chapter sought to devise the contextual sub-theory of human rights planning addressing the role and characteristics of, and interactions among polity, economy, culture, and community and their impacts on implementing human rights. This chapter will advance three sub-theories of planning, substantive, procedural, and analytical, as other parts of the general theory of human rights planning. Whereas a contextual theory of planning examines the societal environment through which planning can effectively work, substantive and procedural theories of planning are in turn concerned with the content and procedure of planning and the analytical theory of human rights planning is a heuristic device for, inter alia, the identification, classification, and prioritization of rights in the course of planning.

The present chapter will start with the origin of the human rights-based approach to development upon which the substantive and procedural theories of planning are based. A human rights-based approach to development as an internationally agreed theoretical framework is flexible enough to act as a guiding star directing the procedure and substance of human rights action plans. The chapter will then present the substantive and procedural theories of human rights planning in turn. The basic idea grounding the substantive and procedural theories, suggested here, is that a human rights action plan, if properly designed and implemented, can indeed pave the way for human rights-based development.

The last section of this chapter is an attempt to build up a novel analytical theory of human rights planning through positive critique of the three major theories of rights, including the interest theory, needs-based approach, and capability approach. This new theory offers an integrated account of basic human rights by explicating the four critical concepts of basic need, interest, capability, and value, and exploring their interrelationships with each other and with the concept of basic rights.

2. Origins of the Human Rights-Based Approach to Development

The human rights-based approach to development arose as a result of two streams: the right to development on the one hand and human development on the other. In what follows, I will quickly review the development of these two steams respectively.

2.1. Development as a human right

Development first entered the human rights discourse through the debate on the right to development.[1] The idea of development as a human right dates back to the ideological debates of the 1950s and 1960s. Whereas socialist countries were pushing for peace and disarmament and launched the idea of the right of people to live in peace, developing countries were trying for economic growth, non-discrimination, and anti-apartheid struggle, and Western countries for the protection of civil and political rights, the 'Non Aligned Movement' (NAM) countries[2] campaigned for the creation of a more just international order and tried to declare development as a right.[3] The debate was also marked by the consequence of the Cold War, which reinforced the distinction between the two sets of human rights, civil and political rights, on the one hand and economic, social, and cultural rights on the other.

In the first place, the idea of the right to development was launched by the Senegalese jurist, Keba M'Baye.[4] Afterwards, this right was recognized legally in Article 22 of the 1981 African Charter on Human and Peoples' Rights, and was later incorporated into the global human rights framework through the adoption in 1986 of the Declaration on the Right to Development. The 1993 Vienna Declaration and Programme of Action, the United Nations Millennium Declaration, and the Durban Declaration and Programme of Action reconfirmed development as a universal and inalienable human right.

Article 1 of the Declaration on the Right to Development states that 'the right to development is an inalienable human right by virtue of which every human person and all peoples are entitled to participate in, contribute to, and enjoy economic, social, cultural and political development, in which all human rights and fundamental

[1] See Alain Pellet, 'The Function of the Right to Development: A Right to Self-Realization' (1984) 3 Third World Legal Studies, Article 9, <http://scholar.valpo.edu/twls/vol3/iss1/9> accessed 20 January 2012; Peter Uvin, *Human Rights and Development* (1st edn, Kumarian Press 2004).

[2] The Non Aligned Movement countries are a group of states which are not formally aligned with or against any major 'power bloc'. Although the Non-Aligned Movement was not set up as a formal organization, NAM became the name to refer to the participants of the *Conference of Heads of State or Government of Non-Aligned Countries* first held in 1961. The term 'non-alignment' itself was first used by VK Krishna Menon in 1953 remarks at the United Nations.

[3] Bonny Ibhawoh, 'The Right to Development: The Politics and Polemics of Power and Resistance' (2011) 33 Human Rights Quarterly 76–104; Ian Brownlie, 'The Human Right to Development: Study Prepared for the Commonwealth Secretariat' (Human Rights Unit occasional paper) (Commonwealth Secretariat 1989).

[4] See Keba M'Baye, 'Le Droit du Développement comme un Droit de l'Homme' (1972) 5 Revue des Droits de l'Homme 503.

freedoms can be fully realized'. The preamble of the Declaration defines development as a 'comprehensive, economic, social, cultural and political process, which aims at the constant improvement of the well-being of the entire population and of all individuals on the basis of their active, free and meaningful participation in development and in the fair distribution of benefits resulting therefrom'.

This right, as one of the several rights belonging to the third generation of human rights, is seen by its advocates as a bridge between the first two generations of rights.[5] As David Beetham argues, the right to development was originally a specific right to the 'Third World countries' and a claim against economically dominant countries.[6] Whereas the hope was that the recognition of development as a right would encourage the economically dominant countries to accept more responsibility for eliminating the causes of underdevelopment, the right was criticized on a broad range of grounds:

The first and most important obstacle is political. The right to development was first formulated by representatives from developing countries for a new international order which would be more favourable to the development of less developed countries and for the full control by people over their own natural resources.[7] However, in 1981, when the drafting process began, the USA stressed that the right to development should not create any right to a transfer of resources. Its representative argued that 'aid is a matter of sovereign decision of donor countries that could not be subject to binding rules under the guise of advancing every human being's right to development'.[8] As Stephen Marks states, 'that bargain was kept insofar as the Declaration of 1986 does not purport to establish any legally binding obligations and remains at the level of general principles'.[9] Even in this form, surprisingly, the United States voted against it.

A second objection to the right to development is concerned with the relationship between the right to development and other basic human rights. Critics argue that the declaration is duplicating other already codified rights and this is nothing more than the sum of civil and political rights, and economic, social, and cultural rights.[10] In response to this objection, Arjun Sengupta, in the Fifth Report of the Independent Expert on the Right to Development, argued that:

> The right to development is a composite right to a process of development; it is not just an 'umbrella' right, or the sum of a set of rights. The integrity of these rights implies that if any one of them is violated, the whole composite right to development is also violated. The independent expert describes this in terms of a 'vector' of human rights composed of various elements that represent the various economic, social and cultural rights as well as the civil

[5] See, eg, Stephen P Marks, 'The Human Right to Development: Between Rhetoric and Reality' (2004) 17 Harvard Human Rights Journal 139.

[6] David Beetham, 'The Right to Development and Its Corresponding Obligations' in Bard A Andreassen and Stephen P Marks (eds), *Development as a Human Rights: Legal, Political and Economic Dimensions* (2nd edn, Intersenita 2010).

[7] ibid.

[8] Marks, 'The Human Right to Development: Between Rhetoric and Reality', note 5 at 143.

[9] ibid.

[10] See Manoj Kumar Sinha, 'Development at the Crossroads-Is Right to Development a Human Right' (2002) 42(4) Indian Journal of International Law 512; Arjun Sengupta, 'On the Theory and Practice of the Right to Development' (2002) 24(4) Human Rights Quarterly 837.

and political rights. The realisation of the right to development requires an improvement of this vector, such that there is improvement of some, or at least one, of those rights without violating any other.[11]

The third objection to the right to development is about its realization in practice—how to make it operational. The challenge here is to make the right to development a priority in development policy as reflected in different national and international strategies. Describing the components of the right to development does not specify the steps required to be taken for implementing it in practice.[12]

Moreover, the right to development poses a number of legal questions. There are arguments about the appropriate place of this right within the body of human rights law.[13] At the international level, the declaration of the right to development does not enjoy a legally binding status. It is not a treaty and therefore with no binding force. It is a soft law that only provides a kind of moral authority rather than a legal one and carries no resource-transfer obligation. Nonetheless, at the national level, states have taken different positions regarding the legal status of development, ranging from rejecting it as a human right at all to the position that it is a core right and should be legally binding.[14]

There are also some difficulties in the identification of beneficiaries and duty-holders of the right to development.[15] While the basic objective of the idea of the right to development was to consider development as a process in which developed countries and some important international financial institutions provide enhanced resources to assist less developed countries in their developmental effort, the Declaration on the Right to Development contains no clear obligation to provide development assistance. According to Article 4(1), 'states have the duty to take steps, individually and collectively, to formulate international development policies with a view to facilitating the full realization of the right to development'. Whereas an effective international co-operation is essential in providing developing countries with appropriate means and facilities to foster their comprehensive development, no reference is made to the duty to provide development assistance.[16] In a 1999 resolution, the General Assembly expressed deep concern about the overall decline in official development assistance flows and called upon developed countries to mobilize their collective resources for development assistance in order to better support the right to development, with a goal of reaching UN targets as soon as possible.[17]

In a nutshell, the idea of the right to development has sought to establish two things. First, it introduces development as a human right in order to provide a legal

[11] Arjun Sengupta, 'Fifth Report of the Independent Expert on the Right to Development', submitted in Accordance with Commission Resolution 2002b/69 (UN Doc E/CN.4/2002/WG.18/6 and Add 1) at 5.

[12] Stephen P Marks, 'Obstacles to the Right to Development' (2003) 5:2–3 Harvard Human Rights Journals 2; Stephen P Marks, 'Human Rights and Development' in Sarah Joseph and Adam MacBeth (eds), *Research Handbook on International Human Rights Law* (1st edn, Edward Elgar Publishing 2010).

[13] Isabella D Bunn, 'The Right to Development: Implications for International Economic Law' (2000) 15(6) American University International Law Review 1425–67.

[14] Marks, 'Human Rights and Development', note 12.

[15] Brownlie, 'The Human Right to Development: Study Prepared for the Commonwealth Secretariat', note 3.

[16] ibid at 23. [17] UNGA Res 53/155.

and moral authority to developing countries' request for the international redistribution of resources to upgrade their level of development and transfer development from the realm of charity to the realm of rights. Second, the idea of the right to development assumes development as the realization of human rights as both civil and political as well as economic, social, and cultural. It confirms that all people have the right to development and that development is achieved through the realization of all kinds of human rights. The first point naturally has not been supported by some of the economically dominant countries, in particular the USA who cast doubt on different facets of this right. Due to all the objections and critiques, the idea of development as a human right has failed to take root and is only recognized as a soft law. But the second point has been elaborated in the form of a human rights-based approach to development.

Discussions of human rights mainstreaming have now been mostly replaced by references to the human rights-based approach to development, though the idea of the right to development has never been put totally aside. Advocates of this approach take the view that development is on a par with realizing human rights without remarking whether development is or is not a human right. Unlike the right to development which was merely focused on underdeveloped and developing countries, the human rights-based approach to development is not limited to these countries, but rather it offers a new look at development which can be applied world-wide.

The change within the UN normative framework is a clear illustration: the UNDP adopted a new policy on integrating human rights with development. In its reports, UNDP affirm that 'human development is essential for realizing human rights and human rights are essential for full human development'.[18] In the words of the Human Development Report:

> Human rights express the bold idea that all people have claims to social arrangements that protect them from the worst abuses and deprivations—and that secure the freedom for a life of dignity. Human development, in turn, is a process of enhancing human capabilities—to expand choices and opportunities so that each person can lead a life of respect and value. When human development and human rights advance together, they reinforce one another—expanding people's capabilities and protecting their rights and fundamental freedoms.[19]

The report highlights the mutual enrichment of the ideas of human rights and human development. As remarked in the UNDP report, the human rights-based approach to development is also rooted in the needs-based approach and the capability approach which all often come together under the name of human development.

2.2. Human development: from needs to rights

Over time, economists have become convinced of the fact that the exclusive focus on the economic dimension of development can lead to forgetting other important

[18] UNDP, Human Development Report, 'Human Rights and Development' (2000) at 2 <http://hdr.undp.org/en> accessed 24 July 2009.

[19] ibid.

aspects.[20] In the place of an economic concept of development, a different response came from Mahbub ul Haq, Paul Streeten, and others in the name of the needs-based approach to development. This approach suggests that all human beings have basic needs, whether material, such as food, water, and shelter, and non-material, such as security and belongingness, and that policies should, first of all, promote the meeting of basic needs. The aim of the approach, at least at a theoretical level, was to provide 'the opportunities for the full physical, mental, and social development of the human personality'.[21] Nonetheless, this approach was faced with serious difficulties in practice. Although at the theoretical level, the approach insisted on both non-material and material needs, in practice, it was focused primarily on material goods and services.[22] Some critics dispute the arbitrariness in choice of basic needs (material goods and services) and argue that this approach can limit individual autonomy.

As a result, due to some shortcomings and misunderstandings which will be discussed in further detail later in this chapter, the needs-based approach has failed to take root.[23] Yet, in the last years of the 1980s, Amartya Sen tried to reformulate the core idea of this approach into a new approach known as the capability approach. The capability approach as another alternative to economic understanding of development defines development as an expansion of human capabilities. The concept of human capability is used in a broad way as 'the alternative combinations of functionings that are feasible for a person to achieve'.[24] The concept of functioning, which has Aristotelian root, reflects 'the various things a person may value doing or being'.[25] In *The Idea of Justice*, Sen argues that:

> [T]he capability perspective is inescapably concerned with a plurality of different features of our lives and concerns. The various attainments in human functioning that we may value are very diverse, varying from being well nourished or avoiding premature mortality to taking part in the life of the community and developing the skill to pursue one's work-related plans and ambitions. The capability that we are concerned with is our ability to achieve various

[20] See eg David Trubek, 'The Rule of Law in Development Assistance: Past, Present and Future' in David M Trubek and Alvaro Santos (eds), *The New Law and Economic Development: A Critical Appraisal* (1st edn, Cambridge University Press 2006); Richard Peet and Elaine Hartwick, *Theories of Development: Concepts, Arguments, Alternatives* (2nd edn, The Guilford Press 2009); James Cypher and James Diestz, *The Process of Economic Development* (3rd edn, Routledge 2009).

[21] Paul Streeten and others, *First Things First: Meeting Basic Human Needs in Developing Countries* (1st edn, Oxford 1981) at 33; see also Frances Stewart, *Planning to Meet Basic Needs* (1st edn, Palgrave Macmillan 1985); Richard Jolly, 'Employment, Basic Needs and Human Development: Elements for a New International Paradigm in Response to Crisis' (2010) 11:1 Journal of Human Development and Capabilities 11.

[22] Frances Stewart, 'Basic Needs Approach' in David Alexander Clark (ed), *The Elgar Companion to Development Studies* (1st edn, Edward Elgar 2006).

[23] In *Resources, Values and Development*, Sen (1984) sought to formulate a fivefold critique of the needs-based approach, though some of his criticisms were challenged as a misrepresentation of the needs-based approach. In particular, his argument that the needs-based approach presents a form of 'commodity fetishism' has been largely criticized (see Sabina Alkire, *Valuing Freedoms. Sen's Capability Approach and Poverty Reduction* (1st edn, Oxford University Press 2002) at 166–70).

[24] Amartya Sen, *Development as Freedom* (1st edn, Oxford University Press 1999) at 75

[25] Polly Vizard, *Poverty and Human Rights: Sen's Capability Perspective' Explored* (1st edn, Oxford University Press 2006) at 108–09.

combinations of functionings that we can compare and judge against each other in terms of what we have reason to value.[26]

This approach has been advanced by, among others, Martha Nussbaum, Desai, Alkire and Black, Clark, and Robeyns.[27] The capability approach has been influential in development thinking, though it has been criticized on a number of grounds which will be examined in the last part of this chapter.

As will be discussed later in the analytical theory of planning, advocates of the capability approach tend to find a link, though somewhat in different directions, between human rights and human capabilities describing human rights as entitlements to essential capabilities.[28] On this account, the human rights-based approach is often seen as an extension of the capability approach. In one of her writings, Nussbaum introduces capabilities and human rights as 'close relatives'.[29] In her paper on 'Capabilities and Human Rights', she states that in some cases, such as the right to religious freedom, 'capabilities and rights should be seen to be equivalent'.[30] In some other cases, such as the right to seek employment, she claims that human rights 'would be prior to capability, and a ground for the securing of a capability'.[31] In a relatively different way, in her *Frontiers of Justice*, she repeatedly emphasizes that 'I view the capabilities approach as one species of a human rights approach'.[32]

Polly Vizard and others argue that the concept of capability can be used as an important entry-point for defending the existence of a broad class of human rights. In this regard, they hold that:

> The concept of capability provides an important entry-point for defining the validity of a broad class of human rights concerns, covering, for example, economic and social rights, such as the human right to an adequate standard of living, including adequate food and shelter, and the human right to health; as well civil and political rights, such as freedom from arbitrary interference, freedom from torture and cruel and inhuman treatment, and the right to a fair trial.[33]

[26] Sen, *Development as Freedom*, note 24 at 233.

[27] Martha Nussbaum, *Women and Human Development: The Capabilities Approach* (1st edn, Cambridge University Press 2000); Martha Nussbaum, *Sex and Social Justice* (1st edn, Oxford University Press 2000); Meghnad Desai, 'Poverty and Capability: Towards an Empirically Implementable Measure' in M Desai (ed), *Poverty, Famine and Economic Development* (1st edn, Edward Elgar 1995); Sabina Alkire and Rufus Black, 'A Practical Reasoning Theory of Development Ethics: Furthering the Capabilities Approach' (1997) 9:2 Journal of International Development 236; David A Clark, *Visions of Development: A Study of Human Values* (1st edn, Edward Elgar 2002); Ingrid Robeyns, 'Sen's Capability Approach and Gender Inequality: Selecting Relevant Capabilities' (2003) 9(2–3) Feminist Economist 61.

[28] Sakiko Fukuda-Parr, 'The Metrics of Human Rights: Complementarities of the Human Development and Capabilities Approach' (2011) 12:1 Journal of Human Development and Capabilities 73.

[29] Martha Nussbaum, *Creating Capabilities: The Human Development Approach* (1st edn, Harvard University Press 2011).

[30] Martha Nussbaum, *Cultivating Humanity: A Classical Defense of Reform in Liberal Education* (1st edn, Harvard University Press 1997) at 293.

[31] ibid.

[32] Martha Nussbaum, *Frontiers of Justice: Disability, Nationality, Species Membership* (1st edn, Harvard University Press 2006) at 78, 284, 285–86, 291.

[33] Polly Vizard, Sakiko Fukuda-Parr, and Diane Elson, 'Introduction: The Capability Approach and Human Rights' (2011) 12(1) Journal of Human Development and Capabilities, at 1.

Taken together, there is a close connection among the needs-based approach, the capability approach, and the human rights-based approach. The major similarity among these three approaches is that all are based on the maxim that individuals should be treated as an end and economic growth is only the means of development. This has been the central message of Human Development Reports released since 1990. The first Human Development Report defines development as 'both the process of widening people's choices and the level of their achieved well-being'.[34] Ten years later, in 2000, the Human Development Report combined this understanding of human development, as the enhancement of capabilities, with the concept of human rights, and started to introduce development as realizing human rights in the form of a human rights-based approach to development.

Although the human rights-based approach to development has emerged following needs-based and capability approaches, it adds further dimensions to development thinking. At the heart of the human rights-based approach to development are concerns with the mechanisms of accountability—what distinguishes rights from needs and capabilities. Rights always trigger obligation(s) whereas needs and capabilities do not imply any duties. While people are often supposed to be grateful when their needs are met or when they receive assistance, it is not expected from right holders when their rights are satisfied.

In sum, two different paths, the path of the right to development and the path of human development paved the way for the rise of the human rights-based approach to development, the core idea of which is that the realization of human rights is both the means and ends of development. The particular strength of this approach is that it entails two sets of principles, substantive and procedural, which are rich enough to guide human rights planning. The next two sections will present the substantive and procedural theories of human rights planning which are mostly derived from the basic idea and principles of the human rights-based approach to development.

3. Substantive Theory of Human Rights Planning

Adopting the human rights-based approach to development, the substantive theory of planning, suggested here, is informed by the comprehensive set of human rights, embodied in the Universal Declaration of Human Rights and subsequent international human rights treaties. Based on the premise that the realization of human rights is both the means and ends of development, the core international human rights treaties,[35] at a minimum, must be addressed in human rights planning

[34] United Nations Human Development Report (Oxford University Press 1990) at 9 <http://hdr.undp.org/sites/default/files/reports/219/hdr_1990_en_complete_nostats.pdf> accessed 9 February 2014.

[35] There are currently nine core human rights treaties. These include: International Covenant on Economic, Social, and Cultural Rights 1966 (ICESCR); International Covenant on Civil and Political Rights 1966 (ICCPR); International Convention on the Elimination of All Forms of Racial Discrimination (ICERD); Convention on the Elimination of All Forms of Discrimination against Women (CEDAW); Convention against Torture and Other Cruel, Inhuman, or Degrading Treatment or Punishment (CAT); Convention on the Rights of the Child (CRC); International

systematically, though this list can be extended to other human rights treaties and declarations, such as the Declaration on the Rights of Indigenous Peoples and the International Convention on the Suppression and Punishment of the Crime of Apartheid and those set out in International Labour Organisation or regional declarations.

The present theory consists of five rights-related and one duty-related principles upon which every human rights planning including NHRAPs should be based. These are the principles of: universality; inalienability; indivisibility; interrelatedness; equality and non-discrimination; and the fourfold principle of obligation. These substantive principles are all equally important.

3.1. Principle of universality of human rights

The universality of human rights is the first and foremost principle of the human rights-based approach to development. As mentioned in Chapter 1, it has been criticized by cultural relativists who argue that human rights, as set forth in international human rights documents, emanate from Western cultural values and, therefore, are not universally valid. Cultural relativists hold that every culture includes different beliefs, values, norms, and practices which are all valid and should be respected.[36] They argue that those norms and practices considered wrong in some cultural contexts are justified in others. Cultural relativism, as a chronic issue in human rights discourse, is somewhat contentious. I will not try to treat this complex subject in its full form here, but instead concentrate my attention on just two significant points. First, the idea of human rights is not Western or Eastern, but rather it is an evolutionary account. In this respect, some scholars have provided various instances, showing that the idea of human rights has no boundaries in time or place. For example, William Talbott in his two-volume book on the universality of basic human rights, adopts the 'Historical-Social Process of Moral Discovery' to show overwhelming evidence of the fact that human rights do not belong to certain cultural traditions.[37] As he argues, it is, for instance, a mistake to think that Western Europe has a tradition of religious tolerance.[38] On the contrary, the first known advocates of religious tolerance were from the East—specifically, Ashoka (third century BC) from India, and Cyrus the Great (sixth

Convention on the Protection of the Rights of All Migrant Workers and Members of Their Families (ICRMW); International Convention for the Protection of All Persons from Enforced Disappearance (ICPPED); Convention on the Rights of Persons with Disabilities (CRPD).

[36] See, eg, John J Tilley, 'Cultural Relativism' (2000) 22(2) Human Rights Quarterly 501–47; James W Nickel, *Making Sense of Human Rights* (2nd edn, Blackwell 2007); James Nickel and David Reidy, 'Relativism, Self-determination and Human Rights' in D Chatterjee (ed), *Democracy in a Global World* (1st edn, Rowman & Littlefield 2008).

[37] William Talbott, *Which Rights Should Be Universal?* (1st edn, Oxford University Press 2005); William Talbott, *Human Rights and Human Well-being* (1st edn, Oxford University Press 2010).

[38] Talbott, 2005, ibid.

century BC), king of Persia (Iran). Whereas in the USA slavery remained a legal institution until the late nineteenth century, as early as the sixth century BC Cyrus had not only strongly opposed slavery but also freed thousands of slaves.[39] Martha Nussbaum likewise mentions that 'we need to remind ourselves that sex equality is an Indian constitutional idea and it is not an American constitutional idea'.[40] In the East, on the other hand, very basic human rights are being violated every day. Infibulation is still approved by some cultures in Sudan, Egypt, and Malaysia, for example. As Michael Freeman argues, cultural relativism is also morally implausible because it accepts cultures and harmful practices that are cruel and unjust such as female genital cutting.[41] Whereas there is a core convention on the rights of people with disabilities, even today an idea common in India is that disability represents a personal flaw and a consequence of karmic retribution for misdeeds.[42]

Second, as will be discussed in the analytical theory of planning later in the present chapter, human rights are grounded in universal objective values which are rooted in basic human needs. Ontologically speaking, human beings have the same basic needs which exist in the external world independently of the knowing subject. Epistemologically, our knowledge of human needs and their corresponding rights has evolved and improved over time. Nonetheless, universality in this form does not refute differences but instead encourages unity through diversity discussed in Chapter 1. There is often a broad range of items (objects or processes) to fulfil basic needs. This is where individual differences and cultural differences in the form of human interests come in. Human interests for the fulfilment of basic needs are dependent on socio-cultural context but it makes no difference to the universality of basic human rights.[43]

3.2. Principle of inalienability of human rights

The second substantive principle which is related to the universality of human rights postulates that rights cannot be taken from or given away from their holders. This is known as the principle of inalienability of rights and must be considered in adopting any human rights action plan.

[39] ibid, 53.

[40] Martha Nussbaum, 'In Defense of Universal Values' in C Wainryb, J Smetana, and E Turiel (eds), *Social Development, Social Inequalities, and Social Justice* (1st edn, Lawrence Erlbaum Associates (LEA) 2008) at 214.

[41] Michael Freeman, 'Universalism of Human Rights and Cultural Relativism' in S Sheeran and N Rodley (eds), *Routledge Handbook of International Human Rights Law* (1st edn, Routledge 2013) 49–63.

[42] Nayreen Daruwalla and others, 'Violence Against Women with Disability in Mumbai, India: A Qualitative Study'. SAGE Open, July–September (2013) Sage Open 1 <http://journals.sagepub.com/doi/pdf/10.1177/2158244013499144> accessed 8 September 2015.

[43] For detailed discussion see Azadeh Chalabi, 'National Human Rights Action Plans: A Roadmap to Development' (2014) 24:8 The Journal of Development in Practice 989–1002.

3.3. Principle of indivisibility of human rights

This substantive principle declares that there is no priority among basic human rights. The fundamental goal of a 'global NHRAP'[44] (not a right-specific plan) is the implementation of all kinds of human rights, civil and political as well as economic, social, and cultural.

3.4. Principle of inter-relatedness of human rights

The fourth principle states that the realization of one right often depends, wholly or in part, on the realization of others. For example, the enjoyment of the right to health is dependent on the right to housing and at least partly the right to education. In a similar fashion, the exercise of political participation is dependent on the vindication of the right to vote and the right to free elections paves the way for enjoyment of that.

3.5. Principle of equality and non-discrimination

The last rights-related principle is equality and non-discrimination which is both a substantive and procedural principle. All individuals are equal as human beings and are entitled to basic human rights without discrimination of any kind, such as race, colour, sex, ethnicity, age, language, religion, political or other opinion, national or social origin, disability, property, birth, or other status. This will be further discussed as a procedural principle shortly.

3.6. Fourfold principle of obligation

This principle implies four main obligations on the states to: respect; protect; promote; and fulfil rights. At a primary level, each state has an obligation not to interfere directly or indirectly with the enjoyment of rights. The right to housing, as an example, is violated if the state engages in arbitrary forced evictions. At a secondary level, the state must provide a system which prevents, protects from, and provides redress for, interference by non-state actors, ranging from neighbours and spouses to multidimensional corporations and international financial institutions. At a tertiary level, the obligation to promote human rights requires raising awareness of human rights, thereby advancing a culture of human rights through, for example, human rights education, research, and dissemination of information and knowledge. At a final level, the obligation to fulfil requires the states to proactively take appropriate legislative, administrative, budgetary, judicial, and other measures towards the full

[44] For further details about different types of national human rights action plans, including global NHRAP (as recommended in the 1993 Vienna Declaration and Programme of Action), rights-specific action plans, National Action Plan on Business and Human Rights (NAP-BHR), and National Action Plan on Women, Peace, and Security (NAR-WPS), see Chapter 4.

realization of rights. Failure to perform any one of these obligations constitutes a violation of human rights.[45]

Having discussed different substantive principles upon which every NHRAP should be based, it is time to turn to the procedural theory as the third part of the general theory of human rights planning.

4. Procedural Theory of Human Rights Planning

Procedurally, at least four main principles, which are not dispensable, need to be employed in every human rights planning, including a NHRAP. These procedural principles, extracted from the human rights-based approach to development,[46] include:

1. Participation
2. Empowerment
3. Non-discrimination
4. Accountability

4.1. Principle of participation

Participation is one of the key bases of human rights planning. This principle entails that in all phases of planning, from preparation to evaluation, participation as a multi-level multi-agent endeavour, should be active, free, and meaningful. This is in marked contrast with central state-centric planning. All stakeholders, including the general public, government, experts, civil society, private sector actors, and donors, both bilateral and multilateral, should have an opportunity to willingly, knowingly, and effectively become involved in the decision-making process in order to reflect their needs and interests.

Participation is much more than informing or consulting the people concerned of the planned project. It should be based on an active engagement of citizens as 'makers and shapers' rather than as 'users and choosers' of interventions designed by others.[47]

[45] For further details, see Henry Shue, *Basic Rights: Substance, Affluence, and US Foreign Policy* (1st edn, Princeton University Press 1980).

[46] Chalabi, 'National Human Rights Action Plans: A Roadmap to Development', note 43; UNDG Human Rights Working Group, The Human Rights Based Approach to Development Cooperation Towards a Common Understanding Among UN Agencies 2003 <https://undg.org/document/the-human-rights-based-approach-to-development-cooperation-towards-a-common-understanding-among-un-agencies/> accessed 17 May 2013; Kirkemann Boesen and Hans-Otto Sano, 'The Implications and Value Added of a Human Rights-Based Approach' in Bård A Andreassen and S Marks (eds), *Development as a Human Right: Legal, Political, and Economic Dimensions* (1st edn, Intersentia 2010); Siobhán McInerney-Lankford, 'Human Rights and Development: a Comment on Challenges and Opportunities from a Legal Perspective' (2009) 1:1 Journal of Human Rights Practice 51.

[47] See, eg, Andrea Cornwall and John Gaventa, 'From Users and Choosers to Makers and Shapers: Repositioning Participation in Social Policy' (2000) 31 IDS Bulletin 50–62; John Gaventa and Andrea Cornwall, 'Challenging the Boundaries of the Possible: Participation, Knowledge and Power' (2006) 37 IDS Bulletin 122–28 <doi:10.1111/j.1759-5436.2006.tb00329.x> accessed 7 April 2013.

To put this principle into practice requires effective methods which will be discussed in Chapter 7.

4.2. Principle of empowerment

Enhancing empowerment of both rights-holders to claim their rights and duty-bearers to meet their obligations is another procedural principle of human rights planning. This principle focuses primarily on how to transform rights-holders from being passive recipients of aid to being empowered claimants.

Needless to say that there is a close linkage between this principle and the participation principle. On the one hand, people must be empowered to be able to knowingly and willingly participate in decision-making that affects their lives. That is citizens' voices should be amplified through awareness-raising and capacity building. On the other hand, participation empowers people to determine their path of development through planning.

4.3. Principle of non-discrimination

This principle prohibits negative discrimination and enjoins positive discrimination. It means that special attention should be paid to the people who lack basic human rights and gives them a sense of prioritization.[48] Human rights planning should be oriented towards those who are deprived of basic human rights or their rights are under threat, such as children, women, racial, linguistic, ethnic, and other minorities, persons with disabilities, elderly persons, refugees, asylum-seekers, and excluded groups. It is strongly against any kinds of social exclusion which is the denial of basic rights of citizens in society or the inability of groups of individuals to participate in the basic political, cultural, economic, and social functionings of their society.[49] By nature, this principle is both substantive and procedural.

4.4. Principle of accountability

This principle declares that states and other duty bearers as lead bodies in different stages of planning should be held into account for their actions or inactions. This can enhance transparency throughout planning. Six types of accountability mechanism will be discussed in Chapter 7.

[48] See Brigitte I Hamm, 'A Human Rights Approach to Development' (2001) 23:4 Human Rights Quarterly 1019; Andrea Cornwall and Celestine Nyamu-Musembi, 'Putting the "Rights-Based Approach" to Development into Perspective' (2004) 25:8 Third World Quarterly 1415; Séverine Deneulin, 'Ideas Related to Human Development' in Séverine Deneulin (with Lila Shahani) (eds), *An Introduction to the Human Development and Capability Approach Freedom and Agency* (1st edn, Earthscan 2009).

[49] See Fotis Papadopoulos and Panos Tsakloglou, 'Social Exclusion in the EU: A Capability-based Approach' in F Comim, M Qizilbash, and S Alkire (eds), *The Capability Approach: Concepts, Measures and Applications* (1st edn, Cambridge University Press 2008).

Let me move on to the last part of our general theory of human rights planning, and that is the analytical theory.

5. Analytical Theory of Human Rights Planning

In this last section, I will make an effort to develop an analytical theory to perform both regulative and heuristic roles for human rights planning and beyond. This will be done through positive critique of the interest theory of rights, the capability approach to human rights, and the needs-based approach to human rights.

Despite sporadic attempts in the literature, the human rights field has been somewhat divided into two groups: those who work more on jurisprudence at the philosophical level such as interest theorists and those who work on rights with regard to policy making such as most advocates of the needs-based approach. Although the work of these groups should inform each other in mutually beneficial ways, they are mostly isolated. In spite of significant differences, these theories have at least one common purpose, that is, what form basic rights or what rights do for those who hold them. To pursue this goal, they have both strengths and weaknesses. Although they are sometimes even seen as in opposition, this section strives for a rapprochement between them. It is a preliminary attempt to go beyond the three theories of rights—the interest theory, capability approach, needs-based approach—with the aim of advancing an integrated account of basic human rights from a scientific realist perspective.

In doing so, I will first offer a critique of the interest theory, needs-based approach, and capability approach respectively, and then provide a new integrated approach which I would call NIC theory (Need, Interest, Capability). This alternative theory is intended to help identify, classify and prioritize basic rights for human rights planning.

5.1. Interest theory of rights

As its name implies, the interest theory of rights places emphasis on individual interests. There are different versions of interest theory, set out by, among others, Joseph Raz, Neil MacCormick, and Matthew H Kramer. A right in different versions of this theory is either grounded in (certain) 'interests' or is to further right-holders' 'interests', though the same linguistic label 'interest' has been used with different connotation across different versions of this theory.[50] More specifically, this theory is subject to at least four criticisms:

[50] See, eg, John Finnis, *Natural Law and Natural Rights* (1st edn, Clarendon Press 1980); Joseph Raz, *The Morality of Freedom* (1st edn, Oxford University Press 1986); Neil MacCormick, *Legal Right and Social Democracy* (1st edn, Oxford University Press 1982); Mathew Kramer, NE Simmonds, and Hillel Steiner, *A Debate Over Rights* (1st edn, Oxford University Press 1998); Mathew Kramer, 'Some Doubts about Alternatives to the Interest Theory' (2013) 123 Ethics 245–63; Neil MacCormick, 'Rights in Legislation' in P Hacker and J Raz (eds), *Law, Morality and Society: Essays in Honour of HLA Hart* (1st edn, Oxford University Press 1977) 189–209.

First, there is a remarkable absence of any coherent discussion about the definition of the concept of 'interest'. To the best of my knowledge, there is no single or agreed definition of interest recognized or acted upon across different versions of this theory. So far, most scholars have used the word 'interest' as if it designated a clear and distinct idea, but it does not, since it is often confused with needs or wants. Interest theorists, like Raz whose version is the most well-known version, are inclined to take the concept of interest for granted ignoring the critical task of examining the very concept of interest which is at the heart of this theory. That is why interest at one time or another has been used to imply different meanings, broadly or narrowly.[51] As Tasioulas mentions 'some interest theorists further restrict or qualify the nature of the interests that can ground human rights. James Griffin, for example, seeks to derive human rights exclusively from the values of personhood, that is autonomy and liberty, thereby conferring a determinate sense on the idea that human rights are protections of a special status, "human dignity".'[52]

Some versions of interest theory implicitly define 'interest' by reference to other contested (often very broad) concepts such as 'good'. For example, MacCormick as one of the most influential figures of the interest theory in one of his latest pieces wrote that:

> [T]hey [rules which confer rights] concern 'goods' (or 'advantages', or 'benefit', or 'interests' or however we may express the point). Whatever x may be, the idea of anyone's having a right to x would be absurd unless it were presupposed that x is normally a good for human beings, at any rate for those people who qualify as having the right in question[53]

It is left unanswered what is a good for human beings? In one of his previous writings, he held that 'it is uncontroversial that the satisfaction of needs, interest, and desires is a part of "the good" for the individual, but it is controversial whether it is exhaustive of and constitutive of the good. A formal account of rights can and should be neutral on that substantive moral question'.[54] Again, it is not clear why an account of rights should leave such critical questions unanswered. How can a human rights action plan be advanced without identifying what is 'good' for a human being? As Jane Fortin rightly argues 'perhaps inevitably, a common criticism of the interest theory is that it is far too broad; the interest relevant to the justification of rights are without clear demarcation'.[55] Campbell who presents his own version of interest theory, admits that it may be a weakness of the interest theory of rights that 'it leaves

[51] See, eg, Jjhon Eekelaar, 'The Emergence of Children's Rights' (1986) 6(2) Oxford Journal of Legal Studies 161–82; Michael Freeman, note 41; John Tobin, 'Justifying Children's Rights' (2013) International Journal of Children's Rights 395–441; MacCormick, 'Rights in Legislation', note 50.

[52] John Tasioulas, 'The Moral Reality of Human Rights' in Thomas Pogge (ed), *Freedom from Poverty as a Human Right: Who Owes What to the Very Poor?* (1st edn, Oxford University Press 2007) 75–103, at 77.

[53] Neil MacCormick, 'Rights in Legislation' in Aileen Kavanagh and John Oberdiek (eds), *Arguing About Law* (1st edn, Routledge 2009) at 330.

[54] Neil MacCormick, 'Children's Rights: A Test-Case for Theories of Rights' in C Nino (ed), *Rights* (1st edn, New York University Press 1992) at 311.

[55] Jane Fortin, *Children's Rights and the Developing Law* (1st edn, Cambridge University Press 1998) at 16.

us with a very open ended basis for determining which interests are to serve as the ground of rights'.[56]

Secondly, there is a network or apparatus of interconnected but distinct concepts—namely basic needs, capabilities, values, wants, preference, happiness, and well-being—which is either overlooked by interest theorists or they use them loosely or interchangeably. For example, MacCormick in his account of rights states that:

> [T]he ascription of a right to some class of beings seems to require the following presuppositions: for the class in question there is some act or omission performance of which in the case of each and every member of the class will satisfy, protect, or advance some need, interest, or desire of each such individual; and secondly: satisfaction of that need, interest, or desire is of such importance that it would be wrong to deny it to any such individual regardless of ulterior advantages in doing so.[57]

Despite the fact that there is a manifest difference, both conceptually and lexically, between 'needs', 'interests', and 'desire', in his account, these three have been left undefined or sometimes used interchangeably. Their failure to adopt a systemic approach has led to a blurred use and polysemous analysis of 'interest' which can distort our understanding of rights.[58]

This problem brings us to a related issue as the third objection—interest theorists have normally ignored some rival theoretical approaches, in particular the needs-based approach and capability approach to rights. The interest theory needs to specify where the line between needs, interests, capabilities, and wants should be drawn. What is the conceptual connection between interests, basic needs, wants, and capabilities?

The fourth challenge is the question of whether (and possibly when) interest is an objective or subjective concept. As mentioned above, in MacCormick's account of rights which is more objective, it remains unclear that where the objective existence of basic needs and subjective existence of desire stand. In some versions, they ground rights in 'universal interests significant enough to generate duties on the part of others'.[59] In this case, seemingly interest is used objectively in the same meaning as 'basic needs' such as health, physical security, friendship, etc.[60] Some other interest theorists in particular Matthew Kramer, in the cases of children and mentally disabled persons, employ an objective understanding of interest and in other settings a subjective context-dependent one. In *Rights, Wrongs and Responsibilities*, he writes that:

56 Tom D Campbell, 'The Rights of the Minor' in P Alston, S Parker, and J A Seymour (eds), *Children, Rights, and the Law* (1st edn, Oxford University Press 1992) at 16.

57 MacCormick, *Legal Right and Social Democracy*, note 50, at 160.

58 As Jassen says, 'the polysemous approach to word meanings should be replaced as much as possible by a monosemous approach'. (Theo AJM Jassen, 'Monosemy vs Polysemy' in H Cuyckens, R Dirven, and J R Taylor (eds), *Cognitive Approaches to Lexical Semantics* (1st edn, Mouton de Gruyter 2003) at 93).

59 Tasioulas, 'The Moral Reality of Human Rights', note 52 at 77; see Kieran Oberman, 'Immigration as a Human Right' in S Fine and L Ypi (eds), *Migration in Political Theory: The Ethics of Movement and Membership* (1st edn, Oxford University Press 2016).

60 See Tasioulas, ibid.

In some settings, the ostensibly suspect entitlements prove amenable to the Interest Theory's analysis when we define human interests objectively rather than subjectively; such an approach is singularly advisable when we confront situations involving children or mentally infirm people. In other settings, where the right-holders are sane human adults, two alternative tacks are available. An Interest Theorist can adopt a context-specific understanding of human interests, or he can recharacterize the tenor of a strange legal right in order to disclose its connections to human interests that are context-transcendent. Whatever might be the best method, the Interest Theorist can chart the intricacies of legal rights more adeptly and meticulously than the Will Theorist.[61]

Although this statement is partially true, '*in some settings*' has been used as a 'residual category', and Kramer provided more a denotative definition for this residual category (and not a connotative one). To a large extent, this shortcoming perhaps is rooted in the fact that he has adopted a functionalist explanation of rights and remained largely silent on the question of what interest exactly is. He has failed to suggest a clear set of criteria against which a line can be drawn between objective and subjective interests.

Having briefly examined the interest theory of rights, let me move on to the needs-based justification of rights as a more practical-oriented account.

5.2. Needs-based approach to rights

Advocates of the needs-based approach such as Doyal and Gough, Jim Ife, and David Miller have attempted to develop a universal theory of needs from which human rights can be derived.[62] David Miller goes on to say that something qualifies to recognize as a human right only if it can be affirmed that having that right can fulfil basic human needs.[63] This argument mirrors the work of Max-Neef, who categorizes human needs in a general framework as a basis for human rights.[64] Rita Floyd similarly believes that human rights should be grounded in something like basic human needs which are both universal and objectively valuable.[65] Otherwise, human rights cannot easily translate from theory into practice. She further argues that:

[H]uman rights and human needs are best thought of as complementary concepts. Thus, unless theories of needs are complemented by human rights they cannot (easily) be realized, because unlike 'rights', 'needs' do not produce duties. Without the capacity to produce obligations in others, the quest for needs fulfillment by needs theorists is likely to remain fruitless, which is why many needs theorists have reverted to linking human needs to the concept of human rights.[66]

[61] Matthew Kramer, *Rights, Wrongs and Responsibilities* (1st edn, Palgrave 2001) at 91.

[62] Len Doyal and Ian Gough, *A Theory of Human Need* (1st edn, Palgrave 1991); Jim Ife, *Human Rights from Below: Achieving Rights Through Community Development* (1st edn, Cambridge University Press 2009); David Miller, *National Responsibility and Global Justice* (1st edn, Oxford University Press 2007).

[63] Miller, ibid.

[64] Manfred A Max-Neef, *Human Scale Development: Conception, Application and Further Reflections* (1st edn, Zed Books 1991).

[65] Rita Floyd, 'Why We Need Needs-Based Justifications of Human Rights' (2011) 7 JIPT 1.

[66] ibid at 113.

Although some historical problems prevent liberal theorists to mention to the objective concept of basic need at the theoretical level, in practice, necessity dictates to employ, more or less, needs at every level of policy making. Policy makers have no option to make constant recourse to the notion of basic needs.[67] Some human rights analysts whose work is more practical-oriented believe that basic human needs can be regarded as a firm ground of human rights employed in human rights programming.[68] Sabina Alkire argues that 'vital needs may have a claim to political attention because even if a person twists and turns to avoid them, the person cannot disrupt laws of nature, unalterable and invariable environmental facts, or facts about the human constitution'.[69]

Needs-based approach sometimes comes under a broader approach called the resource-based approach whose proponents focus on resources and that needs are met when resources are available. As discussed earlier in this chapter, this approach has been criticized on a number of grounds.

First, an important issue with the needs-based approach to human rights is that it often only focuses on the objective concept of basic needs with disregard for individual and cultural differences. This approach has been described as having a one-sided focus that leaves out other aspects such as human freedoms. Dictatorship over needs in Soviet Communism where the 'need-principle', with a particular emphasis on 'material needs' (goods and services), provided a theoretical legitimation for paternalistic politics, has possibly discouraged some jurisprudential writers from any mention of the concept of need in their works.[70]

Second, this approach has failed to take individual interests (as will be explicated shortly in this section) into account. People have the same basic needs but very different interests. This failure can lead to paternalistic planning imposing people's life plan from the top down.

Third, this approach has neglected the fact that people have different capacities to convert resources into what they need or want and may need extra resources.

Fourth, the needs-based approach, at least in practice, has mostly focused on material resources (goods and services) underestimating the importance of non-material needs.

Fifth, this approach has, implicitly or explicitly, ignored other rival theories such as interest theory and the capability approach.

Having said that, the most important advantage of the needs-based approach is that it gives us a universal objective base for the identification of basic human rights.

Let me turn to the capability approach as another account of human rights.

[67] Lawrence A Hamilton, *The Political Philosophy of Needs* (1st edn, Cambridge University Press 2003).

[68] See eg Des Gasper, 'Human Rights, Human Needs, Human Development, Human Security: Relationships between four International "Human" Discourses' (2007), <www2.warwick.ac.uk/fac/soc/garnet/workingpapers/2007.pdf> accessed 12 January 2014.

[69] Sabina Alkire, 'Needs and Capabilities' (2005) 80(57) Royal Institute of Philosophy Supplement 229 at 236 <https://www.cambridge.org/core/journals/royal-institute-of-philosophy-supplements/article/needs-and-capabilities/F76BCFEE57A59EE364F9BE29AB978228> accessed 9 March 2015.

[70] Hamilton, *The Political Philosophy of Needs*, note 67.

5.3. Capability approach to rights

In general, advocates of the capability approach tend to see human rights as entitlements to capabilities that a person has by virtue of being human. Functionings and capabilities are the core concepts in different versions of the approach. As mentioned before, capabilities are defined, almost in all its versions, as what people are able to do and to be and functionings represent parts of the state of a person—in particular the various things that he or she manages to do or be in leading a life. I have no objections at all to their insistence on the importance of the concept of capability and its connection to human rights, quite the contrary I must submit that the very concept of capability is the most important advantage of this approach, absent from other rival theories of rights. However, I think this approach, at least its main version, advanced by Amartya Sen and Martha Nussbaum, suffers from some conceptual difficulties.

First, while it is important to take note of capability, there are some relevant concepts, notably basic needs and human interests, that are, more or less, neglected by the capability approach. As will be discussed later in this chapter, these concepts are as, if not more, important as the concept of capability both in connection with capability itself and basic human rights.

Second, there is a fine distinction between human ability and human liability which has been somewhat ignored by the capability approach. These two are distinct though interdependent. On the causal realist point of view, there are two types of power in a casual transaction of powers: 'active power' and 'passive power'. Whereas active power or ability can affect other things, the passive power or liability can be affected by other things.[71] A well-known example is nothing would be able to cut if nothing were liable to be cut. As Sayer puts it, 'people have the causal powers of being able to work ("labour power"), speak, reason, walk, reproduce, etc., and a host of causal liabilities, such as susceptibility to group pressure, extremes of temperature, etc'.[72] People are different in terms of both their abilities and liabilities. The fact of the matter is that liability and ability together are held to constitute what human capability is. In other words, human capabilities include both what people are able to do or liable to be.

Third, another problem with the capability approach is the lists of basic capabilities suggested by some representatives of this approach such as Nussbaum, Desai, Alkire and Black, Clark, and Robeyns.[73] For example, Martha Nussbaum provided a list of ten basic capabilities as a threshold below which no society should let any

[71] Stephen Mumford, 'Powers, Dispositions, Properties, or a Causal Realist Manifesto' in R Groff (ed), *Revitalizing Causality: Realism About Causality in Philosophy and Social Sciences* (1st edn, Routledge 2008); Brian Ellis, 'Powers and Dispositions' in R Groff (ed), *Revitalizing Causality: Realism about Causality in Philosophy and Social Sciences* (1st edn, Routledge 2008).

[72] Andrew Sayer, *Methods in Social Science: A Realist Approach* (2nd edn, Routledge 2010) at 71.

[73] Nussbaum, *Women and Human Development: The Capabilities Approach,* note 27; Nussbaum, *Sex and Social Justice*, note 27; Desai, 'Poverty and Capability: Towards an empirically implementable measure', note 27; Alkire and Black, 'A Practical Reasoning Theory of Development Ethics: Furthering the Capabilities Approach', note 27; Clark, *Visions of Development: A Study of Human Values*, note 27; Robeyns, 'Sen's Capability Approach and Gender inequality: Selecting relevant Capabilities', note 27.

individual fall. These include 'life', 'bodily health', 'bodily integrity', 'senses, imagination, thought', 'emotions', 'practical reason', 'affiliation', 'other species', 'play', and 'control over one's environment' (political and material).[74] In *Frontiers of Justice*, she states that this list 'can gather cross-cultural agreement, similar to the international agreements that have been reached concerning basic human rights'.[75] Her list has been widely criticized by even some advocates of this approach.[76] There are a number of tensions and contradictions between her proposed methodology and style of essentialism.[77] There seems to be no clear set of criteria against which the exclusiveness or inclusiveness of this list can be judged. Likewise, it has been argued that there are innumerable capabilities and there cannot be a one-size-fit-all list like this.[78] Also, there is always a risk of biases creeping into the list selection. Furthermore, there is a confusion here between basic capabilities (as what people are able to do or be) and basic needs (as the lack of something required). Looking closely at this list, it is easy enough to see that it is very similar to the list of basic needs such as health, shelter, and security.

Fourth, the capability approach, in particular Sen's version, is criticized for its failure to devote sufficient attention to the means or resources required for expanding capabilities or 'freedom' (in his term).[79] Seemingly in response to this line of criticism, Nussbaum sought to include both sides in what she calls 'combined capabilities' and defined it as 'internal capabilities combined with suitable external conditions for the exercise of the function'.[80] She conflates something embodied inside each person ie human capability with external circumstances (opportunities and resources). Such a broad and loose definition would generate further questions about the scientific status of the concept. Perhaps this can also increase the possibility of ignoring or underestimating the importance of the availability of actual opportunities of different kinds for nurturing and nourishing human capabilities.

Fifth, another major challenge for the capability approach is that it is difficult to think of capability as the mere basis of human rights. Why? There are an uncountable number of capabilities people may have, and not all of them can be regarded as positive ones. Instead, some of them have even a negative value. People can make

[74] Nussbaum, *Women and Human Development: The Capabilities Approach*, note 27; Nussbaum, *Sex and Social Justice*, note 27.

[75] Nussbaum, *Frontiers of Justice: Disability, Nationality, Species Membership*, note 32, at 78.

[76] See, eg, Ingrid Robeyns, 'Capabilitarianism' (2016) 17:3 Journal of Human Development and Capabilities 397–414.

[77] David A Clark, 'The Capability Approach: Its Development, Critiques and Recent Advances' 2005, GPRG-WPS-032, Global Poverty Research Group <http://www.gprg.org/> accessed 28 April 2014.

[78] See Robeyns, 'Capabilitarianism', note 76.

[79] See, eg, David A Crocker (1995), 'Functioning and Capability: The Foundation of Senís and Nussbaumís Development Ethic, part II' in Martha C Nussbaum and Jonathan Glover (eds), *Women, Culture and Development* (Clarendon Press 1995) pp 153–98; Mozaffar Qizilbash, 'Capabilities, Well-being and Human Development: A Survey' (1996) 33(2) Journal of Development Studies 143–62; Des Gasper, 'Sen's Capability Approach and Nussbaum's Capabilities Ethic' (1997) 9(2) Journal of International Development 281–302; Des Gasper, 'Is Sen's Capability Approach an Adequate Basis for Considering Human Development?' (2002) 14(4) Review of Political Economy 435–61; Clark, note 77.

[80] Nussbaum, *Sex and Social Justice*, note 27, at 84–85.

mistakes in the process of making choices about the various states of being or doing they can take and this can perhaps justify the need for an objectively universal base (like basic human needs) of rights. In the capability approach, functionings and capabilities are defined in a morally neutral way.[81] Some advocates of the capability approach might object to this argument by pointing out, as Sen has done, that we need to count only those functionings or capabilities that people 'have reason to value' or 'have reason to want to achieve'. However, the concept of value and reason have not been clearly defined here. People may have reasons for valuing diverse and even conflicting 'beings' or 'doings'. They may even have 'reasons' to value something which is even harmful such as FGC. Some people in Sierra Leone or Somalia have their own 'reasons' to value voluntary FGC. Do they have the right to do so? As Robeyns aptly says, 'many specific capability theories make the mistake in defining functionings as those beings and doings that one has reason to value'.[82] How can a fundamentalist Muslim or Jew, a Southern Baptist and a Hollywood liberal all agree on a single set of values? Whose concept of good should come first? The problem is how to ground human rights on a wide range of values including subjective values.

Sixth, what is also quite questionable here is that for the capability approach expanding people's capabilities is defined as an end (not the means). I will get back to this challenge shortly when I try to put forward an integrated account of rights.

5.4. An integrated account of rights: NIC approach

As discussed above, the three major theories of rights—the interest theory, the capability approach, the needs-based approach—have focused on one concept, either interest, capability, or need, and used it in a rather isolated way, if not vaguely and imprecisely. Such deficit has led to conceptual reductionism in these theories. In my view, basic needs, interests, and capabilities are interdependent and all together form the foundations of basic human rights. What follows will be an attempt to build up an integrated account of basic human rights, which I would call 'NIC theory'.[83] The new theory seeks to explicate the concepts in question and explore the relationships among them. This theory begins with basic needs and in particular, addressing three questions: What is basic need? Why can it provide an objective base? And why it cannot be seen as the only base of rights?

A basic human need is a lack of something (object or process)[84] required for the continued healthy existence of every human being. That is something without which

[81] Martha Nussbaum, 'Capabilities as Fundamental Entitlement: Sen and Social Justice' (2003) 9(2–3) Feminist Economics 33–59; Ian Carter, 'Is the Capability Approach Paternalistic?' (2014) 30 Economics and Philosophy 75–98.

[82] Robeyns, 'Capabilitarianism', note 76 at 406.

[83] NIC (Need, Interest, Capability) is one way of breaking down what this integrated model means. NIC in Farsi (Persian) means good.

[84] As Bunge aptly explains 'it is generally admitted that objects can be either material (concrete), like birds and schools, or immaterial (abstract), like concepts and theories. Concrete objects are also called "things" or "existents," and abstract objects "ideal" or "constructs." Correspondingly, the properties of concrete objects, such as viscosity and productivity, may be said to be *substantive*, whereas those

a human being would cease to be alive or serious harm of some specified and objective kind will result.[85] This is what makes basic needs inescapable. Basic needs can be divided into two levels, primary and secondary, and categorized into four types.

Primary needs are necessary for individuals to stay alive such as oxygen, water, food, and light. Without oxygen anyone would be dead in a few minutes; without water no one would survive more than a few days and without food, only a few weeks.[86] Secondary needs are necessary for human beings to keep or regain health such as physical activity and belongingness. For example, as Steptoe and others explain:

> Socially isolated individuals are at increased risk for the development of cardiovascular disease, infectious illness, cognitive deterioration, and mortality. Social isolation also has been associated with elevated blood pressure, C-reactive protein, and fibrinogen and with heightened inflammatory and metabolic responses to stress.[87]

Whereas meeting primary needs is a matter of life and death, meeting secondary needs is a matter of health or sickness. Basic human needs, primary and secondary, provide an objective base, ontologically and epistemologically, for basic human rights. Why? Because, (1) in an ontological sense, basic needs exist in the external world independently of the knowing subject before ratification of any legal rights or any human rights treaty. And (2) in an epistemological sense, basic needs can be known by means of scientific methods, if not recognizable by a normal person. No one would doubt that we cannot survive without food and water or function normally without security. Hence, basic needs can provide a set of objective scientific standards for the identification and prioritization of rights and that is why they can be seen as the root of basic human rights.

Having ranked basic needs into two categories of primary and secondary, horizontally, there are four types of basic needs. These include:

1. Material needs such as food, clean water, clean air, sleep, physical mobility, clothing and shelter

of ideal objects, such as consistency and transitivity, may be said to be *formal*.' (Mario Bunge, *Chasing Reality: Strife over Realism* (1st edn, University of Toronto Press 2006) at 10.) A process, as Falleti and Mahoney state, is 'a particular type of sequence in which the temporarily ordered events belong to a single coherent mode of activity. Processes often describe transitions between states, including movement toward a new state or movement away from a prior state.' Tulia G Falleti and James Mahoney, 'The comparative sequential method' in J Mahoney and K Thelen (eds), *Advances in Comparative-Historical Analysis* (1st edn, Cambridge University Press 2015) at 214.

85 See, eg, David Wiggins, 'Needs, Need, Needing' (1987) Journal of Medical Ethics 13, 62–68; Doyal and Gough, *A Theory of Human Need*, note 62; David Wiggins, *Needs, Values and Truth: Essays in the Philosophy of Values* (1st edn, Oxford University Press 1998); Alkire, note 69; Hamilton, note 67; Björn Hettne, *Development Theory and the Three Worlds: Towards an International Political Economy of Development* (2nd edn, Longman 1995).

86 See Peter Schaber, 'Human Rights and Basic Needs' in M Albers, T Hoffmann, and J Reinhardt (eds), *Human Rights and Human Nature* (1st edn, Springer 2014) 109–19; Wiggins 1998, note 85; Mario Bunge, *Treatise on Basic Philosophy—Ethics: The Good and The Right* (1st edn, Springer 1989).

87 Andrew Steptoe, Aparna Shankar, Panayotes Demakakos, and Jane Wardle, 'Social Isolation, Loneliness, and All-cause Mortality in Older Men and Women' (2013) 110(15) PANS 5797–801, at 5797.

2. Security needs such as the need for freedom from threat to lives and the need to control over environment
3. Cognitive needs such as knowledge and understanding
4. Social needs such as company and belonging

Defining needs in this way makes what is in one's need distinct from what one wants. The concept of want goes beyond basic needs. It is subjective and refers to desire towards something. People sometimes want things that can contribute to their flourishing or advancement of their society such as becoming a mathematician, painter, or 'doctor without border', and sometimes want to indulge themselves in ways dangerous to others or their own health such as smoking. Bunge isolates two types of wants, legitimate and illegitimate,[88] though I would rather divide them into three categories: harming, non-harming, and progressive wants. Something which one desires to have is a legitimate or non-harming want if, to say the least, it can be met without hindering the satisfaction of any basic need of any other person such as mountain climbing. Progressive or advanced wants, as the third category, can contribute to scientific, technological, economic, and cultural advancements through invention and innovation. Remember, for example, the Wright brothers' desire to fly or Bill Gates who pursued his desire (not basic needs) in writing computer programs. Satisfaction of wants, in particular progressive ones, is crucial for social and human development. Nonetheless, since the main focus here is on *basic* rights, I will only mention wants in relation to needs and values, and then restrict my consideration to basic needs. Beyond basic human rights are those rights through which everyone is entitled to satisfy her non-harming and progressive wants, though dealing with that stands well beyond the scope of this chapter.

Basic needs and wants are the roots of human values. From a scientific realist point of view, 'there are no values in themselves but there are valuable items wherever there are organisms'.[89] This is because of the fact that values are not things, properties of things, but rather they are properties we attribute to the former.[90] Values are then relational. As Mario Bunge states, values emerged on our planet about four billion years ago together with the first organisms capable of discriminating what was good for them, ie what was favourable to their survival (as biovalue), and later in the case of human beings (as evaluator) what is normally valuable for their survival (primary needs) and their health (secondary needs) as well as what they desired to have (wants), from what is not or they do not.[91] As Bunge aptly argues, 'the conventional wisdom about values is that all of them are subjective: that value lies only in the mind of the evaluator'.[92] By contrast, whereas some values are based on wants and indeed subjective, others are objective because they are rooted in basic needs. For example, security and peace, health, co-operation, or environmental protection are objective

[88] Bunge, *Treatise on Basic Philosophy—Ethics: The Good and The Right*, note 86, at 27.
[89] ibid, at 13. [90] ibid, at 37. [91] ibid, at 13.
[92] Bunge, *Chasing Reality: Strife over Realism*, note 84, at 266.

values.[93] Whereas objective values are universal and cross-cultural, subjective values are changeable over time and can be traced to both cultural system (at the macro level) and personality system (at the micro level).

Let me return to the question raised at the outset: why basic needs cannot be seen as the only basis of rights? Although basic needs are epistemologically and ontologically objective, what has been largely under-noticed (in particular in the needs-based approach) is that the valuable items (objects, processes, properties of objects, and processes) for the fulfilment of basic needs varies from individual to individual, time to time, place to place, and culture to culture. An important deficit of the needs-based approach is that it solely focuses on basic needs while ignoring or at least underestimating the presence of individual and cultural differences, and the importance of free will. Such deficit can provide a pretext for subsequent paternalistic policies for the fulfilment of basic needs. Dictatorship over needs was seen in the history of Soviet communism and is now observable in North Korea where very basic material needs of the majority may be met though at the cost of individual autonomy.[94] Life plans especially in social, political, and cultural domains are imposed from the top down and heteronomy replaces autonomy. To address the deficit permits us to speak of human interest as another base of basic human rights.

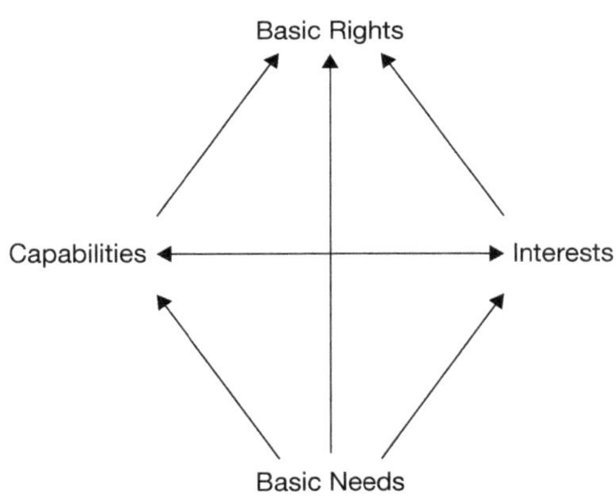

Figure 2.1 Sources of basic rights

The concept of interest is closely related to the concept of basic needs (Figure 2.1). As just remarked, what can meet basic needs are valuable items (objects, processes, properties of objects, properties of processes). Interest is what connects valuable items (from the point of view of an individual evaluator) to basic needs. More precisely, interest pertains to a set of *valuable* items in a given domain (eg economic, social, cultural, or political), evaluated and ranked by individuals who *can* freely choose one or more of the items *in order to meet* her or his basic needs. Note the

[93] ibid. [94] See Hamilton, *The Political Philosophy of Needs*, note 67.

following points: First, '*can*' in this definition is about possibility and/or probability and not actuality. Second, valuable items are not items themselves, instead they are properties (as a second-order or 'third-order' property) we attribute to the former. Third, '*in order to meet*' implies that interest is intentional and goal seeking. Fourth, interests change with the internal and external circumstances of the individual as evaluator. Think of, for instance, different social categories in different life cycle stages and different socio-cultural settings.

Epistemologically, interests are subjective or objective to varying degrees. In the case of primary needs such as the need to water (as a valuable object) or basic learning (as a valuable process), the degree of subjectivity and choicefulness of interest is very low. There is a correlation between these two variables (subjectivity and choicefulness) though this is not necessarily a perfect correlation. There is often no more than one or a few valuable alternatives (objects, processes, properties of objects, properties of objects) to meet such primary needs and therefore we can talk about objective interest (epistemic objectivity). In the latter case, for instance, learning as a process is in the interests of children regardless of their happiness or unhappiness about being required to go to school. People with dementia may rarely feel thirsty or hungry but there is no doubt that food and water are in their objective interest. But even in the case of water as a valuable object, some degree of subjectivity in terms of its properties is present. For instance, one is interested in cold water, the other person in room temperature, and still the third one may be interested in hot water early in the morning.

In contrast with such cases mentioned above, interests are often more subjective than objective. A few examples will clarify the two. Although the level of healthiness of foods can be often objectively (epistemic objectivity) assessed based on scientific standards, various kinds of foods (with the same or different levels of healthiness) and their properties (hot, cold, spicy, etc) are all a matter of subjective interests. Person A may be interested in vegetables (being vegetarian) while person B is more interested in seafood. Take social relations as another example. A is interested to be in a relationship with B rather than with Z—this is subjective interest (individual-mind dependent).

Whereas basic needs are objective, interests are mostly subjective. Contrary to what has been claimed by advocates of the interest theory, human interests cannot be seen as the only base of rights. Why? Because (1) in an ontological sense, the existence of interest is dependent on basic needs; and (2) methodologically speaking, without basic needs which are objective, there would be almost no scientific criteria against which subjective interests can be assessed. The latter is of crucial importance for human rights planning.

As for the satisfaction of interests, one may well ask about what may appear to be expensive tastes (known as expensive tastes objection) which is discussed in some theories of justice and well-being such as in Rawls's account of primary goods,[95] Dworkin's equality of resources,[96] Scanlon's argument for an objective criterion of

[95] John Rawls, 'Social Unity and Primary Goods' in A Sen and B Williams (eds), *Utilitarianism and Beyond* (1st edn, Cambridge University Press 1982) 159–85, at 168–69.

[96] Ronald Dworkin, 'What is Equality? Part 1: Equality of Welfare' (1981) 10 Philosophy and Public Affairs 185–246, at 228–40.

well-being,[97] Elster's discussion on adaptive preferences,[98] and in Arneson's equality of opportunity for welfare.[99] Although the detailed consideration of this matter (such as how an expensive interest is formed and whether people choose to have an expensive interest or not) is beyond the scope of this chapter, three points are noteworthy here.

First, expensive tastes objection would be more an issue in the case of economic interests than others (ie political, social, or cultural interests). Providing alternatives for people to satisfy their interests is not often costly in political, social, or cultural domains. On the contrary, the lack of fulfilment of such interests would involve psychological costs at the micro level, and also social, cultural, political, and even economic costs at the macro level. For instance, free election, freedom of thought and expression, freedom of assembly and association would often involve no economic cost, but rather their restriction or suppression would even have social costs such as social mistrust, hypocrisy, social anomie which in turn can impede economic development. Likewise, ideological censorship or restrictions on art, theatre, and film in cultural domain, for instance, ignore people's interests while their satisfaction involves no economic cost. Removing such restrictions are often accompanied by cultural effervescence and can lead to cultural advancement. Similarly, think of, for example, arranged marriages in the social domain.

Second, the degree of choicefulness of material interests for some very important basic needs in the category of primary needs, such as clean water and a decent toilet, by nature is almost nil. However, such primary needs have been left widely unmet. At present, for instance, 844 million people in the world—one in ten—do not have clean water. 61% of the global population (4.5 billion people) do not have a decent toilet.[100] 289,000 children under five die each year due to diarrhoeal diseases caused by poor water and sanitation. That is 800 a day, or one child every two minutes.[101]

Third, expensive taste is indeed a serious issue with respect to some economic interests. Given that we live in the age of scarcity in food, water, and energy, the range of choices which can satisfy human interests are often bounded by environmental (natural or social) constraints. Therefore, it would be unrealistic to claim that we can become totally free to choose whatever we are interested in. This highlights the need to optimize resources in order to match the interests of different social categories with available resources. For resource optimization, first of all, the public awareness has to be increased so that people become sensitized to the limitations of resources as evidenced by the increasing scarcity of both non-renewables (eg oil and minerals) and renewables (eg fresh water, forests, fertile soils). Moreover, investment

[97] Thomas Scanlon, 'Preference and Urgency' (1975) 72 Journal of Philosophy 655–69, at 650.

[98] Jon Elster, *Sour Grapes: Studies in the Subversion of Rationality* (1st edn, Cambridge University Press 1983).

[99] Richard J Arneson, 'Equality and Equal Opportunity for Welfare' (1989) 56 Philosophical Studies 77–93.

[100] *WHO/UNICEF Joint Monitoring Programme (JMP) Report 2017 update)* <http://www.unwater.org/new-publication-whounicef-joint-monitoring-programme-2017-report/> 12 June 2017.

[101] WASHWatch 2017 <http://www.wateraid.org/what-we-do/the-crisis/statistic> accessed 26 June 2017.

in capacity building can enable individuals to knowingly and willingly adjust their interests to the limitations of resources and ecological crisis. In addition, various alternatives or choices should be evaluated in a participatory top-down bottom-up process where all stakeholders, including the general public, marginalized groups, experts, civil society, private sector actors, and donors, have an opportunity to reflect their interests and become genuinely involved in the process of adjustment of interests with available resources.

Furthermore, as discussed in the contextual theory of planning in Chapter 1, to manage expensive interests the structure of society, distributional and relational, is of crucial importance. The fact of the matter is that in societies where the distribution of resources is highly unequal, the degree of choicefulness of material interests for the majority is low. Only a small portion of society can enjoy various alternatives while the considerable portion is deprived of a minimum subsistence level of living (see Chapter 1).[102] Likewise, as for relational inequality, a society where social exclusion is widespread ie nominal inequality is high, people and different social groups are less inclined to collaborate with each other and to responsibly adjust their interests to available resources and to the interests of others (see Chapter 1).

So far, we have explicated basic needs and interests and explored the relation between the two. Now, the question which remains to be answered is whether being endowed with a basic right consists in being capable of meeting one or more of needs in accordance with interests. Here is where the concept of capability as another base of rights comes in. From a scientific realist point of view, a person's capability is what a person is able to do or liable to be. This concept reflects those abilities or liabilities residing inside a person (basic capabilities at birth) which can be developed through nurturing (trained abilities and skills, eg self-care training) or expanded and nourished with support of external facilities (eg wheelchair, lift, hearing aid, glasses, etc).

As remarked before, basic needs, interests, and capabilities are interdependent. People have different capabilities including (but not limited to) different physical, emotional, and intellectual capacities, skills, and states of bodily fitness, and these all are highly relevant to their choice of interests. One's nurtured intellectual capabilities can advance and improve her judgement in the choice of her interests. Likewise, your interests will direct you to enhance relevant capabilities; those capabilities which can help you satisfy your interests. It goes without saying that one's capabilities enable her to meet her needs, and likewise, meeting needs paves the way for the enhancement of her capabilities through her interests. For example, everyone needs mobility. Her ability (capability) to move from place to place empowers her to fulfil her need. To enhance this capability, she needs food, water, and clothing. Put differently, meeting basic needs for food and clothing can develop her capability, ie being able to move freely about. Sometimes, we need to expand

[102] For inequality between societies and within societies see, eg, Oxfam 2017 report here: <http://www.oxfam.org.uk/media-centre/press-releases/2017/01/eight-people-own-same-wealth-as-half-the-world>.

one's capability in order to be able to meet her need to mobility by providing, for instance, a walking stick.

Praxeologically speaking, human capabilities as a means are required for need/interest satisfactions as an end. Hence, being endowed with a basic right does consist in being capable of meeting one or more needs in accordance with interests.

An important distinction that should be made in order to avoid conceptual confusion, in particular for the purpose of planning, is between internal capabilities and external opportunities and resources. In most cases, being able to meet our needs according to our interests depends more on the availability of resources and opportunities (objects, processes), than merely innate capabilities. Whether a person actually works might depend more on whether there is a job for her than her ability to work. Note the individual-related concepts of needs, interests, and capabilities inside human beings bridge the individual to the external world (resources and opportunities) ie the inner world to the outer one.

Finally, notice that at the ontological level, basic needs, interests, and capabilities are not separate from one another, but at the epistemological level these need to be distinguished in order to sharpen our knowledge for the analysis of rights.

In sum, the theory formulated here, which I call NIC theory of rights, is an integrated one that can perform both heuristic and regulative roles for human rights planning. This analytical theory can serve at least six purposes:

1. This theory as an analytical tool can be employed for building special theories for planning which includes spatio-temporal factors for a given country. While substantive and procedural theories of planning, as two main parts of the general theory, act as a guiding star, they cannot entirely reflect spatio-temporal factors, associated with different rights, ranging from children rights to indigenous rights, contained in a NHRAP which consist of enormously different parts. This analytical theory can help ensure that nothing drop between the cracks and different groups' needs, interests, and capabilities are not overlooked. As will be discussed in Chapter 5, one of the important problems facing NHRAPs today is that different action plans have included different lists of rights some of which are not even in accordance with what is set forth as human rights in regional and international documents. This is related to the questions of where rights come from and whether human rights are or ought to be universal or not. Inquiring into the meaning of rights, needs, interests, and capabilities could help us further our understanding of different phases of planning in accordance with each country's cultural and historical circumstances, limitations, and resources.
2. As will be discussed in Chapter 7, in the preparatory phase of planning, this theory can be a useful heuristic in diagnosing the achievements and shortcomings of a society in terms of implementing basic rights, including needs assessment, interests assessment, and capabilities assessment for different social categories including, among others, gender, age, ethnicity, colour, religion, political opinion or other opinion, and nationality and different life cycle stages (eg foetus, infancy, childhood, adolescence, adulthood, elderly).

3. The new theory also provides criteria for monitoring and evaluating human rights action plans. These criteria can be used for designing both quantitative indicators and qualitative benchmarks.
4. The present theory can be used as a device for prioritization in human rights planning for a given country.
5. After all, this analytical theory can be utilized for reforming the UN human rights instruments. Given the importance of international human rights instruments for human rights planning and beyond that for rights-based development, it seems self-evident that treaties should be based on a firm theoretical base to make them comprehensive, coherent, rational and their monitoring bodies, effective and legitimate. A main challenge of international human rights instruments, however, is that they are not built upon a firm analytical theory of rights and are, to a greater or lesser extent, theoretically baseless. This deficit has given rise to at least two problems. The first one is concerned with a comprehensive identification of rights. A lack of theoretical foundation to guide the development of a treaty can lead to the omission of even a very basic right such as the right to clean and accessible water and the right to safe and hygienic sanitation in the UDHR and ICESCR.[103]

   The second problem pertains to the distinguishment of human rights in international human rights instruments. Despite an extensive use of the classification of economic, social, and cultural rights in various international human rights documents, it still remains widely unclear how to make a distinction between economic rights, social rights, and cultural rights. There is currently no clear set of criteria to distinguish economic rights from social rights and cultural ones. All the rights embodied in the International Covenant on Economic, Social, and Cultural Rights are used as 'economic, social and cultural rights' imprecisely. This is also true of civil and political rights set forth in the International Covenant on Civil and Political Rights. NIC theory can be used for the categorization of rights in regional and international human rights instruments. For instance, the same as needs, basic human rights can be divided into at least four general types. These include: 'economic/material rights' such as the right to adequate standard of living, 'social/relational rights' such as the right to marry, 'cultural/cognitive rights' such as the right to education, and 'political/security rights', such as the right to political participation.
6. NIC theory can be employed not only by planners but also beyond that by human rights policy makers, NGOs, governments, NHRIs, intergovernmental organizations for policy-making, human rights impact assessments, and policy analysis at different levels, from the community level to the national, regional, and international level. In academia likewise this theory

[103] In November 2002, the Committee on Economic, Social, and Cultural Rights adopted General Comment No 15 on the right to water. On 28 July 2010, through Resolution 64/292, the United Nations General Assembly explicitly recognized the human right to water and sanitation and acknowledged that clean drinking water and sanitation are essential to the realization of all human rights.

can be utilized as a heuristic device, especially in case-oriented studies and comparative inquiries.

In short, the three theories of human rights planning—substantive, procedural, and analytica—presented in this chapter formed the three parts of the general theory of planning whose first part was discussed in Chapter 1. The substantive and procedural theories of human rights planning, based on the human rights-based approach to development, offer six substantive and four procedural principles respectively which must be applied in any human rights action plans. In the analytical theory of planning, I have attempted to elucidate the concepts and relationships of needs, values, interests, wants, and capabilities with each other and with basic rights.

PART II
DOCTRINAL PERSPECTIVES

3

Legal Status of NHRAPs in International Human Rights Law

1. Introduction

Despite the fact that the idea of adopting a National Human Rights Action Plan (NHRAP) originates with the 1966 International Covenant on Economic, Social and Cultural Rights (ICESCR), it is surprising that the legal status of these plans has been subjected to very limited commentary in the existing literature and still remains largely unclear. The main purpose of this chapter is to unravel whether states are obliged, under international human rights law, to adopt a NHRAP and if so, what is the nature and the scope of this obligation.

This chapter is divided into three sections. After dealing with the nature of the obligation to adopt a NHRAP in the first section, a textual analysis of all the core human rights treaties, along with General Comments, reports, and Concluding Observations will be conducted in the second section in order to explore the legal status of NHRAPs under these conventions. The final section will briefly examine the fulfilment of this obligation in terms of conduct and result.

2. The Nature of the Obligation to Adopt a NHRAP

The concept of a NHRAP dates back to the ICESCR (16 December 1966). Article 14 of the ICESCR, regarding the right to education, holds that:

> Each State Party to the present Covenant which, at the time of becoming a Party, has not been able to secure in its metropolitan territory or other territories under its jurisdiction compulsory primary education, free of charge, undertakes, within two years, to work out and adopt a detailed plan of action for the progressive implementation, within a reasonable number of years, to be fixed in the plan, of the principle of compulsory education free of charge for all.[1]

Among the existing human rights conventions, Article 14 of the ICESCR is the only article that stipulates expressly the obligation to adopt a NHRAP. However, at different points, in its reports and Concluding Observations the Committee on

[1] International Covenant on Economic, Social, and Cultural Rights, 16 December 1966, S Treaty Doc No 95–19, 6 ILM 360 (1967), 993 UNTS 3, Article 14.

Economic, Social, and Cultural Rights has urged states to develop a human rights plan of action, for instance, for reducing the disparities of living standards,[2] improving the housing situation[3] and social inclusion,[4] reforming the residential system of childcare,[5] preventing suicide,[6] reducing violence against women,[7] eliminating women inequalities,[8] addressing school drop-outs and youth unemployment,[9] eradicating slave labour[10] and female genital mutilation,[11] combating trafficking in human beings[12] and corruption,[13] eliminating violence against children,[14] child labour,[15] sexual abuse, exploitation, and prostitution of children,[16] racism and discrimination,[17] and domestic violence.[18]

Most importantly, the committee has provided, in its General Comments, a legal analysis for this obligation that can be clearly implied to other human rights conventions as well. Whereas General Comments are not legally binding, they are an authoritative source in international human rights law. As Matthew Craven

[2] CESCR, 'Report on the twentieth and twenty-first sessions' UN Doc E/2000/22, E/C.12/1999/11 (18 May 2000) at para 179.

[3] ibid, at para 240; CESCR, 'Report on the twenty-second, twenty-third, and twenty-fourth sessions' E/2001/22, 07/06/2001, at para 179; CESCR, Report on the fortieth and forty-first sessions UN Doc E/2009/22, E/C.12/2008/3 (01 April 2009) at para 287; CESCR, 'Report on the forty-sixth and forty-seventh sessions' UN Doc E/2012/22, E/C.12/2011/3 (23 March 2012) at para 389.

[4] CESCR, 'Report on the thirty-second and thirty-third sessions' (26 April–14 May 2004, 8–26 November 2004), UN Doc E/2005/22, E/C.12/2004/9 (16 March 2005) at paras 242, 261, 333.

[5] CESCR, 'Report on the forty-sixth and forty-seventh sessions' UN Doc E/2012/22, E/C.12/2011/3 (23 March 2012) at para 116.

[6] CESCR, 'Report on the forty-fourth and forty-fifth sessions' (May 2010, 1–19 November 2010, E/2011/22) at para 401; CESCR, 'Report on the thirty-fourth and thirty-fifth sessions' (25 April–13 May 2005, 7–25 November 2005) at para 333, UN Doc E/2006/22, E/C.12/2005/5(16 March 2005); CESCR, 'Report on the thirty-sixth and thirty-seventh sessions' UN Doc E/2007/22, E/C.12/2006/1 (1 October 2007) at para 368.

[7] CESCR, 'Report on the forty-second and forty-third sessions' UN Doc E/2010/22, E/C.12/2009/3 (30 April 2010) at para 95.

[8] CESCR, 'Report on the twenty-second, twenty-third and twenty-fourth sessions', note 3, at para 88.

[9] ibid, at para 139.

[10] CESCR, 'Report on the thirtieth and thirty-first sessions' UN Doc E/2004/22, E/C.12/2003/14 (8 March 2004) at para 154.

[11] Human Rights Committee, UN Doc A/59/40 (Vol I) sec 76 (10).

[12] ibid, at para 309; CESCR, 'Report on the thirty-sixth and thirty-seventh sessions', note 6, at para 559.

[13] CESCR, 'Report on the forty-sixth and forty-seventh session' UN Doc E/2012/22, E/C.12/2011/3 (23 March 2012) at para 152.

[14] UNHRC, 'Report of the Human Rights Committee Seventy-ninth session' UN Doc A/59/40 (Vol I) at para 71(9).

[15] CESCR, 'Report on the thirtieth and thirty-first sessions' UN Doc E/2004/22, E/C 12/2003/14 (8 March 2004) at para 359.

[16] CESCR, 'Report on the twenty-fifth, twenty-sixth, and twenty-seventh sessions' UN Doc E/2002/22, E/C.12/2001/17 (6 June 2002) at paras 127, 147; see CESCR, 'Report on the twenty-eighth and twenty-ninth sessions' UN Doc E/2003/22, E/C.12/2002/13 (21 July 2008) at para 403; CESCR, 'Report on the fortieth and forty-first sessions', note 3, at para 70(C); UN Human Rights Committee, 'Report of the Human Rights Committee Seventy-ninth session' (20 October–7 November 2003) Eightieth session (15 March–2 April 2004) Eighty-first session (5–30 July 2004), UN Doc A/59/40 (Vol I) at para 66(14).

[17] CESCR, 'Report on the thirty-fourth and thirty-fifth sessions' E/2006/22 06/06/2006, at para 333; CESCR, 'Report on the thirty-sixth and thirty-seventh sessions', note 6, at para 487.

[18] ibid, at para 361.

aptly states, it is undoubtedly true that General Comments have considerable legal weight and, thus, it is a fallacy to dismiss such instruments as 'not law', as they can and do contribute to the corpus of international law.[19] In Philip Alston's words, General Comments are 'means by which a UN human rights expert committee distils its considered views on an issue which arises out of the provisions of the treaty whose implementation it supervises and presents those views in the context of a formal statement of its understanding to which it attaches major importance'.[20] The Committee on Economic, Social, and Cultural Rights also takes this view and urges states to act in the light of General Comments. Albania is a clear instance. The Committee in the case of Albania 'urges the state party to take all necessary measures to allocate the required resources to improve the quality of education offered in schools at all levels, 'in line with the Committee's General Comment No 13 on the right to education'.[21] This view can be also confirmed by the fact that the European Court of Human Rights (ECtHR) usually applies General Comments in its decisions.[22] Besides, no state has ever raised any formal objection to the General Comments.[23]

Here, General Comment No 1 is of particular importance to a full understanding of the obligation to adopt a NHRAP. It states that:

> While the Covenant makes this obligation explicit only in article 14 in cases where 'compulsory primary education, free of charge' has not yet been secured for all, a comparable obligation 'to work out and adopt a detailed NHRAP for the progressive implementation' of each of the rights contained in the Covenant is clearly implied by the obligation in article 2, paragraph 1 'to take steps ... by all appropriate means ...'[24]

As the General Comment indicates, the Committee on Economic, Social and Cultural Rights has expanded the obligation 'to work out and adopt a detailed NHRAP for the progressive implementation' of each of the rights contained in the Covenant. Since General Comments are conceived as an authoritative interpretation of the UN treaties which clarify states' obligations,[25] each state party that has ratified

[19] Matthew Craven, *The International Covenant on Economic, Social and Cultural Rights: A Perspective on its Development* (1st edn, Clarendon Press 1998) 212.

[20] Philip Alston, 'The Historical Origins of "General Comments" in Human Rights Law' in Laurence Boisson De Charzournes and Vera Gowlland-Debbas (eds), *The International Legal System in Quest of Equity and Universality* (1st edn, Brill 2001) 764.

[21] CESCR, Consideration of Reports Submitted by States Parties Under Articles 16 and 17 of the Covenant, Concluding Observations of the Committee on Economic, Social and Cultural Rights, Albania, E/C.12/ALB/CO/1, 24 November 2006, at para 66.

[22] See *Hirst v United Kingdom (No 2)* Application No 74025/01 (2005); *Öcalan v Turkey* Application No 46221/99 (2005); *Makaratzis v Greece* Application No 50385/99 (2004); *Melnychenko v Ukraine* Application No 17707/02 (2004); *Kurt v Turkey* Application No 24276/94 [1998] ECHR 44 (25 May 1998).

[23] Manisuli Ssenyonjo, 'Reflections on state obligations with respect to economic, social and cultural rights in international human rights law' (2011) 15(6) The International Journal of Human Rights 969, 975.

[24] CESCR, General Comment No 1, Reporting by States Parties, 13th Sess, UN Doc E/1989/22 (27 July 1981) at para 4.

[25] Henry J Steiner, 'Individual Claims in a World of Massive Violations: What Role for the Human Rights Committee?' in P Alston and J Crawford (eds), *The Future of UN Human Rights Treaty Monitoring* (1st edn, Cambridge University Press 2000) at 21.

the ICESCR, has, therefore, the obligation to adopt a NHRAP for the implementation of the rights set forth in the Covenant. This point is also reaffirmed by the Committee in its Concluding Observations. For instance, in the case of Kazakhstan, 'the Committee urges the state party to review the National Human Rights Action Plan with a view to adopting strategies for promoting and raising awareness of the public regarding human rights in general and economic, social, and cultural rights in particular'.[26] In some other cases, such as the case of the Netherlands, on the other side, the Committee welcomes the adoption of a national human rights action plan.[27]

The Committee in General Comment No 1 not only establishes a clear obligation for the states parties to adopt a NHRAP for implementing all the rights contained in the ICESCR but it also provides a conceptual basis for this obligation which applies readily to other UN human rights conventions. There is nothing here particular to ICESCR. Feldman aptly argues that there are always 'more extensive obligations on the states than are immediately obvious from a superficial perusal of the text'.[28] In order to discover these obligations a dynamic and effective interpretation (effectiveness approach) of the human rights conventions is required.[29]

As the Committee on Economic, Social, and Cultural Rights notes, the obligation to adopt a NHRAP for progressive implementation is clearly implied by the obligation to take steps, that is, the obligation to take steps contains the sub-obligation to adopt a NHRAP. This point has been made in all the General Comments in which adopting a NHRAP has been stipulated by the Committee. More specifically, the Committee in General Comments Nos 4, 12, 13, 14, 15, 18, and 19 has reaffirmed that the obligation to take steps/measures includes an obligation to adopt a NHRAP and, therefore, each state party is duty bound to adopt a NHRAP for implementing certain rights, that is, for housing,[30] food,[31] education,[32] health,[33] water,[34] work,[35]

[26] CESCR, Concluding Observations: Kazakhstan, E/C.12/KAZ/CO/1, 21 May 2010, at para 8; see also, CESCR, Concluding Observations: Sri Lanka, E/C.12/LKA/CO/5, 4 August 2017, at paras 6, 15–16; CESCR, Concluding Observations on the fifth periodic report of Pakistan, E/C.12/PAK/CO/1, 20 July 2017, at para 70.

[27] CESCR, Concluding Observations on the fifth periodic report of the Netherlands, 6 July 2017, E/C.12/NLD/CO/6, at paras 7 and 4; see also CESCR, Concluding Observations: Cyprus, 28 October 2016, E/C.12/CYP/CO/6, at paras 3 and 18.

[28] David Feldman, *Civil Liberties and Human Rights in England and Wales* (2nd edn, Oxford University Press 2002) at 55.

[29] See ibid.

[30] CESCR, General Comment No 4: The Right to Adequate Housing (Art 11(1)): Forced Evictions 6th Sess, UN Doc E/1992/23 (13 December 1991) at para 17.

[31] CESCR, General Comment No 12: The Right to Adequate Food (Art. 11) 20th Sess, at para 21, UN Doc E/C.12/1999/5 (12 May 1999).

[32] CESCR, General Comment No 13: The Right to Education (Art 13 of the Covenant) 21st Sess, UN Doc E/C.12/1999/10 (8 December 1999) at para 52; see United Nations Declaration on Human Rights Education and Training, GA Res (adopted by the Human Rights Council) 16th Sess, UN Doc A/HRC/RES/16/1 (8 April 2011) Article 8.

[33] CESCR, General Comment No 14: The Right to the Highest Attainable Standard of Health (Article 12 of the Covenant) 22nd Sess, UN Doc E/C.12/2000/4 (11 August 2000) at para 53.

[34] CESCR, General Comment No 15: The Right to Water (Articles 11 and 12 of the Covenant) 29th Sess, UN Doc E/C.12/2002/11 (20 January 2003) at para 26.

[35] CESCR, General Comment No 18: The Right to Work (Article 6 of the Covenant) 35th Sess, UN Doc E/C.12/General Comment/18 (6 February 2006) at paras 26, 31.

and social security[36] respectively. In General Comment No 14, for instance, the failure to adopt or implement a NHRAP is part of the failure to take all necessary steps to ensure the realization of the right in question.[37] That is to say, the obligation to take all necessary steps includes the obligation to adopt and implement a NHRAP. The same point has been made in General Comments Nos 15 and 18.[38] Concerning the right to water and the right to work, the Committee clarifies that the obligation to take appropriate measures requires states parties to adopt the necessary measures directed towards the full realization of the right.[39] The Committee reaffirms that this obligation includes, inter alia, the obligation to adopt a NHRAP.[40]

In some of these General Comments even the Committee makes use of terms such as 'clearly'[41] and 'inevitably'[42] to include emphasis on the importance of deriving the obligation to adopt a NHRAP from the obligation to take measures/steps. For example, the Committee in General Comment No 15 states that 'the duty to take steps *clearly* imposes on states parties an obligation to adopt a national strategy or plan of action to realize the right to water'. [43] General Comment No 4 also declares that to take whatever steps are necessary for the full realization of the right in question, *invariably* requires the adoption of a NHRAP.[44]

This interpretation is in line with the 'effectiveness approach' (sometimes known as the principle of effectiveness or '*ut res magis valeat quam pereat*') according to which 'the core interpretive task for any interpreter is to make human rights treaty provisions "effective, real, and practical" for right holders under international law'.[45]As Çalı explains, this means that 'human rights interpretations must have "practical effect" '.[46] The ECtHR case of *Airey* is a good example. The case was about the right to access to court and whether it should involve the obligation to provide legal aid or not. [47] The Irish government argued that there is no obligation to provide such aid because the applicant can exercise her right by appearing in person. The ECtHR rejected this argument on the basis that the human rights treaties require effective rights, not merely formal or illusory rights.

It is important to note that there are some broader obligations, such as the 'obligation to ensure', the 'obligation to provide', the 'obligation to facilitate', and the

[36] CESCR, General Comment No 19: The Right to Social Security (Article 9 of the Covenant) 39th Sess, UN Doc E/C.12/General Comment No 19 (4 February 2008) at paras 48 and 59; see Committee On Economic, Social, and Cultural Rights, Report on the forty-fourth and forty-fifth sessions, note 6, at para 91.

[37] CESCR, General Comment 14, note 33, at para 52, CESCR, General Comment 18, note 35, at para 26.

[38] CESCR, General Comment No 18, note 35, General Comment No 15, note 34.

[39] ibid.

[40] CESCR, General Comment No 18, note 35, at para 26.

[41] CESCR, General Comment No 15, note 34, at para 47; CESCR, General Comment No 19, note 36, at para 68.

[42] CESCR, General Comment No 4, note 30, at para 12.

[43] CESCR, General Comment No 15, note 34, at para 47.

[44] CESCR, General Comment No 4, note 30, at para 12.

[45] Basak Çalı, 'Specialized Rules of Treaty Interpretation: Human Rights', in D B Hollis (ed), *The Oxford Guide to Treaties* (1st edn, Oxford University Press 2012) at 538; see also ECtHR *Loizіou v Turkey* (1995) 20 EHRR 99, 102.

[46] Çalı ibid at 539.

[47] *Airey v Ireland* Application no 6289/73 (1981) 3 EHRR 305.

'obligation to promote' from which the obligation to take steps or measures and, thus, the sub-obligation to adopt a NHRAP can be derived. To meet the obligation to ensure requires each state to take necessary steps, and this includes adopting a NHRAP.[48] The committee, at least in seven General Comments, clearly expresses the view that the core obligation to ensure the satisfaction of, at the very least, minimum essential levels of each of the rights enunciated in the Covenant, includes, inter alia, the obligation to adopt a NHRAP.[49] It is also confirmed by the African Commission when it notes that the states parties to the African Charter have to take 'concrete and targeted steps' while taking full advantage of their available resources, to 'ensure' that economic, social, and cultural rights, such as the right to health, are fully realized in all aspects without discrimination of any kind.[50]

As the Committee in General Comments Nos 13 and 14 notes, all human rights impose at least three different types or levels of obligations on states parties namely the obligations to respect, protect, and fulfil.[51] According to General Comment No 14, the failure to adopt or implement a NHRAP is a violation of the obligation to fulfil.[52] The Committee has noted that the obligation to fulfil incorporates three subcategories: (1) the obligation to facilitate, (2) the obligation to provide, and (3) the obligation to promote.[53] As indicated in General Comments Nos 13, 14, and 19, the obligation to facilitate requires the states to take positive measures/steps to assist individuals and communities to enjoy rights, and, therefore, includes, inter alia, the obligation to adopt a NHRAP.[54] As Sepulveda argues, according to the Committee's view, this obligation implies that each state must take positive steps/measures, aimed at enabling and assisting individuals or communities to enjoy the Covenant's rights.[55] The obligation to provide is applied when right holders, individuals or groups, for reasons beyond their control, are unable to realize their rights by the means at their disposal.[56] The Committee in General Comment No 18

[48] CESCR, General Comment No 12, note 31, at para 21.

[49] ibid, CESCR, General Comment No 14, note 33, at para 43, CESCR, General Comment No 15, note 34, at para 37, CESCR, General Comment No 18, note 35, at para 41; CESCR, General Comment No 19, note 36, at para 59; CESCR, General Comment No 22 (2016) on the right to sexual and reproductive health (Article 12 of the International Covenant on Economic, Social, and Cultural Rights) E/C.12/GC/22, at para 49(b); CESCR, General Comment No 24 (2017) on State obligations under the International Covenant on Economic, Social, and Cultural Rights in the context of business activities, E/C.12/GC/24, at para 58.

[50] African Human Rights Reports, Communication 241/2001, Sixteenth Annual Activity Report (2003) Annex VII 96, at para 84.

[51] CESCR, General Comment No 13, note 32, at paras 46, 55, CESCR, General Comment No 14, note 31, at para 33; see Henry Shue, *Basic Rights: Substance, Affluence, and US Foreign Policy* (1st edn, Princton University Press 1980).

[52] CESCR, General Comment No 14, note 33, at para 52.

[53] Asbjørn Eide, 'Group Accommodation and the Challenges of Education: Multicultural or Intercultural—or a Combination of the Two?' in Jonas Grimheden and Rolf Ring (eds), *Human Rights Law: From Dissemination to Application Essays in Honour of GöranMelander* (1st edn, Martinus Nijhoff Publishers 2006); Magdalena Sepulveda, *The Nature of the Obligation under the International Covenant on Economic, Social and Cultural Rights* (1st edn, Intersentia 2003); CESCR, General Comment No 14, note 33, at para 37.

[54] CESCR, General Comment No 13, note 32, at paras 46, 47, 50; CESCR, General Comment No 14, note 33, at paras 33 and 37; CESCR, General Comment 19, note 36, at para 48.

[55] Sepulveda, *The Nature of the Obligation under the International Covenant on Economic, Social and Cultural Rights*, note 53, at para 239.

[56] ibid, 241; CESCR, General Comment No 14, note 33, at para 37.

expresses the view that the obligation to provide also includes, inter alia, the obligation to adopt a NHRAP. It reads that:

> This obligation [the obligation to provide] includes, inter alia, the obligation to recognize the right to work in national legal systems and to adopt a national policy on the right to work as well as a detailed plan for its realization.[57]

Likewise, the obligation to promote requires the states to undertake actions (steps/measures), such as preparing training programmes to increase public awareness of human rights and, therefore, requires developing a NHRAP.[58]

Nonetheless, it should be stressed that the obligation to adopt a NHRAP is not exclusively concerned with different forms of the obligation to 'fulfil'. If it were, then, the transferability of the Committee's views on this issue might be limited insofar as other human rights conventions might be said to impose less onerous obligations to fulfil the rights specified in those conventions. The obligation to protect also requires states parties to take measures to prevent third parties from interfering with the enjoyment of the right in question. As Alston argues, there is a need for positive measures to be taken to remedy violations or to prevent other actors from violating the declared rights.[59] This, therefore, includes the obligation to adopt a NHRAP. In some General Comments and Concluding Observations, the Committee on Economic, Social, and Cultural Rights has mentioned the obligation to take steps/measures to prevent third parties from interfering with the enjoyment of the Covenant's rights. For example, regarding the right to adequate housing, the Committee has required states to take measures to protect populations from forced evictions by private actors.[60] To 'protect' people from discrimination, as another example, requires adopting legislative measures. Each state is required to reform, amend, and repeal legislation which is manifestly inconsistent with non-discrimination, or adopt new legislation to prevent discrimination. As the Committee addresses this point in General Comment No 5, state parties need to legislate, where necessary, and to eliminate any existing discriminatory legislation.[61] Non-discriminatory legislation or the elimination of any discriminative legislation is precisely a step that must be taken. Concerning the right to work, the Committee, in General Comment No 18, has also noted that 'obligations to protect the right to work include, inter alia, the duties of the states parties to adopt legislation or to take "other measures" ensuring equal access to work and training and to ensure that privatisation measures do not undermine worker's rights'. [62]

57 CESCR, General Comment No 18, note 35, at para 26.

58 CESCR, General Comment No 14, note 33, at para 37.

59 Philip Alston, 'The Contribution of of the Agency to the Realization of Social and Economic Rights' in Philip Alston and Olivier De Schutter (eds), *Monitoring Fundamental Rights in the EU. The Contribution of the Fundamental Rights Agency* (1st edn, Hart Publishing 2005) at 163.

60 General Comment No 4 note 30; CESCR, General Comment No 7, The Right to Adequate Housing (Article 11.1): Forced Evictions, E/1998/22 (20 May 1997); CESCR, Concluding Observations: Jordan E/2001/22, at para 256; CESCR, Concluding Observations: Argentina E/2000/22, at para 284; CESCR, Concluding Observations: Cameroon E/2000/22, at para 355.

61 CESCR, General Comment No 5: Persons with Disabilities, E/1995/22 (9 December 1994) at para 13.

62 CESCR, General Comment No 18, note 35, at para 25.

Although one can still find the view in the literature that economic, social, and cultural rights exclusively pertain to the obligation to fulfil and civil and political rights are concerned with the obligation to respect,[63] the better view is that, as Henry Shue states, all rights including civil and political as well as economic, social, and cultural rights impose all these three obligations on the states.[64] The states are required to take appropriate measures for the full realization of both civil and political rights as well as economic, social and cultural rights. For example, as the Human Rights Committee indicates in its General Comment No 32, the right to a fair trial as protected by Article 14(1) of the ICCPR is concerned with positive obligations, such as providing accessibility to a court in cases of determination of criminal charges and rights and obligations in a suit at law, and the provision of free legal aid if this is 'indispensable for an effective access to court', for instance, for those people who do not have sufficient means to pay for it. [65] This point has been also reiterated by the Maastricht guidelines.[66]

Moreover, as Alston and Quinn argue, although the word 'respect' ordinarily connotes obligations of a generally negative character, the European Court of Human Rights has interpreted it, in the context of family rights, as sometimes giving rise to positive duties.[67] Chapman discusses that to meet the obligation to respect requires the states to take appropriate measures to ensure that their laws, policies, institutions, and means of implementation of rights are all consistent with their human rights commitment.[68]

In sum, the Committee on Economic, Social, and Cultural Rights has provided a conceptual basis for the obligation to adopt a NHRAP which can be applied in other human rights treaties as well. This obligation can be clearly implied in all the rights which require taking steps or measures and is included in the broader obligations to ensure, provide, facilitate, protect, promote, and even, at some points, in the obligation to respect. Apart from all this, the obligation to take all appropriate measures even logically entails the obligation to adopt a NHRAP. States parties are obliged to adopt a NHRAP in order to identify and take appropriate measures for realizing the rights set forth in the conventions.

The next section will explore the obligation to adopt a NHRAP under core human rights treaties.

[63] Kitty Arambulo, *Strengthening the Supervision of the International Covenant on Economic, Social and Cultural Rights: Theoretical and Procedural Aspects* (1st edn, Intersentia-Hart 1999).

[64] Shue, *Basic Rights: Substance, Affluence, and US Foreign Policy*, note 51.

[65] Manisuli Ssenyonjo, 'Economic, Social and Cultural rights: An Examination of State Obligations' in Sarah Joseph and Adam McBeth (eds), *Research Handbook on International Human Rights Law* (1st edn, Edward Elgar Publishing 2010) at 47.

[66] International Commission of Jurists (ICJ), 'Maastricht Guidelines on Violations of Economic, Social and Cultural Rights', 26 January 1997, at 4.

[67] Philip Alston and Gerard Quinn, 'The Nature and Scope of States Parties' Obligations under the International Covenant on Economic, Social and Cultural Rights' (1987) 9(2) Human Rights Quarterly 156.

[68] Audrey R Chapman, 'Towards an Understanding of the Right to Enjoy the Benefits of Scientific Progress and Its Applications' (2009) 8:1 Journal of Human Rights 1–36.

3. The Obligation to Adopt a NHRAP under Core Human Rights Treaties

To unravel the legal status of NHRAPs under various human rights conventions, and to derive the obligation to adopt a NHRAP from the broader obligations addressed above, in what follows, all the core human rights treaties will be examined one by one. This textual analysis will start with the International Covenant on Civil and Political Rights (ICCPR).

3.1. ICCPR

While great emphasis has been placed on the obligation to take steps/measures for implementing economic, social, and cultural rights, it is not often recognized in the literature that there is a significant similarity regarding civil and political rights as well.[69] It is now generally accepted for both civil and political rights as well as economic, social, and cultural rights that states are obliged not merely to refrain from violating these rights but also to take steps to ensure human rights enjoyment.[70] As Alston and Quinn argue, the reality is that the full realization of civil and political rights is heavily dependent on the development of the necessary societal structures[71] and, thus, as Mowbray and Feldman emphasize, each state is required to take measures for the realization of civil and political rights.[72] Alston and Quinn go on to say that 'the suggestion that realization of civil and political rights requires only abstention on the part of the state and can be achieved without significant expenditure is patently at odds with reality'.[73] For example, in the case of physical security rights, each state has not only the duty not to eliminate a person's security but also the duty to take measures, such as legislative measures, and protect people against deprivation of security by other people and also to provide for the security of those unable to provide for their own.[74] The right

[69] Henry J Steiner, 'International Protection of Human Rights' in MD Evans (ed), *International Law* (1st edn, Oxford University Press 2003); Alastair Mowbray, *The Development of Positive Obligations under the European Convention on Human Rights by the European Court of Human Rights* (1st edn, Hart Publishing 2004); Arambulo, *Strengthening the Supervision of the International Covenant on Economic, Social and Cultural Rights: Theoretical and Procedural Aspects*, note 63.

[70] See Sigrun Skogly, 'Extraterritoriality: Universal Human Rights Without Universal Obligations?' in Sarah Joseph and Adam McBeth (eds), *Research Handbook on International Human Rights Law* (1st edn, Edward Elgar Publishing 2010) at 73; Sandra Fredman, 'Human Rights Transformed: Positive Duties and Positive Rights' (2006) 38 Oxford Legal Studies Research Paper; Mowbray, note 69.

[71] Alston and Quinn, 'The Nature and Scope of States Parties' Obligations under the International Covenant on Economic, Social and Cultural Rights', note 67 at 172.

[72] Feldman, *Civil Liberties and Human Rights in England and Wales*, note 28 at 53; Mowbray, *The Development of Positive Obligations under the European Convention on Human Rights by the European Court of Human Rights*, note 69; see Keir Starmer, 'Positive Obligations Under the Convention' in J Jowell and J Cooper (eds), *Understanding Human Rights Principles* (Oxford, Hart Publishing 2001) 159; Ssenyonjo, note 23 at 977.

[73] Alston and Quinn, 'The Nature and Scope of States Parties' Obligations under the International Covenant on Economic, Social and Cultural Rights', note 67 at 172.

[74] Sandra Fredman, *Human Rights Transformed: Positive Rights and Positive Duties* (1st edn, Oxford University Press 2008) 68; Arambulo, *Strengthening the Supervision of the International Covenant on Economic, Social and Cultural Rights: Theoretical and Procedural Aspects*, note 63 at 119.

to a fair trial is another example. As Fredman states, there could be no right to a fair trial without taking steps/measures to set up courts and a criminal judicial system.[75]

The obligation to take steps/measures is clearly found in the International Covenant on Civil and Political Rights (ICCPR).[76] Article 2(1) of the ICCPR states that 'each state party to the present Covenant undertakes to respect and to ensure to all individuals within its territory and subject to its jurisdiction the rights recognised in the present Covenant ...' This article is not restricted to the respect of human rights. It requires the states parties to take steps/measures, enabling right holders to enjoy their rights. Interpreting this article, the Human Rights Committee, in its General Comment No 3, calls for specific 'activities' (steps/measures) by the states parties to enable individuals to enjoy their rights.[77] It reads that:

> The Committee considers it necessary to draw the attention of states parties to the fact that the obligation under the Covenant [Article 2] is not confined to the respect of human rights, but that states parties have also undertaken to ensure the enjoyment of these rights to all individuals under their jurisdiction. This aspect calls for specific activities by the states parties to enable individuals to enjoy their rights.[78]

Whereas the obligation to respect is typically interpreted as a negative obligation to refrain from interference, as discussed before, it also entails some positive obligations on the part of the state.[79]

More importantly, Article 2(2) of the ICCPR expressly states that to give effect to the rights recognized in the Covenant, each state party undertakes to take the necessary steps or measures.[80] To do so, each state party is responsible for adopting a NHRAP to implement all the rights set forth in the Covenant. This point has been also confirmed on different occasions by the Human Rights Committee. The right to personal security is a good example. In the General Comment No 35, which was released on 16 December 2014, the Human Rights Committee stipulated that:

> The right to personal security also obliges States parties to take appropriate measures in response to death threats against persons in the public sphere, and more generally to protect individuals from foreseeable threats to life or bodily integrity proceeding from any governmental or private actors. States parties must take both measures to prevent future injury and retrospective measures, such as enforcement of criminal laws, in response to past injury.[81]

[75] Fredman, ibid.

[76] Craven, *The International Covenant on Economic, Social and Cultural Rights: A Perspective on its Development,* note 19.

[77] Human Rights Committee, General Comment No 3, Article 2 Implementation at the national level (Thirteenth session, 1981), Compilation of General Comments and General Recommendations Adopted by Human Rights Treaty Bodies, UN Doc HRI/GEN/1/Rev.6 at 125 (2003) at para 1.

[78] ibid.

[79] Sepulveda, *The Nature of the Obligation under the International Covenant on Economic, Social and Cultural Rights*, note 53, at 136; see David Harris, 'The International Covenant on Civil and Political Rights and the United Kingdom' in David Harris and Sarah Joseph (eds), *The International Covenant on Civil and Political Rights and United Kingdom Law* (1st edn, Oxford University Press 1995); Manfred Nowak, *UN Covenant on Civil and Political Rights* (2nd edn, Engel 2005).

[80] See also Alex Conte, 'Democratic and Civil Rights' in Alex Conte and Richard Burchill (eds), *Defining Civil and Political Rights* (2nd edn, Ashgate 2009).

[81] Human Rights Committee, General Comment No 35 (Article 9: Liberty and security of person) 16 December 2014, CCPR/C/GC/35, at para 9.

As for the right to liberty of person against deprivations by third parties, as another example of a civil and political right, in this General Comment, the Human Rights Committee also expresses the view that 'states parties have the duty to take appropriate measures to protect the right to liberty of person against deprivation by third parties . . . states parties should do their utmost to take appropriate measures to protect individuals against deprivation of liberty by the action of other States within their territory'.[82] In the case of children, it goes on to say that: 'Article 24, paragraph 1, of the Covenant entitles every child "to such measures of protection as are required by his status as a minor, on the part of his family, society and the state". That article entails the adoption of special measures to protect the personal liberty and security of every child, in addition to the measures generally required by article 9 for everyone.' [83]

The right to life is another example. The Second Optional Protocol to the International Covenant on Civil and Political Rights, which is concerned with the abolition of the death penalty, states that 'all measures of abolition of the death penalty should be considered as progress in the enjoyment of the right to life'[84] and all the measures that the states have adopted to give effect to the present Protocol should be stated in the reports that they submit to the Human Rights Committee.[85] In Article 1, it goes on to state that 'each state party shall take all necessary measures to abolish the death penalty within its jurisdiction'.[86] Regarding the right to marry, as another instance, Article 23 of the Covenant obliges each state party to 'take appropriate steps to ensure equality of rights and responsibilities of spouses as to marriage, during marriage and at its dissolution'.[87] All these examples support the point that the full realization of Civil and Political rights also needs steps to be taken by appropriate means and, therefore, requires adopting a NHRAP. This conclusion is further strengthened by the Human Rights Committee in the 'Focused reports based on replies to lists of issues prior to reporting (LOIPR): Implementation of the new optional reporting procedure (LOIPR procedure)', which asks the states parties to provide detailed information on:

> [N]ew political, administrative and other measures taken to promote and protect human rights at the national level that have occurred since the previous report, including on any national human rights plans or programmes, and the resources allocated thereto, their means, objectives and results.[88]

This point has also been reaffirmed by the Human Rights Committee in different Concluding Observations. For example, in the case of Sudan, for the consideration of reports, the Committee requires the state to 'ensure implementation of the Action

[82] ibid, at para 7. [83] ibid, at para 62.

[84] UN General Assembly, 'Second Optional Protocol to the International Covenant on Civil and Political Rights, Aiming at the Abolition of the Death Penalty', 15 December 1989, A/RES/44/128.

[85] ibid, Article 3. [86] ibid, Article 1.

[87] UN General Assembly, *International Covenant on Civil and Political Rights*, 16 December 1966, United Nations, Treaty Series, Vol 999, 171, Article 23.

[88] Human Rights Committee, Focused reports based on replies to lists of issues prior to reporting (LOIPR): Implementation of the new optional reporting procedure (LOIPR procedure) Ninety-ninth session, CCPR/C/99/4 Geneva, 12–30 July 2010, at para 11.

Plan to combat violence against women in Darfur, and its extension to the rest of the country'.[89]

The next convention to be examined is the Convention against Torture and Other Cruel, Inhuman, or Degrading Treatment or Punishment (CAT).

3.2. CAT

The obligation to adopt a NHRAP is imposed by the language of the CAT. The words 'ensure', 'provide', 'protect', 'take measures', and 'take steps', utilized normally for a positive obligation, are used eight, seven, one, eight, and one times in the CAT respectively. Articles 2 and 16 of the Convention require each state party to 'take effective legislative, administrative, judicial or other measures to prevent acts of torture in any territory under its jurisdiction'.[90] This has also been noted in the preamble of the Optional Protocol to the CAT.[91] This Optional Protocol recalls that 'the *effective* prevention of torture and other cruel, inhuman or degrading treatment or punishment requires education and a combination of various legislative, administrative, judicial and other measures'.[92] Likewise, it obliges states parties to take the necessary measures to *ensure* that the experts of the national preventive mechanism have the required capabilities and professional knowledge.[93]

Despite all the steps mentioned above, the Preamble of the Optional Protocol to the CAT emphasizes that the states parties are convinced that further measures are necessary to achieve the purposes of the CAT and to strengthen the protection of persons deprived of their liberty against torture.[94] The importance of adopting a NHRAP for the fulfilment of the obligation to take steps/measures under the CAT has been noted by the Committee against Torture in some Concluding Observations.[95] For example, in the case of Iceland, the Committee requires the state to establish a national plan of action against trafficking in human beings.[96] Likewise, the General Assembly in a report on Indonesia states that:

> The Government should adopt an anti-torture action plan which foresees awareness-raising programmes and training for all stakeholders, including the National Human Rights

[89] HRC, Ninetieth session 9–27 July 2007, Concluding Observations of the Human Rights Committee, CCPR/C/SDN/CO/3, 29 August 2007.

[90] See Ahcene Boulesbaa, 'The Nature of the Obligations Incurred by States under Article 2 of the UN Convention Against Torture' (1990) 12:1 Human Rights Quarterly 53–93, 80.

[91] UN General Assembly, 'Optional Protocol to the Convention against Torture and other Cruel, Inhuman or Degrading Treatment or Punishment', 22 June 2006, A/RES/57/199, preamble.

[92] ibid. [93] ibid, Article 18(2). [94] ibid, preamble.

[95] CAT, Concluding Observations of the Committee against Torture, Sweden, CAT/C/SWE/CO/5, 4 June 2008; CAT, Consideration of Reports Submitted by States Parties Under Article 19 of the Convention, Concluding Observations of the Committee against Torture, Zambia, CAT/C/ZMB/CO/2, 26 May 2008; see CAT, Consideration of Reports Submitted by States Parties Under Article 19 of the Convention Concluding Observations of the Committee against Torture Indonesia, CAT/C/IDN/CO/2, 2 July 2008; CAT, Concluding Observations of the Committee against Torture Kazakhstan, CAT/C/KAZ/CO/2, 12 December 2008, at para 31.

[96] CAT, Concluding Observations: Iceland, CAT/C/ISL/CO/3, 8 July 2008, Fortieth session, Geneva, 28 April–16 May 2008.

Commission and civil society representatives, in order to lead them to live up to their human rights obligations and fulfil their specific task in the fight against torture.[97]

The next convention to be examined is the International Convention on the Elimination of All Forms of Racial Discrimination (ICERD).

3.3. ICERD

The same as the CAT and ICCPR, to give effect to the ICERD also requires states parties to take measures. The words 'ensure', 'promote', 'protect', and 'measures' which trigger a positive duty on the states are used respectively two, five, six, and eleven times in the text of the ICERD. The convention obliges state parties to 'adopt all necessary measures for speedily eliminating racial discrimination in all its forms and manifestations, and to prevent and combat racist doctrines and practices in order to promote understanding between races and to build an international community free from all forms of racial segregation and racial discrimination'.[98] Article 1 of the Convention also mentions the 'special measures' that should be taken to ensure racial or ethnic groups or individuals equal enjoyment or exercise of human rights and fundamental freedoms. To give effect to the convention 'each state party shall take effective measures to review governmental, national and local policies, and to amend, rescind or nullify any laws and regulations which have the effect of creating or perpetuating racial discrimination wherever it exists'[99] and shall 'prohibit and bring to an end, by all appropriate means, including legislation as required by circumstances, racial discrimination by any persons, group or organisation'.[100] Under Article 2(2) of the ICERD:

> States parties shall, when the circumstances so warrant, take, in the social, economic, cultural and other fields, special and concrete measures to ensure the adequate development and protection of certain racial groups or individuals belonging to them, for the purpose of guaranteeing them the full and equal enjoyment of human rights and fundamental freedoms.[101]

The obligation to take steps/measures is also reaffirmed in Articles 4 and 7 of the Convention obliging the states parties to 'undertake to adopt immediate and positive measures' designed to 'eradicate all incitement to, or acts of, such discrimination'[102] and 'in the fields of teaching, education, culture and information, with a view to combating prejudices which lead to racial discrimination and to promoting understanding, tolerance and friendship among nations and racial or ethnical groups, as well as to propagating the purposes and principles of the Charter of the United Nations, the Universal Declaration of Human Rights, the United Nations

[97] General Assembly, Promotion and Protection of All Human Rights, Civil, Political, Economic, Social, and Cultural Rights, including The Right to Development Report of the Special Rapporteur on torture and other cruel, inhuman or degrading treatment or punishment, Manfred Nowak, Mission to Indonesia, A/HRC/7/3/Add.7, 10 March 2008, at para 76.

[98] UNGA, International Convention on the Elimination of All Forms of Racial Discrimination, 21 December 1965, United Nations, Treaty Series, vol 660, 195.

[99] ibid, Article 2(C). [100] ibid, Article 2(D). [101] ibid, Article 2(2).

[102] ibid, Article 4.

Declaration on the Elimination of All Forms of Racial Discrimination, and this Convention'.[103]

All this imposes an obligation to adopt a NHRAP upon the states. This conclusion is confirmed by the Committee on Elimination of Racial Discrimination in different Concluding Observations.[104] For instance, in the case of New Zealand, 'the Committee notes the lack of a comprehensive national human rights action plan in the state party after the 2005 human rights action plan reached its completion point. However, the Committee notes the state party's intention to develop a new human rights action plan, under the aegis of the national human rights commission, in connection with the Universal Periodic Review process (art. 2)'.[105] In its Concluding Observations, 'the Committee urges the state party to adopt a National Action Plan on Human Rights and ensure that it includes plans on how to combat racial discrimination ...'[106] The Committee, in the cases of Germany and Indonesia, also 'urges' that the state party include, in its next periodic report, specific information on the National Action Plan against Racism and other measures taken to implement the Durban Declaration and Programme of Action at the national level.[107] The Human Rights Council also, in its Report of the Special Rapporteur on racial discrimination, in Russia states that:

> The Government should adopt a comprehensive federal plan for the Roma community, aiming at both promoting and respecting their cultural identity and at eradicating their social and economic marginalisation, in particular, poor housing conditions, lack of documents, the high level of dropouts of Roma children at school and the difficulties of the Roma to access employment. The plan should also aim at sensitizing the Russian society to Roma history and traditions, in order to eliminate the negative stigma and stereotypes Roma are recurrently associated with.[108]

The Committee does not merely express its concern about the lack of NHRAPs, urging the states parties to adopt a NHRAP, but also welcomes and appreciates this step in the case of those states which have already adopted NHRAPs. In the case of Fiji, for example, the Committee 'welcomes the adoption of an action plan to combat racial discrimination in the field of education and to promote integration

[103] UN General Assembly Second Optional Protocol to the International Covenant on Civil and Political Rights 15 December 1989, A/RES/44/128, Article 7.

[104] CERD, Concluding Observations: Belgium, CERD/C/BEL/CO/15, 11 April 2008, Seventy-second session; Concluding Observations of the Committee on the Elimination of Racial Discrimination, Italy, CERD/C/ITA/CO/15, 16 May 2008; CERD, Concluding Observations: United States of America, CERD/C/USA/CO/6, 8 May 2008.

[105] Committee on the Elimination of Racial Discrimination, Concluding Observations: New Zealand, CERD/C/NZL/CO/18-20, 1 March 2013, at para 8.

[106] ibid.

[107] CERD, Concluding Observations: Germany, CERD/C/DEU/CO/18, 21 August 2008, at para 30; Committee on the Elimination of Racial Discrimination, Consideration of Reports Submitted by States Parties under Article 9 of the Convention, Concluding Observations of the Committee on the Elimination of Racial Discrimination, Indonesia, CERD/C/IDN/CO/3, 15 August 2007, at para 26.

[108] Human Rights Council, Implementation of General Assembly Resolution 60/251 of 15 March 2006 entitled 'Human Rights Council', Report of the Special Rapporteur on contemporary forms of racism, racial discrimination, xenophobia and related, intolerance, Doudou Diène, Addendum, Mission to the Russian Federation, A/HRC/4/19/Add.3, 30 May 2007.

of the student body'.[109] Also, in the case of Moldova which already has developed a National Human Rights Action Plan, the Committee notes with appreciation that 'the National Human Rights Plan of Action for 2004–2008 of the state party includes a chapter on the rights of national minorities'.[110]

The next convention to be examined is the International Convention on the Protection of the Rights of All Migrant Workers and Members of Their Families (ICRMW).

3.4. ICRMW

Taking steps by all appropriate measures, which includes the sub-obligation to adopt a NHRAP, is clearly recognized by the ICRMW. The terms 'ensure', 'facilitate', 'promote', and 'measures' are used fourteen, eight, one, and twenty-two times respectively in the text of the ICRMW. Article 3(3) of the ICRMW reads that:

> States parties shall take all appropriate measures to ensure that migrant workers are not deprived of any rights derived from this principle by reason of any irregularity in their stay or employment.[111]

According to Article 84 of the Convention, 'each state party undertakes to adopt the legislative and other measures that are necessary to implement the provisions of the present Convention'. The Committee on the Protection of the Rights of All Migrant Workers and Members of Their Families has noted the need for adopting a NHRAP to identify steps/measures to implement the provisions of the present convention. For instance, in Concluding Observations of the case of Sri Lanka, the Committee notes with interest that:

> the National Action Plan for the Promotion and Protection of Human Rights being developed by the State party will focus on, inter alia, migration issues, including trafficking, irregular migration, strengthening protection of migrants, voting rights of migrants, training and awareness, as well as the situation of migrants workers in Sri Lanka.[112]

It also welcomes the efforts undertaken by Albania to promote and protect the rights of Albania's migrant workers abroad by developing the National Plan on Migration.[113]

The following will examine the obligation to adopt a NHRAP in the Convention on the Rights of the Child (CRC).

109 CERD, Concluding Observations: Fiji, CERD/C/FJI/CO/17, 16 May 2008, at para 24.

110 CERD, Concluding Observations: Moldova, CERD/C/MDA/CO/7, 16 May 2008.

111 UN General Assembly, 'International Convention on the Protection of the Rights of All Migrant Workers and Members of their Families', 18 December 1990, A/RES/45/158, Article 3(3).

112 CMW, Concluding Observations of the Committee on the Protection of the Rights of All Migrant Workers and Members of Their Families, CMW/C/LKA/CO/1, 14 December 2009, at para 37.

113 CMW, Concluding Observations of the Committee on the Protection of the Rights of All Migrant Workers and Members of Their Families, CMW/C/ALB/CO/1, 10 December 2010.

3.5. CRC

The same as previous human rights treaties addressed above, the obligation to take steps/measures is also recognized by the CRC. The terms 'measures', 'ensure', and 'promote' which trigger the obligation to adopt a NHRAP, have been repeated at least thirty, thirty-six, eleven times in the text of CRC, respectively. According to Article 4 of the CRC, states parties shall undertake all appropriate legislative, administrative, and other measures to implement all the rights recognized in the Convention and this inevitably requires adopting a NHRAP.[114]

It is worth noting that even the two optional protocols to the CRC also reaffirm the obligation to take measures. The 'Optional Protocol to the Convention on the Rights of the Child on the Sale of Children, Child Prostitution and Child Pornography' in its preamble declares that to achieve the purposes of the Convention on the Rights of the Child and the implementation of its provisions, it would be appropriate to extend the measures that states parties should undertake in order to guarantee the protection of the child from the sale of children, child prostitution, and child pornography.[115] Likewise, as Article 6 of the 'Optional Protocol to the Convention on the Rights of the Child on the Involvement of Children in Armed Conflict' notes, each state party shall take all necessary legal, administrative, and other measures, set in a NHRAP, in order to ensure the effective implementation and enforcement of the provisions of this Protocol within its jurisdiction.[116] Article 1 of the Optional Protocol also requires 'states parties to take all feasible measures to ensure that members of their armed forces who have not attained the age of eighteen years do not take a direct part in hostilities'.[117] They should also take all feasible measures to prevent armed groups from recruiting or using in hostilities persons under the age of eighteen years.[118]

In order to take all these measures, states are required to adopt a NHRAP and this conclusion is also confirmed by the approach adopted by the Committee on the Rights of the Child in several Concluding Observations.[119] For example, the Committee commends the formulation of several specific plans of action for children and of an overall Afghan National Development Strategy (2008–2013) and urges the state party to fully implement the anti-trafficking plan of action.[120] Also, in the case of Ukraine, the Committee welcomes the adoption of the National Plan of Action for Children 2010–2016 and the National Strategic Action Plan for HIV

[114] UN General Assembly, Convention on the Rights of the Child, 20 November 1989, United Nations, Treaty Series, vol 1577, Article 4.

[115] UN General Assembly, Optional Protocol to the Convention on the Rights of the Child on the Sale of Children, Child Prostitution, and Child Pornography, 16 March 2001, A/RES/54/263, preamble.

[116] UN General Assembly, Optional Protocol to the Convention on the Rights of the Child on the Involvement of Children in Armed Conflict, 12 February 2002, A/RES/54/263, Article 6.

[117] ibid, Article 1. [118] ibid, Article 4.

[119] CRC, Concluding Observations: Belarus, CRC/C/OPSC/BLR/CO/1, 8 April 2011; CRC, Concluding Observations: Panama, CRC/C/PAN/CO/3-4, 21 December 2011.

[120] CRC, Concluding Observations: Afghanistan, CRC/C/AFG/CO/1, 8 April 2011, at paras 11 and 73.

prevention among children and youth at risk of and vulnerable to HIV, care and support for children and youth affected by HIV/AIDS, in May 2010 and urges the state party to ensure effective implementation of the plans.[121] It also urges the state party to develop a national plan of action for human rights education.[122] Each state party shall submit a report to the Committee on the Rights of the Child providing comprehensive information on the measures it has taken to implement the provisions of the Convention and its Protocols.[123] In many cases, the Committee is concerned about the lack of a comprehensive national plan of action for the implementation of the Convention.[124] For example, in the case of Kazakhstan, the Committee notes:

> [T]he state party's efforts to develop a National Plan of Action and the foreseen adoption of the programme entitled 'Children of Kazakhstan' for 2006–2011. However, the Committee is concerned that the programme mainly focuses on protection issues and does not cover the full range of child rights and that it can therefore not be considered as a National Plan of Action as required in the Committee's previous Concluding Observations and the outcome document of the General Assembly special session on children held in May 2002 entitled 'A World Fit for Children'.[125]

In its Concluding Observations, the Committee also welcomes the efforts undertaken by the state party to combat trafficking, such as the implementation of the plan of action to combat and prevent offences involving trafficking in persons for 2004–2005 and its subsequent plan for 2006–2008.[126] In the case of Turkey, the Committee on the Rights of the Child is concerned that 'the state party has yet to establish a plan of action for implementation of the Optional Protocol'.[127] Russia is another example. The Committee notes with concern that since 2000, Russia has not had an overall 'national plan of action'.[128] Nevertheless, it welcomes the information that a national plan, entitled 'Basic directions for improving the situation of children in the Russian Federation', calling for the inclusion of national principles for the implementation of the Convention in various sectoral plans of action, has been established.[129] It is concerned, however, about the integrated and co-ordinated implementation of this strategy via the various sectoral plans of action.[130] In the case of Egypt, the Committee urges the state to intensity efforts to prevent and eliminate all forms of child marriages by pursuing plans of the National Council for Childhood and Motherhood (NCCM) to prepare and adopt an action plan to

121 CRC, Concluding Observations: Ukraine, CRC/C/UKR/CO/3-4, 21 April 2011, at paras 4, 13, and 14.

122 ibid, at para 69.

123 UN General Assembly, 'Optional Protocol to the Convention on the Rights of the Child on the Sale of Children', note 116, Article 8.

124 CRC, Concluding Observations: Cambodia, CRC/C/KHM/CO/2-3, 3 August 2011, at para 12; CRC, Concluding Observations of the Committee on the Rights of the Child: Sweden, CRC/C/SWE/CO/4, 26 June 2009, at para 12.

125 CRC, Concluding Observations: Kazakhstan, CRC/C/KAZ/CO/3, 8 June 2007, at para 12; see also, CRC, Concluding Observations: New Zealand, CRC/C/NZL/3-4, 19 January 2011, at para 15.

126 ibid, at para 67.

127 CRC, Concluding Observations: Turkey, CRC/C/TUR/CO/2-3, 20 July 2012.

128 CRC, Concluding Observations: Russian Federation, CRC/C/RUS/CO/3, 23 November 2005.

129 ibid.

130 ibid.

combat child marriages.[131] In other Concluding Observations, again in the case of Egypt, 'the Committee is concerned at the lack of a comprehensive plan addressing specifically all issues covered under the Optional Protocol'.[132] Also in this regard, in the case of Germany, the Committee recommends that 'the state party expedite the adoption of the National Plan of Action, which should cover all areas of the Convention . . .'[133] More importantly, in the case of Japan, the Committee 'remains concerned at the lack of a comprehensive rights-based national plan of action for children covering all areas of the Convention and which addresses, inter alia, inequalities and disparities among children'.[134]

The next convention to be examined is the Convention on the Elimination of All Forms of Discrimination against Women (CEDAW).

3.6. CEDAW

The CEDAW employs the terms 'ensure', 'provide', protect', and 'measures' which trigger a positive obligation on the states at least twenty-one, two, five, and twenty-three times, respectively. It begins with the point that implementing the principles set forth in the Declaration on the Elimination of Discrimination against Women requires adopting appropriate measures, and to take necessary steps/measures invariably requires the adoption of a NHRAP.[135] Article 24 of the CEDAW goes on to state that 'states parties undertake to adopt all necessary measures at the national level aimed at achieving the full realization of the rights recognised in the present Convention'.[136] This conclusion is further strengthened by the Committee on the Elimination of Discrimination against Women in the Concluding Observations of Slovakia when it states that:

> The Committee also welcomes the adoption of the National Strategy for the Prevention and Elimination of Violence Committed against Women and in Families, in 2004, and the National Action Plan for Combating Trafficking in Persons, in 2006. It notes with appreciation the inclusion of the gender dimension in other strategic plans, including the National Action Plan for Combating Poverty and Social Exclusion, and the National Action Plan of Employment.[137]

Here, the Committee is also concerned at the absence of a 'national action plan on gender equality' with established priorities and based on the evaluation of the previous National Action Plan for Women, which expired in 2007.[138] In the case of Russia, the Committee 'urges the state party to give priority attention to combating

[131] CRC, Concluding Observations: Egypt, CRC/C/EGY/CO/3-4, 20 June 2011, at para 73.
[132] CRC, Concluding Observations: Egypt, CRC/C/OPSC/EGY/1, 20 June 2011, at para 12.
[133] CRC, Concluding Observations: Germany, CRC/C/15/Add.226, 26 February 2004, at para 14.
[134] CRC, Concluding Observations: Japan, CRC/C/JPN/CO/3, 20 June 2010, at para 15.
[135] UN General Assembly, *Convention on the Elimination of All Forms of Discrimination Against Women*, 18 December 1979, United Nations Treaty Series, vol 1249, 13, at preamble.
[136] ibid, Article 24.
[137] CEDAW, Concluding Observations: Slovakia, CEDAW/C/SVK/CO/4, 30 June–18 July 2008, at para 20.
[138] ibid, at para 30.

violence against women and girls and to adopting comprehensive measures to address such violence, in accordance with its General Recommendation. They should also include the development of a coherent and multi sectoral action plan to combat violence against women.'[139] In its Concluding Observations, the Committee urges the state party to fully implement Article 6 of the Convention, including by speedily enacting specific national legislation and a comprehensive policy and action plan on the phenomenon of trafficking, to ensure that perpetrators are punished and victims adequately protected and assisted.[140]

In February 2012, the Committee, in the case of Brazil, urged the state to provide all entities which participate in the implementation of the National Plan to Combat Violence against Women with substantial human, technical, and financial resources, including for the establishment of shelters for women victims of violence.[141] Moreover, in the case of Egypt, the Committee urges the state party to give priority attention to combating violence against women and girls and to adopting comprehensive measures to address such violence. It then goes on to say that 'they should include the development of a coherent and multi sectoral action plan to combat violence against women'.[142] Similarly, in the case of New Zealand, the Committee urges the state to put in place an effective strategy for mainstreaming gender perspectives into all national plans and to strengthen the linkages between the New Zealand Action Plan for Human Rights and the Action Plan for New Zealand Women, with a view to ensuring that the promotion and protection of women's human rights, as enshrined in the Convention, are integrated into all national human rights plans.[143] Likewise, in the case of Indonesia, the Committee 'calls upon the state party to ensure that legislation on trafficking is fully enforced and that the national action plan and other measures to combat human trafficking are fully implemented'.[144] On the other side, in its Concluding Observations on periodic reports of Cyprus, the Committee welcomed the adoption of the National Action Plan on Gender Equality (2007–2013), on Prevention and Handling of Family Violence (2010–2013), and against Trafficking in Human Beings (2013–2015) as the progress achieved by the state concerned.[145] Similarly, in July 2017, in the case of Romania, the Committee welcomed the adoption of 'the National Strategy for Equal Opportunities for women and men 2006–2009, in

[139] CEDAW, Concluding Observations: Russian Federation, CEDAW/C/USR/CO/7, 16 August 2010.

[140] ibid, at para 27.

[141] CEDAW, Concluding Observations: Brazil, CEDAW/C/BRA/CO/7, 23 February 2012, at para 19.

[142] CEDAW, Concluding Observations: Egypt, CEDAW/C/EGY/CO/7, 5 February 2010, at para 24.

[143] CEDAW, Concluding Observations: New Zealand, CEDAW/C/NZL/CO/6, 10 August 2007, at para 15.

[144] CEDAW, Concluding Observations: Indonesia, CEDAW/C/IDN/CO/5, 10 August 2007, at para 25.

[145] CEDAW, Concluding Observations: Cyprus, CEDAW/C/CYP/CO/6-7, 11 February–1 March 2013.

2006, 2010–2012, in 2010 and 2014–2017, with its General Plan of Action for its implementation, in 2014 ...'[146]

In its General Recommendation No 34, the Committee urges the states parties to 'develop action plans that address practical barriers to rural women's participation in community life and implement campaigns to raise awareness about the importance of their participation in community decision-making...'[147]

The following will examine the obligation to adopt a NHRAP in the International Convention for the Protection of All Persons from Enforced Disappearance (ICPPED).

3.7. ICPPED

By imposing the obligation to take steps/measures upon the states, the ICPPED recognizes the obligation to adopt a NHRAP for the states parties.[148] To give effect into the provisions, state parties are obliged to ensure conditions which will allow investigation of the enforced disappearance. To do so, they must take necessary measures, including adopting a NHRAP, to prevent ill-treatment or intimidation of persons involved in the investigation, provide access to documentation and relevant information or places of detention, and to prevent persons suspected of committing crime from influencing or hindering the investigation.[149]

The words 'measures', 'steps', and 'protect' are used at least twenty-eight, two, and five times respectively in the text of the ICPPED. For instance, Article 3 of the convention holds that:

> Each State Party shall take appropriate measures to investigate acts defined in article 2 committed by persons or groups of persons acting without the authorization, support or acquiescence of the State and to bring those responsible to justice.

Article 25(2) and (3), as another example, states that each state party shall take the necessary measures to search and identify children victims of enforced disappearance, to return them to their family, and to co-operate with other state parties to fulfil these obligations. In March 2017, the Committee on Enforced Disappearances states that 'in accordance with Article 30, para 3, of the Convention and Rule 62 of its Rules of procedure, the Committee has requested the states parties concerned to take all the necessary measures, including interim measures, to locate and protect

[146] Committee on CEDAW, Concluding Observations: Romania, CEDAW/C/ROU/CO/7-8, at para 5(e) 24 July 2017.

[147] Committee on CEDAW, General Recommendation No 34, on the rights of rural women, CEDAW/C/GC/34, at para 54(c), 4 March 2016.

[148] UN General Assembly, International Convention for the Protection of All Persons from Enforced Disappearance, 20 December 2006, Articles 3, 4, 6, 8–10, 12, 14, 15, 18, 21–25, 30, 31.

[149] Article 12(1), Article 12(3)(a), Article 12(3)(b), and Article 12(4); see Tatjana Milić, 'International Convention for the Protection of All Persons from Enforced Disappearance', Vol LXII, br 1, str 37–64 Izvorni naučni rad Februar 2010. <http://www.doiserbia.nb.rs/img/doi/0025-8555/2010/0025-85551001037M.pdf> accessed 9 January 2012.

the persons concerned in accordance with the Convention and to inform the Committee, within a specified period of time.' [150]

The next convention to be examined is the Convention on the Rights of Persons with Disabilities (CRPD).

3.8. CRPD

The obligation to adopt a NHRAP can be deduced from the text of the CRPD. As stated in Article 4 of this convention, all the states which are party to the CRPD are duty bound to 'take all appropriate measures' to implement the rights recognized in the Convention.[151] To do so requires developing a NHRAP. It is also confirmed by the Committee on the Rights of Persons with Disabilities in a session on the list of issues to be taken up in connection with the consideration of the initial report of Argentina. Concerning Article 28 of the Convention which requires states parties to take appropriate steps to safeguard and promote the right to adequate standard of living, the Committee in this session asked the states parties to provide detailed information on the specific measures, taken to provide social protection to persons with disabilities, including boys and girls, under a Families Plan of action.[152] Also, in initial reports, submitted by states parties under Article 35 of the Convention (Hong Kong-China), it is noted that the 'Government will, in collaboration with relevant NGOs and Task Force members, develop an action plan to implement specific measures ...'[153]

The Committee, in different Concluding Observations, also 'urges' the state parties to speed up the development and implementation of plans directed to make public facilities, communications, and public transportation, in the urban and rural areas, accessible for persons with disabilities and to ensure that private entities duly take into account all aspects of accessibility for persons with disabilities.[154] In the case of Spain, for instance, 'the Committee welcomes the state's adoption of the Third Plan of Action for persons with disabilities, which addresses disability along gender-analysis lines, as well as the Global Action Strategy for the Employment of Persons with Disabilities 2008–2012, including its first plan of action, covering the years 2008–2010'.[155]

[150] Committee on Enforced Disappearances, Report of the Committee on Enforced Disappearances on its Twelfth Session, Geneva 6–17 March 2017, Twelfth session, at para 13 (see also Committee on Enforced Disappearances, Report of the Committee on Enforced Disappearances on its Eleventh Session, Geneva 3–14 October 2016, Twelfth session, at para 13).

[151] ibid, Article 4(1), at para (a).

[152] Committee on the Rights of Persons with Disabilities, Seventh session Geneva, 16–20 April 2012 Implementation of the Convention on the Rights of Persons with Disabilities, List of issues to be taken up in connection with the consideration of the initial report of Argentina (CRPD/C/ARG/1) concerning Articles 1 to 33 of the Convention, CRPD/C/ARG/Q/1, 16 May 2012, at para 26.

[153] CRPD, Implementation of the Convention on the Rights of Persons with Disabilities, Initial reports submitted by States parties under Article 35 of the Convention (Hong Kong–China), CRPD/C/CHN-HKG/1, 11 February 2011, at para 9.52; see CRPD, Implementation of the Convention on the Rights of Persons with Disabilities Initial reports submitted by States parties under Article 35 of the Convention (Paraguay), CRPD/C/PRY/1, 28 June 2011.

[154] CRPD, Concluding Observations: Peru, CRPD/C/PER/CO/1, 16–20 April 2012, at para 14.

[155] CRPD, Concluding Observations: Spain, CRPD/C/ESP/CO/1, 19 October 2011, at para 7.

The above textual analysis of the core human rights treaties provides significant evidence on the basis of which it is reasonable to conclude that each state which is party to the current human rights conventions and has ratified them has an obligation to adopt a NHRAP. Now, the question arises as to whether the obligation to adopt a NHRAP is an obligation of result or conduct, and what is the consequence of (non-)fulfilment of this obligation.

4. Combination of Obligation of Conduct and of Result

As will be examined in the next chapters, each NHRAP needs to include goals which are general targets explaining what a plan seeks to achieve in the long-term.[156] In the context of international human rights law, goals are typically where the obligation of result comes in. In the case of NHRAPs, the nature of the obligation, imposed upon states parties, makes it abundantly clear that adopting a NHRAP is not enough per se. All the measures identified in a NHRAP should be geared towards achieving the full realization of human rights as set forth in international human rights instruments. Article 14 of the ICESCR, as the key article in the case of NHRAPs, imposes a combination of the obligation of conduct and of result upon states parties. Each state party is obliged to adopt a NHRAP, as an obligation of conduct, for the progressive implementation of the rights in question as an obligation of result. In the case of the right to primary education, as an example, the obligation of conduct could involve the adoption and implementation of an action plan and the obligation of result requires that children are learning to read and write.[157] Similarly, in the case of the right to health, the Maastricht Guideline specifies that:

> [T]he obligation of conduct could involve the adoption and implementation of a plan of action to reduce maternal mortality. The obligation of result requires states to achieve specific targets to satisfy a detailed substantive standard. With respect to the right to health, for example, the obligation of result requires the reduction of maternal mortality to levels agreed at the 1994 Cairo International Conference on Population and Development and the 1995 Beijing Fourth World Conference on Women.[158]

Likewise, Article 2(1) of the ICESCR, as another critical article in the case of NHRAPs, which is also applicable to Article 14, involves a combination of the obligation of conduct and of result.[159] On the one hand, it imposes an obligation of

[156] See Patrick Twomey, 'Human Rights-based Approaches to Development: Towards Accountability' in M A Badering and R MaCorquodale (eds), *Economic, Social and Cultural Rights in Action* (1st edn, Oxford University Press 2007).

[157] Ssenyonjo, 'Economic, Social and Cultural rights: An Examination of State Obligations', note 65 at 43; see Alston and Quinn, 'The Nature and Scope of States Parties' Obligations under the International Covenant on Economic, Social and Cultural Rights', note 67.

[158] International Commission of Jurists (ICJ), 'Maastricht Guidelines on Violations of Economic, Social and Cultural Rights', note 66.

[159] Mashood A Baderin and Robert McCorquodale, 'The International Covenant on Economic, Social and Cultural Rights: Forty Years of Development' in Mashood A Baderin and Robert MacCorquodale (eds), *Economic, Social and Cultural Rights in Action* (1st edn, Oxford University Press 2007); Ssenyonjo, 'Economic, Social and Cultural rights: An Examination of State Obligations', note 65

conduct to take measures, which includes the sub-obligation to adopt a NHRAP. As Alston and Quinn argue, 'where the text of the various "recognized" rights specify the "steps" to be taken for their achievement then the obligations so created can truly be said to be obligations of conduct'.[160] On the other hand, the measures taken should be geared towards achieving the principal obligation of result, that is, the full realization of human rights. The Committee on Economic, Social, and Cultural Rights, in its General Comment No 3, declares that this article imposes an obligation to move, as expeditiously and effectively as possible, towards the goal, that is, the full realization of the recognized rights in the Covenant.[161] If states parties fail to adopt and implement a NHRAP or if their plan is not geared towards achieving the result, a violation may take place, though, as will be discussed in the next chapter, states' compliance or non-compliance should be seen as a matter of degree. There is certainly a difference between state A who has not adopted any plan yet, state B who has adopted two plans, though not well-formulated ones, and state C who has adopted three well-designed plans.

The general goal of the full realization of human rights can be found in all the core human rights treaties, albeit with a different focus of interest.[162] In the case of CEDAW, for instance, the obligation to give effect to the rights means that all the necessary measures must be geared towards eliminating discrimination against women in all its forms and manifestations, by any person, organization, or enterprise.[163] Article 3 of the Convention states that:

> States parties shall take in all fields, in particular in the political, social, economic and cultural fields, all appropriate measures, including legislation, to ensure the full development and advancement of women, for the purpose of guaranteeing them the exercise and enjoyment of human rights and fundamental freedoms on a basis of equality with men.[164]

As far as the CAT is concerned, the necessary steps typically should be taken to prevent all forms of torture.[165] As Ahcene Boulesbaa states, under the CAT, states parties 'have assumed not only the obligations to take the prescribed measures in Article 2, but have also assumed the implied and inherent legal obligation to implement these measures and achieve reasonable results in eradicating the practice of torture as state policy'.[166] As for the ICERD, a NHRAP must be adopted for the purpose of 'speedily eliminating racial discrimination in all its forms and manifestations, and to prevent and combat racist doctrines and practices in order to promote

at 42; UN Committee on Economic, Social, and Cultural Rights (CESCR), General Comment No 3: The Nature of States Parties' Obligations (Art 2, para 1, of the Covenant), 14 December 1990, E/1991/23, at paras 1 and 3.

160 Alston and Quinn, 'The Nature and Scope of States Parties' Obligations under the International Covenant on Economic, Social and Cultural Rights', note 67 at 185.

161 CESCR, General Comment No 3, note 159, at para 9; see Eide, 'Group accommodation and the Challenges of Education: Multicultural or Intercultural—or a Combination of the Two?', note 53.

162 CRC, Article 44; CPED, Article 28(1); CAT, Article 19; ICCPR, Article 2, 40; CEDAW, Article 18; CERD, Article 9; ICPRWN, Article 73; CRPD, Articles 31, 35.

163 CEDAW, Article 2(e) and (preamble).

164 ibid, Article 3.

165 CAT, Article 2(1).

166 Boulesbaa, 'The Nature of the Obligations Incurred by States Under Article 2 of the UN Convention Against Torture', note 90, at 56.

understanding between races and to build an international community free from all forms of racial segregation and racial discrimination'.[167] The CRPD, as another instance, also requires the states parties to adopt a NHRAP for the purpose of enabling persons with disabilities to live independently and participate fully in all aspects of life.[168]

Moreover, it should be noted that the obligation to adopt a NHRAP is an immediate obligation. Whereas the full realization of the rights guaranteed in the conventions, being progressive in nature, may occur over a period of time, each state party is obliged to adopt and implement a NHRAP within a reasonably short time.[169] As the Maastricht Guidelines states:

> The fact that the full realisation of most economic, social and cultural rights can only be achieved progressively, which in fact also applies to most civil and political rights, does not alter the nature of the legal obligation of states which requires that certain steps be taken immediately and others as soon as possible.[170]

It is noteworthy that the recognition of this obligation is in tune with the substantive theory of human rights planning, according to which the adoption of a NHRAP in line with the realization of human rights, as set forth in international human rights instruments, has significant consequences at the outcome level. Whereas a failure to adopt a NHRAP can form a violation, the fulfillment of this obligation can accelerate the process of human rights-based development.

In sum, the foregoing analysis of the nature and scope of the obligation to adopt a NHRAP under international human rights conventions demonstrates that each state which is party to the current human rights treaties and has ratified them has therefore an immediate obligation to adopt and implement a NHRAP for the full realization of the rights concerned. If the states parties fail to adopt a NHRAP or if their action plan is not geared towards the full realization of the rights in question, in either case, they may be deemed to be in violation of the conventions.

Given the fact that states parties have an obligation to adopt a NHRAP, the questions arise as to what is the most suitable way for them to comply with this obligation? Whether states should adopt nine separate convention-specific action plans or just one global action plan covering all the rights at once? Another question to be addressed is how to determine the degree of appropriateness of measures taken by the states through their plans? When states ratify an international human rights treaty, it takes on an obligation to give effect to it, by way of taking appropriate measures or steps. However, it is not clear what an 'appropriate measure' is. These are critical questions that will be addressed in the next chapter.

[167] CERD Preamble.

[168] CRPD, Articles 9(1), 26, 30, 35.

[169] CESCR, General Comment No 13, note 32, at para 52.

[170] International Commission of Jurists (ICJ), 'Maastricht Guidelines on Violations of Economic, Social and Cultural Rights', note 66 at 5.

4

Compliance with the Obligation to Adopt a NHRAP

1. Introduction

In the last chapter, the results of the textual analysis of nine core human rights conventions showed that each of these conventions places upon states parties an immediate obligation to adopt a national human rights action plan (NHRAP) which must be geared towards realizing the rights embodied in the conventions. This chapter focuses on the state's compliance with the obligation to adopt a NHRAP and seeks to address two questions.

First, whether states should adopt separate human rights action plans, including rights-specific plans, the National Action Plan on Women, Peace, and Security (NAP-WPS), the National Action Plan on Business and Human Rights (NAP-BHR), or just one global action plan covering all the conventions and rights-related topics at once. To address this question, I will first present an overview of four different types of human rights action plans, ie rights-specific plans, NAP-WPS, NAP-BHR, and global NHRAP, and then explore two sets of arguments for the 'rights-specific approach' and 'global approach' respectively.

Second, given that the obligation to adopt a NHRAP is substantially tied to the obligation to take all appropriate measures (OTAAM), it still remains largely unclear what 'measure' and 'appropriateness' mean in international human rights law. Under all the nine core human rights treaties, states parties are obliged to adopt appropriate measures through their NHRAP(s) in order to give effect to the rights embodied in the conventions, but it is not clear whether 'measure' means an objective or concrete task. In either case, how can the degree of appropriateness of each measure taken by the state be determined? By adopting a mixed methods approach, including a qualitative textual analysis, a quantitative content analysis, and a fuzzy-set method, in the second part of this chapter, I will seek to unpack and explicate the concept of 'appropriate measures' in international human rights law in order to further clarify state's compliance with the obligation to adopt a NHRAP.

2. Types of Human Rights Action Plans

There are different types of human rights-related action plans, the most important of which can be distinguished as follows.

2.1. Global national human rights action plans

The idea of adopting what I would call a global NHRAP stems from the 1993 Vienna Declaration and Programme of Action which recommended each state to develop a plan of action for implementing human rights in general. This was then included in other regional and international documents. For example, the Council of Europe Commissioner for Human Rights recommended each state to develop an action plan for implementing human rights at the national level.[1] The development of such an action plan is not limited to certain right(s) or convention(s). The Vienna Declaration employs the general term of 'human rights' and declares that:

> The World Conference on Human Rights recommends that each state consider the desirability of drawing up a national action plan identifying steps whereby that state would improve the promotion and protection of human rights.[2]

As the Committee on Economic, Social, and Cultural Rights in its reports states, the term 'human rights' in this paragraph covers all the human rights conventions. For example, in the case of Syria, it states that:

> In the light of paragraph 71 of the Vienna Declaration and Programme of Action … the Committee recommends that the state party prepare a comprehensive national plan of action in relation to the implementation of its obligations under international human rights treaties, including the Covenant.[3]

In the case of Estonia, it goes on to recommend states to prepare and develop a comprehensive NHRAP to implement its obligations under its 'international human rights instruments'.[4] It goes without saying that the international human rights instruments encompass all international human rights treaties and other international

[1] Thomas Hammarberg, Council of Europe Commissioner for Human Rights, Recommendation of the Commissioner for Human Rights on Systematic Work for Implementing Human Rights at the National Level, Strasbourg, 18 February 2009, <https://rm.coe.int/16806da952> accessed 21 March 2013.

[2] UN General Assembly, Vienna Declaration and Programme of Action (1993) Pt 2, at para 71.

[3] CESCR, Report on the Twenty-fifth, Twenty-sixth, and Twenty-seventh Sessions (23 April–11 May 2001, 13–31 August 2001, 12–30 November 2001), 6 June 2002, E/2002/22, E/C.12/2001/17, at para 417.

[4] CESCR, Report on The Fortieth and Forty-First Sessions (28 April–16 May 2008, 3–21 November 2008), UN Doc E/2003/22, E/C.12/2002/13 (21 July 2008), at para 516; see CESCR, Report on the Twenty-second, Twenty-third, and Twenty-fourth Sessions (25 April–12 May 2000, 14 August–1 September 2000, 13 November–1 December 2000), 7 June 2001, E/2001/22; E/C.12/2000/21, at paras 244, 327; CESCR, UN Doc E/2002/22, E/C.12/2001/17 (6 June 2002), note 3, at para 502.

documents relevant to international human rights law and the protection of human rights in general. Although the Vienna Declaration, as soft law, is not obligatory per se, it is an authoritative recommendation for the states.

2.2. Rights-specific action plans

The obligation to adopt a rights-specific (or convention-specific) action plan dates back to the 1966 International Covenant on Economic, Social, and Cultural Rights (ICESCR). Article 14 of the ICESCR, regarding the right to education, holds that:

> Each State Party to the present Covenant which, at the time of becoming a Party, has not been able to secure in its metropolitan territory or other territories under its jurisdiction compulsory primary education, free of charge, undertakes, within two years, to work out and adopt a detailed plan of action for the progressive implementation, within a reasonable number of years, to be fixed in the plan, of the principle of compulsory education free of charge for all.

That requirement was then included in other human rights conventions. The results of the textual analysis of all the nine core human rights treaties in Chapter 3 indicate that under each of these conventions states parties have an immediate obligation to adopt a national action plan for realizing the rights embodied in the convention. Apart from these convention- or rights-specific action plans which are *required* to be adopted, there are some rights-related (subject-specific) action plans which are strongly recommended to be developed and implemented by the states, in particular, National Action Plans on Women, Peace, and Security (NAP-WPS) and National Action Plans on Business and Human Rights (NAP-BHR).

2.3. National Action Plans on Women, Peace, and Security

Development of National Action Plans on Women, Peace, and Security was recommended in eleven of the fifteen Security Council Presidential Statements adopted on Women, Peace, and Security , and in four out of the eight resolutions on Women, Peace, and Security (WPS) released since 2000.[5] National Action Plans on Women, Peace, and Security have come to give effect to the UN Security Council

[5] As of 1 March 2018. For details see United Nations Security Council, S/PRST/2016/9 (15 June 2016); United Nations Security Council, S/PRST/2014/21 (28 October 2014); United Nations Security Council, S/PRST/2012/23 (31 October 2012); United Nations Security Council, S/PRST/2011/20 (28 October 2011); United Nations Security Council, S/PRST/2010/22 (26 October 2010); United Nations Security Council, S/PRST/2007/40 (24 October 2007); United Nations Security Council, S/PRST/2007/5 (7 March 2007); United Nations Security Council, S/PRST/2006/42 (26 October 2006); United Nations Security Council, S/PRST/2005/52 (27 October 2005); United Nations Security Council, S/PRST/2004/40 (28 October 2004); United Nations Security Council, S/PRST/2002/32 (31 October 2002); United Nations Security Council, Resolution 1325 (2000), S/RES/1325 (2000) 31 October 2000; United Nations Security Council, Resolution 1889 (2009) 5 October 2009 S/RES/1889 (2009); United Nations Security Council, Resolution 2122 (2013), S/RES/2122 (2013), 18 October 2013; United Nations Security Council, Resolution 2242 (2015), S/RES/2242 (2015), 13 October 2015.

WPS resolutions in practice and become a proactive tool for implementing the WPS agenda.[6] Denmark advanced the first National Action Plans on Women, Peace, and Security in 2005 and then many countries such as Germany, Ireland, Italy, the Netherlands, Norway, Finland, France, Iraq, Côte d'Ivoire, Philippines, Uganda, and Liberia adopted their plans building on their commitment to implement the UN WPS resolutions.

Despite the complementary nature of the CEDAW and WPS agenda, surprisingly, there has been a gap between the two. Only recently some steps have been taken to start narrowing down the gap, such as through the adoption of CEDAW General Recommendation No 30 or the 2016 'Arria Formula' meeting held by the Security Council on 'Synergies between Security Council Resolutions on Women, Peace and Security and the Convention on the Elimination of All Forms of Discrimination Against Women (CEDAW)'.[7]

Chapter 5 examines some of the problems faced with these plans in practice.

2.4. National Action Plans on Business and Human Rights

With ever-increasing side-effects of multinational corporations like environmental crisis, growing inequality, global poverty, child labour, corruption, and even some forms of modern slavery, it has become more important than ever to address the adverse impacts of business on human rights. In reaction to these side-effects, the UN Human Rights Council unanimously endorsed the Guiding Principles on Business and Human Rights in June 2011. It was the first time that the UN adopted a set of clear standards on the subject of business and human rights and an incredibly positive step forward to mitigate the side effects of business on both those who are directly involved in the business sector such as workers and those who are not involved but are influenced indirectly through for example environmentally degrading activities of the business sector.[8] This guidance is based on three complementary pillars—these are: the state duty to protect against human rights abuses by business; corporate responsibility to respect human rights; and access by victims to effective remedy, both judicial and non-judicial.[9] To put the UN Guiding Principles into

[6] See Aisling Swaine, 'Globalising Women, Peace and Security: Trends in National Action Plans' in S Aroussi (ed), *Rethinking National Action Plans on Women, Peace and Security, NATO Science for Peace and Security Series* (1st edn, IOS Publishing 2017) at 8; Belgin Gumru and Jan Marie Fritz, 'Women, Peace and Security: An Analysis of the National Action Plans Developed in Response to UN Security Council Resolution 1325' (2009) 4(2) Societies Without Borders 209–25. <doi:10.1163/187219109X447485> accessed 20 January 2011.

[7] CEDAW, General Recommendation No 30 on Women in Conflict Prevention, Conflict, and Post-conflict Situations, 1 November 2013, CEDAW/C/GC/30 <http://www.refworld.org/docid/5268d2064.html> accessed 24 January 2017.

[8] See John G Ruggie, Third United Nations Forum on Business and Human Rights Closing Plenary Remarks, Geneva, 3 December 2014; John G Ruggie, *Just Business: Multinational Corporations and Human Rights* (1st edn, W Norton & Company 2013).

[9] United Nations Human Rights Council, Guiding Principles on Business and Human Rights Implementing the United Nations 'Protect, Respect and Remedy' Framework, 2011, <http://www.ohchr.org/Documents/Publications/GuidingPrinciplesBusinessHR_EN.pdf> accessed 2 April 2016.

practice and regulate business sector especially multinational corporations whose economic power can often compete on equal terms (if not higher) with the political power of the states, in 2011 the European Union requested member states to adopt a National Action Plan on Business and Human Rights, and then in 2014 the UN Human Rights Council strongly called on each state to develop such plans. The United Kingdom became the first country to release a National Action Plan on Business and Human Rights in 2013, and following that many countries such as Spain, the Netherlands, Poland, Chile, Colombia, Norway, and Ireland produced their plans.

Parenthetically, in addition to an action planning approach, in 2014 the Human Rights Council adopted a resolution calling for the establishment of an open-ended intergovernmental working group 'to elaborate an international legally binding instrument to regulate, in international human rights law, the activities of transnational corporations and other business enterprises'.[10] It seems that an internationally binding instrument is not to replace other strategies such as implementing the UN Guiding Principles through national action plans or business self-regulation, but to complement them through clarification, elaboration, and enforcement. As Ruggie puts it:

> [G]iven my commitment to 'a smart mix of measures,' I see no intrinsic contradiction between implementing the Guiding Principles, on the one hand, and further international legalization, on the other. Therefore, I urge in the strongest possible terms that as the treaty negotiations unfold, we resist any attempt to polarize the debate as one between the Guiding Principles and a treaty.[11]

Nonetheless, the idea of adopting a legally binding treaty on business and human rights has been challenging and a full discussion of this important idea is well beyond the scope of this book.[12]

The next chapter will be an attempt to unravel different problems facing national action plans of different kinds, including the National Action Plan on Business and Human Rights, in different phases of planning.

[10] United Nations Human Rights Council, 26/9 Elaboration of an international legally binding instrument on transnational corporations and other business enterprises with respect to human rights, Twenty-sixth session, A/HRC/RES/ 26/9, 26 June 2014.

[11] Ruggie, Third United Nations Forum on Business and Human Rights Closing Plenary Remarks, Geneva, note 8.

[12] See, eg, Oliver De Schutter, 'Towards a New Treaty on Business and Human Rights' (2016) 1 Business and Human Rights Journal 41–67; David Bilchitz, 'The Necessity for a Business and Human Rights Treaty' (2016) 1(2) Business and Human Rights Journal 203–27; Jennifer Zerk, 'Corporate liability for gross human rights abuses: Towards a fairer and more effective system of domestic law remedies', A report prepared for the Office of the UN High Commissioner for Human Rights (OHCHR, February 2014); Surya Delva and David Bilchitz, *Building a Treaty on Business and Human Rights* (1st edn, Cambridge University Press 2017); Jolyon Ford, Business and Human Rights: Emerging Challenges to Consensus and Coherence, International Law Programme, February 2015, <https://www.chathamhouse.org/sites/files/chathamhouse/field/field_document/20150226BusinessHumanRightsFord.pdf> accessed September 2016.

3. Integration of Rights-Specific Approach and Global Approach

At this stage, the question to be answered is: what is the most suitable way for the states to comply with their international obligation to adopt a NHRAP? One possible answer to this question is what I would call a convention- or rights-specific approach, that is, the development of nine separate convention-specific action plans as required under each convention as well as National Action Plans on Women, Peace, and Security and National Action Plans on Business and Human Rights separately. Another possible answer is what I would call a global approach, that is, the adoption of a global NHRAP, covering all the human rights conventions or any related topic in particular business-related human rights issues at once.

This question was asked of thirty-seven human rights experts who participated in an online survey conducted by the present author.[13] 62.1% of online survey participants were in favour of the global approach, as recommended at the Vienna conference, and 37.9% were advocates of the convention-specific approach. Each group set out different lines of argumentation. In what follows, I will first review the arguments for each approach and then offer an integrated approach.

3.1. Global approach

The connection between the idea of a global NHRAP, as recommended in the Vienna Declaration and Programme of Action, and the rights-specific plans of action still remains unknown. It is therefore hardly surprising that, on the matters of form and substance, countries stand alone, with each state considering and adopting its own way of developing NHRAPs.[14] Whereas a group of countries, such as Greece, Germany, Ukraine, Singapore, the United Kingdom, and Italy, have developed one or more rights-specific action plans for implementing certain rights such as women's rights and children's rights, another group, such as Sweden, Finland, Republic of Korea, Norway, Nigeria, Spain, Sri Lanka, Indonesia, China, Malawi, and Iraq, have developed one or more global NHRAPs. A number of states likewise have not adopted any plans of this kind yet (see Chapter 5).

Treaty bodies have also taken different positions. For example, the Committee on Economic, Social, and Cultural Rights is primarily in favour of a global NHRAP. In the cases of Kazakhstan, Portugal, Czech Republic, Panama, Belgium, and the United Kingdom and its Crown Dependencies and Overseas Dependent Territories,

[13] The survey was conducted by this author in April–June 2013 as part of another research project on national human rights action plans in Australia. It was based on a purposive sampling technique; participants were mostly selected among those human rights experts who were, directly or indirectly, involved in developing, implementing, monitoring, and/or evaluating such plans. Of the survey respondents, 30.3% were from non-governmental organizations, 15.2% from governmental organizations, 45.5% from academic organizations, 3% from independent consultants, and 6% others.

[14] See Azadeh Chalabi, 'The Problem-Oriented Approach to Improving National Human Rights Action Plans' (2015) 7 The Oxford Journal of Human Rights Practice 272.

for example, the Committee urges the states parties to adopt a comprehensive national plan of action in accordance with Pt II, para 71, of the Vienna Declaration and Programme of Action.[15] In the same way, it notes and regrets the absence of a national plan of action for the protection of human rights in accordance with the Vienna Conference in the cases of the Netherlands and Kuwait.[16]

On the other hand, the Committee on the Rights of the Child, for instance, is mainly in favour of the convention-specific approach.[17] In the case of Sweden, as an example, the Committee requires the state to adopt a specific plan on the rights of children.[18] It holds that:

> While welcoming the adoption of the second National Plan of Action for Human Rights (2006–2009), which includes a number of measures concerning children's rights, the Committee notes with regret the absence of a specific national plan of action on children.[19]

This point has been reaffirmed in the cases of Kazakhstan, New Zealand, Cambodia, Egypt, Japan, and Germany.[20]

As the results of the online survey conducted by the author reveal, the advocates of the global approach put forward four different lines of argumentation:

1. This approach pursues a comprehensive perspective on human rights. According to this approach, domestic lives and society are not divided up according to convention rights. It is sometimes very difficult to answer the question of what type a certain right is. A right at the same time might be a civil and political as well as an economic, social, and cultural right. The right to education is a clear example. This right, recognized in ICESCR as well as in a variety of other international treaties, such as the Convention on the Rights of the Child and the Convention on the Elimination of All Forms of Discrimination against Women, has been variously classified as an economic right, a social right, and a cultural right. It is also, in many ways, a civil right and a political right, since it is central to the full and effective realization of

[15] CESCR, UN Doc E/C.12/KAZ/CO/1 (21 May 2010); CESCR, UN Doc E/2001/22 (7 June 2001), at paras 411 and 469; CESCR, UN Doc E/2003/22, E/C.12/2002/13 (21 July 2008), at paras 93 and 230; CESCR, Report on the forty-second and forty-third sessions, UN Doc E/2010/22, E/C.12/2009/3 (30 April 2010), at para 241; CESCR, UN Doc E/2002/22, E/C.12/2001/17 (6 June 2002) at para 464.

[16] CESCR, UN Doc E/2003/22, E/C.12/2002/13 (21 July 2008) at para 76; CESCR, UN Doc E/2005/22, E/C.12/2004/9 (16 March 2005) at para 183; CESCR, Report on the forty-fourth and forty-fifth sessions (3–21 May 2010, 1–19 November 2010), UN Doc E/2011/22, at para 401; CESCR, Report on the thirty-fourth and thirty-fifth sessions (25 April–13 May 2005, 7–25 November 2005) at para 306; see CESCR, UN Doc E/2002/22, E/C.12/2001/17 (6 June 2002) at para 77.

[17] CRC, Consideration of reports submitted by States parties under Article 12, para 1, of the Optional Protocol to the Convention on the Rights of the Child on the sale of children, child prostitution, and child pornography, Nepal, CRC/C/OPSC/NPL/CO/1, 18 July 2012.

[18] CRC, CRC/C/SWE/CO/4, 26 June 2009, at para 12. [19] ibid.

[20] CRC, CRC/C/KHM/CO/2-3, 3 August 2011, at para 12; CRC, CRC/C/KAZ/CO/3, 8 June 2007, at para 12; see also CRC, CRC/C/NZL/3-4, 19 January 2011, at para 15; CRC, CRC/C/OPSC/EGY/1, 20 June 2011, at para 12; CRC, CRC/C/15/Add.226, 26 February 2004, at para 14. CRC, CRC/C/JPN/CO/3, 20 June 2010, at para 15.

those rights as well.[21] Besides, due to the interdependence between rights of all kinds, to fully implement them requires a global plan of action to set rights in connection to each other. This group of experts believe that one of the values of a NHRAP is that it requires governments to look at the whole corpus of human rights as a comprehensive and indivisible network.

2. This approach is also concerned about the feasibility of adopting nine separate NHRAPs. An argument against the convention-specific approach is that developing even one NHRAP is currently a major undertaking for the states, let alone different convention-specific plans. In the case of Australia, for instance, an online survey participant who was closely involved in the process of developing Australia's NHRAPs stated that: 'For the Australian Government at least, developing even one NHRAP is a major undertaking-especially given the difficulty of involving state governments. There are also relatively few officers in the federal bureaucracy available to work on human rights matters. Multiple NHRAPs would simply be too hard.' According to this approach, the greater the complexity of formulating action plans, the less likely that the government can be held accountable by the general public.
3. Resource optimization is another argument raised by the advocates of the global approach. They argue that multiple NHRAPs would be impossibly complex and very demanding on resources. Different action plans are likely to overlap in terms of target groups, resources, and the types of activities for their implementation. A global NHRAP, by contrast, allows for synergies between resources and obligations relating to different conventions to be highlighted. For example, one action may actually assist individuals/groups to recognize several of their human rights and this can plainly save financial and administrative resources.
4. A global NHRAP addresses large overlaps and avoids the marginalization of either type of rights. The integration of commitments to improve the current situation is important. It is far too confusing to have lots of pieces of plans and far too easy for things to drop through the cracks. If we work in silos, there is too much opportunity for issues to fall between the gaps. This group of experts argue that inviting states to develop more than one NHRAP would encourage the à la carte approach. The 'à la carte approach' to formulating NHRAPs runs a substantial risk that these plans, when implemented independently of one another, may or may not work together as effectively as they would when all the key functions were designed as part of a single plan.

In sum, the advocates of the global approach argue that it might be infeasible to require the states to develop nine different NHRAPs. According to this approach,

[21] CESCR, General Comment No 11, 10 May 1999, E/1992/23, at para 2.

a one-stop-shop for human rights is accessible, and can be readily promoted. Developing multiple action plans is likely to be unwieldy and multiple plans could be at risk of becoming fragmented. Moreover, a global NHRAP allows for resource optimization and can serve the interrelatedness of human rights.

3.2. Rights-specific approach

In contrast with the global approach, the rights-specific (or convention-specific) approach is based on at least four general arguments:

1. The development of nine separate convention-specific action plans helps ensure that nothing falls between the cracks, and vulnerable groups' rights, in particular, are not overlooked. The reason why thematic conventions have been developed is because of the fact that the general conventions, ie ICCPR and ICESCR, have failed to address the specific issues of vulnerable population groups, such as children, women, and persons with disabilities. Thus, to ensure vulnerable population groups' rights are protected, respected, and fulfilled in the state laws, policies, and practices, separate NHRAPs are required. This way of formulating NHRAPs can easily highlight if some human rights conventions or certain human rights issues are stalled. Besides, developing multiple NHRAPs should not be too hard due to the number of core human rights conventions.
2. Due to a hierarchy of priority between various human rights conventions in accordance with each country's circumstances, keeping separate NHRAPs will allow more transparent and effective reporting. Multiple convention-specific action plans would also allow for a greater degree of discussion of the utility and potential application of each convention domestically. Additionally, the process of developing separate NHRAPs in terms of different UN human rights conventions would involve concentration for a period of time on one area of rights, and puts it firmly in the minds of politicians and public servants, at least.
3. It is easier to implement and enforce the more focused and specific action plans than a global NHRAP. Multiple convention-specific action plans would spread accountability and enable progress in specific areas.
4. It is easier to monitor and evaluate separate convention-specific action plans than a global NHRAP. Data can be collected specifically to identify the degree or trajectory of progression of the realization of human rights for those specific population groups.

In short, the advocates of the convention-specific approach argue that each convention is unique and simply requires separate NHRAPs. Keeping separate action plans allows more effective and transparent implementation and helps ensure nothing falls through the cracks. Separate plans are also easier to be monitored and evaluated.

3.3. Towards an integrated approach

Having overviewed the two sets of arguments for a global approach and a convention specific approach in turn, the following will offer an alternative approach:

1. Whereas it might be unrealistic to require the states to develop nine separate convention-specific plans of action, a rights-specific plan is sometimes a plausible solution for the prevalence of human rights abuses in specific areas like women, business and human rights, children, or disabled persons. The results of a research, conducted by the author, on the effectiveness of different NHRAPs in Australia indicate that developing a global plan of action is more feasible than adopting nine separate convention-specific plans of action, but where possible, rights-specific plans are more likely to be effective than a global plan.[22] To strike a balance between feasibility and effectiveness, countries can perhaps develop a global NHRAP covering all human rights issues, and then complete it with one or more rights-specific plans addressing the prevalence of human rights abuses in certain areas. An example which points up this argument is the development of the National Plan to Reduce Violence against Women and their Children 2010–22 (NPRVWC), as a rights-specific plan, side by side with a global NHRAP in Australia. In the experience of Australia, violence against women was one of the most prevalent manifestations of human rights abuses which demanded a long-term focused plan of action. One in three Australian women have experienced physical violence since the age of fifteen, and almost one in five have experienced sexual violence.[23] In response to this problem, the Australian Government released a twelve-year rights-specific action plan, ie NPRVWC. On the other hand, the 2012 global NHRAP linked this rights-specific plan to other relevant policies and programmes in Australia. This co-ordinating role could save resources that may otherwise be spent on inefficient programmes or overlapping activities supported by different plans. Somalia is another example. The highest prevalence rate of Female Genital Mutilation (FGM) is reported in Somalia where 98% of women have undergone the practice.[24] This issue has made the Somali government develop a separate anti-FGM plan (policy) as well as an anti FGM bill and mentioned it in its global action plan (2015–2016).[25]

[22] For details see Azadeh Chalabi, 'Australia's National Human Rights Action Plans: Traditional or Modern Model of Planning?' (2016) 20(7) The International Journal of Human Rights 993–1017.

[23] Australian Bureau of Statistics, Personal Safety Survey Australia, Catalogue No 4906.0 (2006), <http://www.ausstats.abs.gov.au/ausstats/subscriber.nsf/0/056A404DAA576AE6CA2571D000 80E985/$File/49060_2005%20%28reissue%29.pdf> accessed 12 July 2015; see Australian study tour report: Visit of the UN Special Rapporteur on Violence against Women, 2012, at 7 <https://www.humanrights.gov.au/publications/australian-study-tour-report-visit-un-special-rapporteur-violence-against-women> accessed 12 July 2015.

[24] UNICEF report on Female Genital Mutilation <https://www.unicef.org/protection/files/00-FMGC_infographiclow-res.pdf> accessed 20 December 2017.

[25] The Federal Government of Somalia, Ministry of Women and Human Rights Development, Action Plan for the Implementation of the Human Rights Roadmap (HRRM) For Somalia 2015-2016, at 20 <http://www.ohchr.org/Documents/Issues/NHRA/Somalia_en.pdf> accessed 20 December 2017.

2. Since each country starts from different human rights needs and resources, the decision as to whether it should embark on just one global plan, as recommended in the Vienna Declaration and Programme of Action, or whether it should add one or more convention-specific plans, needs to be taken in the light of a realistic appraisal of national human rights problems and resources in the country concerned. Great care is required to ensure that all the human rights issues are taken into account. Human rights planning must begin with a proper understanding of the actual situation in respect of each right embodied in the international human rights conventions. This demands the development of an evidence-based 'baseline study' (also called a 'situation analysis'). As will be discussed in Chapter 7, baseline study is a comprehensive human rights needs assessment which clarifies where a country stands at present and what the main human rights concerns are for now. It seeks to find out detailed conclusions on the state of observance of all areas of human rights by investigation into health care, the education system, and many other areas of service delivery and also into the administration of justice and the relevant areas. It is not merely important for deciding about the number of NHRAPs but also for developing the specific content of each plan.
3. As have been argued by the advocates of both approaches, in the current situation of NHRAPs, things can easily fall between the cracks both in the case of a global plan and rights-specific plans. Whereas multiple convention-specific plans might fail to cover all general human rights issues, keeping a global NHRAP will also allow the specific issues of vulnerable population groups to fall between the gaps. To address this difficulty, perhaps it would be helpful for countries to develop a short plan of NHRAPs as a master plan to locate each of the nine core human rights treaties in separate and/or global NHRAPs and ensure that all the human rights treaties are taken into account and important human rights issues in a given country are not unwillingly overlooked (see Chapter 7). The use of human rights planning theory, both general and special, and the context-specific evidence collected through situation analysis (baseline study) both should be integral to the design of a master plan. Although an evidence-based baseline study is essential to gain in-depth insight into the context-specific conditions of the country concerned, including recurring human rights issues, empirical evidence alone is insufficient to direct practice, and that recourse to the planning theories is crucial to the design of a master plan of plans. Why? Because a general theory of human rights planning, such as the one advanced in Chapters 1 and 2, can serve at least six purposes: (1) to define the scope of interventions and provide guidelines on undertaking systematic review of the issues identified in the baseline study (substantive theory of planning); (2) to shed light on the nature of the problems unearthed in the baseline study (contextual theory of planning and special theory); (3) to give direction to the development of different response strategies required to address the problems identified in the baseline study (substantive, analytical, and contextual theories of human

rights planning); (4) to inform the process of development and implementation of plans of different kinds (procedural theory of human rights planning); (5) to provide inclusion and exclusion criteria (substantive, procedural, and analytical theories of planning); (6) to provide criteria for setting priorities (analytical theory of human rights planning).

In sum, according to this alternative approach, whereas feasibility, interrelatedness, and resource optimization all demand developing a global NHRAP, the prevalence of human rights abuses in certain area(s) calls for one or more rights-specific or convention-specific action plans to involve concentration for a period of time on certain area(s). Hence, in addition to a global national human rights action plan which seems to be necessary for each country, each state may need to advance one or more convention-specific or rights-related action plans as a plausible solution to tackle exclusively the critical human rights issues in the country concerned. These kinds of rights-specific action plans can perfectly complement a global NHRAP and will help strike a balance between feasibility and effectiveness.

Having discussed the first question, let me now return to the second question raised in the introduction: what measures are appropriate and should be adopted in a NHRAP in order to give effect to the rights set forth in the conventions?

4. Appropriate Measures to Implement Human Rights

As discussed in the last chapter, the obligation to take all appropriate measures (OTAAM) inevitably imposes on states an obligation to adopt a national plan of action to realize the rights in question. Since the obligation to adopt a NHRAP is highly dependent on the obligation to take all appropriate measures, to fully understand the nature of the obligation to adopt a NHRAP and states' compliance with it require an examination of OTAAM.

Each of the nine core human rights treaties, that is, ICESCR, ICCPR, ICERD, CAT, CEDAW, CRC, ICRMW, ICPPED, and CRPD, places upon states parties an immediate obligation to take all 'appropriate measures' or 'steps'[26] to implement the rights set forth in the treaties. Overall, as the results of my quantitative content analysis of all the nine core human rights treaties show, the phrase 'take all appropriate measures' has been used 156 times across these nine treaties (Table 4.1). This is apart from some broader obligations, such as the 'obligation to ensure', the 'obligation to provide', the 'obligation to facilitate', and the 'obligation to promote' from which the obligation to take appropriate measures can be derived (see Chapter 3).

Given the degree of prevalence of the usage of OTAAM, it has been widely undernoticed that none of these conventions has established a clear understanding of the intension and extension of the compound concept of appropriate measures. This

[26] In the context of international human rights law, 'measure' and 'step' are used interchangeably and therefore the obligation to take all appropriate measures is the same as the obligation to take all appropriate steps. Hereinafter, I mostly use 'the obligation to take all appropriate measures' (OTAAM).

ambiguity has therefore raised a number of questions. What are the attributes of the OTAAM as a concept? What do 'measure' and 'appropriateness', as two elements of the compound concept of OTAAM, mean? States are obliged to adopt a NHRAP in order to take appropriate measures for realizing human rights as embodied in international human rights documents but the question arises as to who shall determine the 'appropriateness' and 'comprehensiveness' of the measures? To what extent is a state in compliance or in non-compliance with the OTAAM? How to determine and evaluate the degree of appropriateness of each measure taken by the states through their NHRAPs?

To address these questions different methods including a qualitative textual analysis, a quantitative content analysis, and a fuzzy-set method have been utilized. In what follows, I will first explicate the scope and attributes of the concept of 'measure', and then seek to explore 'appropriateness' as a graded concept and show the necessity of the fuzzy-set calibration of the OTAAM.

4.1. Measure: task or objective?

There seems to be an uncertainty about the purpose behind the phrase 'to take (all) appropriate measures' in human rights treaties. As Alston and Quinn explain, during the preparatory work, different phrases were suggested and seemingly the view held by some of the drafters of human rights conventions, in particular the Covenant on Economic, Social, and Cultural Rights was that each Article should specify in detail the particular 'measures' to be undertaken in order to implement the relevant right.[27] On that basis, it would be appropriate for states to undertake the measures thus identified. In practice, however, as the results of this study indicate, the approach adopted in the treaties is extremely uneven.[28] A violation of consistency has created a problem of 'conceptual stretching', that is, the same linguistic label 'appropriate measures' has been used with different connotations across all the nine core human rights treaties. Despite the fact that there is a manifest difference, both conceptually and lexically, between 'objective' and 'task', these two have been often combined and used under the single rubric of 'measure' in various international human rights documents. Table 4.1 illustrates the findings of my quantitative content analysis of all the nine core human rights treaties. As the table shows, only 30% of provisions scrunch 'measure' to cover exclusively concrete 'task'. The term 'measure', in international human rights context, has often (nearly 70% of its usage) been used loosely and broadly covering both 'task' and 'objective' at once.

[27] Philip Alston and Gerard Quinn, 'The Nature and Scope of States Parties' Obligations under the International Covenant on Economic, Social and Cultural Rights' (1987) 9(2) Human Rights Quarterly 156–85, 165.

[28] See, eg, Nadia Bernaz, 'Continuing Evolution of UN Treaty Bodies System' in N Rodley and S Scott (eds), *Routledge Handbook of International Human Rights Law* (1st edn, Routledge 2014); Mashood Baderin and Robert McCorquodale, 'The International Covenant on Economic, Social and Cultural Rights: Forty Years of Development' in M A Baderin and R MacCorquodale (eds), *Economic, Social and Cultural Rights in Action* (1st edn, Oxford University Press 2007).

Take Article 2(1) of the ICESCR as the general legal obligation provision in the ICESCR as an example. The text of this provision states that:

> Each state party to the present Covenant undertakes to take steps, individually and through international assistance and co-operation, especially economic and technical, to the maximum of its available resources, with a view to achieving progressively the full realisation of the rights recognised in the present Covenant by all appropriate means, including particularly the adoption of legislative measures.

This Article is fundamental to the Covenant since it is the general legal obligation provision that can be applied to all of the substantive rights protected in Articles 6 to 15 of the Covenant. The wording of this Article clearly extended the realm of the state discretion. As Matthew Craven argues 'indeed it [Article 2(1) of ICESCR] has been read by some as giving states an almost total freedom of choice and action as to how the rights should be implemented'.[29]

Table 4.1 Frequency distribution of usage of 'OTAAM' and dual meaning of 'measure' in the nine core human rights treaties

Treaties	OTAAM	Measure as task	Measure as objective and task
CEDAW	23	7	16
ICERD	9	1	8
CRC	24	6	18
CAT	8	4	4
CESCR	12	2	10
CRPD	37	18	19
ICCPR	6	0	6
ICRMW	15	1	14
ICPPED	22	8	14
Overall	156	47	109
Percentage	100%	30.12%	69.87%

This reflects a great deal of flexibility in implementing rights, including through the adoption of a NHRAP. On his account, however, to assert that the aims of the Covenant are dynamic in nature is not to suggest that they are deprived of value and should be totally left up to the states to be defined.[30]

Article 2 of ICESCR is only one example. This unfettered model of discretion, as a general pattern, can be traced through other human rights treaties as well. For example, Article 2(2) of the ICCPR expressly states that to give effect to the rights

[29] Matthew Craven, *The International Covenant on Economic, Social, and Cultural Rights: A Perspective on its Development* (1st edn, Oxford University Press 1998) at 5.

[30] ibid, at 129.

recognized in the Covenant, each state party undertakes to take legislative or other measures. Article 2 of the CRC, as another instance, states that 'states parties shall take all appropriate measures to ensure that the child is protected against all forms of discrimination or punishment on the basis of the status, activities, expressed opinions, or beliefs of the child's parents, legal guardians, or family members'. According to Article 4 of the CRC, similarly, states parties shall undertake all appropriate legislative, administrative, and other measures to implement all the rights recognized in the Convention. In a similar vein, Article 25(3) of the ICRMW reads that 'states parties shall take all appropriate measures to ensure that migrant workers are not deprived of any rights derived from this principle by reason of any irregularity in their stay or employment'. Likewise, as stated in Article 4 of the CRPD, all the states which are party to this convention are duty bound to take all appropriate measures to implement the rights recognized in the Convention. Article 24 of the CEDAW similarly declares that 'states parties undertake to adopt all necessary measures at the national level aimed at achieving the full realization of the rights recognized in the present Convention'. What are legislative measures? What does 'other measures' mean? It is largely unclear what all appropriate or necessary measures mean. For example, Article 2(e) of CEDAW states that: '[states parties undertake] to take all appropriate measures to eliminate discrimination against women by any person, organization or enterprise …'

The scope of OTAAM across all the nine core human rights treaties is vast and unbounded. It scarcely identifies clear borders for 'appropriate measures'. This level of flexibility in the wording of human rights provisions has not only introduced ambiguity in the work of human rights committees[31] but also provided an extremely large scope of discretion for the states as to the implementation of human rights and made it much easier for delinquent states to comply with treaties, including with the obligation to adopt a NHRAP, without changing their behaviour. In the extant model of discretion, predictability is diminished and the result would only depend on the humane volition and good faith of states.[32]

To set limits on such unlimited discretionary power of the states requires narrowing the scope of 'measure' down to convey exclusively 'task' while objectives can

[31] Michael O'Flaherty, 'Towards Integration of United Nations Human Rights Treaty Body Recommendations: The Rights-Based Approach Model' in M A Baderin and R MacCorquodale (eds), *Economic, Social and Cultural Rights In Action* (1st edn, Oxford University Press 2007); Michael O'Flaherty, 'Reform of the UN Human Rights Treaty Body System: Locating the Dublin Statement' (2010) 10(2) HRLRev 319–35; Joanne Pedone and Andrew R Kloster, 'New Proposals for Human Rights Treaty Body Reform' (2012) 22 Journal of Transnational Law & Policy 29; Christian Tomuschat, *Human Rights between Idealism and Realism* (1st edn, Oxford University Press 2003); Aslan Abashidze, 'The Process of Strengthening the Human Rights Treaty Body System' (2014) 5 Czech Yearbook of International Law 3–18; Office of the United Nations High Commissioner for Human Rights, Strengthening the United Nations Human Rights Treaty Body System: A report by the United Nations High Commissioner for Human Rights, Navanethem Pillay, 26 June 2012, A/66/860 <http://www2.ohchr.org/english/bodies/HRTD/> accessed 29 October 2016.

[32] See eg Eric Posner, 'A Human Welfare, Not Human Rights' (2008) 108(7) Columbia Law Review 1758–801; Azadeh Chalabi, 'Law as a System of Rights: A Critical Perspective' (2013) 15 HRRev 117–38.

be set out systematically in advance. To clarify this point, let me move on with a three-level ladder of implementation:

(1) Goals
(2) Objectives
(3) Tasks

At the topmost rung, 'goals' outline the fundamental long-term targets. In the context of international human rights law, as discussed in the last chapter, goals are where the obligation of result comes in. In this context, the full realization of or giving effect to the relevant right(s) is the fundamental goal which can be found in all the core human rights treaties, albeit with a different focus of interest. In the case of the CAT, as an example, the main goal is the prevention of all forms of torture.[33] In the case of CEDAW, for example, it means the elimination of discrimination against women in all its forms and manifestations, by any person, organization, or enterprise.[34]

The next rung is concerned with 'objectives' which are more detailed than goals and describe the way by which we can reach the goals. There may be more than one objective to help achieve a goal. For example, to give effect to the rights embodied in the CEDAW, the following objectives, inter alia, must be accomplished:

1. modification or abolition of existing discriminatory regulations and laws (Article 2)
2. modification of the social and cultural patterns of conduct (Article 5(a))
3. suppression of all forms of traffic in women and exploitation of prostitution of women (Article 6)
4. facilitation of the political participation of women (Articles 7 and 8)
5. providing equal access to education (Article 10)
6. elimination of any stereotyped concept of the roles of men and women (Article 10)
7. ensuring the equality of women and men in the field of employment (Article 11), health care (Article 12), and other areas of economic and social life (Article 13), such as for acquiring, changing, or retaining their nationality (Article 9(1))
8. elimination of discrimination against women in rural areas (Article 14) and in all matters relating to marriage and family relations (Article 16(1))
9. providing access to specific educational information helpful to the health and well-being of families (Article 10(h))

Although some objectives are already set out in the conventions, a great many of them are notoriously indeterminate and open-ended and thus are left up to the states. I will return to this point again later in this section.

[33] UN General Assembly, *Convention Against Torture and Other Cruel, Inhuman or Degrading Treatment or Punishment*, 10 December 1984, United Nations, Treaty Series, vol 1465, Article 2(1).
[34] ibid, Article 2(e).

The next subordinate level is related to what is called 'task' which includes concrete actions accompanying with target date, lead body, and performance indicator(s) (see Chapter 7). This rung of the ladder is time-specific and action-oriented involving a list of concrete actions to reach objectives in accordance with each country's circumstances. Tasks aim to address specifically 'how', 'when', and 'by whom' objectives can be achieved. In other words, each objective will have a sequence of tasks, and each task will tell us how the objective will be accomplished and by when. It will also indicate who will be involved. Tasks are very specific, and will help the states to assign responsibilities for implementing objectives. For example, to modify or abolish existing discriminatory regulations and laws as an objective, a series of tasks with a timeline has been set out by the Australian government in its National Human Rights Action Plan (2012), such as: (1) the Australian Government will develop legislation to consolidate Commonwealth anti-discrimination laws to remove unnecessary regulatory overlap, address inconsistencies across laws, and make the system more user-friendly; (2) the South Australian Equal Opportunities Commission should accept and conciliate complaints made by disadvantaged and vulnerable groups who experience discrimination in areas of public life; (3) the Tasmanian Government should bring amendments before Parliament in 2012 following a review of its Anti-Discrimination Act 1998 (Tas); (4) The Department of Justice should monitor the effectiveness of the new Equal Opportunity Act 2010 (Vic), which commenced operation on 1 August 2011.[35] All these actions should include an exact time-frame.

If states had unlimited latitude as to defining the appropriateness of objectives as well as concrete tasks, there would be little basis upon which to judge whether or not they were acting in good faith. Unlike the current usage which has often included both tasks and objectives in the single label of 'measures', and thus left a wide latitude to the discretion of states, it would be better to use 'measures' in a narrow sense to convey exclusively 'tasks'. This usage would set some limits on such unlimited discretionary power of the states and instead would allow some room for international human rights bodies to set out 'objectives' in advance. In other words, while the responsibility for the identification of general context-independent objectives[36] can primarily rest with the relevant international supervisory organ, this is a matter for each state to specify 'tasks', that is, 'how' (setting concrete actions and resources), 'when', and 'by whom' objectives can be accomplished domestically. This can establish an internationally agreed framework within which the specifics could be subsequently developed by each country. At this juncture, the question arises how to set general objectives at the international level? Where do objectives come from?

Treaty provisions are the first source to set out objectives which do not pertain exclusively to a particular country but rather address issues of general relevance to all or many countries.

[35] Australia's National Human Rights Action Plan (2012) <http://www.ohchr.org/Documents/Issues/NHRA/NHRPAustralia2012.pdf> accessed 25 September 2013.

[36] As will be discussed in Chapter 7, there should be always a space for those who are involved in developing NHRAP at the national level to add further context-dependent objectives which are appropriate for implementing human rights within the given context of a particular country.

For example, to give effect to the CRC, the following objectives, inter alia, must be achieved:

1. combating the illicit transfer and non-return of children abroad (Article 11(1))
2. providing health care (Article 24(2)b and 24(2)c), education (Article 28(a)) and social security for all children (Article 26)
3. abolishing traditional practices prejudicial to the health of children (Article 24(3))
4. securing the recovery of maintenance for the child from the parents or other persons having financial responsibility for the child (Article 27(4))
5. providing appropriate regulation of the age, hours, and conditions of employment (Article 32(2))

Nonetheless, the adoption of objectives should be an ongoing job rather than a single event; a systemic endeavour to respond to changing circumstances. For being adequate to respond to the contingency of the empirical world, treaties' provisions often tend to be broad and flexible. Despite the fact that such loosely worded provisions can increase the possibility of dynamic interpretations of rights, it seems that the onus should primarily rest on the relevant international supervisory organs to flesh out, in a co-operative way through a global human rights network (see Chapter 6), the levels of obligation involved rather than international human rights law in its treaty text. In particular, the UN human rights bodies have the potential to map out a coherent set of context-free objectives for the states as regards the framing of measures appropriate for implementing human rights. As Wakefield mentions, a unique and very important feature of the UN treaty bodies is that they have the capacity to contribute to the progressive development of international human rights law through authoritative interpretations of treaty provisions and recommendations to the states and other stakeholders on human rights issues.[37]

Objective setting can be done by treaty bodies through, for example, the development of an international human rights action plan (see Chapter 6). Building upon the existing mechanisms, however, the adoption of General Comments seems to be a suitable tool available to each of the UN human rights bodies to systematically identify objectives appropriate to give effect to the rights embodied in the conventions.[38] General Comments are useful jurisprudential tools which can potentially address matters of relevance to all or many states parties to a particular treaty. As Philip Alston notes, the potential significance of these tools derived from the fact that a great many international human rights norms are notoriously, but

[37] Megan Wakefield, 'The International Human Rights Treaty System: Impact at the Domestic and International Levels' (2014) 21:1 Human Rights Brief 32–36.

[38] Although under current settings, General Comments are perhaps a suitable tool for objective setting, this task should extend beyond a particular UN committiee to include inputs from other relevant human rights bodies, including but not limited to civil society, human rights institutions, human rights academics and practitioners, UPR working group, and other human rights bodies, inter-governmental and non-governmental (local, national, and international), that have relevant experience and knowledge which can inform the process of objective setting.

unavoidably, open-ended.[39] General Comments can provide a sort of guidance for the states in better understanding, implementing, and monitoring the implementation of human rights conventions.[40] Although General Comments are soft law instruments, they are authoritative sources and have a persuasive effect setting interpretive positions around which state and non-state practices can unite. General Comments can potentially provide detailed content in a systematic, comprehensive, and coherent way to the rather vague and generally worded provisions of treaties.[41] While traditional accounts of international law-making assume a monolithic state voice that tend to often silence other voices if they are not in line with their interests, General Comments, by elaborating progressive and professional interpretations, can potentially 'operate as a counter-hegemonic balance to these deleterious influences of state sovereignty and international human rights realpolitik'.[42]

At present, however, the approach adopted by different treaty bodies is widely uneven.[43] Objective setting is not particularly new to the work of UN treaty bodies, though in a fragmented, inconsistent, and unsystematic way.[44] Among other factors, this problem can be attributed to the lack of a firm theoretical framework underlying human rights treaties around which the work of human rights bodies can unite. In particular, the UN human rights bodies lack any analytical theory of human rights, such as that developed in Chapter 2, which can not only be used as a heuristic device in diagnosing human rights shortcomings but also provide criteria for objective setting and prioritization. This deficit has reduced the degree of comprehensiveness, clarity, and depth of treaties themselves and their complementary documents such as General Comments and Concluding Observations. For example,

[39] Philip Alston, 'The Historical Origins of the Concept of "General Comments"' in L Boisson de Chazournes and V Gowland Debbas (eds), *Human Rights Law* (1st edn, Brill 2001).

[40] Ziba Vaghri, Adem Arkadas, Sami Kruse, and Clyde Hertzman, 'CRC General Comment 7 Indicators Framework: A Tool for Monitoring the Implementation of Child Rights in Early Childhood' (2011) 10(2) Journal of Human Rights 178.

[41] Kerstin Mechlem, 'Treaty Bodies and the Interpretation of Human Rights' (2009) 42 Vanderbilt Journal of Transnational Law 905.

[42] Conway Blake, Normative Instruments in International Human Rights Law: Locating the General Comment, Center for Human Rights and Global Justice Working Paper Number 17, 2008 at 13 <http://chrgj.org/wp-content/uploads/2012/07/blake.pdf> accessed 12 January 2017; see also, Hilary Charlesworth and Christine Chinkin, *The Boundaries of International Law: A Feminist Analysis* (1st edn, Manchester University Press 2000).

[43] Suzanne Egan, 'Strengthening the United Nations Human Rights Treaty Body System' (2013) 13(2) HRL Rev 209–43; Eric Tistounet, 'The Problem of Overlapping Among Different Treaty Bodies,' in P Alston and J Crawford (eds), *The Future of UN Human Rights Treaty Monitoring* (1st edn, Cambridge University Press 2000); Philip Alston, *The United Nations and Human Rights: A Critical Appraisal* (1st edn, Clarendon Press 1992); John Morijn, 'Reforming United Nations Human Rights Treaty Monitoring Reform' (2011) 58:3 Neth Int'l L Rev 295; Abashidze, 'The Process of Strengthening the Human Rights Treaty Body System', note 31; Pedone and Kloster, 'New Proposals for Human Rights Treaty Body Reform', note 31; O'Flaherty, 'Towards Integration of United Nations Human Rights Treaty Body Recommendations: The Rights-Based Approach Model', note 31.

[44] As Steiner argues, 'the accumulated General Comments range from spelling out the internal procedures of the committees or requiring states to include certain information in their periodic reports, to making general interpretations of the substantive provisions of the Covenants' (Henry J. Steiner, 'Individual Claims in a World of Massive Violations: What Role for the Human Rights Committee' in P Alston and J Crawford (eds), *The Future of UN Human Rights Treaty Monitoring* (1st edn, Cambridge University Press 2000) at 22);

it is still largely unclear what is the relationship between basic rights, basic needs (primary and secondary), human capabilities, and human interests. There is no theoretical frame of reference against which the content of basic rights can be comprehensively formed and general objectives can be set out systematically. This failure has led to not only vagueness and ambiguity of the content of rights but also lack of comprehensiveness in the identification of rights. Think of for instance the omission of a very basic right to clean and accessible water or the right to safe and hygienic sanitation in the ICESCR. The analytical theory of human rights suggested in Chapter 2 can be employed for the modification of treaties and served as a frame of reference for the work of human rights bodies.

Moreover, the lack of systematic adoption of and coherent form and substance of General Comments of different treaties at least partly stem from the fact that the international human rights system, in particular the UN human rights system, is operating under a fragmented governance structure. As Michael O'Flaherty argues, on matter of form and substance, each treaty body considers and adopts its own recommendations without reference to the other committees or other relevant human rights bodies.[45] States sometimes must address multiple sets of recommendations, concerning the same or closely related issues.[46] They sometimes have to contend with 'clashes of approach by distinct treaty bodies, including cases of inconsistent or contradictory recommendations'.[47] This problem will be examined in further detail in Chapter 6.

Although narrowing the scope of 'measure' down to only include 'tasks' can advance the degree of conceptual adequacy of the obligation to take all appropriate measures (OTAAM), it is still unclear how to determine the degree of appropriateness of one measure relative to other. The following is an attempt to address this question.

4.2. Degree of appropriateness

In terms of appropriateness, the question to be answered is how qualitatively different are measures taken by the states in their NHRAPs? This ambiguity stems from the fact that the obligation to take all appropriate measures has not been adequately calibrated. By calibration, I mean marking the intervals of scale instrument. Before I suggest a method for calibration of the obligation to take all appropriate measures, I need to examine different approaches through which the attributes of OTAAM can be defined. In the literature, more or less, two approaches have been adopted: minimal and maximal.

see also, Philip Alston, 'Out of the Abyss: The Challenges Confronting the New UN Committee on Economic, Social and Cultural Rights' (1987) 9 Human Rights Quarterly 332–81.

[45] Michael O'Flaherty 'Towards Integration of United Nations Human Rights Treaty Body Recommendations: The Rights-Based Approach Model', note 31 at 30; Michael O'Flaherty, 'The Concluding Observations of United Nations Human Rights Treaty Bodies' (2006) 6(1) Human Rights Law Review 27–52.

[46] Tomuschat, *Human Rights between Idealism and Realism*, note 31.

[47] O'Flaherty, 'Towards Integration of United Nations Human Rights Treaty Body Recommendations: The Rights-Based Approach Model', note 31.

A minimalist approach seeks to establish a minimal threshold as the bare essentials of the obligation to take all appropriate measures. For example, one might argue that Article 24(2) of CRC constitutes attributes of the obligation to take all appropriate measures in the case of the right of the child to the enjoyment of the highest attainable standard of health where it requires states to take measures to:

1. diminish infant and child mortality
2. provide necessary medical assistance and health care to all children with emphasis on the development of primary health care
3. combat disease and malnutrition
4. provide pre-natal and post-natal health care for mothers
5. promote basic knowledge of child health and nutrition

Although the above list might arguably provide the minimum core content and thus offers a very primitive ordinal scale[48]—'core content' and 'non-core content'—for the measurement of the appropriateness of measures taken by the states, it has at least two caveats. The first one is that we are defining the obligation to take all appropriate measures in a very minimalist fashion, leaving other possible attributes often associated with the concept in abeyance. This can provide a legitimate basis for the states to make do with a minimalist approach to their obligations. Using a minimalist approach can indeed limit the full guarantee of a right by setting a low standard for the states to meet and thus impose significant costs in practice.[49] The second caveat is that the concept of 'minimum core content' used in human rights discourse is often very vague, broad, and loosely defined.[50] Measures with different levels of importance are categorized broadly in the same category of 'the minimum core'.

A maximal approach, by contrast, seeks to include all possible measures that might be defined as 'appropriate' in its fullest form in the list of the obligation's attributes. This approach, which is the predominant one, has at least three caveats. First, perhaps listing all possible measures is not feasible and that is why it has often left it totally up to the states to define both objectives and tasks. Second,

[48] There are different scales of measurement: nominal, ordinal, interval, and ratio. A nominal scale refers to mere classification with respect to a certain characteristic, such as classification of crimes into two categories of 'property crimes' and 'personal crimes'. When measuring using an ordinal scale, one simply orders among all categories with respect to the degree with which they possess a certain characteristic, such as the seriousness of crimes based on their penalties, for instance, infractions, misdemeanours, and felonies. Interval scales are numerical scales in which intervals have the same distances, for example, the penalty for a crime is between two to fifteen years. The ratio scale of measurement includes a true zero such as the rate of crime. The difference between interval and ratio is that the interval scale employs an arbitrary zero point, whereas the ratio scale employs a true zero point. In a fuzzy-based approach, even for ordinal scale we can have a meaningful zero.

[49] Azadeh Chalabi, 'Law as a System of Rights: A Critical Perspective', note 32.

[50] Katharine G Young, 'The Minimum Core of Economic and Social Rights: A Concept in Search of Content' (2008) 33 Yale International Law Journal 113–75; Audrey R Chapman and Sage Russell, *Core Obligations: Building a Framework for Economic, Social and Cultural Rights* (1st edn, Intersentia 2002); Maritza Prada Formisano, *Empowering the Poor: Through Human Rights Litigation* (1st edn, UNESCO 2012).

listing all attributes in the same order of importance gives us no clear scale against which the appropriateness of measures taken by the states can be assessed. There is no sense in which measure A is more appropriate than measures B and C. The third caveat to this approach is that it is based on crisp logic (binary logic). As the results of my textual analysis indicate the conceptualization of OTAAM is based on a two-valued logic (0 or 1). States are either in compliance with the obligation (if they take 'all' appropriate measures) or in non-compliance (if they do not take 'all' appropriate measures). Likewise, measures are either appropriate or non-appropriate. Unlike this way of conceptualization which is based on the law of excluded middle, in reality, however, a measure might be to some extent appropriate for the realization of a given right. Likewise, a state might be to some degree in compliance with OTAAM and to some degree in non-compliance, that is to say, this is all a matter of degree.

An alternative approach is to rank the attributes of the obligation to take appropriate measures in a more cumulative fashion, that is, as more or less essential to the concept of OTAAM for the implementation of a given right. As Figure 4.1 indicates, one can envision a cumulative scale indicator of appropriate measures for implementing, say for instance, the right of the child to the enjoyment of the highest attainable standard of health that begins with a list of objectives (A and B) such as those embodied in Article 24(2) of CRC—as the minimum core content—and proceeds through additional sets of objectives of C, D, E, and F to advance the degree of compliance with the obligation to take appropriate measures, that is, objective setting in order of centrality. A and B, as the minimum core content of a given right, are those objectives that must be met in any situation. These are the bare essentials (necessary conditions) of appropriate measures. There are also additional attributes such as C and D (as the second order of appropriateness) and E and F (as the third order of appropriateness) which increase the level of state compliance with the obligation to take appropriate measures.

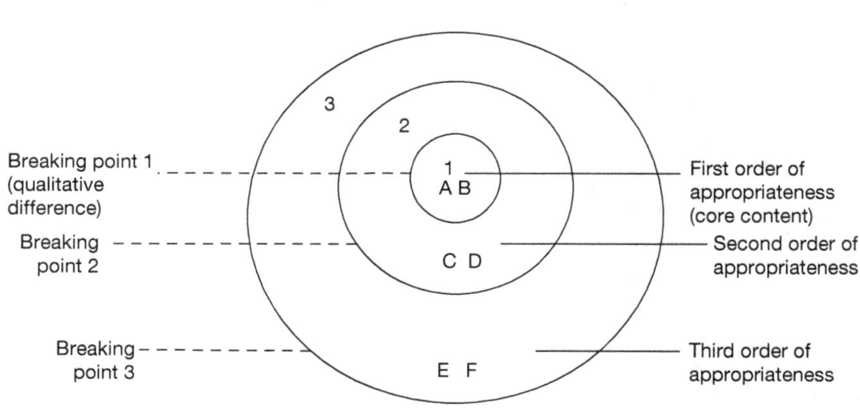

Figure 4.1 Concentric circles diagram of OTAAM

For example, the ESCR Committee in its General Comment No 14 has listed the minimum core content (as the necessary conditions) of the right to essential primary health care.[51] These include:

1. access to health facilities, goods and services on a non-discriminatory basis, especially for vulnerable or marginalized groups
2. access to the minimum essential food which is nutritionally adequate and safe
3. providing essential drugs, as from time to time defined under the WHO Action Programme on Essential Drugs
4. equitable distribution of all health facilities, goods, and services

Then, the committee in the same General Comment provides another list of attributes which are not considered as 'core content' but supplementary conditions of the right, such as (1) immunization against the major infectious diseases; (2) prevent, treat, and control epidemic and endemic diseases; (3) access to information concerning the main health problems; (4) appropriate training for health personnel.[52] Arguably, this presents the second most important set of attributes. We can add more sets as 'additional attributes' such as preventing obesity.

If it is agreed that for the implementation of the right to essential primary health care the first set of objectives is more essential than the second, and the second is more essential than the third, then it may be possible to arrive at a graded concept of appropriate measures that incorporates many of the attributes commonly associated with the term, while also recognizing the relative importance of each of these attributes.

Nevertheless, this is certainly not an easy task to unambiguously and sharply define and order the attributes of OTAAM for a given right. To address the questions as to what the minimum core content is and where the boundary between the sets of essential and additional attributes lies requires using theory-driven criteria. As remarked before, however, the UN human rights instruments are not based on a firm analytical theory of rights from which a comprehensive and coherent set of criteria can be derived. The analytical theory of human rights, developed in Chapter 2, can be employed as a heuristic device for the identification and prioritization of the attributes of the obligation to take all appropriate measures for realizing basic human rights. In this case, the core content may include those measures required for meeting the most basic human needs (primary needs) upon which the right in question is based, and following that the set of measures which are necessary for meeting secondary needs, and then the measures appropriate for the enhancement of capabilities and fulfilment of interests (in so far as resources permit) etc.

Based on a set of theory-driven criteria, the attributes of OTAAM and their centrality to the concept (relative importance of each of the attributes) for each basic

[51] UN Committee on Economic, Social, and Cultural Rights (CESCR), General Comment No 14: The Right to the Highest Attainable Standard of Health (Art 12 of the Covenant), 11 August 2000, E/C.12/2000/4, at para 43.

[52] ibid, at para 44.

right need to be set out separately. Depending on the right in question, this task may demand co-operation among experts of different disciplines such as law, sociology, economics, political science, anthropology, psychology, ecology, and possibly human biology. Different methods can be employed for ordering the attributes of this obligation.[53] Although addressing the question as to what method(s) can be employed here stands well beyond the scope of this chapter, I would tentatively suggest the 'Delphi method' as a method well suited for consensus-building. Parenthetically, the Delphi method has been accepted as a method for gathering data from experts within their field of expertise. It has been widely used in various areas such as needs assessment, planning, policy formation, and resource allocation to explore a wide range of alternatives.[54] The method encompasses an expert group communication process which seeks to achieve a convergence of opinion on a specific matter or issue, in our case, the obligation's attributes and their centrality to the concept.[55] The goal is to integrate and reduce the range of responses of a group of experts coming up with something as expert consensus.[56]

A graded concept of OTAAM is not any more on the basis of binary logic (the traditional two-valued logic) but rather on fuzzy logic. Fuzzy logic, as a multiple-valued logic, offers a more realistic framework for human reasoning than binary logic which is based on the law of excluded middle.[57] Classical logic sees the attributes as binary and cannot solve the 'problem of approximation'.[58] As Zadeh argues in fuzzy logic, in contrast with crispy logic, everything, including truth, is a matter of degree.[59] Fuzzy logic is flexible and adaptable to the empirical cases and its application in concept formation is a way to address the above mentioned problems.[60] Whereas in the maximal approach, states are either in compliance or non-compliance with the obligation to take all appropriate measures, in the alternative approach, depending on the degree of the appropriateness of the measures taken by the states through their NHRAPs, each state can stand at different levels of compliance. For illustration purposes, let me return to Figure 4.1 and this time, for the sake of parsimony, only focus on the first and second order of attributes, ie A, B, C, and D. A and B as the minimum core content are the necessary conditions of OTAAM and thus have to be present in every set of state compliance. Otherwise, the negation of (A^B) is non-compliance. If this ordering of attributes is accepted—if,

[53] See eg John Gerring, *Social Science Methodology: A Unified Framework* (2nd edn, Cambridge University Press 2012).

[54] Ravonne A Green, 'The Delphi Technique in Educational Research' (2014) SAGE Open, April–June 1–8 <DOI: 10.1177/2158244014529773> accessed 24 March 2017.

[55] Chia-Chien Hsu and Brian A Sandford, 'The Delphi Technique: Making Sense of Consensus' (2007) 12(10) Practical Assessment, Research and Evaluation; Shawn J Adams, 'Projecting the next decade in safety management: A Delphi technique study' (2001) 46(10) Professional Safety 26–29.

[56] ibid.

[57] Lotfi A Zadeh, 'The Concept of A Linguistic Variable and Its Application to Approximate Reasoning' (1975) 8(3) J Inf Sci 67, 199–249.

[58] Hans-Jürgen Zimmermann, *Fuzzy Set Theory and Its Applications* (4th edn, Springer 2001); Charles Ragin, *Fuzzy-Set Social Science* (1st edn, University of Chicago Press 2000).

[59] Lotfi A Zadeh, 'Fuzzy Logic' (1988) 21(4) Computer Volume at 84.

[60] Mario Quaranta, Concept Structures and Fuzzy Set Theory: A Proposal for Concept Formation and Operationalization, COMPASSS Working Paper 2010-62 <http://www.compasss.org/wpseries/Quaranta2010.pdf> accessed 18 September 2016.

that is, it is agreed through objective setting that A and B are necessary conditions of OTAAM and C and D are in the second order of appropriateness, then at least four levels of state compliance with this obligation can be distinguished here:

Non-compliance = (avb) v (CvD) [61]
Minimal compliance = (A^B) ^ (dvc)
Substantial compliance= (A^B) ^ (CvD)
Full compliance= A ^ B ^ C ^ D

If the measures adopted in a NHRAP do not include A and B at all (as the necessary condition of obligation to take appropriate measures) even if they include C and/or D, the state would be in non-compliance with the obligation to take appropriate measures. If the measures taken by the state include exclusively A and B, then the state would be in minimal compliance with OTAAM. If the measures taken by the state through developing a NHRAP include A and B as the necessary condition of OTAAM and also C or D, then the state would be substantially in compliance with OTAAM. If the measures adopted in a NHRAP include A and B as the necessary condition of OTAAM and also C and D both, then the state would be fully in compliance with OTAAM. Let me stress that these four sets (types) of compliance with the obligation to take appropriate measures are defined just for the sake of illustration (and not suggestion).

Having suggested a graded concept of the obligation to take all appropriate measures, still two sets of questions remain unanswered. The first one pertains to the 'qualitative difference' between circles (Figure 4.1). The difference between circle 1 (the first order attributes) and circle 2 (the second order attributes) is not equivalent to the difference between circle 2 and circle 3. The difference between the levels of state compliance cannot be explained by merely a graded concept of this obligation. The qualitative difference between for example 'non-compliance' and 'minimal-compliance' cannot be assumed to be the same as the difference between two other levels.

Put differently, each circle in Figure 4.1 represents a different level of state compliance with the obligation to take appropriate measures which is qualitatively different from other circles. For example, the first circle (core content) may include those measures which are appropriate for the fulfilment of the most basic human needs with respect to the right in question. At this level, every effort must be made to use all resources ('maximum available resources'), as a matter of priority, to satisfy the minimum core obligation.[62] Taking two measures addressing the most basic need for physical survival such as providing accessibility to the minimum essential food (primary needs) is qualitatively different (and comes first in terms of importance) from taking even ten measures to control obesity among children (secondary needs and interests). Even if providing essential drugs is very important for the realization of the right to essential healthcare but in terms of level of appropriateness, it comes

[61] ^ = logical 'And'
v = logical 'OR'
*Capital letters to indicate 'presence' and lower case to indicate 'absence'.

[62] An important factor which should be taken into account when defining different levels of compliance with OTAAM is concerned with availability and allocation of resources—whether states have enough resources and if so, how they have allocated them for each circle. This stands well beyond the scope of this chapter though. For further details, see Chapters 1 and 2.

after providing essential food. As Charles Bukowski in one of his famous quotes nicely puts it, 'we decided to take some medicine to Africa but all the prescriptions said: take after meal'.

The second set of questions is concerned with the quantitative difference between real cases at the same level of compliance, that is, the difference of degree (in contrast with the difference of kind) within each circle itself. Looking at real cases as in-or-out instances (compliance/non-compliance) may lead us to overlook the differences that are present among states in practice. A set of measures taken by state X and state Y through their NHRAPs may have the same features A, B, C, but to a different degree. Would you say that measures taken by state X and state Y through their NHRAPs are instances of the same level of compliance? Yes, they are instances of the same level, but to a different degree. State X and Y both may take measures to provide training for health personnel but one only for 30% of personnel and one for more than 80%.

To address these questions there is a need for a fuzzy-set calibration of OTAAM. Whereas conventional measurement (uncalibrated measures) simply shows the positions of cases relative to each other, calibrated measure (fuzzy-set calibration) can indicate both qualitative and quantitative differences.[63]

In a fuzzy-set method, concepts are conceived as sets, defined in terms of boundaries that clarify zones of inclusion and exclusion, then '[c]ases are measured according to their fit within the boundaries of a set'.[64] The values of a membership function, called membership degrees, specify the degree to which case X belongs to a fuzzy set.[65] As Ragin states 'fuzzy sets are especially powerful because they allow us to calibrate partial membership in sets using values in the interval between 0.0 (non-membership) and 1.0 (full membership)'.[66] For example, the three sets of 'compliant states', 'partially compliant states', and 'non-compliant states' are qualitatively different. This should not be regarded as a continuum with one pole full compliance and the other non-compliance. The membership function of state X for the set of 'compliant states' might be 0.20 (more out than in) and for the set of 'partially compliant states' might be 0.65 (more in than out).

From a fuzzy set approach, OTAAM is a linguistic variable whose values are words or sentences in a natural or artificial language, that is, they are linguistic rather than numerical. A linguistic variable is characterized by at least four parameters (*X, T, U, M*) in the literature, where *X* is the name of the variable, *T* is the set of terms of *X*, *U* is the range of all possible values applicable to a chosen variable, and *M* is a semantic rule for associating each term with its meaning, ie a fuzzy set defined on *U*.[67]

[63] Charles Ragin, *Redesigning Social Inquiry: Fuzzy Sets and Beyond* (1st edn, University of Chicago Press 2008).

[64] James Mahoney, 'What is a concept? Two definitions and their research implications' (2010) Mimeo, North Western University, Evanston, IL, 7.

[65] See, eg, Carsten Q Schneider and Claudius Wagemann, *Set-Theoretic Methods for the Social Sciences: A Guide to Qualitative Comparative Analysis* (1st edn, Cambridge University Press 2012).

[66] Ragin, *Redesigning Social Inquiry: Fuzzy Sets and Beyond*, note 63, at 29.

[67] Zadeh, 'The Concept of a Linguistic Variable and its Application to Approximate Reasoning', note 57; Badredine Arfi, 'Fuzzy Decision Making in Politics: A Linguistic Fuzzy-Set Approach (LFSA)' (2005) 13 Political Analysis 23–56; Nurnadiah Zamria and Lazim Abdullah, 'A New linguistic Variable in Interval Type-2 Fuzzy Entropy Weight of a Decision Making Method' (2013) 24 Procedia Computer

In our case, *X* is the obligation to take all appropriate measures, *T* is the term-set of X namely the collection of its linguistic values such as {compliance, non-compliance}. M is a semantic rule which associates with each linguistic value X its meaning, that is, it specifies for each term a corresponding fuzzy set on the universe *U* which can be, for example, between 0 and 100. M and U need to be generated purposefully using theoretical and substantive knowledge.[68] This theoretically and empirically founded external knowledge should determine the qualitative breakpoints or thresholds, based on which we can determine the degree of membership of each set—at least three qualitative breakpoints are needed here: threshold for full membership, threshold for full non-membership, and cross-over point. This three-value set is a very basic fuzzy set. A more fine-grained fuzzy set uses four, six, or even nine values.[69] For example, the four-value scheme, that is, 0.1, 0.67, 0.33, and 0.0 (indicating 'fully in', 'more in than out', 'more out than in', and 'fully out' respectively), is especially useful in situations where researchers have a substantial amount of information about cases, but the evidence is not systematic or strictly comparable from case to case.[70]

The types of expertise required for the specification of qualitative breakpoints (where the qualitative change is made) might be different for each right. For instance, when it comes to the specification of breakpoints for the right to health, we may need to refer to not only human rights scholars and practitioners but also medical specialists, psychologists, and biologists.

There are different methodological strategies, numerical and linguistic, for finding a qualitatively satisfying boundary between words such as compliance and non-compliance or minimal compliance and non-compliance.[71] The most common strategies for assigning membership used by researchers employing fuzzy sets include (but not limited to) direct assignment, indirect assignment, assignment by transformation.[72] Bear in mind that the assignment methods are not mutually exclusive, but rather the aspects of each method can be a part of the other.[73] In direct assignment, a group of experts provides a membership value, numeric, or linguistic, based on their expert knowledge.[74] Indirect assignment also uses a group of experts as judges to generate membership but as its name implies in an indirect way.[75] Indirect assignment draws out responses from experts and then 'applies a model to the judgments to generate membership values'.[76] As Verkuilen argues, 'the basic

Science 42–53; Michael Smithson and Jay Verkuilen, *Fuzzy Set Theory: Application in Social Sciences* (1st edn, Sage Publications 2006).

[68] Ragin, *Redesigning Social Inquiry: Fuzzy Sets and Beyond*, note 63. [69] ibid.

[70] ibid, at 31.

[71] See eg Achille Lemmi and Gianni Betti, *Fuzzy Set Approach to Multidimensional Poverty Measurement* (1st edn, Springer 2006); Zimmermann, *Fuzzy Set Theory and Its Applications*, note 58.

[72] Jay Verkuilen, 'Assigning Membership in a Fuzzy Set Analysis' (2005) 33(4) Sociol Methods Res 462–96.

[73] ibid.

[74] Alrik Thiem and Adrian Dusa, *Qualitative Comparative Analysis with R* (1st edn, Springer 2013).

[75] Qing Li, 'Indirect Membership Function Assignment Based on Ordinal Regression' (2016) 43(3) J Appl Stat 441–60.

[76] Verkuilen, 'Assigning Membership in a Fuzzy Set Analysis', note 72, at 474.

idea in transformation is to take a numerical variable, usually one or more previously existing variables, and then map it into membership values with a theoretically motivated transformation'.[77] The answer to the question as to what strategy would be the most suitable one for calibrating the obligation to take all appropriate measures in practice stands well beyond the scope of this chapter and demands a separate research project involving the collaboration of human rights academics, practitioners, and methodologists.

In a nutshell, the results of the content analysis of all the nine core human rights treaties indicate that the term 'appropriate measures' has been used 156 times across all these treaties and that OTAAM is the most prevalent obligation under all the nine core human rights treaties. However, the way it has been used in international human rights treaties lacks the clarity and constancy required. In almost 70% of its usage, 'measure' as one of the key elements of this compound concept has been used loosely and broadly covering both 'concrete task' and 'objective'. Only 30% of provisions scrunch 'measure' to cover exclusively 'concrete task'. This level of flexibility and inconsistency has left a wide latitude to the discretion of states as to implementing human rights and made it much easier for delinquent states to comply with treaties without meaningfully changing their behaviour. Although the appropriateness of measures is sometimes context-dependent and reflects the necessity of flexibility in implementing human rights, these measures should be predictable in the sense that they must be geared towards the principal obligation of result, that is, the realization of human rights as enshrined in international human rights instruments and not a mere facade. If states had an unfettered level of discretion as to defining the appropriateness of both tasks and objectives, it would be hardly surprising if they made do with rights on the cheap. The confusion does not end here. With no clear set of attributes, there is also a great deal of ambiguity about the referents of the obligation to take all appropriate measures and the way we can assess the degree of states compliance in practice. This ambiguity can be easily traced to the states' reports to human rights committees, states' NHRAPs, and even through the work of UN treaty bodies themselves. To address these ambiguities, the following strategic implications are suggested.

First, to set limits on such unlimited discretionary power of the states, which has diminished predictability, requires narrowing the scope of 'measure' down to convey exclusively 'concrete task' while context-independent objectives can be set out systematically in advance.

Second, to reconcile the 'maximal' and 'minimal' approaches currently adopted, an alternative approach, suggested here, is to rank the attributes of appropriate measures cumulatively, that is, as more or less 'appropriate' for the implementation of a given right. This approach employs OTAAM as a graded concept in order to determine the degree of appropriateness of one measure relative to other. Whereas in the maximal approach, states are either in compliance or non-compliance with obligation to take all appropriate measures, in the alternative approach, depending

[77] ibid, at 479.

on the degree of the appropriateness of the measures taken by the states, each state can stand at different levels of compliance. A graded concept of OTAAM for each right can be used as a frame of reference against which to not only develop different human rights policies and action plans for the fulfilment of different levels of compliance but also monitor and evaluate the appropriateness of different measures (relative to each other) already taken by the states through their NHRAP or other policies and programming.

Finally, to determine the qualitative differences between different levels of state compliance (specification of qualitative breakpoints) and quantitative differences of those states which stand at the same level of compliance demand a fuzzy-set calibration of OTAAM. A calibrated scale of this concept can be utilized by UN human rights bodies, governments, human rights NGOs, practitioners and human rights commissions for the measurement of the degree (between 0 to 1) of membership of each state in qualitatively different sets of, for instance, 'non-compliant states', 'partially compliant states', and 'fully compliant states'.[78]

[78] Fuzzification and calibration of OTAAM demand at least three multi-disciplinary group projects to (1) define and order the attributes of the obligation to take appropriate measures for a given right; (2) construct performance scales in the form of simple or composite index(es) for the measurement of defined attributes; and (3) specify qualitative breakpoints where qualitative change between different levels of compliance is made.

PART III

EMPIRICAL PERSPECTIVES

5

A Cross-Case Analysis of NHRAPs of Fifty-Three Countries

1. Introduction

This chapter presents the results of a qualitative comparative analysis of National Human Rights Action Plans (NHRAPs) of fifty-three countries. This comparative analysis includes four types of NHRAPs: (1) global NHRAPs as recommended in the 1993 Vienna Declaration and Programme of Action; (2) rights-specific (or convention-specific) action plans required under core human rights treaties (discussed in Chapter 3); (3) National Action Plans on Business and Human Rights (NAP-BHR) as recommended by the UN Human Rights Council; and (4) National Action Plans on Women, Peace, and Security (NAP-WPS) as recommended in the Security Council resolutions on WPS, though the main focus will be on the first two ones.

In the first section, seventeen major problems of NHRAPs in the 'pre-phase' and the four phases of planning, unravelled through a textual analysis of action plans of fifty-three countries—directly or indirectly through treaty bodies' Concluding Observations—will be presented. Adopting purposive sampling, these countries are selected on the basis of four main criteria: (1) human rights record (positive and negative cases); (2) geographical diversity; (3) political regimes (ideology); and (4) cultural diversity.[1]

To improve NHRAPs requires addressing the root causes of the problems. To pave the way for generating response strategies, in the second section of the chapter, the underlying causes of these problems will be explored.

2. NHRAP Problems in Different Phases

By adopting a problem-oriented approach, this section provides a profile of the main problems of NHRAPs of different kinds in the pre-phase and the four phases

[1] These countries include: Afghanistan, Australia, Azerbaijan, Bolivia, Brazil, Bosnia and Herzegovina, Canada, Cape Verde, China, Colombia, Ecuador, Egypt, Ethiopia, Finland, Georgia, Germany, Greece, Iceland, Indonesia, Iraq, Ireland, Italy, Japan, Kazakhstan, Latvia, Lebanon, Liberia, Lithuania, Malawi, Mauritania, Mexico, Moldova, Mongolia, Nepal, the Netherlands, New Zealand, Nigeria, Pakistan, Philippines, Russia, Serbia, Singapore, Somalia, South Africa, South Korea, Sri Lanka, Sierra Leone, Sweden, Tanzania, Turkey, Uganda, Ukraine, and the United Kingdom.

National Human Rights Action Planning. Azadeh Chalabi. © Azadeh Chalabi 2018. Published 2018 by Oxford University Press.

of planning, including the preparatory phase, development phase, implementation phase, and assessment phase. The problem-oriented approach seeks to fully research all of the sources available in order to identify significant problems faced by or within NHRAPs. This enables those involved in the exercise to pinpoint exactly where, and often how, a response strategy needs to be generated.

2.1. Problems in the pre-phase

A 'pre-phase' is the stage before planning, in which a preliminary decision on whether or not to proceed with a plan is made. In this stage, two significant problems can be identified.

2.1.1. Non-compliance problem

The first and most important challenge surrounding NHRAPs is that whilst each state is obliged, under the nine core human rights treaties, to develop a NHRAP for implementing the rights contained in the conventions (see Chapter 3), a number of states have not adopted any plan yet.[2] Despite a rapidly growing number of NHRAPs, there is still a number of states who are reluctant to develop such plans. This difficulty has been reflected through the human rights treaty supervisory system. For instance, in the case of Turkmenistan, the Committee on the Elimination of Discrimination against Women is 'concerned at the absence of a National Action Plan for implementation of the Convention'.[3] Similarly, the Committee on the Elimination of Racial Discrimination, in the cases of Switzerland and the United States, reiterated its concern at the lack of a National Action Plan to combat racial discrimination.[4]

This problem is likewise observed in the case of the NHRAP as recommended in the Vienna Conference in 1993. Although the Vienna Declaration, as soft law, is not legally binding *per se*, it is a strong recommendation for the states to develop a NHRAP. However, many countries, with different cultural traditions, economic systems and political regimes, such as the United States, Cuba, Syria, Saudi Arabia, Israel, North Korea, the United Arab Emirates, Iran, and Colombia have not developed even one NHRAP in accordance with paragraph 71 of the Vienna Declaration and Programme of Action yet.[5]

Similarly, in the case of NAPs on Business and Human Rights (NAP-BHR), a number of countries have not adopted any plan yet, though many countries such as the United Kingdom, Finland, the Netherlands, Italy, Denmark, Spain, Norway,

[2] Obviously this group of countries could not be included in my research sample.

[3] CEDAW, Concluding Observations on the third to fourth periodic report of Turkmenistan adopted by the Committee at its fifty-third session (1–19 October 2012) CEDAW/C/TKM/CO/3-4, 24 October 2012, at para 14.

[4] CERD, Committee on the Elimination of Racial Discrimination to hold eighty-fourth session in Geneva from 3 to 21 February 2014, CERD/C/CHE/CO/7-9, 21 February 2014, at para 18; CERD, Concluding Observations on the combined seventh to ninth periodic reports of the United States of America CERD/C/USA/CO/7-9, 25 September 2014, at para 25.

[5] As of 20 January 2018.

Lithuania, Sweden, Colombia, and Ireland have released one or even two National Action Plans on Business and Human Rights. This problem can be seen to a lesser extent in the case of National Action Plans on Women, Peace, and Security (NAP-WPS) as well. Of the 193 member states of the UN, more than seventy countries such as the Central African Republic, Rwanda, Tajikistan, Italy, Spain, Germany, Ireland, the Netherlands, Norway, Finland, France, Iraq, Sweden, New Zealand, Australia, and Liberia have adopted one or more such plans, though still around 120 countries have not adopted any National Action Plan on Women, Peace, and Security.[6] Surprisingly, two permanent members of the Security Council, Russia and China, have not released any National Action Plan on Women, Peace, and Security yet.[7] But it should be noted that whereas Russia has not developed any global NHRAP as recommended in the Vienna Declaration and Programme of Action, China has developed three global NHRAPs which will be examined throughout this chapter.

2.1.2. Tardiness problem

Another challenge is that some states have been developing their plans with considerable delays. As reported by the UNDP in a Desk Study of National Human Rights Action Plans, the process of developing NHRAPs has been delayed in some countries, such as Mauritania, Nepal, and Cape Verde.[8] Likewise, the Committee on the Elimination of Discrimination against Women, in its Concluding Observations, in the case of Serbia, as another example, remained concerned about the 'significant delays in the adoption of a new action plan to combat trafficking in human beings' and, thus, recommended the state to adopt it without further delay.[9]

It seems that the two problems of non-compliance and tardiness in the pre-phase mostly stem from the lack of political will. Perhaps these problems are also related to the traditional model of planning upon which most NHRAPs are based. Traditional planning as a mirror image of central planning of the former Soviet Union can discourage political elites and those who are in power to adopt a NHRAP and thereby intensify the lack of political will to use planning for implementing human rights. Hence, a distinction could be made between the lack of political will to implement human rights and the lack of political will to use planning for the implementation of human rights.[10] While the former seems to be an issue of many countries and can

[6] As of 1 March 2018, 74 UN member states (38% of all UN member states) have adopted one or more NAP-WPS. See Women's Internationa League for Peace and Freedom < http://www.peacewomen.org/member-states> accessed 24 March 2018.

[7] As of 14 September 2017.

[8] UN Development Programme (UNDP). 2003. A Desk Study of National Human Rights Action Plans <http://www.undp.org/content/undp/en/home/librarypage/democratic-governance/cslo_governance_centre/a-desk-study-on-national-human-rights-action-plans.html> accessed 2 December 2012.

[9] CEDAW/C/SRB/CO/2-3, 25 July 2013, at paras 24–25; See CEDAW, Concluding Observations on the combined third and fourth periodic reports of Turkmenistan CEDAW/C/TKM/CO/3-4 10 August 2012, at para 49.

[10] Azadeh Chalabi, 'Australia's National Human Rights Action Plans: Traditional or Modern Model of Planning?' (2016) 20(7) International Journal of Human Rights 993–1017.

be found mostly in authoritarian regimes, the latter would be a concern of mostly democratic countries where planning, in its traditional form, reminds them of central top-down planning used in the former Soviet Union (see Chapter 1).

2.2. Problems in the preparatory phase

The preparatory phase is the very early stage of planning in which a situation analysis is conducted. The difficulties facing NHRAPs in this phase are concerned with the development of baseline study and meaningful participation which will be discussed in turn as follows.

2.2.1. Baseline study problem

Whereas each planning should be grounded in a situation analysis, known as a 'baseline study', most of the NHRAPs such as those of Ecuador (1998), Latvia (1995), and China (2009–2010) are not grounded in any comprehensive and participatory baseline study or only relied on the government's own assessment of the status of human rights observance.[11]

If properly conducted, a comprehensive baseline study supports human rights planning by firm evidence. The National Plan of Action against Trafficking in Children and Women for Sexual and Labour Exploitation of Nepal (2001), as an example, is not developed upon adequate data on the trafficking of women, and that is why the Committee on the Elimination of Discrimination against Women expressed its concern over the lack of specific data on trafficking of women and girls in which the plan can be grounded.[12] In a similar vein, this concern was also raised by the Committee in the cases of Iceland and Tanzania.[13]

Without a proper baseline study, it is difficult to comprehensively and adequately address various human rights issues in the country in question and measure progress, if any, towards realizing human rights. Likewise, the lack of a baseline study can somewhat undermine the credibility and legitimacy of the planning process. For example, whereas child poverty is one of the most important problems in Moldova, the state did not address it in its action plan, entitled 'National Development Strategy' (2008–2011). That is why the Committee on the Rights of the Child observes in its Concluding Observations on the report of Moldova that the NHRAP (2008–2011)

[11] Ecuador, National Human Rights Program (1998) <http://www.ohchr.org/EN/Issues/PlansActions/Pages/PlansofActionIndex.aspx> accessed 01 December 2017; Latvia, National Programmes for the Protection and Promotion of Human Rights (1995) <http://www.ohchr.org/EN/Issues/PlansActions/Pages/PlansofActionIndex.aspx> accessed 1 December 2017; National Human Rights Action Plan of China (2009–2010) <http://www.ohchr.org/EN/Issues/PlansActions/Pages/PlansofActionIndex.aspx> accessed 01 December 2017.

[12] CEDAW/C/NPL/CO/4-5, 29 July 2011, at para 21.

[13] CEDAW, Concluding Observations of the Committee on the Elimination of Discrimination against Women: Iceland CEDAW/C/ICE/CO/6, 18 July 2008, at para 224; CEDAW/C/TZA/CO/6, 16 July 2008, at para 123.

does not specifically address child poverty and that poverty has been given lower priority under the plan.[14]

Another related problem here is that some countries have not followed the sequential logic of planning. For example, Pakistan included a baseline study in its NHRAP (2013–2016), though a baseline study should be conducted in advance, preparing the ground for planning.

The lack of a systematic and comprehensive baseline study has been likewise an important problem across most National Action Plans on Women, Peace, and Security. Only some countries such as Bosnia and Herzegovina have developed their plan on the basis of a baseline study. This has been an issue in the case of National Action Plans on Business and Human Rights as well. Except in a few cases such as Mozambique where the government has developed a relatively comprehensive baseline study on the UN Guiding Principles implementation with multi-stakeholder involvement,[15] most states that have adopted such plans so far have failed to conduct any comprehensive evidence-based situation analysis. In the case of the Netherlands, an internal mapping of government policies was carried out by the inter-ministerial working group but it comes nowhere close to the level of an evidence-based situation analysis required for an effective action plan. Similarly, the Finish National Action Plan on Business and Human Rights (2014) is based on a background memorandum which was carried out by government ministries. This memorandum included information on 'Finnish legislation, provisions on fundamental rights and international conventions, and other measures and practices of the authorities in relation to the UN principles.'[16] However, this memorandum did not address the key questions of the UN Guiding Principles, and non-state actors were not actively involved in its development.[17]

On a positive side, a group of countries have developed their global NHRAPs, recommended in the 1993 Vienna Declaration and Programme of Action, based on a comprehensive baseline study. For example, the New Zealand action plan for implementing human rights (2005–2010) was advanced based on 'the contributions of over 5,000 individuals, groups and organisations who made submissions and participated in nationwide consultations and in the extensive public opinion research'.[18] As highlighted in the plan, this was the first comprehensive assessment of the status of human rights in New Zealand. This assessment was based on the

[14] CRC/C/MDA/CO/3, 20 February 2009.

[15] In the case of Mozambique, although a comprehensive baseline study has already been conducted, the government has not yet (as of 1 March 2018) adopted a National Action Plan on Business and Human Rights.

[16] Finnish National Action Plan for the Implementation of the UN Guiding Principles on Business and Human Rights (2014) at 1 (Forward) <http://www.ohchr.org/EN/Issues/Business/Pages/NationalActionPlans.aspx> accessed 9 October 2016.

[17] ICAR and European Coalition for Corporate Justice, 'Assessments of Existing National Action Plans (NAPs) on Business and Human Rights' (2014) at 15–16 <http://accountabilityroundtable.org/wp-content/uploads/2014/10/ICAR-ECCJ-Assessments-of-Existing-NAPs.pdf> accessed 14 August 2015.

[18] The New Zealand Action Plan for Human Rights (2005–2010) at 3 <http://www.ohchr.org/Documents/Issues/NHRA/New_Zealand.pdf> accessed 12 January 2018.

rights set out in the Universal Declaration of Human Rights (UDHR) and codified into international law through United Nations Covenants and Conventions and the eight core International Labour Organisation (ILO) labour standards.[19]

2.2.2. Participation problem

As mentioned in the procedural theory of human rights planning in Chapter 2, there is a big difference between informing or consulting with stakeholders and meaningful participation. Unlike informing and consulting where government defines the issues, sets the questions, manages the process from top-down, and takes feedbacks selectively, in a meaningful participation, NGOs, National Human Rights Institutions (NHRIs), the public, and other stakeholders have an opportunity to get genuinely involved in the process of decision making throughout planning.[20]

Consultation with civil society is common among existing NHRAPs of different kinds such as those of Sierra Leonean and Liberian plans in the case of National Action Plans on Women, Peace, and Security and the Dutch, Swedish, and Australian ones in the case of global NHRAPs as recommended in the Vienna Conference. For the sake of illustration, I will focus on global NHRAPs in Australia. In contrast with the first two NHRAPs, the third Australian plan (2012) was developed in consultation with the public, particularly non-government organizations. As part of the preparatory phase of the third NHRAP in Australia, in June 2011, the government released a baseline study and asked the public and NGOs for their comments and feedbacks. Almost fifty submissions, mostly from non-governmental organizations, were received by the Attorney-General's Department. This consultation generated a great deal of public and media attention and played a part in raising awareness of such plans which should not be degraded.[21] However, there was no guarantee that the comments made in the submissions are to be taken into considerations by the government. And this is what can render all the submissions ineffective. As Sarah Joseph and Adam Fletcher argue:

> Strong and robust they [comments] may be, but even formal recommendations by the Parliamentary Committees or the Australian Human Rights Commission (AHRC) are at best persuasive, and can be ignored if the Government of the day declines to accept them. This should be acknowledged as a significant protection gap.[22]

Without a meaningful participation of different stakeholders, in particular NGOs and NHRIs which can provide insights from the bottom-up, it would be hardly

[19] ibid, at 4.

[20] See Sherry Arnstein, 'A Ladder of Citizen Participation' (1969) 35(4) Journal of American Planning 216–24; Roger Hart, 'Children's participation: from tokenism to citizenship' (1992), Essay for UNICEF, Innocenti Essay No 4, UNICEF International Child Development Centre; Scott Davidson, 'Spinning the Wheel of Empowerment' (1998) 1262 Planning.

[21] Chalabi, 'Australia's National Human Rights Action Plans: Traditional or Modern Model of Planning?', note 10.

[22] Sarah Joseph and Adam Fletcher, 2012. Castan Centre For Human Rights Law: National Human Rights Action Plan: Draft Baseline Study, 9 <http://www.law.monash.edu.au/castancentre/policywork/national-hr-action-plan-sub.pdf> accessed 5 September 2013.

surprising if the baseline study and thereby the plan itself cannot reflect a comprehensive picture of the status of human rights in the country concerned (see Chapter 7).

In some cases, such as China, notwithstanding a large number of NGOs, a strong and vibrant civil society and an independent National Human Rights Institution (NHRI) has not been formed so that they can willingly, knowingly, and effectively participate in the identification of problems and prioritization of solutions.[23] This is related to the lack of political will to get civil society and NHRIs genuinely involved in human rights planning.

In some other cases, despite the presence of political will to include different views from the bottom-up, there is no or little social will to become involved in developing such plans. For example, in the case Female Genital Cutting (FGC) in Somalia, it would be hardly surprising if government had difficulty to get the public involved in the process of planning. As reported by Crawford and Ali:

> Until recently, FGC was considered to be a taboo issue in Somalia. It was often avoided, even in health programmes concerned with maternal and neonatal, and sexual and reproductive, health and well-being. With estimates of FGC prevalence of up to 98% amongst women in all zones of Somalia, FGC was so much a part of normal life, so much a part of cultural practice and such a deeply embedded social norm, that it was possible to work for women's health and well-being without challenging FGC or specifically addressing the trauma it causes. FGC is a social issue, but it has often been ignored. For example, in Somalia, whilst issues such as fistula were addressed, the major underlying cause – FGC – remains a gap.[24]

Here is where the necessity of a contextual theory of human rights planning becomes apparent. As indicated in Chapter 1, it is of crucial importance to take contextual factors into account when designing a plan. A NHRAP cannot achieve its goals effectively if it ignores both general and spatio-temporal contexts.[25]

2.3. Problems in the development phase

As its name implies, the development phase is the stage during which a plan itself is formulated. This phase of the NHRAPs has been beset by at least seven inter-related pitfalls, including the 'non-correspondence problem', 'ideological-orientation problem', 'supporting the status quo problem', 'incomprehensiveness problem', 'lack of prioritization problem', 'lack of time-frame problem', and 'contextual ignorance problem'.

[23] See Philip Alston, United Nations Special Rapporteur on extreme poverty and human rights, End-of-mission statement on China, 23 August 2016 <http://www.ohchr.org/en/NewsEvents/Pages/DisplayNews.aspx?NewsID=20402&LangID=E> accessed 28 January 2018.

[24] Sheena Crawford and Sagal Ali, Situational Analysis of FGM/C Stakeholders and Interventions in Somalia, 2015, Health and Education advice and resource team, UNICEF and UNFPA <http://orchidproject.org/wp-content/uploads/2015/02/Situational-Analysis-of-FGMC-Stakeholders-and-Interventions-in-Somalia1.pdf> accessed 12 January 2017.

[25] For further clarification about 'spatio-temporal context' and 'general context' refer to the first footnote in Chapter 1.

2.3.1. Non-correspondence problem

Whereas the universality of human rights serves to highlight the fact that the state is not entitled to treat as optional the decision as to whether or not a right, enshrined in the human rights conventions should be implemented, different existing NHRAPs have suggested different lists of human rights which do not necessarily correspond with the rights set forth in the international human rights instruments. For example, rights such as 'the right to oversee', embodied in the second NHRAP of China (2012–2015), is something new which is not in correspondence with international human rights instruments. Surprisingly, this plan did not contain, for example, the right to freedom of expression or thought as current critical issues in China. In its third NHRAP (2016–2020), China removed the right to oversee. In this new plan, it included the 'rights of expression and supervision'. The combination of expression and supervision is again something new and relatively vague.[26]

That said, it has to be stressed that China in its third plan has made a rather good effort to strengthen its human rights protection system. Despite the fact that over the last three decades or so, China has experienced extensive economic development, like many other countries it still needs to work on a more well-balanced and multi-dimensional development in which human rights of all kinds are respected. Adopting three NHRAPs have been certainly a very positive step forward. Nonetheless, human rights action planning would be much more effective in China if it was based on a participatory, top-down bottom-up, and theory-laden model of planning where vibrant civil society and an independent national human rights institution could get genuinely involved in developing, implementing, and monitoring such plans. This could and indeed can, if followed in future planning, get China closer to a more well-balanced development.

The non-correspondence problem, to a lesser extent, can be seen in the case of the United Kingdom as well. In this case, the Committee on the Rights of the Child remains concerned that the Convention is not regularly used as a framework for the development of action plans. Finland is another example.[27] The Finnish NHRAP (2012–2013), entitled 'National Action Plan of Fundamental and Human Rights', in a relatively unjustified way distinguished between 'fundamental rights' which refer to the rights of the individual laid down in the Constitution, and 'human rights' which refer to the basic rights of the individual guaranteed in international human rights documents in general.

The Scottish action plan (2013–2017) sought to adopt a 'human rights-based approach' which is a promising step, though its content is not 'pragmatic' enough to put this approach into practice. The theoretical approach adopted in this plan is not translated into effective interventions with detailed steps, explicit lead bodies, and a clear time frame in a coherent way. There is also no analytical and contextual theory of planning to include contextual factors and guide its priority setting.

[26] National Human Rights Action Plan of China (2016–2020) <http://english.gov.cn/archive/publications/2016/09/29/content_281475454482622.htm> accessed 9 January 2018.

[27] CRC, Concluding observations: United Kingdom of Great Britain and Northern Ireland, CRC/C/GBR/CO/4, 20 October 2008, at para 14.

A group of plans such as those of New Zealand (2005–2010), Lebanon (2014–2019), and Nigeria (2009–2013) has made a good effort to ground their plan on the Universal Declaration of Human Rights (UDHR) and core human rights treaties.[28] A number of countries such as Iraq and Australia (its third NHRAP) based their plan on the Universal Periodic Review's recommendations which is a positive move, though it is not necessarily sufficient for the implementation of human rights as set forth in international human rights instruments.[29] Why is it a positive move and why is it not necessarily sufficient?

One of the strengths of the UPR is that the standard for the measurement of a state's human rights performance involves a full range of human rights, no matter whether or not the state has ratified the relevant treaty. This can be very important, given the relatively low rate of treaty ratification in some cases.[30] This makes the recommendations comprehensive. However, grounding a NHRAP merely on UPR recommendations may have at least five limitations: (1) It is totally left up to each state to accept recommendations made at UPR. (2) Due to the game of tit-for-tat, there sometimes (if not often) exists an unwritten agreement among the states to save each other's international image. Hence, issues raised at UPR are not always comprehensive and factual enough.[31] (3) Sometimes during the interactive dialogue states are talking past each other.[32] (4) Many of the issues raised during the UPR merely focus on legal limitations (such as failure to ratify certain treaties and discriminatory laws) and disregard social and cultural factors which are as, if not more, important as legal factors.[33] That is why the Iraqi plan of action which is based on UPR recommendations, for example, mostly contains legal measures. (5) While national NGOs can potentially participate in the process, they often do not have the resources to engage in lobbying other states in Geneva before and during the interactive dialogue.[34]

To indicate these limitations, let me focus on the case of Australia. In 2011, Australia participated in its first UPR before the United Nations Human Rights Council. The Australian government accepted almost 95% of the council's recommendations made in its first UPR and committed to using them to inform the development of Australia's new NHRAP. In the words of the 2012 NHRAP:

[28] The New Zealand Action Plan for Human Rights (2005–2010), note 18; The Parliamentary Human Rights Committee, The National Action Plan for Human Rights in Lebanon 2014–2019 <http://www.ohchr.org/Documents/Issues/NHRA/Lebanon_en.pdf> accessed 25 January 2018; National Action Plan for the Promotion and Protection of Human Rights in Nigeria (2009–2013) <http://www.ohchr.org/EN/Issues/PlansActions/Pages/PlansofActionIndex.aspx> accessed 1 December 2017.

[29] The Iraqi National Human Rights Action Plan (2011) <http://www.ohchr.org/EN/Issues/PlansActions/Pages/PlansofActionIndex.aspx> accessed 1 December 2017; Australia's National Human Rights Action Plan (2012) <http://www.ohchr.org/Documents/Issues/NHRA/NHRPAustralia2012.pdf> accessed 12 January 2018.

[30] Natalie Baird, 'The Universal Periodic Review: building a bridge between the Pacific and Geneva?' in H Charlesworth and E Larking (eds), *Human Rights and the Universal Periodic Review* (1st edn, Cambridge University Press 2015) at 207.

[31] See Takele Soboka Bulto, 'Africa's engagement with the Universal Periodic Review: Commitment or Capitulation?' in H Charlesworth and E Larking (eds), *Human Rights and the Universal Periodic Review* (1st edn, Cambridge University Press 2015) at 235–55.

[32] Baird, 'The Universal Periodic Review: building a bridge between the Pacific and Geneva?', note 30 at 208.

[33] ibid, at 208. [34] ibid, at 209.

Consequently, the Action Plan demonstrates how Australia is turning the commitments made at the UPR into specific actions to improve and promote human rights. All UPR recommendations accepted or accepted-in-part by Australia are referenced against specific measures in the Action Plan.[35]

Undoubtedly, this was a positive step towards incorporating the international community's human rights concerns into national human rights planning. As Anna Brown puts it 'the NHRAP helps Australia move from "talking the talk" to "walking the walk" when it comes to implementing commitments made during Australia's Universal Periodic Review by the UN Human Rights Council'.[36] Nonetheless, references to the UPR recommendations throughout the plan are often cursory or partial. There is a list of the recommendations that Australia accepted but to which the plan makes no reference.[37] Additionally, a number of UPR recommendations, accepted by the Australian government, are broadly addressed but not explicitly referred to in the plan.[38]

In addition to that, the Australian government failed to observe the other human rights treaties and instruments to which it is a signatory in its NHRAP such as the United Nations Declaration on the Rights of Indigenous Peoples (UNDRIP). As Joseph and Fletcher argue, 'the UPR process is undeniably important, but the treaty bodies comprise experts in human rights law who (generally) make targeted, detailed and well-informed recommendations which are just as (if not more) important to consider in the development of the Action Plan'.[39]

So far I have striven to indicate some of the limitations of designing NHRAPs merely on the basis of UPR recommendations. On a positive side, there is another group of plans such as the Dutch NHRAP which are designed to cover not only the UPR's recommendations but also the UN human rights committees' recommendations (mostly under the guise of Concluding Observations). As stated in the Dutch NHRAP (2014):

> It [NHRAP] may serve as a source document for the individual government reports to committees set up to monitor compliance with human rights conventions and for contributions to the UN's four-yearly examination of human rights known as the Universal Periodic Review. [40]

[35] Australia's National Human Rights Action Plan (2012), note 29.

[36] Anna Brown, 'New Human Rights Action Plan a Step Forward for Rights but Needs Stronger Accountability Measures', 18 December 2012 <http://www.humanrightsactionplan.org.au/nhrap-blogs/new-national-human-rights-action-plan-a-modest-success> accessed 25 December 2014.

[37] United Nations Human Rights Council, Report of the Working Group on the Universal Periodic Review, 24 March 2011, A/HRC/17/10, 2 March 2011 Recommendations Nos 31, 34, 94, 98, 100, 103, 108, 136.

[38] ibid, Recommendations Nos 6–9, 11–12, 57–58, 59–65, 96, 135.

[39] Joseph and Fletcher, Castan Centre For Human Rights Law: National Human Rights Action Plan: Draft Baseline Study, note 22 at 3.

[40] Dutch Ministry of the Interior and Kingdom Relations, National Action Plan on Human Rights: The protection and promotion of human rights within the Netherlands, February 2014, at 8 <https://www.government.nl/documents/policy-notes/2014/03/19/national-action-plan-on-human-rights> accessed 24 January 2018.

In practice, however, the Dutch Ministry of the Interior and Kingdom Relations has somewhat failed to address this comprehensive set of recommendations systematically throughout the plan.

2.3.2. Ideological orientation problem

Most troublingly, the universal idea of human rights in NHRAPs developed to date is somehow contaminated with political ideologies, that is, the term 'human rights' in the existing NHRAPs has become, more or less, politicized and divorced from the original meaning of human rights in the international human rights instruments. For example, the second National Human Rights Action Plan of China (2012–2015) in its 'Introduction' holds that:

> The Action Plan was formulated in accordance with the following guidelines: holding high the flag of socialism with Chinese characteristics, taking Deng Xiaoping Theory and the important thought of 'Three Represents' as guidance.[41]

Although the overall compatibility of the third NHRAP of China (2016–2020) with universal human rights standards has been improved, yet, this plan similarly repeated this ideological statement with an even stronger voice as follows:

> The guiding ideology for formulating and implementing the Action Plan is as follows: Upholding socialism with Chinese characteristics, fully implementing the guiding principles of the 18th National Congress of the Communist Party of China (CPC) and the third, fourth and fifth plenary sessions of the 18th CPC Central Committee, following the guidance of Marxism-Leninism, Mao Zedong Thought, Deng Xiaoping Theory, the important thought of the Three Represents, and the Scientific Outlook on Development, implementing the spirit of a series of important speeches made by General Secretary Xi Jinping, following the strategic arrangement of building China into a moderately prosperous society in an all-around way, advancing reform in an all-around way, comprehensively promoting law-based government, and running the Party with strict discipline, and sticking to the innovative, coordinated, green, open and sharing development concept.[42]

Nonetheless, it does not mean that a national human rights action plan should not be sensitive to social and cultural context where it is going to be implemented. Although political ideology may be an impediment to effective human rights action planning, a special theory of planning in which spatio-temporal factors are taken into account can enhance its effectiveness in practice. Again, in the case of China, whereas having Marxism-Leninism, Mao Zedong Thought, and Deng Xiaoping Theory as a guidance of the plan can be a serious threat to its effectiveness, being compatible with Chinese culture ('Chinese characteristics') may foster

[41] Deng Xiaoping Theory is an ideological foundation of the Communist Party of China (CPC), developed by Chinese leader Deng Xiaoping. The important thought of 'Three Represents', credited to Jiang Zemin, is also another ideological guideline of the CPC. At its Sixteenth National Congress in November 2002, the CPC established the important thought of 'Three Represents', together with Marxism-Leninism, Mao Zedong Thought, and Deng Xiaoping Theory, as the long-term guiding ideology that it must uphold.

[42] National Human Rights Action Plan of China (2016–2020), note 26.

the legitimacy and even effectiveness of the plan in practice. As fully discussed in Chapter 1, the combination of moderate relativism and moderate universalism is where identity and difference are reconciled. Such a combination which promotes unity through diversity can not only pave the way for the protection of universal rights which are based on ontologically universal objective values but also respect individual and cultural differences.

The National Plans of Action for the Promotion and Protection of Human Rights of Indonesia (1998–2003) provides another example for the ideological orientation problem. The preamble of this plan states that 'Indonesia's commitment to the promotion and protection of human rights in the entire Indonesian territory is derived from Pancasila (Five Pillars) ... as well as relevant articles in the "1945 Constitutions" which came into being prior to the adoption of the United Nations Universal Declaration of Human Rights in 1948'.

As for the 'Pancasila', it is worth mentioning that the first pillar is a religious one and thus is not consistent with the right to freedom of thought and religion.[43] Moreover, it must be noted that the original text of the 1945 Constitution, as another conceptual ground for Indonesia's NHRAP, only contains six provisions that explicitly talk about human rights with fifteen human rights principles included.[44] As Susanti argues, 'human rights provisions in the 1945 Constitution are problematic because there were too many further regulations delegated to laws/statutes. Thus, they could be easily "twisted" according to those in power'.[45]

In the case of Australia, as another example, the 'Shared Responsibility Agreements' (SRA) upon which the 'indigenous rights' part of the second NHRAP in Australia is based, is clearly based on the conservative government's general move away from a rights-based agenda in Aboriginal and Torres Strait Islander affairs to one based on 'practical reconciliation' or 'obligation-based approach'.[46] As a UN special Rapporteur states:

> The Liberal Party of Prime Minister John Howard came to power in 1996 on the basis of a programme under which the Aboriginal question would be given secondary importance and drastic measures in relation to immigration and asylum-seekers would be proposed.[47]

A NHRAP should not be structured so that it is seen as reflecting the policies or political ideology of one political party. Given the universality of human rights, a

[43] 'Pancasila' encompasses five principles including: 1) believe in the one and only God, 2) just and civilized humanity, 3) the unity of Indonesia, 4) democracy led by the wisdom of deliberations among representatives, and 5) social justice for the whole of the people of Indonesia.

[44] Bivitri Susanti, 'Constitution and Human Rights Provisions in Indonesia: An Unfinished Task in the Transitional Process' (2001) Paper presented at the Conference on 'Constitution and Human Rights in a Global Age: An Asia-Pacific History', Canberra, 30 November–3 December 2001.

[45] ibid, at 3.

[46] Ian PS Anderson, 'Mutual obligation, shared responsibility agreements and indigenous health strategy' (2006) 3:10 Australia and New Zealand Health Policy <http://www.publish.csiro.au/hp/pdf/HP060310> accessed 21 January 2018.

[47] Anand Grover, 'Report of the Special Rapporteur on the right of everyone to the enjoyment of the highest attainable standard of physical and mental health: Mission to Australia', UN Doc A/HRC/14/30/Add.4 (2010) 21–24, 10 <http://www.unhcr.org/refworld/docid/49faf7652.html> accessed on 6 June 2013.

NHRAP should be able to survive a change of government.[48] An interrelated issue is that NHRAPs do not often enjoy a firm legal status and usually have the status of a government policy—that is, they have no legal status as such in domestic legal systems.

The ideological orientation problem is rooted in the state-centric and non-participatory planning which is currently predominant. Many of the NHRAPs are not grounded in a free ideological theory to guide its process and content professionally in accordance with internationally agreed standards. Leaving human rights planning entirely up to the states has often led to the one-sided dominance of the political system over other systems in society, and thereby an unbalanced attention to the functions of other societal systems in planning. As examined in our contextual theory of planning in Chapter 1, the relative autonomy of societal systems lets the major steering mechanism of each of them work and this provides suitable context for planning. Moreover, the presence of a strong civil society, which acts as a mediated sphere between political, cultural, economic, and community systems, in developing and implementing NHRAPs alongside the states, can not only help sustain the relative autonomy of the systems but also directly lessen the likelihood of this problem's occurrence.

2.3.3. *Supporting the status quo problem*

Supporting the status quo, which is a trend common to almost all the existing NHRAPs, is another shortcoming of these plans in the development phase. Take the first Chinese action plan (2009–2010) as an example. It states that 'by putting people first, the Chinese government makes sure the constitutional principle that "the state respects and protects the human rights of its citizens" is implemented'.[49] As Human Rights Watch stated in its assessment of China's NHRAPs:

> The Chinese NHRAP characterises the government's participation in the UN Human Rights Council's first Universal Periodic Review (UPR) of China's human rights record in February 2009, as consisting of 'constructive dialogues' and the execution of 'rational proposals.' Yet the Chinese government rejected every recommendation made during the process that related to the country's key human rights issues. Its officials refused to answer any of the questions submitted by UN members in writing in advance of China's UPR session and failed to provide reasoning for the rejection of recommendations. It also made manifestly false statements about its human rights record in its UPR report. Those included, 'There is no censorship in the country,' 'No individual or press has been penalized for voicing their opinions or views,' and, 'There are no black jails in the country.' This raises questions about the Chinese government's willingness to fulfill its requirement as a member of the HRC to 'fully cooperate with the Council' (as set out in UN General Assembly resolution 60/251).[50]

[48] Chalabi, 'Australia's National Human Rights Action Plans: Traditional or Modern Model of Planning?', note 10.

[49] National Human Rights Action Plan of China (2009–2010) at 3 <https://www.law.hku.hk/ccpl/research/NationalHumanRightsActionPlan_ChinaV1.1.pdf> accessed 17 January 2018.

[50] Human Rights Watch. 2011. Promises Unfulfilled: An Assessment of China's National Human Rights Action Plan, at 52–53.

It stands in conflict with the main goal of developing NHRAPs, that is, improving the status quo in terms of the human rights situation.[51] This problem partly stems from the fact that many states fail to develop a baseline study which is necessary for the evaluation of the human rights situation in the country concerned.

In contrast with China, for instance, the NHRAP of New Zealand (2005–2010) states that: 'it [the plan] identifies what must be done over the next five years so that the human rights of everyone who lives in New Zealand are better recognised, protected and respected ... it reflects the evidence that in some crucial areas, New Zealand falls well short of fully recognising and actively respecting the human rights of all its people.'[52] As remarked before, the Action Plan of New Zealand (2005–2010) draws on 'Human Rights in New Zealand Today', the first comprehensive assessment of the status of human rights in New Zealand, and the contributions of over 5,000 individuals, groups, and organizations who made submissions and participated in nationwide consultations and in the extensive public opinion research.[53] As highlighted in the plan, this situation analysis 'showed where New Zealand is doing well in protecting human rights and where we must do better'.[54]

Mongolia is another example. After unearthing the limitations of the status quo, the Mongolian plan (2003) has made an attempt to move from the current state to the preferred state. Following conducting a baseline study, this plan acknowledges that 'according to the study [baseline study], the promotion and protection of human rights are not meeting national and international human rights standards and there are widespread violations of human rights'.[55]

The absence of specific proposals for future action is another objection of these plans which is closely tied to the problem of supporting the status quo. Strikingly, the first plan of action in Australia failed to include any new initiatives that were not already part of existing policies. Likewise, there is nearly no new initiative in the second plan (2004) to improve the human rights situation in Australia. This is to the extent that the Human Rights Law Resource Centre goes on to say that:

> At no point did the 2004 action plan set out any proposals for change. An action plan of this nature serves merely to serve as a cover for human rights failures and undermines the very purpose and aim of an action plan that is conceived and executed in good faith.[56]

In this regard, Chris Hartley argues that while the 2004 action plan emphasized Australia's commitment to human rights and international law, it failed to include any active measure that would lead to a greater realization of rights.[57] In the

[51] UNOHCHR, Handbook on National Human Rights Plans of Action, 29 August 2002 <http://www.ohchr.org/Documents/Publications/training10en.pdf> accessed 24 January 2018.

[52] The New Zealand Action Plan for Human Rights, note 18, at 2.

[53] ibid, at 2–3.

[54] ibid at 4.

[55] National Human Rights Action Programme of Mongolia (2003) at 2.

[56] Human Rights Law Resource Centre. 2011. Making rights real: A National Human Rights Action Plan for Australia, Submission to the Attorney-General's Department on the development of a National Human Rights Action Plan, February 2011 <https://static1.squarespace.com/static/580025f66b8f5b2dabbe4291/t/599e7cebe58c62bd9c76059a/1503558899844/National-Human-Rights-Action-Plan-for-Australia-HRLRC-Submission.pdf> accessed 2 March 2013.

[57] Chris Hartley, 2012. Your voice is required <http://www.humanrightsactionplan.org.au/nhrap-blogs/your-voice-is-required-participate-in-the-development-of-the-national-human-rights-action-plan> accessed 9 March 2013.

same vein, Bill Barker explains that 'the plan focuses heavily on describing existing programs. To the extent that it provides for future action, it usually refers to ongoing programs that do not owe their existence to the plan.'[58] As the UN Handbook on NHRAP states:

> [I]t is important for those involved in the development and implementation of the plan to prevent it from being limited to a public relations exercise. For example, there may be a temptation simply to include ongoing programmes in relevant areas and to re-label them as human rights programmes. While this may entail some benefit, as it may promote awareness of human rights and a rights-based approach to social and development programming, if it is the only or the main content of the plan in the area concerned, it will fall well short of what might be achieved using the mechanism of a national action plan.[59]

Promising talk rather than real action is also an important issue of some NHRAPs such as the third NHRAP of Australia. Under the title of 'Action', the Australian plan, as an instance, sometimes simply uses 'promise to consider further' (and not 'promise to change') and 'will review' rather than 'real action'. For example, it states that 'the Australian Government will **review** its reservations under the following international human rights instruments ...'.[60] NHRAPs are the place of actions. 'Reviews' should be done as much as possible in the 'preparatory phase' through the baseline study. Similarly, the same plan of Australia includes a considerable number of 'actions' which include only 'considering something by government' rather than a 'specific clear action'. [61]

2.3.4. Incomprehensiveness problem

Whereas a NHRPA (mostly in its global form) should be comprehensive, encompassing all the critical issues relating to the protection of human rights at the national level and in a relatively detailed way, some of the existing plans either have not reflected in depth upon the key problems of human rights within the country concerned or are very selective. For example, the Malawian National Plan of Action (1995–1996) is set out in a three-page document structured around five very general sections, including:

1. The Creation of an Effective Legal Framework for the Promotion and Protection of Human Rights
2. The Strengthening of Implementation Mechanisms
3. Public Information and Training Campaigns
4. The Strengthening of National Monitoring Capacity
5. Implementation of the National Plan of Action.

[58] Bill Barker, Protecting, Promoting and Fulfilling Human Rights in Australia: A National Human Rights Action, A paper prepared for the Australian Human Rights Commission (January 2011) at 14.
[59] UNOHCHR, Handbook on National Human Rights Plans of Action, note 51, at 73.
[60] Australia's National Human Rights Action Plan (2012), note 29.
[61] ibid, at 25.

This is also true of, for instance, the Azerbaijani (2011); Brazilian (1996); Bolivian (1999); Filipino (1996–2000); Indonesian (1998); and Mexican plans of action (1998) for human rights. They all comprise very general sections without laying the issues out in detail.

The second NHRAP in Australia is another example. It has been criticized of being 'selective'. As Chris Hartley states, this plan failed to respond to a number of human rights concerns in Australia and thus some human rights problems were simply overlooked.[62] The protection of asylum seekers' rights is an example. Given consistent criticism of the government's record on the rights of asylum seekers and refugees and its often fractious relationship with the UN human rights bodies in this area it is regarded by several commentators as extraordinary that the 2004 NHRAP did not even reflect this human rights issue in its main text. As Bill Barker states, the plan's self-satisfied rhetoric and its failure to deal with many important human rights issues seem to be main reasons behind its ineffectiveness in certain areas.[63]

The importance of comprehensiveness of NHRAPs is reaffirmed by different UN human rights bodies. As for convention-specific action plans, for example, in the cases of Kazakhstan, Singapore, Germany, Brazil, Egypt, and New Zealand, the UN Committee on the Rights of the Child was concerned that the action plan adopted by the states did not cover the full range of child rights contained in the Convention and, therefore, encouraged them to adopt a comprehensive corresponding national plan of action for the implementation of the Convention.[64] Similarly, the Committee on the Elimination of Discrimination against Women calls upon Finland, Tanzania, and New Zealand to put in place a comprehensive action plan to prevent and eliminate all forms of violence against women and girls.[65]

The UN Committee on Economic, Social, and Cultural Rights, which was concerned about the large number of homeless persons throughout Japan, was also concerned that the state has no comprehensive plan to combat homelessness.[66] Similarly, the report of the Special Rapporteur on violence against women to the UN Commission on Human Rights, in the case of Russia, recommended the state to 'develop and implement a national human rights action plan, which provides for the full protection of all human rights for all persons in the Federation'.[67]

In contrast, for example, the South African Plan (1998) and Ethiopian plan (2013–2015), formulated in a 151-page and 199-page document respectively, are

[62] ibid.

[63] Barker, note 58, Protecting, Promoting and Fulfilling Human Rights in Australia: A National Human Rights Action, at 15.

[64] CRC/C/KAZ/CO/3, 8 June 2007, at para 12; CRC, Concluding Observations: Singapore, 4 May 2011, CRC/C/SGP/CO/2-3, at para 13; CRC/C/NZL/3-4, 19 January 2011, at paras 14–15; CRC/C/15/Add.226, 26 February 2004, at paras 13–14; CRC/C/OPSC/EGY/1, 20 June 2011, at para 12; CRC, Concluding Observations: Brazil, 3 November 2004, CRC/C/15/Add.241, at paras 17–18.

[65] CEDAW, Concluding Observations: Finland, CEDAW/C/FIN/CO/6, 15 July 2008, at para 174; CEDAW, Concluding Observations: United Republic of Tanzania, CEDAW/C/TZA/CO/6, 16 July 2008, at para 124; CEDAW/C/NZL/CO/6, 10 August 2007, at para 16.

[66] CESCE, Consideration of Reports Submitted by States Parties under Articles 16 and 17 of the Covenant, Twenty-sixth (extraordinary) session, 13–31 August 2001, E/C.12/1/Add.67, 2001, at para 29.

[67] UN Commission on Human Rights, 2006. Report of the Special Rapporteur on violence against women, its causes and consequences, Yakin Erturk: Mission to the Russian Federation. E/CN.4/2006/61/Add.2, at para 86.

somewhat comprehensive in planning (if not necessarily in practice).[68] They included almost all types of rights, civil and political rights (equality, freedom and security of the person, life, access to justice, refugees, freedom of expression, the rights of arrested, detained, convicted or accused, etc), social and cultural rights (employment, housing and shelter, health, food, water, land, social security, education, rights of children and young people, etc) and even the rights to development, self-determination, peace, and a protected environment. Also, the Lebanese plan of action (2014–2019) has covered twenty-one areas, in a 151-page document, including both civil and political rights as well as economic, social, and cultural ones.[69] The third NHRAP of China (2016–2020) is also broad in scope. However, it goes without saying that the quality of any NHRAP is not guaranteed by its length.

The incomprehensiveness problem is also found in the case of National Action Plans on Business and Human Rights. Whereas such action plans should be comprehensive, encompassing all the principles set forth in the UN Guiding Principles, many of the extant plans have been selective in their approach to these principles. These plans are mostly focused on one or two of the Pillars of the UNGPs, leaving other Pillars inadequately addressed. In particular, while Pillar III has been highlighted as an essential Pillar of the UN Guiding Principles, this has either not been addressed or very broadly. The Dutch National Action Plan on Business and Human Rights, for instance, focused mostly on Pillar II, with much less attention given to Pillars I and III. Although a positive aspect of the Danish National Action Plan on Business and Human Rights is that it comes ahead principle by principle in its Annexes, it does not give equal attention to all the pillars. In a similar way, whereas the first National Action Plan on Business and Human Rights of the UK is organized around all the three Pillars of the UNGPs, it primarily focused on Pillar II, with little attention to Pillar I and Pillar III.

The incomprehensiveness problem can be seen in the case of National Action Plan on Women, Peace, and Security as well. Most of these plans are dedicated mostly to resolution 1325 (2000) such as those of Denmark (2005), Norway (2006), the Netherlands (2007), Rwanda (2009), Chile (2009), and also to a lesser extent to resolution 1820 (2008) such as the action plan of Uganda (2008) and Sierra Leone (2010).[70] Almost no National Action Plan on Women, Peace, and Security

[68] South Africa, National Action Plan for the Protection and Promotion of Human Rights (1998) <http://www.ohchr.org/EN/Issues/PlansActions/Pages/PlansofActionIndex.aspx> accessed 9 May 2013; The Federal Democratic Republic of Ethiopia, National Human Rights Action Plan 2013–2015 <http://www.ohchr.org/Documents/Issues/Education/Training/actions-plans/Excerpts/NHRAP%20Ethiopia%20Draft%20213-2015.pdf.pdf> 2 January 2018.

[69] The Parliamentary Human Rights Committee, The National Action Plan for Human Rights in Lebanon 2014–2019, note 28.

[70] Denmark's Action Plan on Implementation of Security Council Resolution 1325 on Women, Peace, and Security <http://peacewomen.org/nap-denmark> accessed 25 May 2016; The Norwegian Government's Action Plan for the Implementation of UN Security Council Resolution 1325 (2000) on Women, Peace, and Security <http://peacewomen.org/sites/default/files/norway-nationalactionplan_march2006.pdf> accessed 2 January 2015; Dutch National Action Plan on Resolution 1325: Taking a stand for women, peace, and security (2007) <http://peacewomen.org/sites/default/files/dutch_nationalactionplan_december2007.pdf> accessed 8 September 2015; Republic of Rwanda, National Action Plan 2009–2012, The United Nations Security Council Resolution 1325/2000 on Women, Peace, and Security (2009) <http://peacewomen.org/sites/default/files/rwandan_national_

has specifically and systematically covered all eight Women, Peace, and Security resolutions.[71]

2.3.5. *Lack of prioritization problem*

Considering the limit of resources, NHRAPs should strike a balance between prioritization and pursuit of a wide spectrum of rights (comprehensiveness). However, in many cases, no or little prioritization has been made to the list of rights. Take Ethiopia as an example. 61 million Ethiopians lack access to safe water and 65 million lack access to improved sanitation. Of those who lack access to improved sanitation, a staggering 27 million practice open defecation.[72] Despite the importance of priority setting, however, the violation of these very basic rights have been recognized as the same as other rights such as rights of persons held in custody.[73] China's NHRAP (2009–2010) is another example. In this regard, the Human Rights Watch declares that:

> The NHRAP devoted considerable attention to issues that are at best secondary to China's urgent human rights problem, such as increasing community sports facilities to 1.4 square meters per capita by 2010 and 'overall promotion of digitalised movie, radio and TV service.' Yet the NHRAP does not address several major human rights issues prioritised by both Chinese and foreign human rights activists: China's *hukou*, or household registration system; rights abuses related to rising numbers of property disputes; and human rights concerns related to China's increasingly active diplomatic, development, and investment activities in the developing world.[74]

In the case of Moldovan plan (2004–2008), as the assessment report on the implementation of this plan declares:[75]

> certain important deficiencies have been identified in the document [the first NHRAP (2004–2008)]: ... it contains wide human rights scopes, no priorities being defined, ... unreal priorities are defined in the context of the demand for preliminary reforms or the preparation of assessment studies.

action_plan_1325.pdf> accessed 21 January 2015; Republic of Chile, National Plan of Action for the Implementation of the UN Security Council Resolution No 1325/2000 (2009) <http://peacewomen.org/sites/default/files/chile_nap_2009_english.pdf> accessed 24 September 2017; The Republic of Uganda, The Uganda Action Plan on UN Security Council Resolutions 1325 and 1820 and the Goma Declaration (2008) <http://peacewomen.org/sites/default/files/uganda_nationalactionplan_december2008.pdf> accessed 12 September 2017; The Sierra Leone National Action Plan for the Full Implementation of United Nations Security Council Resolutions 1325 (2000) and 1820 (2008) <http://peacewomen.org/sites/default/files/sierra_leone_nap.pdf> accessed 2 March 2016.

[71] Aisling Swaine, 'Globalising Women, Peace and Security: Trends in National Action Plans' in S Aroussi (ed), *Rethinking National Action Plans on Women, Peace and Security, NATO Science for Peace and Security Series* (1st edn, IOS Publishing 2017) at 16–17.

[72] Ethiopia's water and sanitation crisis, <https://water.org/our-impact/ethiopia/> accessed 27 December 2017.

[73] The Federal Democratic Republic of Ethiopia, National Human Rights Action Plan 2013–2015.

[74] Human Rights Watch, Promises Unfulfilled: An Assessment of China's National Human Rights Action Plan, note 50 at 65.

[75] Assessment Report on the Implementation of the National Human Rights Action Plan (2004–2008 and 2011–2014) at 7 <https://rm.coe.int/1680597a50> accessed 23 December 2017.

Think of child poverty which has been overlooked in Moldovan NHRAP (2008–2011) as an example here.[76]

There is also a group of plans that have set out priorities though with no clear set of criteria. The Scotland's National Action Plan for Human Rights (SNAP) (2013–2017) offers an example here.[77] It is not clear enough where the plan's priorities come from.

2.3.6. Lack of time-frame problem

A NHRAP is required to set a fixed target date within a reasonable number of years for the achievement of its goals.[78] In addition to a time frame for the plan as a whole, each plan must also specifically set out a series of targeted implementation dates for each stage of the implementation of the plan.[79] The lack of time frame, however, is a pervasive problem of NHRAPs in practice. Some countries such as Latvia (1995) and Ecuador (1998) have not even established any time frame for their NHRAPs as a whole.[80] It goes without saying that to monitor a NHRAP effectively requires, inter alia, an exact timetable. The UN Committee on the Rights of the Child, in the case of Greece, for instance, regretted the lack of information on the period of action of the NHRAP for Children's Rights in 2007 and its specific time-bound and measurable goals for effectively monitoring progress in the implementation of the rights.[81]

Moreover, whereas each specific action identified through a NHRAP should be defined within reasonable timeframes, some plans like Mongolian (2003), Scottish (2013–2017), Chinese (2016–2020), and Swedish (2006–2009) have failed to set any corresponding timeframe for the specific actions contained in them.[82] In some plans, for many actions, the timeline is simply marked as 'ongoing'.

Similarly, some National Action Plans on Women, Peace, and Security such as Ireland's and the Federal Republic of Germany's plans, and also National Action Plans on Business and Human Rights such as the Polish and Italian plans have not established a clear timeframe for their identified actions.[83]

[76] Moldova's National Development Strategy (2008–2011) <http://www.legislationline.org/documents/id/16659> accessed 21 February 2014.

[77] Scotland's National Action Plan for Human Rights (SNAP) 2013–2017 <http://www.snaprights.info> accessed 8 October 2017.

[78] CESCR, General Comment No 14, E/C.12/2000/4, at para 56.

[79] CESCR, General Comment No 1, at para 10; CESCR, General Comment 12, C.12/1999/5, at para 24.

[80] Latvia. National Programmes for the Protection and Promotion of Human Rights (1995), note 11; Ecuador. National Human Rights Program (1998), note 11.

[81] CRC, Consideration of reports submitted by States parties under Article 44 of the Convention: Convention on the Rights of the Child: Concluding Observations: Greece, 13 August 2012, CRC/C/GRC/CO/2-3, at para 13.

[82] National Human Rights Action Programme of Mongolia (2003) <http://www.ohchr.org/EN/Issues/PlansActions/Pages/PlansofActionIndex.aspx> accessed 17 March 2012; Scotland's National Action Plan for Human Rights (SNAP) 2013–2017, note 77; National Human Rights Action Plan of China (2016–2020), note 26; Sweden's National Action Plan for Human Rights (2006–2009) < http://www.ohchr.org/EN/Issues/PlansActions/Pages/PlansofActionIndex.aspx> accessed 17 March 2015.

[83] Ireland's Second National Action Plan on Women, Peace and Security 2015–2018 <http://peacewomen.org/sites/default/files/Revised%20NAP%20Ireland%20(2015-2018).pdf> accessed 25 January 2018; Action Plan of the Government of the Federal Republic of Germany on the Implementation

By contrast, one of the positive aspects of the NHRAP of Lithuania (2002), Georgia (2014–2016), Pakistan (2016), and Australia (2012) is that for each action, they often included relatively clear timeline.[84] For example, 'Australian Government funding for the Reconciliation Australia led community awareness initiative covers a two year period, ending 30 June 2014.'[85]

2.3.7. *Contextual ignorance problem*

Another critical problem of most NHRAPs in the development phase is what I would call the contextual ignorance problem. Whereas contextual factors can play a key role in making guided institutional changes (see Chapter 1), most action plans for implementing human rights are developed in a context-independent way with a main focus on legal mechanisms and formal reforms from the top down. Bear in mind that here 'context' is used in two senses: (1) 'general context' at the high level of abstract discussed as part of the general theory of human rights planning in Chapter 1; and (2) 'spatio-temporal context' which, as its name implies, is what is bounded by spatio-temporal factors. The latter is the central concern of the special theory of planning for a given country which can complement a general theory of planning.

For the sake of illustration, let me focus on the case of indigenous Australians. As Australia's Department of Social Services reports, 'too many indigenous Australians experience unacceptable levels of disadvantage in living standards, life expectancy, education, health and employment. Current data shows a significant gap in these critical areas between indigenous and non-indigenous population'.[86] To address these difficulties, the 2012 NHRAP of Australia, among other things,[87] focuses on the Closing the Gap strategy, as a separate rights-specific plan, and stresses that:

of United Nations Security Council Resolution 1325 on Women, Peace and Security for the Period 2017–2020 <http://peacewomen.org/sites/default/files/170111_Aktionsplan_1325.pdf> accessed 25 January 2018; Polish National Action Plan for the Implementation of the United Nations Guiding Principles on Business and Human Rights (2017–2020) <http://www.ohchr.org/Documents/Issues/Business/NationalPlans/PolandNationalPland_BHR.pdf> accessed 1 February 2018; Italian National Action Plan on Business and Human Rights (2016–2021) <http://www.cidu.esteri.it/resource/2016/12/49117_f_NAPBHRENGFINALEDEC152017.pdf> accessed 25 January 2018.

[84] Lithuania. National Programmes for the Protection and Promotion of Human Rights (2002) <http://www.ohchr.org/EN/Issues/PlansActions/Pages/PlansofActionIndex.aspx> accessed 17 March 2015; Action Plan of the Government of Georgia on the Protection of Human Rights 2014–2016 <https://www.coe.int/t/commissioner/source/NAP/Georgia-National-Action-Plan-on-Human-Rights.pdf> accessed 28 December 2017; Ministry of Human Rights, Government of Pakistan, Action Plan for Human Rights 2016 <http://www.mohr.gov.pk/userfiles/APBL.pdf> accessed 21 January 2018; Australia's National Human Rights Action Plan (2012), note 29.

[85] Australia's National Human Rights Action Plan (2012), note 29, at 25.

[86] Australian Government, Department of Social Services, Closing the Gap on Indigenous Disadvantage: The Challenge for Australia <http://www.dss.gov.au/our-responsibilities/indigenous-australians/publications-articles/closing-the-gap/closing-the-gap-on-indigenous-disadvantage-the-challenge-for-australia-2009?HTML#ft4> accessed 10 January 2014.

[87] As far as indigenous rights are concerned, the 2012 plan includes different initiatives such as 'Constitutional recognition for Indigenous Australians', 'reinstating the Racial Discrimination Act 1975 (Cth)' and 'The Stronger Futures', but its main focus is on the Closing the Gap strategy.

The Australian Government's priority action to address Indigenous disadvantage is the *Closing the Gap Strategy*. The Strategy covers the key areas of health, housing, work and education through mainstream and Indigenous Specific National Agreements.[88]

However, as the result of a recent survey, conducted by the present author, indicates, this part of the plan was not very effective.[89] An important concern with the Closing the Gap strategy is that the social and cultural determinants of 'the gap' are somewhat disregarded in this rights-specific action plan. The main objective of this strategy is merely achieving a statistical equality, however, it is largely overlooked that this statistical gap, more importantly, indicates a culture gap between indigenous Australians and non-indigenous Australians.[90] Although indigenous and non-indigenous Australians live in the same territory, their normative and cognitive environments are very different. This is to the extent that, as Simmel explains, they are physically near and conceptually distant simultaneously.[91] Whereas this culture gap is a significant barrier to an effective communication, it is not effectively reflected in the third NHRAP and the Closing the Gap Strategy in particular. Considerable emphasis, for example in the case of health issues, is given to various disease-focused programs, incentives for health workforces, health service infrastructure, though the communication gap between indigenous and non-indigenous Australians remains overlooked. Although cross-cultural miscommunications between indigenous clients and non-indigenous health professionals, as an important instance, are commonly documented, the Australia's NHRAP lacks a contextual theory, both general and special, to address this problem.

The NHRAP of Iraq is another instance. It is mostly focused on legal reforms such as the ratification of human rights treaties, revising its criminal law, amending its anti-terrorism law and prison law, and supporting an independent judiciary authority.[92] Although this is a positive move forward and it should not be underestimated, this plan is hardly sensitive to the context through which actions can take place and legal reforms can be realized.

Chinese NHRAP provides another example. Recently, the UN Special Rapporteur on extreme poverty and human rights, Philip Alston, presented his country visit report on China to the Human Rights Council. His report cautions that, despite economic development, structural inequalities are exacerbated by the absence of an independent and vibrant civil society. As his report indicates, China employs a top-down approach to poverty alleviation, which marginalizes the role of civil society

[88] Australia's National Human Rights Action Plan (2012), note 29.

[89] For details see Chalabi, 'Australia's National Human Rights Action Plans: Traditional or Modern Model of Planning?', note 10.

[90] Kerryn Pholi, Dan Black, and Craig Richards, 'Is "Close the Gap" a useful approach to improving the health and wellbeing of Indigenous Australians?' (2009) 9:2 Australian Review of Public Affairs 1; see also, Karen B Murray, 'Do not disturb: "Vulnerable populations" in federal government policy discourse' (2004) 13:1 Canadian Journal of Urban Research 50.

[91] William D Gudykunst, 'Anxiety/Uncertainty Management (AUM) Theory: Current Status' in R L Wiseman (ed), *International and Intercultural Communication Annual, Vol 19. Intercultural Communication Theory*, 8–58 (1st edn, Sage Publications 1995).

[92] The Iraqi National Human Rights Action Plan (2011), note 29.

in shaping effective planning.[93] As mentioned in the contextual theory of human rights planning advanced in Chapter 1, a vibrant civil society can contribute to the relative autonomy of each of the major systems of society. By providing environmental immunity, a vibrant and strong civil society can also contribute to the prevention of corruption and nepotism which is of crucial importance for an effective development and implementation of human rights action planning.

On the positive side, a number of NHRAPs have mentioned some structural bottlenecks even if they have not addressed them comprehensively and adequately. For instance, the NHRAP of Ethiopia (2013–2015) states that:

> Over the past long years Ethiopia has suffered under the unrelenting oppression of anti-democratic and despotic rulers . . . The country never had a multi-party system, nor was there any indication of democracy. Basic group and individual human rights and freedoms were not respected. Instead, the Ethiopian people were long victims of wars and subjected to political crises and never-ending conflicts deliberately instigated and exacerbated by undemocratic rulers . . . There is no gainsaying the fact the historical inequalities and natural disasters, particularly the residuals of wars, underdevelopment, droughts and poverty, as well as the low level of economic and human development, etc., have their negative impact.[94]

The plan expresses its commitment to the 'creation of a strong and capable government structure; overall transparency and elimination of corruption; inclusion of multi-facetted issues into the civil service; and reinforcing administrative decentralization through building the capacity of the *woreda* and area councils'.[95] With regard to changing the social attitudes on harmful traditional practices and revenge killings, the plan declares that 'efforts will continue reinforced with the co-operation and support of women's, youth and professional associations, religious institutions, *Idirs*, and other social organizations, through educating public and in the arrest, prosecution and conviction of offenders.'[96]

Let me recapitulate that an effective NHRAP needs to take contextual factors into consideration. To do so, it should adopt both a contextual theory of human rights planning and special theory (see Chapter 1).

2.4. Problems in the implementation phase

The implementation phase is the critical stage, during which the NHRAP is brought into practice. The following shall illustrate four important difficulties facing NHRAPs in this phase. These include the 'lack of coordination problem', 'lack of transparency problem', 'lack of accountability problem', and 'resources problem'.

[93] Philip Alston, United Nations Special Rapporteur on extreme poverty and human rights End-of-mission statement on China, 23 August 2016 <http://www.ohchr.org/en/NewsEvents/Pages/DisplayNews.aspx?NewsID=20402&LangID=E> accessed 14 November 2017; also see ISHR, China | UN expert says respect for human rights and civil society essential to development and poverty alleviation <https://www.ishr.ch/news/china-un-expert-says-respect-human-rights-and-civil-society-essential-development-and-poverty> 14 November 2017.

[94] The Federal Democratic Republic of Ethiopia, National Human Rights Action Plan 2013–2015, at 11–12.

[95] ibid, at 12. [96] ibid, at 22.

2.4.1. Lack of co-ordination problem

One of the significant challenges around NHRAPs is that there is no or limited co-ordination among different NHRAPs *inter se*, and between NHRAPs and other policies and plans, in particular economic and development planning. For example, in the case of Finland, the Committee on the Elimination of Discrimination against Women expresses its concern about the proliferation of plans of action against trafficking and the lack of co-ordination among them.[97]

By the same token, the Committee on the Rights of the Child, in the case of Singapore, recommends that the state party harmonize its various action plans on children and families, under a comprehensive national plan of action for children, to ensure full implementation of the Convention.[98] This problem stems from the lack of a systemic view in planning (see Chapter 1).

A positive aspect of the third NHRAP of China (2016–2020) is its advancement in co-ordination with the Thirteenth Five-Year Plan for National Economic and Social Development of the People's Republic of China which is very comprehensive and of crucial importance in China.[99] There is also a harmony in terms of time between these two national plans—both are set out for the period between 2016 and 2020.

2.4.2. Lack of transparency problem

As discussed in our procedural theory of human rights planning, the formulation and implementation of a NHRAP should respect, inter alia, the principle of transparency (see Chapter 2). Nevertheless, another defect of many NHRAPs in practice is that those countries that have developed a NHRAP have not spelled out transparently the process of developing and implementing them, for example, the NHRAPs of Indonesia (1998–2003), Malawi (1995–96), and Mexico (1998).[100] The lack of transparency can be found as an important issue in the case of National Action Plans on Women, Peace, and Security and National Action Plan on Business and Human Rights as well.[101]

[97] CEDAW/C/FIN/CO/6, 15 July 2008, at para 175.

[98] CRC/C/SGP/CO/2-3, 4 May 2011, at para 13.

[99] China's Five-Year Plans are a series of social and economic development initiatives, available at <http://en.ndrc.gov.cn/newsrelease/201612/P020161207645765233498.pdf> accessed 2 December 2017.

[100] National Plans of Action for the Promotion and Protection of Human Rights-Indonesia (1998–2003) <http://www.ohchr.org/EN/Issues/PlansActions/Pages/PlansofActionIndex.aspx> accessed 23 February 2014; Malawi, National Plan of Action in the Field of Human Rights (1995–96) <http://www.ohchr.org/EN/Issues/PlansActions/Pages/PlansofActionIndex.aspx> accessed 7 May 2015; Mexico, National Program to Promote and Strengthen Human Rights (1998)) <http://www.ohchr.org/EN/Issues/PlansActions/Pages/PlansofActionIndex.aspx> accessed 23 February 2014.

[101] See, eg, Claire Methven O'Brien, Amol Mehra, Sara Blackwell, and Cathrine Bloch Poulsen-Hansen, 'National Action Plans: Current Status and Future Prospects for a New Business and Human Rights Governance Tool' (2016) 1 Business and Human Rights Journal 117–26.

2.4.3. Lack of accountability problem

Establishing accountability mechanisms is central to ensuring the plan's effectiveness. It is not enough to find fault or pass the buck when a plan fails. It pertains to the question of whether the implementing bodies did what they were going to do in a particular period of time. It is critical to understand why the intervention failed, who is responsible, and what actions need to be taken to meet the objectives and goals.[102]

Whereas accountability is one of the most important procedural principles upon which a NHRAP should be based (see Chapter 7), most states which have developed NHRAPs have not established any clear accountability mechanism to ensure the implementation of their plans. This applies, for example, to the Brazilian (1996), Malawian (1995–1996), Chinese (2009–2010), and first Australian (1994) plans.[103] Due to the lack of accountability, as the characteristics of the technocrat concept of planning, the process of the NHRAPs was delayed in some countries, like Mauritania, Nepal, and Cape Verde.[104] Similarly, the Committee on the Elimination of Discrimination against Women, in the case of Sweden, also calls upon the state to introduce effective accountability mechanisms in the context of the plan for gender mainstreaming in Government offices 2004–2009, and that such mechanisms include sanctions for non-compliance.[105] Likewise, in some cases like Sri Lanka, accountability mechanisms in a NHRAP are described vaguely.[106]

One of the most important ways to promote transparency and accountability is using performance indicators that can demonstrate to the public and NGOs what the government is doing. Information of this type is also important for combating corruption. If the states maintain secrecy about different phases of planning, there is little chance for the public and NGOs to impose effective control over government and provide feedback for the improvement of action plans. Some action plans such of those of Georgia (2014–2016), Finland (2012–2013), and Tanzania (2013–2017) have specified some form of performance indicators.[107] Likewise, in

[102] See United Nations Development Programme, 'Development Effectiveness—Spotlight on performance: Why Some Countries Do Better Than Others', 2003, at 7.

[103] Brazil, National Action Plan for Human Rights (1996) <http://www.ohchr.org/EN/Issues/PlansActions/Pages/PlansofActionIndex.aspx> accessed 2 November 2016; Malawi, National Plan of Action in the Field of Human Rights (1995–1996), note 100; National Human Rights Action Plan of China (2009–2010), note 49; Australia's National Action Plan on Human Rights (1996, 1997 Update) <http://www.ohchr.org/EN/Issues/PlansActions/Pages/PlansofActionIndex.aspx> accessed 2 May 2012.

[104] UN Development Programme (UNDP). 2003. A Desk Study of National Human Rights Action Plans, note 8; CEDAW, Concluding Observations of the Committee on the Elimination of Discrimination against Women: Nepal, CEDAW/C/NPL/CO/4-5, 29 July 2011, at para 35.

[105] CEDAW, Concluding Observations of the Committee on the Elimination of Discrimination against Women: Sweden, CEDAW/C/SWE/CO/7, 8 April 2008, at para 21; CRC/C/SWE/CO/4, 26 June 2009, at para 67(a).

[106] UN Human Rights Council (2012) No Real Will to Account: Shortcomings in Sri Lanka's National Plan of Action to Implement the Recommendations of the LLRC, A/HRC/21/NGO/72. 5 September, at 2.

[107] Action Plan of the Government of Georgia on the Protection of Human Rights 2014–2016, note 84; Finland, National Action Plan on Fundamental and Human Rights 2012–2013 <http://www.ohchr.org/EN/Issues/PlansActions/Pages/PlansofActionIndex.aspx> accessed 1 June 2015; Ministry of

the case of National Action Plans on Women, Peace, and Security, some plans such as Ireland's second plan (2015–2018) have identified a set of performance indicators.[108] Ireland, however, has failed to include such set of indicators in its National Action Plan on Business and Human Rights (2017–2020) recently released.[109]

Different types of performance indicators, including process indicators and result indicators (output indicators, outcome indicators, and impact indicators) as well as accountability mechanisms will be explored in Chapter 7.

2.4.4. *Lack of resources problem*

Another problem of NHRAPs in the implementation phase pertains to resources. Every action planning, the NHRAPs among them, should identify resources available to attain the objectives. Nevertheless, some of the existing NHRAPs, such as the global NHRAP of Nepal, have not allocated enough resources to attain their goals.[110] As a result, the implementation of these plans has been delayed for a long time.[111]

Rights-specific action plans of Italy, Nigeria, Moldova, Brazil, Tanzania, and Russia provide other examples. The Committee on the Rights of the Child was particularly concerned that the Italian National Plan of Action has not yet been implemented and that no budget has been allocated for the implementation of the plan.[112] Similarly, in the cases of Nigeria and Moldova, the Committee was concerned that the impact of the NHRAPs for the protection of children's rights is very limited due to inadequate financial support out of the state budget.[113] The Committee on the Elimination of Racial Discrimination also regrets the lack of resources to effectively implement the 2007–2010 Action Plan (Articles 2 and 5) in Moldova as a right-specific plan.[114] This is also true of the global NHRAP in Moldova (2004–2008) in that there is no financial coverage or quantification of costs.[115]

Constitutional and Legal Affairs, United Republic of Tanzania National Human Rights Action Plan 2013–2017 <http://www.ohchr.org/Documents/Issues/Education/Training/actions-plans/Excerpts/Tanzania_en%202013-2017.pdf> accessed 10 December 2017.

[108] Ireland's second National Action Plan on Women, Peace and Security (2015–2018), note 83.

[109] Ireland's National Plan on Business and Human Rights (2017–2020) <http://www.ohchr.org/EN/Issues/Business/Pages/NationalActionPlans.aspx> accessed 1 February 2018.

[110] Nepal, Office of the Prime Minister and Council of Ministers Singh Durbar, National Human Rights Action Plan (2004) <http://www.ohchr.org/Documents/Issues/NHRA/Nepal_NHRAP.pdf> accessed 28 January 2018.

[111] UN Development Programme (UNDP). 2003. A Desk Study of National Human Rights Action Plans, note 8, at 33.

[112] CRC/C/ITA/CO/3-4, 31 October 2011, at para 10.

[113] CRC, Consideration of Reports Submitted by States Parties under Article 44 of the Convention: Concluding Observations—Nigeria, 21 June 2010, CRC/C/NGA/CO/3-4, at paras 12–13; CRC, Consideration of reports submitted by States parties under Article 44 of the Convention: Convention on the Rights of the Child: Concluding Observations: Republic of Moldova, 20 February 2009, CRC/C/MDA/CO/3; see CEDAW/C/SWE/CO/7, 8 April 2008; E/C.12/TUR/CO/1, 12 July 2011, at para 23.

[114] CERD, Consideration of reports submitted by States parties under Article 9 of the Convention: Republic of Moldova, CERD/C/MDA/CO/8-9, 10 March 2011, at para 15.

[115] Assessment Report on the Implementation of the National Human Rights Action Plan (2004–2008 and 2011–2014) at 7 <https://rm.coe.int/1680597a50> accessed 3 September 2017.

In the cases of Brazil and Tanzania, likewise, the Committee on the Elimination of Discrimination against Women expresses its concern at the inadequate funding for the implementation of the National Action Plan.[116] This point has been also emphasized by the Committee on Economic, Social, and Cultural Rights in the case of Russia. It requests the Russian state to allocate sufficient resources for the implementation of its national strategy and national plan to combat corruption.[117]

Some plans such as NHRAP of Iraq (2011), instead of considering the budget in the preparatory phase before the advancement of the plan, in the main text of the plan itself proposed generating sources for adequate budget from the state general budget and international financial support. In contrast, the NHRAP of Somalia (2015–2016) has included a separate row specifically on budget aimed at determining how much needs to be spent on each activity.[118]

The critical point is that as the Committee on Economic, Social, and Cultural Rights, in its General Comment No 11 states, 'a state party cannot escape the unequivocal obligation to adopt a plan of action on the grounds that the necessary resources are not available'.[119] Where a state is clearly lacking in the financial resources and/or expertise required to develop and implement a NHRAP, the international community has a clear obligation to assist.[120] The Committee also encourages states parties to seek the assistance of relevant international agencies, including the International Labour Organisation (ILO), the United Nations Development Programme (UNDP), the United Nations Educational, Scientific, and Cultural Organisation (UNESCO), the United Nations Children's Fund (UNICEF), the International Monetary Fund (IMF), and the World Bank, in relation both to the preparation of NHRAPs and their subsequent implementation. It also calls upon the relevant international agencies to assist states parties, to the greatest extent possible, to meet their obligations on an urgent basis.[121]

Nonetheless, as John Friedmann aptly argues, insufficient resources are only part of the problem. Governments' will to enforce and implement the plan, or allocate enough resources is sometimes very weak.[122] Matthew Craven also believes that 'the failure of many states fully to implement economic, social and cultural rights can

[116] CEDAW/C/TZA/CO/6, 16 July 2008, note 65, at para 119; CEDAW/C/BRA/CO/7, 23 February 2012, at para 18; see CRC/C/JPN/CO/3, 20 June 2010, at para 16; CRC, Consideration of reports submitted by States parties under Article 12, paragraph 1, of the Optional Protocol to the Convention on the Rights of the Child on the Sale of Children, Child Prostitution and Child Pornography: Concluding Observations: Japan, 22 June 2010, CRC/C/OPSC/JPN/CO/1, at para 10.

[117] CESCR, Consideration of reports submitted by States parties under Articles 16 and 17 of the Covenant, Forty Sixth Session, E/C.12/RUS/CO/5, 20 May 2011, at para 6.

[118] Action Plan for the Implementation of the Human Rights Roadmap (HRRM) For Somalia 2015–2016 <http://www.ohchr.org/EN/Issues/PlansActions/Pages/PlansofActionIndex.aspx> accessed 9 December 2017.

[119] UN Committee on Economic, Social, and Cultural Rights (CESCR), General Comment No 11: Plans of Action for Primary Education (Art 14 of the Covenant), 10 May 1999, E/1992/23, at para 9.

[120] ibid.

[121] ibid, at para 11.

[122] John Friedmann, 'Planning Cultures in Transition' in B Sanyal (ed), *Comparative Planning Cultures* (1st edn, Routledge 2005) 29–44.

often be more clearly attributed to a lack of political will than any matter of resources scarcity'.[123] This can be a result of political and/or administrative corruption.[124]

As fully discussed in Chapter 1, central planning (the traditional model of planning) is a model well fitted for the corrupt states to misuse funds. It allows government officials 'unfettered' discretion to allocate resources—the resources that would otherwise be used for implementing NHRAPs. Those plans which are developed through the traditional model of planning with no or little input from the bottom up, are often not respected even by those governments and politicians who developed them in the first place. This type of planning can result in state monopoly in developing and implementing NHRAPs and this monopoly is very likely to lead to favouritism, nepotism, biased allocation of resources, distorted priorities, and stifling of local and NGOs initiatives and innovations.[125] As the human rights Council panel on anti-corruption states, corruption typically diverts funding from state budgets that should be dedicated to the realization of basic human rights.[126] That is why, under international human rights law, a NHRAP should clearly identify resources available to attain the goals.[127]

2.5. Problems in the assessment phase

The need to demonstrate performance places demands on monitoring and evaluating NHRAPs, known as the assessment phase. Two problems of the lack of monitoring mechanism and the lack of evaluation mechanism will be discussed in this phase.

2.5.1. *Lack of monitoring problem*

Monitoring involves a process of adjustment of plan objectives and activities in the light of circumstances.[128] A NHRAP should include a periodic review and effective mechanisms for monitoring.[129] Monitoring provides ongoing, systematic

[123] Matthew C R Craven, *The International Covenant on Economic, Social and Cultural Rights: A Perspective on its Development* (1st edn, Clarendon Press 1998), at 106.

[124] ibid.

[125] See Susan Rose-Ackerman, *From Elections to Democracy Building Accountable Government in Hungary and Poland* (1st edn, Cambridge University Press 2005); Susan Rose-Ackerman, *International Handbook on the Economics of Corruption* (1st edn, Edward Elgar 2006).

[126] Council panel on anti-corruption (2013) <http://www.ohchr.org/EN/Issues/Development/GoodGovernance/Pages/AntiCorruptionPanel.aspx> accessed 20 January 2018.

[127] See UN Committee on Economic, Social, and Cultural Rights (CESCR), General Comment No 15: The Right to Water (Arts 11 and 12 of the Covenant), 20 January 2003, E/C.12/2002/11, at para 47.

[128] UNOHCHR, Handbook on National Human Rights Plans of Action, note 51 at 41.

[129] See UN Committee on Economic, Social, and Cultural Rights (CESCR), General Comment No 15: The Right to Water (Arts 11 and 12 of the Covenant), 20 January 2003, E/C.12/2002/11, at para 53; UN Committee on Economic, Social, and Cultural Rights (CESCR), General Comment No 14: The Right to the Highest Attainable Standard of Health (Art 12 of the Covenant), 11 August 2000, E/C.12/2000/4, at para 43(f); UN Committee on Economic, Social, and Cultural Rights (CESCR), General Comment No 11: Plans of Action for Primary Education (Art 14 of the Covenant), 10 May 1999, E/1992/23, at para 8; UN Committee on Economic, Social, and Cultural Rights (CESCR), General Comment No 20: Non-discrimination in economic, social, and cultural rights (Art 2, para 2, of the International Covenant on Economic, Social, and Cultural Rights), 2 July 2009, E/C.12/GC/20,

information in order to determine whether sufficient progress is being made toward achieving expected results and processes comparing implementation efforts with original targets. It allows plans to assess what is actually happening versus what was planned. The monitoring mechanisms should meet at reasonable intervals during the life of the plan. The reviews should honestly identify shortcomings and obstacles and propose remedies to ensure that objectives are met.[130]

Nonetheless, most of the existing NHRAPs have failed to provide adequately any mechanism for monitoring their current situation. For example, the NHRAPs of the Netherlands (2014), Mongolia (2003), Brazil (1996), Ecuador (1998), Somalia (2015–2016), and Bolivia (1999) omitted any clear monitoring mechanism.[131]

This problem is seen in the case of rights-specific plans as well. Regarding the Italian NHRAP, for instance, the Committee on the Rights of the Child expresses its concern that 'the Plan of Action lacks a specific monitoring and evaluation system'.[132] The Committee on the Elimination of Discrimination against Women also calls on Nepal to strengthen its monitoring mechanisms for the implementation of plans of action aimed at achieving de facto equality between women and men, and the development of a comprehensive gender indicator system, with a view to improving the collection of sex-disaggregated data as a means of assessing the impact and effectiveness of plans aimed at mainstreaming gender equality and enhancing women's enjoyment of their human rights.[133]

In contrast, another group of plans such as the Tanzanian NHRAP (2013–2017) clarified its monitoring mechanisms in greater depth.[134] This plan required each of the implementing actors and organizations responsible for implementing sections of the plan to provide a progressive report to the Commission on Human Rights and Good Governance (CHRAGG), as the central monitoring body, setting out broad

at para 41; UN Committee on Economic, Social, and Cultural Rights (CESCR), General Comment No 18: The Right to Work (Art 6 of the Covenant), 6 February 2006, E/C.12/GC/18, at para 38; UN Committee on Economic, Social, and Cultural Rights (CESCR), General Comment No 19: The right to social security (Art 9 of the Covenant), 4 February 2008, E/C.12/GC/19, at para 68; UN Committee on Economic, Social, and Cultural Rights (CESCR), General Comment No 12: The Right to Adequate Food (Art 11 of the Covenant), 12 May 1999, at para 29.

130 UNOHCHR, Handbook on National Human Rights Plans of Action, note 51 at 20.

131 National Action Plan on Human Rights: The protection and promotion of human rights within the Netherlands, note 40; National Human Rights Action Programme of Mongolia (2003), note 82, Brazil, National Action Plan for Human Rights (1996), note 103; Ecuador, National Human Rights Program (1998), note 11; Action Plan for the Implementation of the Human Rights Roadmap (HRRM) For Somalia 2015–2016, note 118; Bolivia. National Plan of Action for the Promotion and Protection of Human Rights in the Medium and Long Term (1999) <http://www.ohchr.org/EN/Issues/PlansActions/Pages/PlansofActionIndex.aspx> accessed 12 January 2013.

132 CRC, Consideration of reports submitted by States parties under Article 44 of the Convention: Convention on the Rights of the Child: Concluding Observations: Italy, 31 October 2011, CRC/C/ITA/CO/3-4, at para 10.

133 CEDAW, Concluding Observations of the Committee on the Elimination of Discrimination against Women: Nepal, CEDAW/C/NPL/CO/4-5, 29 July 2011, at para 14.

134 Tanzania, National Action Plan for Human Rights (2013–2017) <http://www.ohchr.org/EN/Issues/PlansActions/Pages/PlansofActionIndex.aspx> accessed 28 December 2017.

and specific objectives, the performance indicators, what the implementing actor has done to achieve the objectives, and how their activity satisfies the performance indicators.[135]

In between, a number of action plans such as the Iraqi NHRAP (2011), Finnish NHRAP (2012–2013), Swedish NHRAP (2006–2009), and Chinese NHRAP (2012–2015) included follow up and monitoring mechanisms though in a general way and with rather vague wording.[136]

The lack of monitoring mechanisms is an important issue in the case of National Action Plans on Women, Peace, and Security and National Action Plans on Business and Human Rights as well. Whereas Finland (2010), Ireland (2011–2014), Canada (2012–2013), and Norway (2012), for example, released annual/progress reports on the implementation of their National Action Plan on Women, Peace, and Security and made them publically available, some countries such as Uganda and the Philippines, did not release any comprehensive progress report during the implementation phase. In the case of the National Action Plan on Business and Human Rights, similarly, some plans such as the UK and Finnish National Action Plan on Business and Human Rights established some sort of monitoring mechanisms, though many others such as the Dutch and Danish NAPs failed to do so.[137]

2.5.2. Lack of evaluation problem

Evaluation means that the achievement of the plan's goals is systematically assessed with a view to laying the foundation for a successor plan.[138] Towards the end of the life of the plan, the plan's achievements and challenges should be assessed and recommendations should be made for subsequent plans.[139] Most states, nonetheless, have failed to develop any mechanism for evaluating their plans. Examples include Russia, Turkey, Greece, Somalia, and Australia. In the case of Russia, the Committee on the Elimination of Racial Discrimination was concerned that specific evaluation mechanisms have not yet been established through the adoption of an action

[135] United Republic of Tanzania National Human Rights Action Plan 2013–2017, note 97, at 55.

[136] The Iraqi National Human Rights Action Plan (2011), note 29, Finland, National Action Plan on Fundamental and Human Rights 2012–2013, note 107; Sweden's National Action Plan for Human Rights (2006–2009), note 82; National Human Rights Action Plan of China (2012–2015) <http://news.xinhuanet.com/english/china/2012-06/11/c_131645029.htm> accessed 23 January 2016.

[137] United Kingdom, Good Business: Implementing the UN Guiding Principles on Business and Human Rights <https://www.gov.uk/government/uploads/system/uploads/attachment_data/file/236901/BHR_Action_Plan_-_final_online_version_1_.pdf> accessed 20 March 2017; Finland, Ministry of the Employment and the Economy, National Action Plan for the implementation of the UN Guiding Principles on Business and Human Rights (2014) <http://tem.fi/documents/1410877/3084000/National%20action%20plan%20for%20the%20implementation%20of%20the%20UN%20guiding%20pronciples%20on%20business%20and%20human%20rights/1bc35feb-d35a-438f-af56-aec16adfcbae> accessed 5 April 2016.

[138] UNOHCHR, Handbook on National Human Rights Plans of Action, note 51, at 41.

[139] ibid, at 20.

plan.[140] Also, the Committee on Economic, Social, and Cultural Rights noted the lack of information on the impact of, and the results achieved by, the Gender Equality National Action Plan of Turkey (2008–2013) and requests the state party to include, in its next periodic report, information on the outcomes of the monitoring and evaluation of the Gender Equality National Action Plan.[141] Similarly, the Committee on the Elimination of Discrimination against Women was concerned at the lack of information on its effective implementation of the National Action Plan to combat trafficking for 2010–2012 in Greece.[142] Likewise, no mechanism can be found for monitoring and evaluation of the NHRAP of Somalia (2015–2016) and the first two NHRAPs of Australia.

In the case of National Action Plans on Women, Peace, and Security, only a few countries such as Ireland (2011–2014) and the United Kingdom (2013) released a final evaluation report on the implementation of their plan. Needless to say that developing a plan without any proper mechanisms for monitoring and evaluation can lead to a huge difference between the plan on the papers and the plan in reality.[143] This problem is also seen across National Action Plans on Business and Human Rights. For instance, the Dutch National Action Plan on Business and Human Rights failed to specify any follow up procedures for implementation of the actions identified in the plan. In the case of Denmark, although there is a reference to the fact that Denmark's earlier CSR NAP will be continually updated, it is not clear how or when that will happen.[144]

Having identified major problems of NHRAPs in different phases, the next step is to ascertain the underlying causes of the problems.

3. Root Cause Analysis of the Problems

So far, seventeen problems have been identified in the pre-phase and the four phases of planning. Although the causes of these problems are various and may differ from time to time and case to case, there seems to be some causes that tend to be common, more or less, in a wide range of cases. These include the lack of political will, the lack

[140] CERD, Concluding Observations on the 20th to the 22nd periodic reports of the Russian Federation, adopted by the Committee at its 82nd session, 11 February–1 March 2013: Committee on the Elimination of Racial Discrimination, 17 April 2013, CERD/C/RUS/CO/20–22, at para 15.

[141] CESCR, Consideration of reports submitted by States parties under Articles 16 and 17 of the Covenant E/C.12/TUR/CO/1, Forty Sixth session, 12 July 2011, at para 14; Republic of Turkey Prime Ministry: General Directorate on the Status of Women. National Action Plan: Gender Equality (2008–2013). Ankara 2008 <http://www.huksam.hacettepe.edu.tr/English/Files/NAP_GE.pdf> accessed 25 March 2016.

[142] CEDAW, Concluding Observations on the seventh periodic report of Greece adopted by the Committee at its fifty fourth session (11 February–1 March 2013) CEDAW/C/GRC/CO/7, 1 March 2013, at para 22.

[143] James Simmie, *Planning at the Crossroads* (1st edn, Routledge 1993); Ernest Alexander, *Evaluation in Planning: Evolution and Prospects. Contributions in Honour of Nathaniel Lichfield* (1st edn, Ashgate 2006).

[144] ICAR and European Coalition for Corporate Justice, 'Assessments of Existing National Action Plans (NAPs) on Business and Human Rights', note 17, at 6.

of social will, social inequalities, traditional planning, lack of stakeholder awareness of various features of NHRAPs, lack of systemic relative autonomy among the major systems of society (polity, culture, community, economy), and cultural particularism. Since dealing with all these factors stands well beyond the scope of this chapter, here, I will concentrate on three of them: the traditional model of planning, lack of stakeholder awareness, and lack of political will.

3.1. Traditional model of planning

An invisible factor underlying many of the above-mentioned problems is the traditional model of planning upon which most of the existing NHRAPs are based. As discussed in Chapter 1, this state-centric model of planning has a very shaky ground in that it is not only theory-neutral but also directed from the top down.[145] It assumes that the political establishment is perfect and there is a general agreement on values in society.[146] As John Friedmann states:

> The old view of planning was of a relatively static world in which planners were objective analysts who had access to pertinent knowledge about the future and could effectively communicate what they knew to political decision-makers through written documents, such as policy drafts or a plan. The articulation of values implicit in this view was not the planners' responsibility but politicians'. Planning was understood to be essentially a technical, value-free activity in the public realm.[147]

All the materials, directly or indirectly concerned with NHRAPs, reflect the fact that the traditional concept of planning is still the predominant model in international human rights law. For example, Article 2 of the International Covenant on Economic, Social, and Cultural Rights (ICESCR), which is of vital importance in the case of NHRAPs, has provided a broad discretion for states to formulate the necessary steps/measures for implementing human rights from the top down (see Chapter 4). Whilst the UN Committee on Economic, Social, and Cultural Rights requires states to show 'the progress achieved' and the difficulties encountered, it has not established a clear understanding of the 'appropriate measures' and the criteria against which these measures can be evaluated. As explored in Chapter 4, this unlimited discretion of the states, as a general pattern, can be found across other human rights treaties. By the same token, the Vienna Declaration, as another most relevant source here, does not precisely describe what is required for a plausible NHRAP. It states that:

> The World Conference on Human Rights recommends that each State consider the desirability of drawing up a national action plan identifying steps whereby that State would improve the promotion and protection of human rights.[148]

[145] See Azadeh Chalabi, 'The Problem-Oriented Approach to Improving National Human Rights Action Plans' (2015) 7(2) Oxford Journal of Human Rights Practice 272–98.

[146] ibid.

[147] John Friedmann, *Insurgencies: Essays in Planning Theory* (1st edn, Routledge 2011) at 15.

[148] UN General Assembly, Vienna Declaration and Programme of Action, 12 July 1993, A/CONF.157/23, at para 71 <http://www.refworld.org/docid/3ae6b39ec.html> accessed 21 January 2018.

As Bill Barker, the author of the UN handbook on NHRAPs, argues, this paragraph 'gives little guidance as to what the structure or content of such a plan might be. The idea of voluntarism was implicit in the formulation, but the rest was left up to each state to fill in for itself'.[149] It is thus hardly surprising that governments can invoke the vagueness of these documents and sometimes creatively develop NHRAPs in accordance with their own political ideology and at other times brazenly skip some significant rights from their plans.

All in all, the traditional model of planning, to a greater or lesser extent, causes most of the above-mentioned problems. Let me start with the baseline study problem. To conduct a baseline study requires a set of criteria against which to assess the status of human rights in the country concerned, that is, the diagnosis of the current problems depends on an image of the desired state which acts as a point of reference. This set of criteria is derived from substantive, contextual, and analytical theories of human rights planning. However, the traditional planning upon which most plans are based is theoretically baseless. Planning theories provide a set of general criteria for initiating baseline study, and then, based on the evidence collected during baseline study, planners can construct or modify their special theory of planning taking into consideration spatio-temporal factors. It means that logically an 'abductive approach'[150] may need to be adopted here, that is, there might be a back-and-forth between special theory and evidence in order to improve the special theory of planning where necessary.

Bearing in mind that baseline study, monitoring, and evaluation are closely connected, the lack of monitoring mechanism and lack of evaluation mechanism can be seen as other outcomes of a theoretically baseless planning. Monitoring and evaluation are aimed at the collection and analysis of information to track changes from baseline to the desired outcome (see Chapters 1 and 2). Without planning theory, there would be no frame of reference for conducting baseline studies, developing the content, prioritization, monitoring, and evaluating NHRAPs. As Jim Ife holds:

> Theory and practice cannot be understood separately but are part of each other; in fact neither makes sense without the other. If practice is totally divorced from theory it leads to an unthinking anti-intellectualism. Frames of reference and critical reflection are gone and one simply does, for the sake of doing.[151]

Another difficulty which stems from the traditional model of planning is the supporting the status quo problem. Traditional planning is criticized not merely because of its anti-democratic manner of planning from the top down. Many also have

[149] Barker, Protecting, Promoting and Fulfilling Human Rights in Australia: A National Human Rights Action, note 58, at 7.

[150] See Stefan Timmermans and Iddo Tavory, 'Theory Construction in Qualitative Research: From Grounded Theory to Abductive Analysis' (2012) 30(3) Sociological Theory 167–86 <http://journals.sagepub.com/doi/abs/10.1177/0735275112457914> accessed 27 January 2018.

[151] Jim Ife, *Human Rights from Below: Achieving Rights through Community Development* (1st edn, Cambridge University Press 2009) at 208.

disagreed with this model because it encourages 'acceptance of the status quo and support of the current political establishment'.[152]

The ideological orientation problem, non-correspondence problem, and incomprehensiveness problem likewise can be seen as a result of traditional planning. Whilst international human rights law could establish an internationally agreed frame of reference to guide the substance and the process of NHRAPs, the current situation of these plans is theoretically debased and a number of states simply develop NHRAPs for the sake of doing them and as a kind of window dressing. They start planning with no or little ideologically free concept of an appropriate societal environment for implementing human rights. This weakness can reinforce the limited political will of states to develop a NHRAP in accordance with international human rights standards and makes it much easier for governments to get around their international human rights commitments. In other words, a theoretically baseless model of planning is like an empty box which can be filled from top down by any political ideologies ranging from fascism and populism to neoliberalism. Depending on the nature of the state, it is shaped differently. Hence, this paternalistic model is always criticized for its bias toward central control in the definition of problems and solutions, in the evaluation of alternatives, and in the implementation of decisions.

Some problems in particular, the participation problem, the lack of transparency problem, and the lack of accountability problem are mostly rooted in the lack of procedural theory of human rights planning discussed in Chapter 2. Likewise, the lack of co-ordination problem is due to the fact that most plans explored in this cross-case analysis have not adopted a systemic approach as elaborated in our contextual theory of planning in Chapter 1.

In sum, there is a need to shift from the traditional planning which is top-down, state centric, and theoretically baseless to a participatory, top-down bottom-up, and theory-laden planning.

3.2. Lack of stakeholder awareness

An effective development, implementation, monitoring, and evaluation of a NHRAP can only be achieved through an informed and continued demand by, and meaningful participation of stakeholders. As the UN Handbook emphasizes, 'if the plan is to be effective, it is crucial that all relevant actors as well as the general public are aware of it and give it their support'.[153] At present, however, the lack of awareness of various aspects of the NHRAPs can be found among many levels of stakeholders, ranging from the local to the global level and this can lead to, or reinforce most of the difficulties explored in this chapter.

Firstly, whereas general public awareness and support is fundamental for formulating and implementing NHRAPs, basic knowledge of these plans is unquestionably

[152] Walter Schonwandt, *Planning in Crisis? Theoretical Orientations for Architecture and Planning* (1st edn, Ashgate 2008) at 6.

[153] UNOHCHR, Handbook on National Human Rights Plans of Action, note 51, at 88.

non-existent among the public and remains isolated from the media. Increasing public awareness of NHRAPs is a core element of any successful development and implementation of them in practice. To enhance people's participation in developing and implementing these plans, there should be an effective mechanism to transmit basic knowledge of such plans and foster its integration into public values in advance.

Secondly, bearing in mind that the obligation to adopt a NHRAP dates back to 1966 in the ICESCR, the necessary knowledge and skills for developing and implementing these plans are little known even in academic circles and among those who are expected to be directly or indirectly associated with developing, implementing, and/or evaluating these plans, such as NGOs, NHRIs, human rights practitioners, government agencies, and human rights lawyers. Human rights practitioners and civil society actors are typically unaware of such plans' potentials. They are unfamiliar with the different phases of NHRAPs and the way by which they can participate in developing, implementing, and monitoring these plans. At the academic level, for instance, too little literature can be found on NHRAPs. At the practical level, likewise, there is merely one 108-page practical handbook on NHRAP, released by the OHCHR in 2002, which is not yet available in any language other than English and is not any more up to date. Moreover, that handbook is prepared on the basis of the idea of action plans for implementing human rights in accordance with paragraph 71 of the Vienna Declaration and Programme of Action, and, therefore, it contains no mention of action plans as required by the ICESCR and other human rights treaties. It therefore takes the view that the states are only recommended (not required) to develop any plan of action.[154] It is unfortunate that no more guidance has been released by the UN on the fulfilment of the state's obligation to adopt a NHRAP as required under international human rights treaties.

Thirdly, whereas NHRAPs should, among others, target disadvantaged and marginalized individuals and groups and empower them to participate in developing NHRAPs, there is effectively no special mechanism dedicated to informing them on the way in which they can participate in designing such plans.[155] As media coverage is very poor, vulnerable groups, as part of the whole society, are typically unaware of the existence of such plans, let alone providing opportunities to become involved in the process of developing and evaluating such plans.

Fourthly and more surprisingly, even at the international level, the potentials of NHRAPs and the form and substance of such plans have not been systematically and adequately reflected through the work of the UN human rights bodies, and this failure can increasingly reinforce the low level of stakeholder awareness of the NHRAPs at the national level. Whereas treaty bodies constantly have stressed the states' obligation to adopt a NHRAP (see Chapter 3), they have failed to clarify systematically how to fulfil this obligation and what measures need to be identified in these plans (see Chapter 4).

[154] ibid, at 16.

[155] See CESCR, General Comment No 20, note 129, at paras 38–39; CESCR, General Comment No 18, note 129, at paras 18 and 31(C); CESCR, General Comment No 14, note 129, at para 54; CESCR, General Comment No 19, note 129, at para 68.

Moreover, treaty bodies have failed to address this obligation systematically by way of Concluding Observations. The UN Committee on the Rights of the Child, in some of its Concluding Observations (for example, in the cases of Afghanistan, the United Kingdom, and Singapore—under the 'main area of concern and recommendation'), has provided an independent subtitle 'National Plan of Action', in order to investigate the obligation to adopt a NHRAP. For the sake of example, in the case of Singapore, it states that:

> [the Committee] is concerned that the strategies are rarely accompanied by concrete action plans for implementation. The Committee remains concerned that the State party has not developed a comprehensive national plan of action (NPA) for the implementation of the Convention.[156]

But in some other cases, such as Ukraine, the Committee has not even mentioned such plans.[157] As Alston notes, this weakness is a result of the ineffectual working methods used by the treaty bodies.[158] It is unfortunate that treaty bodies' outputs vary considerably from one case to other both in form and substance. As will be discussed in the next chapter, there is a need to put an end to the fragmented and unpredictable way in which the UN human rights treaty bodies currently work.

Another related weakness in the UN human rights treaty system which can exacerbate the low level of awareness of NHRAPs among stakeholders is that treaty bodies' views with respect to NHRAPs vary from each other, to the extent that there sometimes even appears to be no concurrence over what a NHRAP is for and where such plans stand in the whole international human rights system. This inconsistency can possibly reinforce the non-compliance problem, the non-correspondence problem, and the lack of co-ordination problem discussed above. This is because there is currently little connection among the treaty body reporting processes. As O'Flaherty generally notes, governments may have to sometimes deal with inconsistent or even contradictory recommendations released by different treaty bodies.[159] O'Flaherty further argues that the 'weakness of such fragmented and mutually unsupportive approaches appear to be obvious in terms of diminished impact and missed opportunities'.[160]

Likewise, the importance of NHRAPs is not the same in all committees and needs to be aligned. For example, whereas the UN Committee on the Rights of the Child

[156] CRC, Consideration of Reports submitted by States Parties under Article 44 of the Convention, Singapore, CRC/C/SGP/CO/2-3, 4 May 2011, at para 12.

[157] CRC, Concluding Observations: Afghanistan. CRC/C/AFG/CO/1, 4 February 2011; CRC, Concluding Observations: Ukraine, CRC/C/OPAC/UKR/CO/1, 21 April 2011; CRC, Concluding Observations: United Kingdom of Great Britain and Northern Ireland, note 27.

[158] Philip Alston, 'Beyond "Them" and "Us": Putting Treaty Body Reform into Perspective' in P Alston and J Crawford (eds), *The Future of UN Human Rights Treaty Monitoring* (1st edn, Cambridge University Press 2000) 501–27; see also, Egan, 'Strengthening the United Nations Human Rights Treaty Body System', note 43.

[159] Michael O'Flaherty, 'Towards Integration of United Nations Human Rights Treaty Body Recommendations: The Rights-Based Approach Model' in M A Baderin and R McCorquodale (eds), *Economic, Social, and Cultural Rights in Action* (1st edn, Oxford University Press 2007) at 30.

[160] ibid.

has often emphasized the importance of NHRAPs in its Concluding Observations, the UN Committee against Torture rarely refers to these plans.[161] It seems that these plans would only be investigated by the Committee against Torture if the given state has already developed a plan.[162]

As will be discussed in Chapter 6, the fragmented nature of the UN treaty bodies is problematic as it has led to inconsistent or contradictory recommendations which can pave the way for problems such as the 'tardiness problem' and the 'ideological orientation problem'.

Taken together, raising stakeholder awareness as a response strategy can influence implementing human rights through NHRAPs in many ways. First, it can promote understanding of the rationale of such NHRAPs among the public and practitioners. Second, raising awareness can help the more effective monitoring of existing NHRAPs in a way that a halt can be called to illegitimate and perverse plans. Third, it can also help secure more effective participation in all stages of planning. It can significantly enable those communities most affected to participate in developing NHRAPs. Fourth, raising stakeholders awareness can help secure the accountability of human rights actors with respect to NHRAPs.

3.3. Lack of political will

Lack of political will is at the core of most problems discussed above. In an online survey conducted by the author, 74% of respondents who are experts in NHRAPs, in reaction to an open-ended question about the root cause preventing most countries from adopting a NHRAP for implementing human rights, put their finger on the lack of political will.[163]

Whereas any failure to adopt NHRAPs constitutes a violation (see Chapter 3), ironically the key role of states in deciding on the appropriateness of developing NHRAPs—as well as the form and the substance of such plans—has come to be viewed as a normal and legitimate way of planning in international human rights law. Reliance on states and leaving human rights planning entirely up to them (who

[161] UN Committee against Torture, Concluding Observations: Australia, CAT/C/ AUS/CO/3, 22 May 2008; UN Committee against Torture, Conclusions and Recommendations: Costa Rica. CAT/C/ CRI/CO/2, 7 July 2008.

[162] Similar difficulties can be observed in the UN Charter-based mechanisms, and in particular the Universal Periodic Review (UPR) during which each state must be assessed against its overall human rights obligations. Take the UPR national report as an example. The national report of the state for the UPR must be prepared on the basis of general guidelines adopted by the UN Human Rights Council at its sixth session in September 2007. Nonetheless, the Human Rights Council has failed to name NHRAPs as an important element in every national human rights system when it lists national human rights framework and infrastructure. Despite the fact that every state, under the nine core human rights treaties, is obliged to adopt a NHRAP, these plans are brought up in the process of the UPR only if the country under review has already developed or promised to develop such plans.

[163] This online survey was conducted by this author in April–June 2013 as part of another research project on 'Australia's National Human Rights Action Plans in Practice'. Participants, who were experts on NHRAPs, were identified from four main groups, ie governmental organizations; NGOs; academic organizations; and independent consultants. See Chalabi, 'Australia's National Human Rights Action Plans: Traditional or Modern Model of Planning?', note 10.

are at the same time also the principal duty bearer) would be fairly senseless. State monopoly in preparing, implementing, and evaluating NHRAPs will also open the door to corruption and violation of human rights.[164] The absence of intergovernmental organizations, national and international human rights NGOs and NHRIs, as key participants in monitoring NHRAPs alongside states, increases the likelihood of violation by the states.

The traditional notion of hierarchical, top-down government has always been an imperfect match for implementing the universal idea of human rights. Even at the supranational level, despite significant efforts to incorporate non-state actors in global human rights governance, it still remains largely state-centric. Apart from states' unwillingness, the crux of the matter is that states alone are sometimes unable to address many of the human rights-related challenges—such as the environmental crisis, immigration, growing inequality, conflict-related issues—which are crossing sovereign boundaries. This point is of particular importance in the area of business and human rights. The rise of the modern corporation has brought a concentration of economic power which can compete on equal terms with the political power of the state.[165] Of the 100 largest economies in the world, fifty-one are corporations; only forty-nine are countries.[166] As Shields argues:

> State power has been hollowed out by corporate power and states often do not have the strength to refuse the will of corporate interests. Not only do the Guiding Principles rely on an out-dated faith in state sovereignty but they also negate any progress towards the evolution of third generation extraterritorial human rights responsibilities. The UN Guiding Principles explicitly entrench the status quo of human rights obligations as exclusively state-held duties to protect against human rights abuses by non-state actors, including by business, affecting persons within their territory or jurisdiction.[167]

In the extant state-centric model of governance, it comes as no surprise that NGOs, NHRIs, and at-risk groups are not often actively and meaningfully involved in the process of designing, implementing, and evaluating action plans and policies.

These chronic challenges call for new approaches to human rights governance. Realizing human rights demands a multi-layered model of governance. The idea of a networked model of governance appears to be a plausible response strategy for addressing or mitigating the lack of political will. Unlike conventional government-led actions to further citizen participation, in networked governance the scope of

[164] See Rose-Ackerman, *International Handbook on the Economics of Corruption*, note 125; Susan Rose-Ackerman, *Corruption and Government: Causes, Consequences, and Reform* (1st edn, Cambridge University Press 1999).

[165] Patricia Feeney, 'Business and Human Rights: The struggle for accountability in the UN and the future direction of the advocacy agenda' (2009) V 6, N 11, Dec, 161–75, 165; see Julian Arato, 'Corporations as Lawmakers' (2015) 56(2) Harvard International Law Journal 229.

[166] Manfred B Steger, *Globalisation: A Very Short Introduction* (2nd edn, Oxford University Press 2008) at 51.

[167] Kirsteen Shields, 'Ethical Trade Networks as a Catalyst for Corporate Compliance with Human Rights' in M Fenwick, S Van Uytsel, and S Wrbka (eds), *Networked Governance, Transnational Business and the Law* (1st edn, Springer 2014) at 130; see Nicholas Connolly and Manette Kaisershot 'Corporate power and human rights' (2015) 19:6 International Journal of Human Rights 663–72 <DOI: 10.1080/13642987.2015.1074458> accessed 21 January 2017.

cooperation is not defined solely by government. Instead, in networks all stakeholders, directly or indirectly, can provide inputs to the identification of problems, the investigation of options, the development of solutions, and monitoring and evaluation of the plan.[168] The idea of advancing a networked model of governance for implementing human rights and its feasibility will be discussed in the next chapter.

[168] See eg Keith G Provan and Patrick Kenis, 'Modes of Network Governance: Structure, Management, and Effectiveness' (2007) 18 JPART 229–52.

PART IV

PRACTICAL PERSPECTIVES

6

A Networked Model of Global Governance for Implementing Human Rights

1. Introduction

Global human rights governance architecture as it currently stands is not only *state-centric* but also *fragmented*; two significant problems that have undermined its effectiveness in implementing human rights in practice. While global governance is expected to play a key role in mitigating various global problems such as the environmental crisis (global warning, pollution, natural resource depletion, deforestation, etc), growing inequality, conflict-related issues, and the rise of populism, there is almost no conclusive evidence. It is now widely accepted that the international human rights 'system' needs to be redesigned in order to work as an integrated 'system'. More specifically, we can talk about what I would call the 'UN five-gap problem'. The gaps are between: (1) the Universal Periodic Review (UPR), treaty bodies, and the Special Procedures; (2) human rights treaty bodies *inter se*; (3) the UN development programming and UN human rights bodies; (4) national human rights actors and the UN human rights bodies; and (5) the UN human rights bodies and regional human rights systems. The lack of an integrated system of operations in such a state-centric governance framework can not only decrease the overall performance of global human rights governance but also exacerbate the problem of the lack of political will of the states to implement human rights.

These pressing challenges call for new approaches to global human rights governance. The present chapter is a preliminary attempt to explore the idea of a networked model of global governance as a promising way to address the UN five-gap problem enhancing the overall functioning of the international human rights 'system'. This chapter proceeds as follows. The first section examines the UN five-gap problem. The networked model of governance as a possible response strategy is suggested in the second section. Then, the question of who are required to be included in a global-wide network for implementing human rights is addressed. It then explores the role of network facilitator and suggests orchestration as a powerful practical strategy which can be approached by a facilitator and other network partners in certain circumstances. Afterwards, the idea of developing an international human rights action plan as a roadmap through which network activities can be crystallized is proposed. Finally the four types of accountability mechanisms in a global human rights network are briefly examined.

2. The UN Five-Gap Problem

Whereas all human rights bodies and mechanisms must act in synergy to realize human rights, the effectiveness of global governance in addressing human rights challenges is hindered by the system's fragmentation. There is an increasing recognition that the UN human rights system is disintegrated and hardly works like a 'system'.[1] At least five gaps can be identified in the international human rights system in particular the UN human rights architecture. These gaps are described as follows.

2.1. The gap among the UPR, treaty bodies, and the Special Procedures

Under the present arrangements, there is no effective and systematic mechanisms to link the outcome of the Universal Periodic Review process with recommendations of treaty bodies and the Special Procedures. In the absence of consolidation of treaty bodies, the Special Procedures and the UPR's recommendations into a unified position, the UN human rights system cannot work efficiently. For example, there is an absence of follow-up mechanism of the recommendations of UPR through other human rights bodies and this can render the process somewhat ineffective. As Surya Subedi states:

> Although the UPR subjects all member States of the UN to a 4-yearly scrutiny, most States with a dubious human rights record seem to have learned how to 'play the game' within the Human Rights Council ... Many countries were willing to accept most, if not all, of the UPR recommendations. This is most likely because there is no proper mechanism to follow up the extent to which those recommendations accepted are subsequently implemented by the State under review and the State has another 4 years before it will be called upon again to report the progress made.[2]

Hence, it comes as no surprise if their operations would create internal contradictions leading to failure or paradoxical outcomes. As Nigel Rodley says, 'the current

[1] See, eg, Michael O'Flaherty, 'Towards Integration of United Nations Human Rights Treaty Body Recommendations: The Rights-Based Approach Model' in Mashood Baderin and Robert McCorquodale (eds), *Economic, Social and Cultural Rights in Action* (Oxford University Press 2007); Homayoun Alizadeh, 'A Proposal for How to Realize Human Rights at the National and Regional Level: A Three-Pillar Strategy' (2011) 33(3) Human Rights Quarterly, 826–55, 830; Anne Gallagher, 'Making Human Rights Treaty Obligations a Reality: Working with New Actors and Partners' in P Alston and J Crawford (eds), *The Future of UN Human Rights Treaty Monitoring* (1st edn, Cambridge University Press 2000); Anne F Bayefsky, *The UN Human Rights Treaty System: Universality at the Crossroads* (1st edn, Martinus Nijhof 2001); Martti Koskenniemi and Päivi Leino, 'Fragmentation of International Law? Postmodern Anxieties' (2002) 15 Leiden Journal of International Law 553–79; Frank Biermann, Philipp Pattberg, Harro van Asselt, and Fariborz Zelli, 'The Fragmentation of Global Governance Architectures: A Framework for Analysis' (2009) 9 Global Environmental Politics 14–40; Joost Pauwelyn, Ramses A Wessel, and Jan Wouters, 'The Stagnation of International Law', Working Paper No 97, Leuven Centre for Global Governance Studies, October 2012, Social Science Research Network <http://ssrn.com/ abstract=2271862> accessed 23 April 2015.

[2] Surya P Subedi, *The Effectiveness of the UN Human Rights System: Reform and the Judicialisation of Human Rights* (1st edn, Routledge 2017) at 118.

challenge will be to find ways of indeed making the two processes [the UPR and treaty reporting] complementary and productive, rather than competitive and injurious to the promotion of the better enjoyment of human rights. This not insignificant dimension apart, the existence of the two systems cannot be properly understood as creating substantial duplication and overlap'.[3] It is important that the UN partners engage throughout a cycle. The treaty body process, as a cyclical engagement, should not be only limited to the dialogue in Geneva.[4] There should be a mutual sharing of information and expertise between the UPR, Special Procedures, and treaty body processes.

2.2. The gap between human rights treaty bodies *inter se*

Whereas human rights are interrelated, surprisingly the link among the UN human rights treaty bodies themselves remains remarkably weak. Treaty body after treaty body was established with no systematic relationship to each other. The result has been a burgeoning reporting burden, duplication of procedures, little effort to synchronize substantive outcomes, and rudimentary follow-up processes and responsibilities.[5] Speaking at the drafting meeting for the Dublin Statement, the then UN High Commissioner for Human Rights, Navanethem Pillay described the treaty body system as:

> facing at least two major challenges. The first is related to resources, while the second pertains to coherence . . . In fact, the impressive growth of the treaty body system, although very positive in absolute terms, has also adversely affected the coherence of the system and its ability to coordinate work. Various initiatives aimed at addressing these problems have had the unintended and perverse effect of creating additional and cumbersome layers. As a result, the system often seems paralyzed . . . (T)he treaty body end product, that is its sets of recommendations, at times can also appear unmanageable for States and other stakeholders . . . (P)redictably, the result is an overlap or even duplication of requests. Worse, at times recommendations from different human rights mechanisms contradict one another. This conundrum may weaken the very impact of treaty bodies at the country level.[6]

A lack of co-ordination and collaboration among the treaty bodies has not only raised serious concerns regarding the risk of conflicting or inconsistent recommendations but also provided significant difficulties in achieving synergies capable of producing the desired outcomes in the most administratively and cost effective manner.[7]

[3] Nigel Rodley, 'The United Nations Human Rights Council, Its Special Procedures, and Its Relationship with the Treaty Bodies: Complementarity or Competition?' in Kevin Boyle (ed), *New Institutions for Human Rights Protection* (1st edn, Oxford University Press 2009) 49–73, at 71.

[4] UNOHCHR, 'Consultation on treaty body strengthening with UN entities and specialized agencies', 28 November 2011, at 8 <https://www.ishr.ch/sites/default/files/article/files/report_of_the_consultation_with_un_entities_and_specialized_agencies.pdf> accessed 27 January 2018.

[5] Bayefsky, *The UN Human Rights Treaty System: Universality at the Crossroads*, above note 1.

[6] Navanethem Pillay, United Nations High Commissioner for Human Rights, Dublin Statement, 19 December 2009 <http://www.ohchr.org/en/NewsEvents/Pages/DisplayNews.aspx?NewsID1/49642&LangID1/4E> accessed 24 March 2011.

[7] The Concept Paper on the High Commissioner's Proposal for a Unified Standing Treaty Body, 14 March 2006, HRI/MC/2006/2, at paras 16–26; O'Flaherty, 'Towards Integration of United Nations

2.3. The gap between UN development programming and UN human rights bodies

Despite significant progress in integrating human rights in the UN's development work, in particular the establishment of the United Nations Development Group's Human Rights Working Group (UNDG-HRWG),[8] the connection still needs to be tightened.[9] Most financial assistance, including that provided by the UN and its agencies—is often designed, executed, and evaluated in a human rights vacuum and thereby the opportunity to institutionalize international human rights standards is more or less wasted.[10] Still, no systematic connection exists between the Common Country Assessment (CCA),[11] United Nations Development Assistance Framework (UNDAF), and other UN development assistance programs, on the one hand, and the recommendations of the UN human rights bodies including the treaty bodies, the UPR process, and the Special Procedures, on the other.[12] Although some promising steps have been taken by the OHCHR through UNDG-HRWG, the UN Country Teams (UNCTs)[13] are not systematically involved in the

Human Rights Treaty Body Recommendations: The Rights-Based Approach Model', note 1, at 30; Helen Keller and Geir Ulfstein, 'Introduction' in Helen Keller and Geir Ulfstein (eds), *UN Human Rights Treaty Bodies: Law and Legitimacy* (1st edn, Cambridge University Press 2012) at 6.

[8] Recognizing the increased emphasis on human rights as a cornerstone of the Post-2015 development agenda, as well as renewed commitment by the UN system to uphold its human rights responsibilities, the UNDG transformed the Human Rights Mainstreaming mechanism into the Human Rights Working Group, effective as of January 2015. <http://www.ohchr.org/EN/NewYork/Pages/MainstreamingHR.aspx> accessed 8 October 2016.

[9] The United Nations Development Group (UNDG) unites the UN funds, programmes, specialized agencies, departments, and offices that play a role in development in over 160 countries. The UNDG was constituted in 1997 following the UN General Assembly's endorsement of UN Secretary-General Kofi Annan's report 'Renewing the United Nations: A Programme of Reform' (A/51/950, at para 73).

[10] Gallagher, 'Making Human Rights Treaty Obligations a Reality: Working with New Actors and Partners', note 1, at 224.

[11] The Common Country Assessment analyses the national development situation and identifies key development issues with a focus on the Millennium Development Goals and the other commitments, goals, and targets of the Millennium Declaration.

[12] Alizadeh, 'A Proposal for How to Realize Human Rights at the National and Regional Level: A Three-Pillar Strategy', note 1, at 830.

[13] The UNCT encompasses all the entities of the UN system that carry out operational activities for development, emergency, recovery, and transition in programme countries. More specifically, the UNCTs unite 32 UN bodies. These bodies include: United Nations Development Programme (UNDP); United Nations Children's Fund (UNICEF); United Nations Population Fund (UNFPA); World Food Programme (WFP); Office of the High Commissioner for Human Rights (OHCHR); United Nations Women (UN Women); United Nations Office for Project Services (UNOPS); Joint United Nations Programme on HIV/AIDS (UNAIDS); United Nations Human Settlements Programme (UN Habitat); United Nations Office on Drugs and Crime (UNODC); World Health Organization (WHO); Department of Economic and Social Affairs (DESA); International Fund for Agricultural Development (IFAD); United Nations Conference on Trade and Development (UNCTAD); United Nations Educational, Scientific and Cultural Organization (UNESCO); Food and Agriculture Organization of the United Nations (FAO); United Nations Industrial Development Organization (UNIDO); International Labour Organization (ILO); United Nations Department of Public Information (UNDPI); Regional Commissions (ECA, ECE, ECLAC, ESCAP, ESCWA—rotating annually); Office of the High Representative for the Least Developed Countries, Landlocked Developing Countries & Small Island Developing Countries (OHRLLS); Special Representative of the Secretary-General for Children and Armed Conflict (SRSG/CAC); United Nations Environment

implementation process of treaty bodies, the Special Procedures, and UPR's recommendations.[14] As the representatives of the various UN entities and specialized agencies in their report notes, 'there is a general lack of understanding and awareness of the UNCTs about the treaty body system, particularly in cases where there is no OHCHR presence or human rights adviser in the country'.[15] They stress that there is 'a need to awaken the interest of the UNCTs and alert them to the added value of contributing to the work of the treaty bodies, including by using the treaty body Concluding Observations in areas where the UNCTs might experience difficulties in getting the governments on board'.[16]

2.4. The gap between national human rights actors and UN human rights bodies

Although these days through the provision of shadow reports and oral presentations, National Human Rights Institutions (NHRIs) and NGOs have begun to deepen their engagement with treaty bodies,[17] as Egan puts it, 'an obvious source of frustration for both groups, however, is the lack of coherence and alignment in the modes of engagement deployed by individual treaty bodies in interacting with them'.[18] Representatives of NHRIs are not always present during the 'constructive dialogue' and, when present, the role of NHRIs is often limited to providing comments as an 'advisor' to the official delegation but it comes nowhere close to the level of involvement required for an active and meaningful participation (see Chapters 2 and 7).[19] As stated in the report of the UN High Commissioner for Human Rights:

Programme (UNEP); United Nations High Commissioner for Refugees (UNHCR); Office of USG—Special Advisor on Africa (OSAA); United Nations World Tourism Organization (UNWTO); World Meteorological Organization (WMO); International Telecommunications Union (ITU); World Bank; United Nations Fund for International Partnerships; Office for the Coordination of Humanitarian Affairs; Spokesman for the Secretary-General.

[14] Alizadeh, 'A Proposal for How to Realize Human Rights at the National and Regional Level: A Three-Pillar Strategy', note 1, at 830.

[15] UNOHCHR, 'Consultation on treaty body strengthening with UN entities and specialized agencies', note 4, at 2.

[16] ibid at 2.

[17] While some treaty bodies, such as the Committee on the Rights of the Child, have sought to formalize their interaction with NGOs, others simply rely on informal briefings and written communications (see Andrew Clapham, 'The Use of International Human Rights Law by Civil Society Organizations' in N Rodley and S Sheeran (eds), *Routledge Handbook of International Human Rights Law* (1st edn, Routledge 2014)); CRC, 'Guidelines for the participation of partners (NGOs and individual experts) in the pre-sessional working group of the Committee on the Rights of the Child' (CRC/C/90, Annex VIII); The Concept Paper on the High Commissioner's Proposal for a Unified Standing Treaty Body, 14 March 2006, HRI/MC/2006/2, at paras 16–26).

[18] Suzanne Egan, 'Strengthening the United Nations Human Rights Treaty Body System' (2013) 13(2) Human Rights Law Review 209–43, 227; see Marrakech Statement on Strengthening the Relationship Between NHRIs and the Human Rights Treaty Body System, Marrakech, 9–10 June 2010 ('Marrakech Statement') <http://www2.ohchr.org/english/bodies/HRTD/docs/MarrakeshStatement_en.pdf> accessed 24 January 2018.

[19] See Gallagher, 'Making Human Rights Treaty Obligations a Reality: Working with New Actors and Partners', note 1 at 208.

the effective engagement of NHRIs and civil society organizations with the treaty body system is hampered by numerous factors including limited awareness, capacity and resources, the multiplicity of models of interactions with the treaty bodies, and in some cases alleged reprisals from the State party. Furthermore, as each treaty body has different engagement rules, national actors are not gaining from their experience, rather having to learn each time again how to cooperate with individual treaty bodies.[20]

As a result, opportunities to assist the growth of national-level human rights capacity have been more or less lost.[21] This indicates a significant 'orchestration' deficit in the work of international human rights regimes which will be discussed later in this chapter.

2.5. The gap between UN human rights bodies and regional human rights systems

A further gap that may be mentioned here is that of the UN human rights bodies and the regional human rights systems which can increase the risk of the development of inconsistent or contradictory systems of law and practice across regions.[22] As highlighted in the European parliament report:

> Although the main common goal of both the UN and the regional mechanisms is the enhancement of human rights protection throughout the world, cooperation between them remains often minimal, ineffective and at a technical rather than fully institutionalized. Moreover, besides missed opportunities, many areas covered by UN mechanism, especially in the case of thematic mandates, are covered by regional procedures as well. Even though these overlaps do not entail a weakening of human rights protection, in times of limited resources and insufficient capacities to address the burgeoning human rights issues, coordination and cooperation between the UN and the various regional human rights mechanism appears to be necessary.[23]

Although there is no systematic co-operation between the two, some sporadic good efforts have been made in particular from the side of the UN such as using the country reports of the Council of Europe Commissioner for Human Rights

[20] Navanethem Pillay, 'Strengthening the United Nations human rights treaty body system. A report by the United Nations High Commissioner for Human Rights', June 2012, at 65 <http://www2.ohchr.org/english/bodies/HRTD/docs/HCReportTBStrengthening.pdf> accessed 25 February 2017.

[21] See Michael O'Flaherty and Claire O'Brien, 'Reform of UN Human Rights Treaty Monitoring Bodies: A Critique of the Concept Paper on the High Commissioner's Proposal for a Unified Standing Treaty Body' (2007) 7:1 Human Rights Law Review 141–72, 143; Michael O'Flaherty, 'The United Nations Human Rights Treaty Bodies as Diplomatic Actors' in M O'Flaherty, Z Kędzia, A Müller, and G Ulrich (eds), *Human Rights Diplomacy: Contemporary Perspectives* (1st edn, Brill 2011).

[22] Michael O'Flaherty, 'Reform of the UN Human Rights Treaty Body System: Locating the Dublin Statement' (2010) 10(2) Human Rights Law Review 322; see also, HRC Res 6/20, 28 September 2007, A/HRC/6/20; HRC Res 12/15, 1 October 2009, A/HRC/12/15.

[23] European Parliament, Directorate-General for External Policies Policy Department, 'The Role of Regional Human Rights Mechanisms', 2010, at 27 <http://www.europarl.europa.eu/RegData/etudes/etudes/join/2010/410206/EXPO-DROI_ET(2010)410206_EN.pdf> accessed 21 December 2015.

in the UPR process or occasional (but not systematic) reference to the regional human rights jurisprudence (if there is a court established within the regional mechanism).

Moreover, while there is a clear rationale for collaboration among regional human rights systems *inter se* to define human rights challenges and implement coherent response strategies, no specific mechanism has been established to link these systems to each other.

In such a fragmented structure of regional and international human rights systems, it is hardly surprising that many states view the international human rights instruments as impotent and, therefore, often accede to or ratify them knowing that they do not intend to fully implement them.[24] Fragmentation can make a system inefficient reducing capacity and performance, and making difficult to optimize resources. What is required is a new governance model under which different human rights bodies and the fragmented system can become aligned through a coherent multi-layered network with varying degrees of non-hierarchical but systematic and coherent relations, out of which guided changes can evolve.

The next section will propose the idea of a networked model of global governance as a possible response strategy to narrow the gaps leading to greater integration of global human rights system which includes other (sub-)systems.

3. Networked Governance: A Promising Way Forward

The current mode of governance in the international human rights system is either hierarchical and hard[25] (mostly in the form of treaty-based governance, and rarely in the form of the Responsibility to Protect (RtoP) doctrine and the rules under Chapter VII of the UN Charter) or soft and collaborative (such as what is undertaken under UPR process and technical assistance of the UN agencies). The critical point is that both forms are centralized around the states and place them in the first line of defence against human rights violation and that affected groups, NGOs, and NHRIs play little or no substantive role in governance. As Cherif Bassiouni mentions, there is an inherent tension here: on the one hand this model is meant to recognize and vindicate rights, and on the other hand, the strength and effectiveness of its enforcement relies wholly on the will of the states who are themselves responsible for the violations identified in international human rights instruments.[26] John

[24] See Makau Mutua, 'Standard Setting in Human Rights: Critique and Prognosis' (2007) 29 Human Rights Quarterly 547–630, 573; Paul W Zagorski, *Comparative Politics: Continuity and Breakdown in the Contemporary World* (1st edn, Routledge 2009) at 55; Azadeh Chalabi, 'Law as a System of Rights: A Critical Perspective' (2013) 15(2) Human Rights Review 117–38.

[25] 'Hard' in a sense that they are often legally binding and mandatory.

[26] M Cherif Bassiouni, 'A Critical Introduction Assessment of the UN Human Rights Mechanisms' in M Cherif Bassiouni and W A Schabas (eds), *New Challenges for the UN Human Rights Machinery* (1st edn, Intersentia 2011) at 3.

Ruggie aptly says that if there is only one thing on which all governance scholars agree, it is that the hierarchical current governance model has limited utility in dealing with many of today's most significant human rights global challenges.[27] Although different reforms have been suggested, it is evident that the need for reform still remains as compelling as ever.

Unlike the predominant mode of international human rights governance which is state-centric and mostly hierarchical, the networked model of governance, suggested here, is based on multi-layered co-operation among 'a group of goal-oriented interdependent but autonomous actors that come together to produce a collective output (tangible or intangible) that no one actor could produce on its own'.[28] The networked model of governance for implementing human rights is a promising way to integrate various currently fragmented actors and stand-alone mechanisms established to implement human rights. It can mobilize a wide range of human rights actors and mechanisms in a coherent way addressing disparities and disintegration of human rights systems and contribute to ensuring optimum utilization of resources.

In its normative and prescriptive *gestalt*, the network model of governance is an institutional innovation for our time.[29] Over the last decade or so, networked governance has gained increasing prominence in different policy areas.[30] Networked governance moves from vertical to more horizontal modes of decision making and is characterized by systems of communications, knowledge exchange, and open dialogues. According to Eva Sorensen, the political systems slowly and gradually change from hierarchically organized unitary systems of government to more horizontally

[27] John Gerard Ruggi, 'Global Governance and "New Governance Theory": Lessons from Business and Human Rights' (2014) 20(1) Global Governance: A Review of Multilateralism and International Organizations: January–March 2014 5–17, at 8; see also Philip Alston, 'The Populist Challenge to Human Rights' (2017) 9 Journal of Human Rights Practice 1–15.

[28] Kimberly Isett, Ines Mergel, Kelly Leroux, Pamela Mischen, and Karl Rethemeyer, 'Networks in Public Administration Scholarship: Understanding Where We Are and Where We Need to Go' (2011) 21 (Suppl 1) Journal of Public Administration Research and Theory 157–73, at 161.

[29] Koppenjan and Klijn, 2004 cited in Nils Hertting and Evert Vedung, 'Purposes and criteria in network governance evaluation: How far does standard evaluation vocabulary takes us?' (2012) 18(1) Evaluation 27–46; Paul Fawcett and Carsten Daugbjerg, 'Explaining Governance Outcomes: Epistemology, Network Governance and Policy Network' (2012) 10 Political Studies Review 195–207; Michael Pirson and Shann Turnbull, 'Toward a More Humanistic Governance Model: Network Governance Structures' (2011) 99 Journal of Business Ethics 101–14; Eva Sørensen, 'Introduction Governance Network Research: Towards a Second Generation' in E Sørensen and J Torfing (eds), *Theories of Democratic Network Governance* (Houndmills: Palgrave 2007); Eva Sørensen and Jacob Torfing, 'Making Governance Networks Effective and Democratic through Metagovernance' (2009) 87(2) Public Administration 234–58.

[30] See Kimberley R Isett and Keith G Provan, 'The evolution of interorganizational network relationships over time: Does sector matter?' (2005) 15 Journal of Public Administration Research and Theory 149–65; Martino Maggetti and Fabrizio Gilardi, 'Network Governance and the Domestic Adoption of Soft Rules' (2014) 21:9 Journal of European Public Policy 1293–310; Keith G Provan and Patrick Kenis, 'Modes of Network Governance: Structure, Management, and Effectiveness' (2007) 18 JPART 229–52, 229; Patrick Kenis and Keith G Provan, 'The Control of Public Networks' (2006) 9 International Public Management Journal 227–47.

organized systems of networked governance that govern through the regulation of networks at different levels from the local to the global.[31]

Networked governance theory rests on the premise that none of the human rights relevant actors (it can be states, intergovernmental organizations, NGOs, NHRIs, etc) by itself can do all the heavy lifting required to meet most pressing human rights challenges and that they therefore need to engage other actors to leverage their capacities. As Reinicke and Deng stress, 'complementarity of resources is the key to the success of networks. Networks do not merely aggregate resources, but are structured to take advantage of the fact that each participating sector brings different resources to the fore'.[32] In this functional perspective, governance is accomplished through decentralized networks of various actors associated to governmental, non-governmental, and inter-governmental organizations.[33]

Ideally, in networks all relevant actors will be able to, directly or indirectly, provide inputs to the identification of problems and development of solutions.[34] The aim of network governance is to create synergies between different competences and sources of knowledge, legitimacy, voluntary energy, management, regulatory authority, capacity building, and financial resources in order to deal with complex and interlinked problems such as the non-realization of human rights. Networked model of governance seeks to integrate and harmonize different human rights related bodies and actors with different competencies in order to achieve common goals and optimum utilization of resources.

In such a soft mode of governance which is voluntary and decentralized, the state remains a significant player but not the predominant authority within the governance. Although there has been a clear shift in attitudes towards human rights standards by the states, moving from considerations of human rights as a matter of national sovereignty to a more universal concern, the network model of participation is not to erode state sovereignty.[35] As Julia Steets states:

> Some local and national governments are wary of engaging in forms of networked governance, because they feel this might erode their power and sovereignty. However, this view of

[31] Eva Sorensen, 'Democratic Theory and Network Governance' (2002) 24(4) Administrative Theory and Praxis 693–721.

[32] Wolfgang H Reinicke and Francis M Deng, 'The United Nations, Networks, and the Future of Global Governance', IDRC 2000, at 23–24 <http://www.gppi.net/fileadmin/user_upload/media/pub/2000/Reinicke_Deng-2000-Critical_Choices.pdf> accessed 21 February 2014.

[33] Tom Dedeurwaerdere (2005) 'The Contribution of Network Governance to Sustainable Development' <http://www.iddri.org/Evenements/Seminaires-reguliers/s13_dedeurwaerdere.pdf> accessed 9 March 2016; See Roger Gould, 'Why do networks matter? Rationalist and structuralist interpretations' in M Diani and D McAdam (eds), *Social Movements and Networks: Relational Approaches to Collective Action* (1st edn, Oxford University Press 2003); Gabriel A Huppé, Heather Creech, and Doris Knoblauch, 'The Frontiers of Networked Governance' (2012) The International Institute for Sustainable Development.<www.iisd.org> accessed 4 October 2016.

[34] See Martin Kilduff and Wenpin Tsai, *Social Networks and Organizations* (1st edn, Sage Press 2003); Provan and Kenis, 'Modes of Network Governance: Structure, Management, and Effectiveness', note 30.

[35] William O'Neill and Vegard Bye, 'From High Principles to Operational Practice: Strengthening OHCHR Capacity to Support UN Country Teams to Integrate Human Rights in Development Programming' (2002). Geneva: Geneva, Consultancy Report to the Office of the High Commissioner for Human Rights OHCHR, at 13.

'networked governance' misconceives its effects. Rather than limiting the power and effectiveness of traditional government institutions, networks are a way of reasserting some of the influence lost through the impacts of globalisation and falling public engagement in politics. It is by co-operating with other parties whose activities can help to solve complex public policy issues transcending national borders that governments regain some of their ability to solve problems and serve their communities.[36]

Networks are typically loose and self-governing structures. They are based on what is called 'structured informality', that is, keeping relationships loose and non-confining while at the same time building in enough organization and framework to get things done.[37] Global public policy networks are not just another attempt at bureaucratic organization building. Networks are flexible, adapting their structures and working procedures to the problem at hand as well as the stage reached in solving the problem and thus shaping them does not necessarily require very formal procedures.[38] Networks are dynamic in both process and structure and this gives them an advantage over hierarchies which are typically cumbersome. At present, the UN's bureaucratic system is rigid and therefore not effectively responsive to urgent human rights' needs.[39] This problem restricts its functionality in practice. Human rights networked governance must focus on maintaining the principle of structured informality through which various players, public or private, from the local to the global, can work with one another to achieve specific goals that require combined resources and expertise in a way that hierarchies alone could not readily accomplish.[40]

Because this model lacks a 'hard' element (ie regulations are not often legally binding), one may wonder how it can work effectively? There are different mechanisms through which networked governance can affect changes. These mechanisms of influence which are not mutually exclusive include, but are not limited to, shaming, diffusion through mimesis or discourse, deliberation, and learning.[41] There are also four types of accountability mechanisms which will be discussed later in this chapter.

[36] Julia Steets, 'Networks: Engaging Governance? The Case of Transparency International', Paper presented at the United Nations Interregional Workshop on 'Engaged Governance', Colombo, Sri Lanka, 9–11 December 2003, at 5; see also, Walter W Powell, Douglas R White, Kenneth W Koput, and Jason Owen-Smith, 'Network Dynamics and Field Evolution: The Growth of Interorganizational Collaboration in the Life Sciences' (2005) 110 American Journal of Sociology 1132–205; Erik-Hans Klijn and Chris Skelcher, 'Democracy and Governance Networks: Compatible or Not?' (2007) 85(3) Public Administration 587–608.

[37] Reinicke and Deng, 'The United Nations, Networks, and the Future of Global Governance', note 32, at xii.

[38] Steets, 'Networks: Engaging Governance? The Case of Transparency International', note 36.

[39] Bassiouni, 'A Critical Introduction Assessment of the UN Human Rights Mechanisms', note 26 at 11.

[40] Provan and Kenis, 'Modes of Network Governance: Structure, Management, and Effectiveness', note 30, at 244; see Naim Kapucu and Montgomery Van Wart, 'The evolving role of the public sector in managing catastrophic disasters: Lessons learned' (2006) 38 Administration and Society 279–308; Grace Skogstad, 'Legitimacy and/or Policy Effectiveness?: Network Governance and GMO Regulation in the European Union' (2003) 10(3) Journal of European Public Policy 321–38.

[41] See David M Trubek and Louise G Trubek, 'Hard and Soft Law in the Construction of Social Europe: the Role of the Open Method of Co-ordination' (2005) 11(3) European Law Journal 343–64, at 365, May 2005; Jelle Visser, 'Neither convergence nor frozen paths: bounded learning, international diffusion of reforms, and the open method of coordination' in M Heidenreich and J Zeitlin (eds), *Changing European Employment and Welfare Regimes: The Influence of the Open Method of Coordination on National Reforms* (1st edn, Routledge 2009) at 51.

One way to affect guided changes through networking is reputation loss through naming and shaming—what is also used in the current mode of human rights governance such as treaty-based human rights system.

Discursive diffusion is another mechanism of influence through networked governance.[42] This mechanism suggests that various processes through networking, such as the requirements for state and non-state reports, network partners meetings of various types, different monitoring efforts, the adoption of new theoretical frameworks and heuristic devices can transform human rights discourse and thus human rights planning and policy at the local, national, regional, and international levels. For example, one of the major effects of networking on human rights planning can be the adoption and diffusion of a shared planning theory for implementing human rights such as what is discussed in Chapters 1 and 2. This mechanism can also be used to transform current or form new conceptual frameworks upon which human rights instruments are based. As discussed in Chapter 2, despite an undeniable significant contribution of human rights treaties in the development of an international human rights system, in their current form, they are not grounded in a firm theoretical framework. This deficit has reduced the degree of comprehensiveness of these instruments, for instance, the omission of a very basic right to clean and accessible water or the right to safe and hygienic sanitation in the ICESCR. Lack of a firm theoretical base has also given rise to ambiguity in the identification of different types of rights such as the distinction between economic rights, social rights, and cultural rights. Diffusion through discourse can be used for the amendment and unification of existing human rights instruments and policies.

Change can also come about through the diffusion of continuous practical guidelines as implementation models (diffusion through mimesis), perhaps in the form of regional and international human rights action plans. As will be explored later in this chapter, this mechanism can put a coherent and comprehensive action-oriented policy model before different national, regional, and international actors who are one way or another involved in implementing human rights.

Moreover, through networking diverse sets of network partners at different levels can deliberate possible response strategies while exchanging different local and expert knowledge in order to deal with common problems in particular those that go beyond national borders such as human rights related issues of immigrants, workers, and environment. To this we can also add mutual learning of good practices. The emergence of a network of human rights actors can capitalize on a coherent and diverse body of knowledge and experience from both top-down and bottom-up. As Trubek and Mosher note policy learning can be facilitated by:

> mechanisms that destabilize existing understandings; bring together people with diverse viewpoints in settings that require sustained deliberation about problem-solving; facilitate erosion of boundaries between both policy domains and stakeholders; reconfigure policy networks; encourage decentralized experimentation; produce information on innovation; require sharing of good practice and experimental results; encourage actors to compare results

[42] Trubek and Trubek, ibid, at 365.

with those of the best performers in any area; and oblige actors collectively to redefine objectives and policies.[43]

These are all soft mechanisms of influence through networking. Nonetheless, the critical point is that the networked model of governance for implementing human rights is meant not to replace the legally-binding treaty-based system for human rights protection or different current mechanisms established by the Human Rights Council, but rather to complement them. A networked model of governance for implementing human rights seeks to be an instrument of integration among others, and can therefore be combined with and linked to other instruments and mechanisms of the implementation of human rights. Hence, we have to get beyond the idea that there must be a choice between these two. These forms of governance are not mutually incompatible, and perhaps the most promising ideas are those that would combine the two together. The regulatory power of the hierarchical mode of human rights governance currently performed lurks in the background. If necessary, it can step in with mandatory regulation, and the threat of such hierarchical intervention reinforces those soft mechanisms used in the networked model, including, among others, action-oriented measures identified in an international human rights action plans which will be dealt with shortly.

At this juncture, the question arises as to who are required to be included in a global-wide network for implementing human rights and how these partners can effectively co-operate?

4. Network Partners and Lead Bodies

There is no specific number that is likely to be 'correct' for a network model of governance and this is all flexible.[44] Nonetheless, networks must avoid falling into the trap of becoming just another institution, with an established bureaucracy and a rigid hierarchy. One way to dodge the institutional trap is to build the network as much as possible on existing institutions, keeping the network's own secretariat to a minimum.[45] Networking for implementing human rights does not necessarily imply full harmony among partners or the absence of any conflict, but only the common goal and interest to implement human rights.

Human rights network partners share and pursue the basic goal of implementing human rights as set forth in international human rights instruments. There are already a wide range of actors, bodies, and mechanisms involved in implementing

[43] David Trubek and James Mosher, 'New Governance, Employment Policy, and the European Social Model' in J Zeitlin and D M Trubek (eds), *Governing Work and Welfare in a New Economy: European and American Experiments* (1st edn, Oxford University Press 2003) at 46–47; see also David Trubeck, Patrick Cottell, and Mark Nance, 'Soft Law, Hard Law and the EU Integration' in Gráinne de Búrca and Joanne Scott (eds), *Law and New Governance in the EU and the US* (1st edn, Hart Publishing 2006) at 79.

[44] Provan and Kenis, 'Modes of Network Governance: Structure, Management, and Effectiveness', note 30, at 238.

[45] Reinicke and Deng, 'The United Nations, Networks, and the Future of Global Governance', note 32, at xii.

human rights from the local to regional and international levels, though in a fragmented way. These actors are often deficient in certain required capabilities for implementing human rights, yet possess certain capacities to offer such as regulatory competence, operational capacity, expertise, financial resources, technologies, or legitimate authority. Collaboration in networks creates synergy as well as regularity and predictability in the participants' relationships, generating a viable institutional framework for fruitful co-operation.[46] Building upon existing human rights bodies, in my view, a global-wide network for implementing human rights can include at least seven sets of partners:

1. States: One of the most important partners of a global-wide network for implementing human rights are the states. The enforcement capacity and rule making power are the most important sources shared by this set of partners.
2. UN human rights bodies: The second set of partners involves the UN human rights bodies, in particular, at a minimum, the OHCHR, treaty bodies, the Universal Periodic Review (UPR) Working Group, and the Special Procedures. This internationally legitimate set of partners can bring expertise and knowledge of human rights, as set forth in international human rights instruments, to the fore. This set of participants, as a sub-network, can be extended to other UN human rights bodies such as the UN Women, the International Labour Organization (ILO), and the UN working group on Business and Human Rights.
3. Technical and financial assistance agencies and programmes: The third set includes those who can offer technical and financial assistance for implementing human rights in a given country or region in particular UNDG Human Rights Working Group, the UNCTs (which encompass United Nations funds and programmes, the specialized agencies, and the World Bank), the Technical Cooperation Programme, and the non-UN aid donors. The work of such partners has a direct impact on the capacity of the states to implement their human rights commitments. This also refers to external assistance and support to NGOs and NHRIs for the purpose of strengthening national structures and institutions for implementing human rights.
4. Non-Governmental Organizations: The fourth set of partners for a global human rights network involves national and international non-governmental organizations who can provide their independent information, specialized local knowledge and expertise, and dedicate their voluntary energy to address human rights thematic issues.
5. National Human Rights Institutions: The fifth set of partners can encompass NHRIs as independent state sector institutions. If in full compliance with the Paris Principles, their unique status as state agency while being independent

[46] Reinicke and Deng, 'The United Nations, Networks, and the Future of Global Governance', note 32, at 23–24; see David Lazer, 'Global and Domestic Governance: Modes of Interdependence in Regulatory Policymaking' (2006) 12(4) European Law Journal 455–68.

gives them an opportunity to play an incredible role in bridging the gap between states, NGOs and intergovernmental organizations.[47]

6. Regional human rights systems: An effective regional human rights system can strengthen operational capacity and regulatory competence of a global-wide network for implementing human rights reflecting the particular human rights concerns of the region and provide regional input to the development of international human rights strategies.
7. Human rights academics: Such a network can certainly benefit from academic expertise, including research institutes, individual experts, and relevant educational institutions.

At a minimum, engagement with these bodies seems to be indispensable in a global-wide human rights network, though this set can be extended to other relevant actors. When working on business and human rights, as an example, such a network can involve businesses, including those representing the largest sectors within countries, small and medium enterprises, and business associations as well as the UN working group on business and human rights.[48]

Facilitating the free flow of views and information and deliberative dialogues are crucial within network governance. With dialogue and discussion at the very heart of the networked governance approach, network partners can jointly produce a collective understanding of human rights problems, priorities, and possible response strategies.[49] As networks get larger with more actors being drawn into the policy formulation and implementation processes, effective communication among partners will be an apparent challenge and can greatly influence the successful culmination of the networks' objectives or contribute to the failure of policy networks.[50] A possible pragmatic solution to enhance feasibility of networking in practice is to centralize network governance activities around a number of 'lead bodies'.[51] By centralizing governance through lead bodies, participants no longer need to interact directly with each other, but rather, they can interact directly with their lead body for the purposes of co-ordinating network-level needs. A global network for implementing

[47] See Linda C Reif, 'The UN Guiding Principles on Business and Human Rights and Networked Governance: Improving the Role of Human Rights Ombudsman Institutions as National Remedies' (2017) 17(4) Human Rights Law Review 603–32, at 606.

[48] See Danish toolkit on business and human rights, 2014, at 37 <https://www.humanrights.dk/business/tools/national-action-plans-business-human-rights> accessed 16 May 2017.

[49] See Frank Fischer, 'Beyond empiricism: policy analysis as deliberative practice' in MA Hajer and H Wagenaar (eds), *Deliberative Policy Analysis. Understanding Governance in the Network Society* (Cambridge University Press 2003) 137; Nils Hertting and Evert Vedung, 'Purposes and criteria in network governance evaluation: How far does standard evaluation vocabulary takes us?' (2012) 18(1) Evaluation 27–46.

[50] Viliame Wilikilagi, 'What is Network Governance and its Implications for Public Policy Formulation?' (23 October 2009) at 12 <http://dx.doi.org/10.2139/ssrn.1494757> accessed 23 April 2016; see Adrienne Héritier, 'New modes of governance in Europe: policy-making without legislating?' in Adrienne Windhoff-Héritier (ed), *Common Goods: Reinventing European and International Governance* (1st edn, Rowman & Littlefield Publishers 2002) 185–206.

[51] Provan and Kenis, 'Modes of Network Governance: Structure, Management, and Effectiveness', note 30, at 238.

human rights can bring together diverse actors through the establishment of some form of global alliances.

There is already a Global Alliance of National Human Rights Institutions (GANHRI)—formerly called the International Coordinating Committee of National Institutions for the Promotion and Protection of Human Rights (ICC)—through which NHRIs are aligned. The GANHRI who has been fairly successful in co-ordinating the relationship between NHRIs and the UN human rights bodies can act as a sub-network of a global human rights network.

In a similar vein, a preliminary suggestion would be to set up at least five further global alliances as sub-networks of a global network for implementing human rights. These may include:

1. Global Alliance of United Nations Human Rights Bodies: To link and align the UN human rights bodies, my suggestion would be to design what I would call a Global Alliance of United Nations Human Rights Bodies (GAUNHRB). This may include, at a minimum, independent experts of different human rights treaty bodies, the Special Procedures, and UPR Working Group. Such a sub-network as a lead body can unite the UN human rights mechanisms, harmonize recommendations of different bodies, address large overlaps, and avoid the marginalization of either type of rights.
2. Global Alliance of Aid Agencies: In trying to create synergies among various key UN and non-UN aid agencies, it seems useful to establish what I would call a Global Alliance of Aid Agencies (GAAA). Such a sub-network may encompass representatives of at least the non-UN aid donors, the Technical Cooperation Programme, and the UN Resident Coordinators (RC).
3. Global Alliance of Non-Governmental Organizations: To ensure an active participation of NGOs in the process of human rights policy making and policy implementation and facilitate communication among them, my suggestion would be to create what can be called a Global Alliance of Non-Governmental Organizations (GANGO) composed of representatives of national and international human rights NGOs.[52]
4. Global Alliance of Regional Human Rights Systems: In order to enhance a worldwide co-operative relationship among regional human rights systems, it seems inevitable to shape what I would call a Global Alliance of Regional Human Rights Systems (GARHRS).
5. Global Academic Human Rights Alliance: In my view, the establishment of what can be named a Global Academic Human Rights Alliance (GAHRA) can not only facilitate conducting innovative and collaborative human rights researches but also narrow the current gap between human rights academics and human rights practitioners.

[52] Some good efforts have already been made such as the establishment of Civil Society Section as a unit in the OHCHR dedicated to strengthening engagement between civil society and the United Nations human rights programme.

These five global alliances listed as a preliminary suggestion above along with the Global Alliance of National Human Rights Institutions which has already existed together can have an obvious capacity to maintain network stability over time. They can make frequent dialogues and meetings of all participants possible and thereby advance the feasibility of networking at different levels. These subnets which interact across borders can form a global system of human rights as a cross-border network of networks.

5. Network Facilitator and Orchestrator

Global networks for implementing human rights do not emerge spontaneously. Each network requires at least one 'facilitator' which plays a central role in initiating the network and making co-operation and co-ordination easier for partners within the network. In order to persuade different human rights-related actors of the network's potentials and inform them about the co-operative process, the network facilitator may sometimes need to employ what is known as the orchestration strategy in which a lead body (the orchestrator) enlists an intermediary body to influence the behaviour of other body/ies (the target). Orchestration can draw on a range of potential orchestrators and intermediaries and the same parties may take on different roles as orchestrator, intermediator, or target.[53] Hence, a network facilitator can sometimes act as orchestrator as well. Now the question arises as to who is the most suitable one to act as network facilitator and when the orchestration can be a useful practical strategy to be employed?

It is crucial for the network facilitator to be seen as legitimate by the network partners and targets it aims to work with. For a global network for implementing human rights, the Office of the High Commissioner for Human Rights (OHCHR) which has a distinct role within the UN human rights system appears to be the best choice to act as a network facilitator taking the lead in initiating and facilitating such a global-wide network of sub-networks. It is a focal body in the area of human rights which has occupied a central position in the UN human rights system and can legitimately, as an uncontested facilitator, take steps to draw human rights partners of different kinds together ensuring that protection responsibilities are discharged effectively. The Mission Statement of OHCHR assumes a leadership role for the OHCHR while stating that:

> OHCHR aims to ensure the practical implementation of universally recognized human rights norms. It is committed to ... providing the United Nations treaty monitoring bodies ... with the highest quality support ... OHCHR is committed to working with other

[53] Kenneth W Abbott, Philipp Genschel, Duncan Snidal, and Bernhard Zangl, 'Orchestration: Global Governance Through Intermediaries' in K Abbott, P Genschel, D Snidal, and B Zangl (eds), *International Organizations as Orchestrators* (1st edn, Cambridge University Press 2015); see Kenneth Abbott and Duncan Snidal, 'The Governance Triangle: Regulatory standards institutions and the shadow of the state' in K W Abbott and D Snidal (eds), *The Politics of Global Regulation* (1st edn, Princeton University Press 2009); Philipp Genschel and Bernhard Zangl, *Transformations of the State: From Monopolist to Manager of Political Authority* (1st edn, Univ Sonderforschungsbereich 2008).

parts of the United Nations to integrate human rights standards throughout the work of the Organization . . . A number of OHCHR field presences have been established with a view to ensuring that international human rights standards are progressively implemented and realized at country level, both in law and practice.[54]

According to the UN Charter and the mandate of the UN High Commissioner for Human Rights, as set out in General Assembly Resolution 48/141 of 20 December 1993, OHCHR Regional Offices, together with Country Offices, are at the forefront of OHCHR's efforts to engage effectively with governments, inter-governmental and nongovernmental organizations, as well as relevant UN partners, in order to formulate and implement strategies, programs, and activities for the promotion and protection of all human rights in different countries.[55]

In some cases, the network facilitator by itself may not be able to directly get the actors on board and therefore may need to play a catalytic role in creating sub-networks, that is, to orchestrate and work through intermediaries including focal and legitimate bodies and actors in each set of potential network partners that can legitimately and effectively reach out to a wide range of relevant actors and engage in advocacy, campaigning, lobbying, or other possible forms of persuasion. Orchestration thus can be sometimes a powerful strategy for a network facilitator like the OHCHR who seeks to effect beneficial change but lacks the authority to mandate it.[56] Orchestration occurs when neither orchestrator nor intermediaries can alone achieve their shared goal or objective. They are mutually dependent because each lacks certain required capabilities for direct and independent action. Networking allows orchestrators and intermediacies to pursue complementary goals and combine complementary competencies. Orchestration is indirect (through intermediaries) and soft (because the orchestrator lacks control over intermediaries) and can take different forms such as convening and endorsement (political, legal, or material).[57] For example, an orchestrator like an intergovernmental organization (IGO) by using their formal legitimate mandate, can empower intermediaries by endorsing them formally as competent and legitimate actors in a specific field.[58]

Taken together, the network facilitator can benefit from employing the orchestration strategy to catalyse, mobilize, support, and/or enable each partner or subnetworks, as an intermediary, so that they can take action and work with targets in line with the network's goals and objectives set out in an international human rights action plan which will be discussed shortly. Similarly, this strategy can be adopted by

[54] Mission Statement of OHCHR (2000) <http://www.ohchr.org/EN/AboutUs/Pages/MissionStatement.aspx> accessed 12 May 2017.

[55] See General Assembly, Resolution 48/141, A/RES/48/141, 20 December 1993; Alizadeh, 'A Proposal for How to Realize Human Rights at the National and Regional Level: A Three-Pillar Strategy', note 1, at 844.

[56] Kenneth W Abbott and Thomas Hale, 'Orchestrating Global Solution Networks: A Guide for Organizational Entrepreneurs' (4 April 2014), <https://ssrn.com/abstract=2431956> accessed 12 September 2017.

[57] Abbott, Genschel, Snidal, and Zangl, 'Orchestration: Global Governance Through Intermediaries', note 53.

[58] ibid.

other network partners in different stages of human rights networking across a wide range of issue areas. When it comes to communities' rights practices, for example, the state itself can act as an orchestrator supporting NGOs (as intermediators) and local authorities to help change the collectively accepted set of 'rights' and 'obligations' which is not in accordance with the set of rights and obligations embodied in international human rights instruments (see Chapter 1). Although NGOs and NHRIs are the most likely potential intermediaries in human rights governance, this role can also be played by business organizations, public-private partnerships, trans-governmental networks, and IGOs on some occasions.

To foster networked co-ordination including orchestration and to develop a unified position on human rights protection throughout the network, in my view, demand international human rights action planning. Some important features of such planning are depicted in the following section.

6. International Human Rights Action Plan

Once a global-wide network for implementing human rights is established, it requires adoption of what I would call an International Human Rights Action Plan (IHRAP) through which network activities can be identified. Such a plan is distinct from national human rights action planning and can serve at least seven purposes. These include:

1. Integrated and effective co-operation and co-ordination among various human rights related actors in a global-wide network require realistic action planning on how and when each actor must act. To keep various partners in line with the network's goals and priorities, human rights network may seek to shape a human rights action plan. It can also open the discussion for the adoption of different practical strategies such as orchestration and 'stewardship'[59] for the implementation of human rights in a particular time and place.
2. For a human rights treaty to be implemented effectively, it has to be accompanied by realistic and periodic action planning. A considerable body of international human rights instruments including core human rights treaties have been developed, though there is as yet no consensus on how to put them into practice in a coherent and systematic way. To give effect to human rights instruments and to cope with ongoing and upcoming human rights challenges in a volatile world require a more proactive and systematic move than merely releasing Concluding Observations, which are idiosyncratic and ad hoc, or advancing sporadic General Comments. Implementation of a treaty needs to be guided by action planning as an ongoing process so as to respond to new challenges as they arise.

[59] For further details on stewardship as a strategy, see Tom Pegram, 'Regulatory Stewardship and Intermediation: Lessons from Human Rights Governance' (2017) 670(1) The ANNALS of the American Academy of Political and Social Science 225–44, March 2017.

3. IHRAP as the product of a multi-level governance can serve as an international platform around which national and regional human rights systems can unite and interact within and across borders. In particular, for human rights-related issues which are shaped by the complex interplay of factors at different levels and cross sovereign boundaries such as environmental disasters, human trafficking, and refugee crisis, IHRAPs can increase the impact of national and regional plans by synchronizing their ultimate goals and priorities. It should be noted that international human rights action planning is not a one-way relationship imposing guidance from international to national and regional levels, but rather inputs and feedbacks flow through governance at different levels. In particular, national and regional action planning can provide context-specific insights which can help revising international human rights planning. Furthermore, sharing national and regional human rights action plans through networked governance enables states and other human rights-related actors to benefit from good practice by other actors.
4. At the regional level, in particular, an IHRAP can provide practical inputs to strengthen co-operation within regional human rights systems and help develop a unified position on human rights protection issues across regions. In line with an IHRAP, each regional human rights system can advance a context-specific Regional Human Rights Action Plan (RHRAP). A RHRAP can help a better understanding of the problems, concerns, and shortcomings encountered in efforts to realize a wide range of rights in the region concerned. The EU has already developed two regional action plans on human rights and democracy.[60] This is a positive step forward and an illustration of a good practice at the regional level. The Council of Europe has also encouraged its member states to advance a national human rights action plan as a continuous, participatory, and transparent process.[61]
5. An IHRAP can serve as a coherent guiding template against which states and non-state human rights performance can be assessed by the UN human rights bodies. Such a plan wields great influence in bringing issues to the attention of human rights bodies evenly. This can improve the integrity of the system of inter-related rights and avoid duplicity. Moreover, adopting a comprehensive national human rights action plan in line with an IHRAP can facilitate knowledge-sharing with regard to measures taken by each country to implement human rights treaties, and thereby address the problem of the overloading reporting requirements. At present, many states are struggling to submit various periodic reports to various human rights bodies, some of which

[60] Council of the European Union, EU Strategic Framework and Action Plan on Human Rights and Democracy, Luxembourg, 25 June 2012 11855/12, <https://www.consilium.europa.eu/uedocs/cms_data/docs/pressdata/EN/foraff/131181.pdf; https://ec.europa.eu/anti-trafficking/sites/antitrafficking/files/joint_communication_on_human_rights_and_democracy_en.pdf> accessed 19 January 2018.

[61] Council of Europe, Workshop on Developing and Implementing National Action Plans for Human Rights, Strasbourg, 27–28 March 2014 <https://rm.coe.int/16806daabd> accessed 23 May 2017.

have overlapping competence.[62] That is why the current level of overdue reports is a big issue within the UN human rights system. To ensure that states adhere to international human rights standards as recognized in human rights treaties, instead of submitting various different reports with overlaps to different treaty bodies and also in response to the UPR working group, each state can submit its up-to-date national action plan as one point of reference. Different phases of a national human rights action plan are discussed in the next chapter.

6. Although international human rights action plans cannot create new international law obligations, they can contribute to the clarification of the scope of the state's extra-territorial obligations and provide incentives for the states to engage in regulating extraterritorial side effects of, say for instance, business activities on human rights. Moreover, examination and elaboration of legally binding instruments in the form of legal and regulatory reforms can be suggested in an IHRAP.
7. Finally, of course, what is required is not just some insights, priorities, and a set of time bound actions that need to be taken, but the tools to make these happen. An international human rights action plan can be seen as a platform where the UN Technical Cooperation Programme, UNCTs, relevant NGOs, and NHRIs can develop collaborative initiatives to assist states and non-states actors in implementing human rights in practice.

Allowing national and international NGOs, NHRIs, UNCTs, treaty bodies, and governments to form horizontal networks across borders and jurisdictions to identify human rights problems, develop objectives, and adopt action plans may be a reasonable governance strategy, but who is responsible for what is performing in such a horizontal network among equals and how all the activities should be monitored through networking? The next section will examine different types of accountability mechanisms which can complement other mechanisms of influence such as orchestration discussed before.

7. Four Types of Accountability Mechanisms

In general, there are at least four types of accountability mechanisms which facilitate policy reformulation, institutional learning, and monitoring in global governance for implementing human rights.[63] These include: mutual accountability among network partners, accountability within network partners, accountability of network

[62] Pillay, United Nations High Commissioner for Human Rights, Dublin Statement, note 6.

[63] Hertting and Vedung, 'Purposes and criteria in network governance evaluation: How far does standard evaluation vocabulary takes us?', note 49; see also, Pirson and Turnbull, 'Towards a More Humanistic Governance Model: Networked Governance Structure', note 29; Janet Newman, 'Constructing Accountability: Network Governance and Managerial Agency' (2004) 19 Public Policy and Administration 17–33; Julia Steets, *Accountability in Public Policy Partnerships* (1st edn, Palgrave Macmillan 2010).

partners to constituencies, and accountability of network partners to an external network governor. I will briefly discuss them separately.

7.1. Mutual accountability among network partners

A world-wide network for implementing human rights consists of a set of parties in horizontal relationships. An important prerequisite for successful horizontal co-operation within a network like this is that co-operating partners themselves jointly organize mutual monitoring of each other.[64]

7.2. Accountability within network partners

Whereas partners are equal within a network, they are put into a vertical relationship with their own parent organization. This forms some vertical accountability relationships in the network governance approach. Each networking parent organization is a principal with motives to control her agents representing it in face-to-face collaboration processes and asks whether the agent is a good representative of their interests in the operative collaboration processes?[65]

7.3. Accountability of network partners to constituencies

This type of accountability is about the network parties' shared responsibility to relevant outsider stakeholders such as marginalized and vulnerable groups who do not have representatives in the network.[66] As Hertting and Vedung argue:

> This accountability perspective can be formulated in terms of responsivity. The issue is not whether the network has acted within the limits of its prior mandate, but whether those who are not among the networking players and are affected and concerned experience *ex post* that the network has been effective in realizing their wishes.[67]

The networked governance approach strongly emphasizes the significance of discussion, dialogue, and communication among those affected by or with a stake in a plan like human rights action plans. In the case of a global network for implementing human rights, this demands an acute need to create feedback loops between the OHCHR as the network facilitator and the public. Efforts should be made to ensure that people have access to relevant information and can provide feedback and input to the network. Feedback loops can be established by different methods for capturing people's inputs such as effective use of social media, dialogues, meetings,

[64] See Raw Rhodes, *Understanding Governance: Policy Networks, Governance, Reflexivity, and Accountability* (1st edn, Open University Press 1997); Joop Koppenjan and Erik-Hans Klijn, *Managing Uncertainties in Networks: A Network Approach to Problem Solving and Decision Making* (1st edn, Routledge 2004).

[65] Hertting and Vedung, 'Purposes and criteria in network governance evaluation: How far does standard evaluation vocabulary takes us?', note 49, at 38–39.

[66] ibid, at 39. [67] ibid.

focus groups, and surveys.[68] These loops could be a powerful tool in helping network partners to better monitor and evaluate the tasks in place and to be more sensitive to the needs of vulnerable groups in society. Received feedbacks can be analysed with respect to, inter alia:

1. Frequency: How many people bring up a specific human rights issue?
2. Priority: What level of importance do people give to a specific human rights issue?
3. Origin: Do certain stakeholder groups in particular bring up a particular point or issue?
4. Time: Do people consider a specific human rights issue as more important now than before?
5. Resonance: Is there a high level of energy when people talk about a particular human rights issue? Is there any conflict of interests in this issue?

Claims, concerns, and issues of various stakeholders could serve as points of departure for monitoring of different features of human rights planning.

7.4. Accountability of network partners to an external network governor

The last type of accountability in networking arises in the case where an external network governor such as the European Commission or the UN Human Rights Council may intervene in their external and vertical relationship with relevant actors, through financial or other incentives, to get states or other related actors on board.[69] Moreover, as mentioned before, a binding treaty-based system can coexist with global networked governance. It can step in with mandatory regulation should network partners fail to comply with soft measures.

In a nutshell, fragmentations abound in the international human rights 'system', leading to failures in that the predominant mode of human rights governance not only often fails to systematically change behaviours and achieve its stated goals and objectives, but even sometimes produces the opposite effects from those intended. This failure is also because of the fact that states have still remained the predominant authority within the current global human rights governance system. The networked model of governance as an alternative suggested here appears to be a promising way to enhance system-wide coherence among various players involved in realizing human rights at different levels. Such a global-wide network draws its strength from the complementarity of resources, capabilities, legitimacy, expertise, and knowledge of the diverse partners involved. This can not only build up channels of communications among various human rights-related actors and mechanisms

[68] See Post-2015 Development Agenda: Guidelines for Country Dialogue, United Nation Development Group, June 2012, <http://www.unicef.org/earlychildhood/files/Final_Post-2015_Country_Guidelines_10_June_2012.pdf> accessed 28 January 2018.

[69] Hertting and Vedung, 'Purposes and criteria in network governance evaluation: How far does standard evaluation vocabulary takes us?', note 49, at 39.

from the local to the global level, and thereby enhance the overall functioning of the international human rights system as a whole, but also to mitigate the lack of political will of the states to implement their international human rights commitments.

The next chapter will briefly discuss the establishment of a national network for implementing human rights and examine different phases of national human rights action planning from the preparatory phase to assessment phase.

7

Phases of Human Rights Action Planning in Practice

1. Introduction

It is now widely acknowledged that the ratification and legalization of human rights treaties are not enough for realizing human rights in practice.[1] To implement human rights as the ultimate goal of development requires a much more proactive move than merely ratifying treaties, enacting bills of rights, or offering judicial remedies. To take concrete practical-oriented steps towards better human rights observance, countries need to put in place effective action plans to ensure compliance with the human rights treaties they have committed themselves to. As remarked in the Vienna Declaration and Programme of Action, special attention should be given to action plans to assist in 'building and strengthening national structures which have a direct impact on the overall observance of human rights and the maintenance of the rule of law'.[2] Similarly, the Council of Europe Commissioner for Human Rights has recommended the development of national action plans as a way of bridging the 'implementation gap' between international commitments and national implementation.[3] A national action plan for implementing human rights, if properly designed, can be an important vehicle taking forward a proactive strategy for implementing human rights in a coherent way, in accordance with each country's social, political, cultural, economic, and legal circumstances. A well formulated NHRAP can not only enhance a more focused political commitment to the observance of human rights and integrate human rights agenda throughout

[1] See eg Emilie M Hafner-Burton, 'Human rights in a globalizing world: the paradox of empty promises' (2005) 110(5) American Journal of Sociology (AJS) 1373–411; Emilie M Hafner-Burton, Kiyoteru Tsutsui, and John W Mayer, 'International human rights law and the politics of legitimation: repressive states and human rights treaties' (2008) 23 International Sociology 115–27; David S Law and Mila Versteeg, 'The evolution and ideology of global constitutionalism' (2011) 99(5) California Law Review 1163–174.

[2] UN General Assembly, *Vienna Declaration and Programme of Action*, 12 July 1993, A/CONF.157/23, at para 69, <http://www.refworld.org/docid/3ae6b39ec.html> accessed 10 November 2017.

[3] Council of Europe, Conclusions of a Workshop on Developing and Implementing National Action Plans for Human Rights, Strasbourg, 27–28 March 2014 <https://rm.coe.int/16806daabd> accessed 24 March 2017.

government administration,[4] but also increase public awareness of human rights and social will to protect international human rights standards. Aside from this, such plans can also be used as a good basis for the UN human rights treaty committees and possibly the UPR working group to examine a country's situation, helping co-ordinate cross-treaty efforts and reduce the burden upon states parties faced with producing multiple reports to different treaty bodies and the UPR working group.

However, despite the fact that many countries have developed one or more global or rights-specific action plans for implementing human rights, most of which are, to a greater or lesser extent, ill-designed and lacking the integral parts of an effective action plan in practice. This was reflected in the result of the cross case analysis of NHRAPs of fifty-three countries presented in Chapter 5.

The Office of the UN High Commissioner for Human Rights (OHCHR) and the United Nations Development Programme in its 'HURIST' (Human Rights Strengthening) Programme have made some efforts towards improving the advancement of NHRAPs in practice. In particular, the OHCHR released a 108-page Handbook on National Human Rights Plans of Action in 2002, which seeks to provide guidance on the development of such plans. Although this was a positive and promising move forward, the handbook is no longer up-to-date. It is also theoretically baseless and has provided a large scope of discretion for the states to form the substance of these plans. Besides, although NHRAPs are sporadically referred to in the context of reports to and recommendations from the Human Rights Council's Universal Periodic Review process and the human rights treaty bodies (in particular, General Comments and Concluding Observations), it has failed to adopt a systematic, comprehensive, coherent, and consistent approach to the form and substance of such plans. Hence, it is hardly surprising that most states are still wrestling with the question of how to put an effective plan in place. As a result, different countries have adopted their own approach, developing significantly different action plans, ranging from a two-page plan to a 200-page one.

This chapter aims to examine different phases of human rights planning at the practical level. These include the preparatory phase, development phase, implementation phase, and assessment phase. In the preparatory phase, the idea of establishing a national human rights network and the importance of conducting a comprehensive baseline study will be discussed. Before proceeding with the content of a NHRAP, in the development phase, the necessity of advancing a master plan of action plans will be briefly examined. Then, in the implementation phase, the sustainability of a NHRAP, emerging a complex situation during implementation, and six types of accountability mechanisms will be discussed in turn. This chapter ends with proposing a seven-feature model of assessment in the final phase.

[4] See UNOHCHR, Handbook on National Human Rights Plans of Action, 29 August 2002 <http://www.ohchr.org/Documents/Publications/training10en.pdf> accessed 24 January 2018.

2. Preparatory Phase

The preparatory phase is the critical stage of planning in which participants, administrative and management structures, human rights problems, and available resources are identified. In this section, I will first suggest the idea of establishing a nationwide network of different stakeholders for implementing human rights and then examine five key elements of a comprehensive baseline study.

2.1. National human rights network

Although it is an obligation of the states to adopt an action plan for implementing human rights as embodied in international human rights conventions (see Chapter 3), consideration should be given to the critical role of national human rights institutions, NGOs, and regional and international human rights bodies, in particular treaty bodies and the Human Rights Council's Universal Periodic Review, in creating impetus on the states to respond to their obligations. Currently, most NHRAPs are initiated, developed, and implemented by government alone with limited or no meaningful participation from other stakeholders. The findings of the cross-case analysis of these plans in Chapter 5 show that a state-centric plan is at the risk of suffering different problems such as ideological orientation, non-correspondence, supporting the status quo, incomprehensiveness, and the lack of accountability. When government has privileged status it can easily intimidate or silence civil society, NHRIs, and community stakeholders. As the procedural theory of human rights planning in Chapter 2 suggests, the process of developing a NHRAP is as important as its result, and should be participatory, non-discriminatory, empowering, accountable, and top-down bottom-up. It should aim to reach out to different sectors of society at different levels in order to avoid a situation in which the plan becomes an exercise focused narrowly on government or civil society elites exclusively.

Despite significant progress and the widespread use of the 'participatory approach' in policy making and planning, some of which, in particular those initiated by governments, still remain mostly at the rhetorical level. Although most states make a point of claiming to have prepared their NHRAPs in *participation* with stakeholders, they cannot be taken at face value. The crux of the matter is that participation is a categorical term for citizen power and varies in terms of (1) degree; (2) level; (3) composition (participants); and (4) phases.[5]

In terms of degree, participation can be seen along a continuum, ranging from non-participation (like manipulation, decoration, and therapy) and tokenism (eg, informing and consultation) to powerful citizenship (ie, partnership, shared

[5] See John Gaventa, 'Finding the Spaces for Change: A Power Analysis' (2006) 37(6) IDS Bulletin; Lisa VeneKlasen and Valerie Miller, *A New Weave of People, Power and Politics: The Action Guide for Advocacy and Citizen Participation* (2nd edn, World Neighbors 2007).

decision making, and control).[6] As mentioned in Chapter 2, meaningful participation is much more than informing or even consulting with the people concerned in planning. It includes an active and genuine engagement of citizens as decision makers rather than as merely users or choosers of interventions developed by others from the top-down.[7]

In terms of the level of participation, the approach adopted in practice varies, ranging from a 'populist form of participation' focusing on very local issues at the community level to structural development interventions dealing with broad societal changes at the meso and macro level.[8] The populist form of participation treats participation as a technical method of community project work rather than a human right or a method of empowerment and capacity building.[9]

In terms of composition (participants), it ranges from involving exclusively government organizations to all stakeholders, governmental and non-governmental, including the general public, government, experts, civil society, national human rights institutions, private sector actors, and donors, both bilateral and multilateral. This is close to what is known as 'spaces for participation' in the literature. The 'spaces for participation' refers to opportunities and channels citizens have to willingly, knowingly, and effectively get involved in planning that affects their lives. There is a continuum of spaces ranging from 'closed' or 'provided spaces', where decisions are made only by the state or experts from the top-down, to 'claimed' or 'created spaces' where all stakeholders have an opportunity to actively participate.[10]

In terms of phases of participation, it can range from engaging participants in only the preparatory phase to all phases of planning namely the preparatory phase, development phase, implementation phase, monitoring and evaluation phase.

To develop an effective NHRAP requires an acknowledgment of equal standing for all stakeholders as genuine participants at different levels and in all phases of planning, from the preparatory phase to assessment phase. This includes the participation of, among others, the following:

1. Government
2. National human rights institutions

[6] See Sherry Arnstein, 'A Ladder of Citizen Participation' (1969) 35(4) Journal of American Planning 216–24; Roger Hart, 'Children's Participation: From Tokenism to Citizenship' (1992) Essay for UNICEF, Innocenti Essay No 4; Scott Davidson, 'Spinning the Wheel of Empowerment' (1998) 1262 Planning.

[7] See, eg, John Graventa, 'Towards Participatory Local Governance: Assessing the Transformative Possibilities' in S Hickey and G Mohan (eds), *Participation: from Tyranny to Transformation: Exploring New Approaches to Participation in Development* (1st edn, Zed Books 2004); Andrea Cornwall and John Gaventa, 'From Users and Choosers to Makers and Shapers Repositioning Participation in Social Policy' (2000) 31 IDS Bulletin 50–62.

[8] See Sam Hickey and Giles Mohan, 'Towards Participation as Transformation: Critical Themes and Challenges' in S Hickey and G Mohan (eds), *Participation: from Tyranny to Transformation: Exploring New Approaches to Participation in Development* (1st edn, Zed Books 2004).

[9] ibid, at 10.

[10] See Gaventa, 'Finding the Spaces for Change: A Power Analysis', note 5.

3. Civil society, including specialized organizations such as those focusing on the rights of women, disabled persons, the elderly, and children; community organizations, particularly those that may not normally be regarded as human rights organizations because they deal with social issues such as health, housing, education, development assistance, minorities, asylum seekers, as well as labour unions and professional groups, including associations of teachers, lawyers, journalists, and so on.
4. Representative members of vulnerable groups
5. Human rights experts including academics and practitioners
6. Business sector and private foundations including corporate representatives, and industry associations

In some situations, it may be useful to have representatives of international organizations as participants in planning, particularly where the development and implementation of the plan draw on international technical co-operation.[11]

To ensure that a NHRAP, in its different phases, derives full benefit from varying complementary insights, expertise, and experiences, a co-ordinating committee composed of representatives of the participant groups, mentioned before, can be set up. Since different governmental and non-governmental bodies are involved in developing, implementing, and assessing the plan, it may not be feasible to have more than those with broad responsibilities on the co-ordinating committee itself.[12] In order to ensure a comprehensive representation from participant groups and to mobilize effectively different inputs, knowledge, experience, activities, and resources, different sub-committees with respect to specific rights or groups of right holders can be established. These sub-committees should be genuinely involved in the process of planning and channelled directly to the co-ordinating committee.[13] The establishment of sub-committees can help set up a national network of various stakeholders involved in implementing human rights in the country concerned.

A national network for implementing human rights should work in partnership with all stakeholders, opening up communication among them at all levels of plan operations. Stakeholders should have an opportunity to directly (in the co-ordinating committee) or indirectly (through sub-committees) become involved in the process of decision making in different phases of planning. Human rights planning through such network needs to reflect upon collaboration and inclusivity in an ongoing dialogue among all partners. Collaboration and co-operation should happen in all stages of planning—including needs assessment, problems definition, prioritization, examination of possible response strategies, implementation, and assessment of NHRAPs. This national network can become part (as a sub-network) of a global-wide network for implementing human rights as suggested in the last

[11] See UNOHCHR, Handbook on National Human Rights Plans of Action, note 4.
[12] ibid, at 46.
[13] ibid, at 47.

chapter. Building a nationwide network for implementing human rights itself can serve different purposes:

First and perhaps the most important use of such networked co-operation that should not be overlooked is awareness-raising and capacity building (transformative role). An important function of this network is to facilitate, train, and educate network partners (in particular community members) to become aware of human rights and build up a shared understanding of human rights issues, motivate them to tackle the problems, and enable them to willingly, knowingly, and effectively become involved in the process of planning. It is of critical importance that human rights networking at different levels can foster a human rights culture through awareness-raising.

Second, such a multi-level multi-agent network can be used as a possible response strategy against the lack of political will of states to implement human rights. It can also enhance the social will of communities to implement human rights as set forth in international human rights instruments, and thereby makes implementation more effective (see Chapter 1). By involving stakeholders in the process of planning and by taking an essentially non-confrontational approach, it can generate a commitment to the observance of human rights that would not otherwise exist. Free and meaningful participation must be incorporated in different phases of planning if the plan is to have credibility, legitimacy, and public support. Otherwise, success is improbable due to the lack of social will to implement it.

Third, a multi-layered network is better able to plan creatively and strategize how to identify and deal with complex human rights issues in a particular time and place. Planning that involves all stakeholders is more likely to find socially legitimate and sustainable response strategies that are applicable and meaningful to the lives of those affected by the plan. Human rights networking is more likely to ensure that the concerns of vulnerable groups, such as women, children, the elderly, disabled persons, and minorities are more effectively addressed. Detailed local insights are valuable contributions that local partners can bring from the bottom-up, while academics and human rights practitioners bring valuable expert knowledge and technical knowledge, and others such as UN Country Teams (UNCTs) may be able to offer additional technical and financial resources.

Fourth, by putting human rights on the national agenda, such a network can mobilize a wide range of people and organizations at different levels in support of human rights activity. The distinct roles and competencies of each partner in the network can generate synergies that would not otherwise exist. Such an inclusive approach throughout planning creates shared ownership and contributes to the legitimacy of a NHRAP.

Having suggested the idea of advancing a nationwide network for implementing human rights and explored different features of such a network, let me move on to the second element of the preparatory phase: conducting a baseline study which is of critical importance in advancing an effective and evidence-based plan of action.

2.2. Baseline study

A baseline study is an analysis of the current human rights situation in the country concerned in order to identify human rights problems as well as resources and opportunities available. For a country to move forward towards the realization of human rights, it is important to know where it stands at present. A comprehensive and accurate baseline study informed by reliable evidence provides an objective depiction of the state of human rights in the country concerned and helps specify and concretize the objectives of NHRAP and thereby particular tasks (activities) which can be initiated to accomplish a plan's objectives. Moreover, baseline information is a crucial input for both monitoring and evaluating a plan. It can be used as a reference point at a later date for monitoring in the course of implementation and also for evaluating the plan when assessing its results at the end.

In conducting a baseline study, the quality and reliability of the evidence and information upon which it is based are crucial. A baseline study achieves its purpose through well-established methods. As will be discussed later in the assessment phase, to gain a full picture of the situation, it is always worthwhile to use a mixed methods strategy. Moreover, a comprehensive baseline study requires both expert knowledge from the top-down and local knowledge from the bottom-up to come to the fore. Depending on different practical considerations such as how much time, money, and social and political support is available at the time of conducting a baseline study, a range of methods can be used, such as analysis of available information and existing reports (secondary data); public meeting; public hearing; participant observation; interview with key informants including experts, practitioners, and local authorities; focus group studies with stakeholders (target population) or their representatives and key members of NGOs; telephone, mail, and online surveys; and diagrammatic methods.

In keeping with the general theory of human rights planning advanced in Chapters 1 and 2, a human rights baseline study should be comprehensive in scope reflecting, at a minimum, human rights as embodied in the core human rights treaties, and include at least the following elements:

1. target population
2. legal framework assessment
3. needs assessment
4. interests assessment
5. capabilities assessment
6. resources assessment

2.2.1. *Target population*

The first job is to identify the intended beneficiaries of the plan in an all-inclusive and comprehensive way. One way is to set them out in terms of different social categories which include, among others, gender, ethnicity, colour, religion, political opinion or other opinion, nationality, and different life cycle stages (eg foetus, infancy, childhood, adolescence, adulthood, elderly). This can also be set out in terms of target groups such as women, children, indigenous peoples, minorities (racial, ethnic, religious, linguistic, etc), persons living in extreme poverty, persons with disabilities, persons living with HIV/AIDS, older persons, the mentally ill, refugees and asylum-seekers, and migrant workers.

2.2.2. *Legal framework assessment*

A proper incorporation of human rights standards and norms on the books is a prerequisite for putting them into practice. International human rights instruments are insufficient without strong counterparts in domestic law. That is why a critical part of a baseline study for developing a NHRAP is to address the questions as to whether international human rights instruments are adopted and ratified without any significant reservation and whether international human rights standards are effectively and genuinely incorporated in domestic law. Due to the importance of incorporation of international human rights standards in domestic law, let me digress a little to demonstrate that the way by which human rights have been textualized on the books can have direct effects on the practices of the states.

Over time, domestic laws are becoming increasingly similar in terms of the name and number of rights. These days, it is quite common for current legal systems to adopt a similar set of rights, in the name of 'human rights', such as the right to education, the right to political participation, the right to freedom of expression and press. This is at least partly due to the fact that countries have faced international pressure to conform to human rights standards in order to enjoy legitimacy and win financial and political support in the international arena. The legalization of human rights conventions in domestic laws has become a way for governments to align themselves with externally legitimated models of statehood.[14] Some scholars interpret the legalization of human rights as an attempt to secure human rights ideals by domestic law.[15] However, there is often a huge difference between what is legalized as 'human rights' in domestic laws and what is set forth as 'human rights' in international human rights instruments. As Meyer and Rowan argue, the ratification and legalization of human rights treaties often function as myths that are taken for granted as legitimate, apart from evaluations of their impact in practice.[16] Much research has shown that even there is sometimes a perverse association between ratification and repression.[17]

[14] Linda Camp Keith, 'Constitutional provisions for individual human rights (1976–1996): are they more than mere "window dressing?"' (2002) 55 Political Research Quarterly 111–43; Emilie M Hafner-Burton, Kiyoteru Tsutsui, and John W Meyer, 'International human rights law and the politics of legitimation: repressive states and human rights treaties' (2008) 23 International Sociology 115–27.

[15] Saladin Mackled-Garcia and Basak Cali, *The Legalization of Human Rights: Multidisciplinary Perspectives on Human Rights and Human Rights Law* (1st edn, Routledge 2006).

[16] John W Meyer, and Brian Rowan, 'Institutionalized organizations: formal structure as myth and ceremony' (1977) 83 American Journal of Sociology 340–63, at 344.

[17] Wade M Cole, 'Human rights as myth and ceremony? Reevaluating the effectiveness of human rights treaties, 1981 to 2007' (2012) 117(4) American Journal of Sociology 1131–171.

The process of codification of human rights in domestic laws is a critical stage that unfortunately has been largely overlooked in the literature. Elsewhere, the author, by adopting the critical system approach, has made an attempt to show that law as a soft system on the books is more than the name and number of rights.[18] It is a complex whole whose function depends on not only the name and number of rights but also different features of rights and the relationships among them. These features include: (1) the frame of reference; (2) the scope of rights; (3) the orientation of rights; (4) the enforceability of rights; and (5) the realizability of rights. The way of codification of human rights with respect to each of these five features makes a big difference in implementing human rights in practice.

The frame of reference in legal systems is either 'external' or 'internal'. The internal frame of reference means that legal rules (including rights and obligations) are recognized on the basis of legal criteria which come from within legal systems professionally. The external frame of reference, by contrast, means that legal rules are recognized by extra-legal criteria. These are non-legal criteria by nature though contained within the system. Law and Versteeg in their empirical study demonstrate the ideological character of national constitutions and how this can allow the states to easily violate international human rights standards by appealing to their domestic laws.[19] In a legal system such as Saudi Arabia, criteria stem from their political ideology (ie state religion).

The scope of rights as another feature of the law on the books refers to possible ways by which right holders can exercise their right. In this regard, rights are decomposed into 'narrow-scope' and 'broad-scope'. The right to marry, as an example, is included in all legal systems, though its scope is different across current legal systems. Whereas in some countries, women have the right to marry anybody without any limitation as to race, nationality, religion, or even sex; in Pakistan, Muslim women are unable to marry officially non-Muslims. In this case, women have a narrow scope right to marry. The scope of rights can be narrowed by exception clause(s), imposing negative duties and/or ambiguous criminalization. Take the right to freedom of speech, assembly, and association as another example. In Singapore, for instance, these rights are all contained in the constitution (Article 14(1)). However, the scope of them are restricted by laws imposed by the Parliament of Singapore on the grounds stated in Article 14(2) of the constitution. That is to say, in Singapore it can be shown that restricting the rights is 'necessary or expedient in the interest' of 'the security of Singapore and public order', 'morality', and 'friendly relations with other countries'.

The orientation of rights, as another feature of the law on the books, indicates the normative horizon or normative boundary of the system of rights. Whose rights are in and whose rights are out of the system of rights? This is the value orientation of the system of rights which can be either universal or particular. For example, as

[18] Azadeh Chalabi, 'Law as a System of Rights: A Critical Perspective' (2013) 15(2) Human Rights Review 117–38.

[19] Law and Versteeg, 'The Evolution and Ideology of Global Constitutionalism', note 1.

Kashyap argues, Bangladesh uses discriminatory personal laws governing marriage, separation, and divorce.[20] These laws set out separate rules for Muslims, Hindus, and Christians. Indonesia provides another example. Whereas religious freedom is guaranteed in the Indonesian Constitution, due to a blasphemy law in Indonesia, the orientation of the right to freedom of religion is particularistic.

The enforceability of the system of rights is another feature of the system of rights. With respect to this dimension, rights can be divided into 'operative rights' and 'in-operative rights'.[21] For example, the right not to be tortured is recognized in most constitutions. The critical point is whether all forms of torture are offences under criminal law or not.

The realizability of the system of rights is the last feature of law as a soft conceptual system on the books. Take the right to education as an example. Although the right to education can be found everywhere, the degree to which it is realizable varies across legal systems. To make the right to education realizable requires the states to ensure that education at least in the elementary stage is free. There are still some countries where primary school is not free (eg South Africa, Zimbabwe, Zambia, Somalia, and Guinea) or not compulsory (eg Saudi Arabia, Oman, Nepal, and Botswana).[22] As reported by UNESCO, more than 72 million children around the world remain unschooled.[23] Sub-Saharan Africa is the most affected area with over 32 million children of primary school age remaining uneducated.[24]

In a nutshell, although the successful establishment of human rights as legal rights on the books is the first step for providing strong counterparts of international human rights law in domestic law, some states have selected and 'textualized' human rights norms in their domestic law in a manner that can free governments from their international obligations to protect and promote human rights. This is in opposition with the purpose behind international human rights instruments.

The next important element of a comprehensive baseline study is needs assessment.

2.2.3. Needs assessment

A basic human need is the lack of something required for the continued healthy existence of every human being. As indicated in the analytical theory of human rights planning, basic human needs, primary and secondary, provide an objective base, ontologically and epistemologically, for basic human rights (see Chapter 2).

[20] Aruna Kashyap, 'Laws Hurting Bangladesh Women Linger on the Books' (2012) <http://womensenews.org/story/law/121221/laws-hurting-bangladesh-women-linger-the-books> accessed 9 January 2013.

[21] For further details, see Chalabi, 'Law as a System of Rights: A Critical Perspective', note 18.

[22] UNESCO, Regional Overview: Sub-Saharan Africa <https://en.unesco.org/gem-report/sites/gem-report/files/157229E.pdf> accessed 28 January 2018.

[23] UNESCO report 2017 <http://cfmunesco.it/media/uploads/ckeditor/2017/11/07/chairreport_unesco_schoolsystem_vulicjulia_.pdf>

[24] ibid.

A comprehensive needs assessment should identify what is needed for different social categories at different life cycle stages. Different indicators should be used in order to assess both quantitative and qualitative aspects.

2.2.4. Interests assessment

Even if what can potentially meet basic needs is available, adequate, accessible, and with reasonable quality and cost, still the question remains as to whether it is acceptable and adaptable to individual and cultural differences (in so far as resources permit). Each category of the target population may have different interests (see Chapter 2). As discussed in the analytical theory of human rights planning, there is often more than one valuable item (objects, processes, properties of objects, properties of processes) to meet basic needs, that is, a degree of choicefulness of interests for meeting basic needs often exists. What valuable items are in the target population's interest? Different social categories in different life cycle stages may have different interests some of which are culture dependent. Interests assessment seeks to address the question as to what range of options should and can, depending on the resources available, be provided in order to satisfy right holders' interests.

2.2.5. Capabilities assessment

A capabilities assessment is concerned with the question of what capabilities need to be developed for different social categories at different life cycle stages through nurturing (the trained abilities and skills eg self-care training) or basic external means and facilities for expanding capabilities (eg wheelchair, lift, hearing aid, glasses, etc) in order for right holders to be able to meet their needs in accordance with their interests.

2.2.6. Resources assessment

Availability and accessibility of resources are fundamental for implementing an action plan. A baseline study should take into account the constraints that resources pose to the realization of human rights. Are there enough financial, human (skills, knowledge, commitment, etc), and organizational resources available for implementing bodies to take action? What kinds (if any) of outside support, eg international financial or technical support, is needed to accomplish a plan's activities?

The main purpose of all these assessments, from legal framework assessment to resources assessment, in a baseline study is to determine the nature, scope, and causes of human rights problems in the country concerned as well as resources available to address them. The plan should certainly not fail to give proper expression to the most urgent problems identified in all these assessments. Special theory can be formulated simultaneously on the basis of both general theory (such as the one depicted in Chapters 1 and 2) and the evidence collected in the preparatory phase. The accumulation of empirical evidence about the situation of human rights in the country concerned is of limited value unless accompanied by a general and special theory of planning to guide process and substance of planning. Without reference to planning theories, planners risk being submerged by a morass of empirical data, which, on its own, can do little to guide practice. Based on planning theory on the one hand, and the results of legal framework-, needs-, interests-, capabilities-, and resources-assessments on the other hand, the plan's objectives and activities can be prioritized.

The next phase of planning is the development phase which will be explored in the following section.

3. Development Phase

The development phase is the stage during which the plan itself is designed. Before addressing the content of a NHRAP, this section will briefly discuss the advantage of advancing a master plan of action plans for co-ordination among different NHRAPs.

3.1. Co-ordination of plans

As discussed in Chapter 5, one of the challenges facing NHRAPs is that there is no or limited co-ordination among different national action plans and policies. Given the interrelatedness of human rights, a master plan of plans has to be developed to present a coherent system-wide picture of human rights planning in a given country depicting the relationships among different human rights action plans themselves and their lead bodies. Based on the findings of the baseline study, general and special theories of human rights planning, recommendations received from regional and international human rights bodies such as Concluding Observations, General Comments, and the UPR recommendations, an effort should be made to develop a short master plan of plans indicating what role each plan is to perform in strengthening the human rights system of the country concerned. Such a plan can be of overarching significance serving at least five purposes as follows.

First, as mentioned in Chapter 4, without a master plan in place, it is difficult to ensure that nothing falls between the cracks and that enough attention has been given to human rights issues, in particular the rights of vulnerable and marginalized groups. Second, a master plan can set national strategic priorities indicating which area is in urgent need of a separate rights-specific plan and which areas can be effectively covered by a global NHRAP. Third, such a master plan can incorporate linkage between governmental and non-governmental policies and planning at the local, national, regional, and international levels in relevant areas. Fourth, it can help ensure that different types of human rights action plans (global NHRAPs, rights-specific plans, National Action Plan on Women, Peace, and Security, and National Action Plan on Business and Human Rights) are consistent with each other and with other national plans and policies, and that the plans' human rights objectives are reflected in other relevant policies such as those relating to development. Furthermore, each NHRAP's value additional to the value of already existing plans should be clarified in this master plan. Otherwise, developing different plans and policies without a meaningful synergistic linkage among them inevitably leads to duplication and possible inefficiency. Fifth, such a master plan can advance general strategies to address structural bottlenecks (contextual factors) in different domains of societies, for example, general strategies aimed at facilitating the activities of non-governmental organizations, legal reforms, and also different strategies to raise public awareness of human rights.

Focusing on global NHRAPs, as recommended in the 1993 Vienna Declaration and Programme of Action, the following is dedicated to developing the content.

3.2. Plan's content

Each NHRAP should have a clear, comprehensive, and logical structure. In harmony with the universality, indivisibility, and interrelatedness of human rights, as set out in the substantive theory of human rights planning in Chapter 2, a global NHRAP should be broad in scope covering, at a minimum, the core international human rights treaties, unless conventions have already been included in one or more convention-specific action plan(s). This list can be extended to other human rights instruments, such as the ILO conventions, Declaration on the Rights of Indigenous Peoples, and the International Convention on the Suppression and Punishment of the Crime of Apartheid. At the same time, enough attention should be made that the plan is structured so that it is manageable. It has been a problem that some NHRAPs have a comprehensive but shallow scope which makes management difficult. It is therefore crucial to ensure that a balance is made between comprehensiveness, depth, and manageability.

Although each plan must be tailored to the circumstances of the country concerned, every NHRAP must at least encompasses eleven headings:

a) *Goals*: a common ultimate goal of each NHRAP is broadly 'the full realization of human rights of different kinds for all'.
b) *Objectives*: at the next subordinate level, as discussed in Chapter 4, each NHRAP should outline more specific and detailed targets as objectives. Apart from context-independent objectives which may be set out by an international human rights supervisory system in advance, each country needs to identify a set of country-specific objectives based on its baseline study and special theory of planning. Objectives should be carefully selected. The critical point in the development of a NHRAP is that it should be credible and achievable. Otherwise, a NHRAP with unrealistic objectives would run into the sand without substantive achievements at the end.
c) *Priorities*: in the context of scarce resources, prioritization is often inevitable. Prioritization has to be context-specific, as circumstances differ from country to country. Upon completing the legal framework-, needs-, interests-, capabilities-, and resources-assessments in the preparatory phase, areas of

intervention should be weighted properly, to account for differences in context, and beneficiaries' needs and capabilities.

d) *Activities (tasks)*: to develop a NHRAP, each state requires identification of the most appropriate concrete activities responsive to its objectives. The identification of tasks should be evidence-based linking clearly to the baseline study that stands behind the plan and in line with the four types of obligations to respect, protect, promote, and fulfil human rights. Moreover, tasks should be very clear, specific, and achievable (feasible). They should clearly address the questions as to what is going to be accomplished? What need(s) is going to be met by the identified task? What capability is enhanced by this activity? Who will benefit as a result? What set of valuable items (based on available resources) will be provided for the target population to meet their needs in accordance with their interests? Continuous development of tasks may occur in response to dynamic conditions and constant monitoring about what is working and what is not working as planned. In particular, where predictability is relatively low, such as 'complicated' and 'complex' situations (which will be discussed later in this chapter), tasks can be to some degree emergent and changing rather than totally predetermined and fixed.

e) *Lead bodies*: each NHRAP should clearly map out how responsibility to deliver tasks is distributed among those governmental and non-governmental bodies involved in implementing the plan. Specification of lead bodies responsible for carrying out each activity can enhance transparency and accountability as the two procedural principles upon which a NHRAP is based (see Chapter 2).

f) *Time frames*: each NHRAP should include both a timeframe for the plan as a whole and a time frame for each of its individual activity. Without a clear timeframe, it is almost impossible to monitor and evaluate the implementation of NHRAPs, and measure the degree of accountability of the bodies involved.

g) *Resources*: providing sufficient resources (including human, technical, organizational, natural, and information ones)[25] devoted exclusively to the objectives and activities identified in an action plan for implementing human rights is an integral part of effective planning for implementing human rights. Here is where the concept of the 'maximum available resources' comes in. As first recognized by the Covenant on Economic, Social, and Cultural Rights, states have an obligation to use 'maximum available resources' to achieve the full realization of human rights.[26] This refers to 'both the resources existing within

[25] See, eg, Working Group Paper 3: 'States parties' obligations: realizing economic, social and cultural rights. Are child rights a luxury during an economic crisis?', prepared for the Celebration of the 20th Anniversary of the Adoption of the Convention on the Rights of the Child <http://www2.ohchr.org/english/bodies/ crc/docs/20th/BackDocWG3.doc> accessed 19 May 2017.

[26] ICESCR, Article 2(1); see International Commission of Jurists (ICJ), *Maastricht Guidelines on Violations of Economic, Social and Cultural Rights*, 26 January 1997 <http://www.refworld.org/docid/48abd5730.html> accessed 20 December 2017.

a state as well as those available from the international community through international cooperation and assistance'.[27] As Balakrishnan and others in their analytical report on maximum available resources (MAR) state, sustainably maximizing resource availability to realize human rights depends on different factors, including: (1) government expenditure; (2) government revenue (including taxation and official development assistance); (3) development assistance (both official development assistance and private resource flows); (4) debt and deficit financing; and (5) monetary policy and financial regulation.[28]

Government expenditure which is of critical importance must be efficient and effective.[29] Both the total level of expenditures and the allocation of spending to human rights areas such as health and education (and not for instance to support military purposes) matter to the realization of human rights through NHRAPs.[30] Where national resources are inadequate, the state must do all it can to secure international assistance.[31] A critical factor which negatively affects the availability of resources and their allocation to the realization of human rights is corruption. As stated in a recent report by the OHCHR, 'because corruption is an inefficient use of available resources, failure to curb corruption is also a failure to comply with MAR [maximum available resources]. Corruption can often be spotted through monitoring revenue, allocations and expenditure in the budget.'[32] Hence, it is crucial to collect and allocate an adequate budget to implement human rights in a participatory, accountable, and transparent process; three important principles which are integral to successful anti-corruption strategies. In countries where corruption is pervasive, NHRAPs must be designed to contribute to anti-corruption efforts such as legal and institutional reforms.

h) *Performance indicators*: performance indicators play a key role in raising accountability, transparency, and assessment of the plan's performance. Given

[27] The UN Committee on Economic, Social, and Cultural Rights, 'An Evaluation of the Obligation to Take Steps to the "Maximum of Available Resources" Under an Optional Protocol to the Covenant', Thirty-eighth session, 10 May 2007, E/C.12/2007/1, at para 5 <http://www2.ohchr.org/english/issues/escr/docs/e_c12_2007_1.pdf> accessed 28 January 2018.

[28] Radhika Balakrishnan, Diane Elson, James Heintz, and Nicholas Lusiani, 'Maximum Available Resources & Human Rights: Analytical Report' (2011) Center for Women's Global Leadership Rutgers, The State University of New Jersey, at 5 <http://www.cwgl.rutgers.edu/docman/economic-and-social-rights-publications/362-maximumavailableresources-pdf/file> accessed 23 November 2014.

[29] Realizing Human Rights Through Government Budget, OHCHR, 2017, HR/PUB/17/3, at 29 <http://creativecommons.org/licenses/by/3.0/igo/> accessed 25 January 2018.

[30] Balakrishnan and others, 'Maximum Available Resources & Human Rights: Analytical Report', note 28, at 6.

[31] See UN Committee on Economic, Social and Cultural Rights (CESCR), General Comment No 3: The Nature of States Parties' Obligations (Art 2, para 1, of the Covenant), 14 December 1990, E/1991/23; Radhika Balakrishnan, 'Taxation and Economic and Social Rights in the US' in R Balakrishnan and D S Elson (eds), *Economic Policy and Human Rights: Holding Governments to Account* (1st edn, Zed Books Ltd 2011) Chapter 6.

[32] United Nations, OHCHR, Realizing Human Rights Through Government Budget, 2017, HR/PUB/17/3, at 30 <http://creativecommons.org/licenses/by/3.0/igo/> accessed 26 January 2018.

that in human rights planning, process is as important as the result achieved, two types of performance indicators need to be set up: process indicators and result indicators. Process indicators measure the process through which a NHRAP is formed and implemented whereas result indicators are intended to measure short-, mediate-, and long-term results of a NHRAP on the identified tasks, objectives, and goals.

In line with the procedural theory of human rights planning depicted in Chapter 2, process indicators measure planning process in terms of accountability, participation, non-discrimination, and empowerment.

Adopting a logical model of output-outcome-impact, in each area of intervention, three types of result indicators in a chronological order can be distinguished—(1) output indicators, (2) outcome indicators, and (3) impact indicators—which will be briefly discussed here:

h.1. To ensure activities are achievable and fit for intended objectives requires a set of output performance indicators driven from the theory of planning and the baseline study upon which a NHRAP is based. Outputs refer to the immediate result of activities, that is, what is expected to be produced or delivered by activities ie products, goods, training, or services provided to the plan's direct beneficiaries or the target population. Outputs indicators serve to monitor the rate of progress so that adjustment can be made if progress is not being achieved.

h.2. Outcome is what happens directly as a result of outputs. It pertains to the results of the entire plan intervention immediately after its completion, that is to say, whether objectives are achieved and if so, to what extent such as an increase of school enrolment from 70% to 78%.

h.3. Impact is the wider developmental effect (change) such as contribution to poverty reduction because of improved educational outcomes. It is concerned with the intended and unintended results of the plan in the long term, that is, whether plans' goals are achieved, and if so, to what extent, such as reducing rates of illiteracy from 20% to 12%, and higher percentage of disabled people of working age in employment.

Assumptions about activities and how they lead to realizing intended objectives and goals are derived from both general and special theories of planning. As McLaughlin and Jordan mention, planning theory prior to the monitoring and evaluation is considered most beneficial for predicting cause and effect relationships and for setting performance indicators.[33] Some evaluators believe that making explicit the underlying assumptions about how a plan is supposed to form and work increases the potential for evaluation

[33] John A McLaughlin and Gretchen B Jordan, 'Using Logic Models' in J S Wholey, H P Hatry, K E Newcomer (eds), *Handbook of Practical Programme Evaluation* (2nd edn, Jossey-Bass 2004) at 11.

utility.[34] Likewise, planning theory at the end of the evaluation helps explain observed causal relationships.[35]

It is useful to include both fact-based indicators, eg reducing the percentage of illiteracy, underweight children under five years old, or number of recorded arbitrary executions to a certain level within a specific period of time, and also judgment-based indicators, eg reducing the percentage of people who feel safe when walking alone at night to a certain level or how independent and fair the judiciary system is, though both sets of performance indicators should be transparent, specific, and universally recognized.[36]

A NHRAP is almost never implemented exactly as expected, and consequently monitoring mechanisms must have the flexibility to adapt to changing circumstances by, for example: making adjustment to tasks; definition of the target population; output indicators; outcome indicators; or impact indicators. Although general goals and objectives are often fixed during the course of implementation, as the plan unfolds, tasks, target population, and performance indicators may need to adjust to unexpected situations and factors.

i) *Accountability mechanism*: it is fundamental for a NHRAP to develop an effective system of accountability for all responsible parties on how well they are achieving the targets established in the plan and whether the time schedule is observed. It should clarify what mechanisms are at work to hold all bodies with implementation responsibilities accountable for their performance and the results achieved. There are at least six types of accountability mechanism which will be explored later in the implementation phase.

j) *Monitoring mechanism*: monitoring is a form of assessment which takes place throughout the course of implementation of a NHRAP as a tool to improve ongoing process performance. It allows the plan to determine what is and is not working well, so that adjustments can be made along the way. It can also enhance accountability and transparency throughout planning. It supports innovation by bringing evidence-based updates to bear to inform ongoing decision making and adjustments. Further details will be discussed shortly in this chapter.

k) *Evaluation mechanism*: evaluation mechanisms aim to document and examine the results of a plan at its completion and to learn from the experience of intervention. That is, evaluation is both backward-looking (was it a successful or unsuccessful plan, and to what extent?) and also forward-looking, as well as

[34] See Patricia J Rogers, Anthony Petrosino, Tracy A Huebner, and Timothy A Hacsi, 'Program theory evaluation: Practice, promise, and problems' (2000) 87 New Directions for Evaluation 5–13 <doi:10.1002/ev.1177> accessed 25 January 2012.

[35] McLaughlin and Jordan, 'Using Logic Models', note 33, at 11.

[36] The Office of the High Commissioner for Human Rights (OHCHR) has published Human Rights Indicators: A Guide to Measurement and Implementation, 2012, <http://www.ohchr.org/EN/Issues/Indicators/Pages/documents.aspx> accessed 1 February 2014.

process-oriented (what can we learn for the future?).[37] If a NHRAP is not accompanied by clear mechanisms for valid and reliable assessment, both monitoring and evaluation, it would be more like a rhetorical gesture rather than an effective plan for implementing human rights.

4. Implementation Phase

In order for a NHRAP to be implemented effectively, it must be, among others, well-designed (ie based on a comprehensive and evidence-based situation analysis, a general and special theory of planning, a realistic set of objectives, clear activities, realistic timeframe, and performance indicators, etc), backed by adequate resources (technical, financial, and human), enough social and political will, and carried out through a participatory, accountable, transparent, and empowering process.

Having all these elements in play, however, does not always guarantee that the plans produce tangible outcomes or achieve objectives simply on the basis of clearly formulated goals and objectives. Different factors, antecedent and mediating, external to the plan and not often under its control can positively or negatively influence its performance. Hence, three interconnected issues will be raised here: the sustainability of plan over time; 'complex situations'; and accountability mechanisms which will be discussed respectively in this section.

4.1. Sustainability

Developing and implementing NHRAPs is an ongoing and relatively long term job which often coincides with national elections and a change of government. As mentioned in Chapter 5, political changes sometimes delay, retard, or even reverse the course of planning. For instance, the third NHRAP of Australia, which was based on a wide range of inputs from NGOs and was intended to address the UPR recommendations, was totally left aside and even its website was shut down by the then new government elected after the launch of the plan.

To enhance the plan's sustainability, support, commitment, impetus, and legitimacy are required at different levels as follows:

1. Broad political consensus from the main political parties and active participation by representatives of them can create ownership for the planned activities and enhance the plan's sustainability.
2. One way of ensuring sustainability and continuity is to adopt a legal status for NHRAPs which can manifest itself through parliamentary endorsement of the plan, incorporating the plan in a government decree, or enacting legislation,

[37] See Joseph S Wholey, 'Exploratory Evaluation' in JS Wholey, H P Hatry, and K E Newcomer (eds), *Handbook of Practical Programme Evaluation* (3rd edn, Jossey-Bass 2010).

though this way may be a lengthy process and therefore not necessarily suitable for any context.

3. Systematic monitoring and evaluation of the state's performance on developing and implementing NHRAPs should be carried out by international and regional human rights bodies through, among others, the UPR recommendations and Concluding Observations. How widely the plan is recognized and supported by human rights systems at the regional and international levels is of crucial importance in its sustainability in practice. As mentioned in Chapter 5, however, the form, function, and substance of NHRAPs have not been systematically and adequately reflected in the work of the UN human rights bodies. Hence, it is important to develop awareness of all aspects of NHRAPs among those working in diverse but relevant bodies of the UN human rights system. Perhaps a more theoretically laden guidance should be provided pinpointing the role of NHRAPs in advancing human rights-based development.[38] Such guidance can help to clear up any possible misunderstandings about the function of NHRAPs among human rights bodies.
4. Enough and constant international funding and technical assistance for the development and implementation of national action plans is essential for a plan's sustainability.
5. It is vital that civil society capacity both at the national and international level as well as human rights institutions are strengthened to enable increased advocacy on NHRAPs and to create a greater impetus on states to respond to their obligation to adopt and implement a NHRAP.
6. If a NHRAP is to be effective, it is extremely important that all stakeholders including the general public are aware of planning and give it their support.[39] To this end, a culture of participatory planning for implementing human rights should be developed from the local to the global level. Such a culture can change underlying attitudes about planning, enhance public awareness of the role of NHRAPs in improving human rights-based development, and thereby advance the legitimacy of planning for implementing human rights among the public, civil society, and even state functionaries, and form a social basis for an effective development and implementation of NHRAPs.

4.2. Complex situation

When we start implementing a NHRAP some of what is planned may be implemented as expected in accordance with the logical model of inputs-outputs-outcomes-impacts specified in the plan, some may go unrealized, and some new things may emerge unexpectedly. If things go unrealized, this can be attributed to

[38] See Azadeh Chalabi, 'National Human Rights Action Plans: A Roadmap to Development' (2014) 28(8) The Journal of Development in Practice 989–1002.

[39] See UNOHCHR, Handbook on National Human Rights Plans of Action, note 4, at 88–89.

the lack of perfect delivery of tasks or an emerging unexpected situation. Let me focus on the latter. The former will be discussed shortly with respect to accountability mechanisms.

The actual nature of the situation that the plan is going to deal with is of crucial importance. Considering situations as totally predictable or unpredictable is not always realistic when planning. The 'Cynefin framework', developed by David Snowden and Cynthia Kurtz, is a helpful heuristic device which can be employed for the identification of four behaviours a situation may display: simple, complicated, complex, and chaotic. The Cynefin framework draws on network theory, learning theories, and third-generation knowledge management.[40] The chaos situation, which is where no patterns can be observed, is an exception in the case of human rights planning. Therefore, I will focus on and examine the other three situations in turn.

When a situation is defined as 'simple' it implies that there is a predictable linear pattern of cause and effect: if X, then Y will almost certainly happen. For example, to deal with malnutrition certain foods should be provided immediately. To advance health care in a rural area, health care facilities should be available and accessible. People at risk of malaria should sleep under long-lasting treated bednets. To eradicate polio, all children should be immunized. A simple situation is one in which there is widespread agreement about what should be done and what will be the result.[41]

The Cynefin framework suggests 'sense-categorise-response' strategy to deal with a simple situation. It means that first, data should be collected to identify the characteristics of the situation (this is what accomplished in a baseline study) and then, by referring to relevant theory and method, the 'best practice' (ie a context-free application of theory to the situation) should be identified and implemented.

As the situation becomes less predictable and producing desired outcomes becomes less certain, it moves into 'complicated territory'.[42] In a complicated situation, the situation is not known when data is collected but a pattern of changes is 'knowable' by referring to relevant theory (including general and special theories of planning), and both local knowledge of those affected and expert knowledge. The relationship between cause and effect can be *known*: Y is predictable if you know X and the details of the relationships between the elements.[43] Most of the time the situations with which human rights planning deals are complicated.

The Cynefin framework suggests 'sense-analyse-response' strategy to deal with a complicated situation. It means that the data and evidence collected must be analysed through a theoretical framework (planning theory and other context-relevant

40 Bob Williams and Richard Hummelbrunner, *Systems Concepts in Action: A Practitioner's Toolkit* (1st edn, Stanford University Press 2011).

41 Michael Quinn Patton, *Developmental Evaluation: Applying Complexity Concepts to Enhance Innovation and Use* (1st edn, The Guilford Press 2011) at 86.

42 ibid, at 87.

43 Williams and Hummelbrunner, *Systems Concepts in Action*, note 40, at 166.

theories) in order to identify the 'good practice' (ie context-modified application of theory and evidence to the situation). In such situations, which are predominant in the case of human rights planning and implementation, both expert and local knowledge from top down and bottom up are needed to identify tasks and implement them in practice.

If simple or complicated, planning can be implemented based on the logical model of cause and effect where predicted outputs appear after activities and will lead to an expected outcome and then long-term impacts in practice. In this case, outputs, outcome, and impacts can and should be tracked periodically through accountability and monitoring mechanisms.

Things might not always go as planned. Then a simple or complicated situation may turn into a *complex* or even *chaotic* arena. As Paton states, a situation is complicated when there is either a high degree of uncertainty (certainty about what should be done to solve a problem) *or* a high degree of disagreement (about what to do). And 'if there is *both* high uncertainty and high disagreement (eg, uncertainty is a primary source of disagreements and disagreements contribute to the uncertainty), we have moved into the arena of complexity.'[44]

When a situation, in part or in whole, is complex or turns into a complex situation, then it is or becomes impossible to expect or track any predetermined logical model of output-outcome-impact. Unpredictability of a situation may be predictable at the beginning when designing the plan though often it appears in the phase of implementation. Sometimes many factors are interacting, some of which not only unknown but unknowable.[45] In a complex situation, different possible factors which are at work can be determined only during or after the delivery of a task. It means 'cause and effect is unknown *and* unknowable until after the effect has emerged, at which point some retrospective tracing and patterning may be possible'.[46] X may result in Y or Z or A, but you will be unable to predict which outcome on the basis of knowing X or any of the details until after implementation.[47]

Sometime when a plan is being developed, the patterns of change are unpredictable and it is rather impossible to specify all the variables that may come into play. For example, when planning on a very cultural sensitive issue for the first time in a remote area and there is no clear information about different possible factors which might be at work. The Cynefin model offers the strategy of 'probe-sense-respond' for the management of complex situations. It means a close examination of different possible strategies, track changes closely and constantly, spot the patterns that emerge (emerging patterns), and see what works best for whom. Whereas in other situation, some improvements may seem necessary during implementation, in a complex situation there is often a need for ongoing developments as adaptive

[44] Patton, *Developmental Evaluation: Applying Complexity Concepts to Enhance Innovation and Use,* note 41, at 90.

[45] ibid, at 90. [46] ibid, at 92.

[47] Williams and Hummelbrunner, *Systems Concepts in Action*, note 40, at 167.

strategies, changing even the entire intervention, lead bodies, etc.[48] In such situation, the role of those affected in monitoring the plan is even more important than in the simple or complicated situations.

4.3. Accountability mechanisms

Accountability mechanisms as an integral part of human rights planning is not only a means through which duty holders are held accountable for their performance and/or the results achieved but also an intrinsic end itself.[49] A comprehensive well-designed accountability system makes all the activities from those related to resource allocation (inputs), to performing tasks (process) and the result achieved (output and outcome) transparent, reducing information asymmetries during planning, and making the whole system of planning more self-reflective and self-correcting. A self-reflective system can serve to reduce the likelihood of corruption in different phases of planning while enhancing the sustainability and legitimacy of the plan.

There are at least six types of accountability mechanism, each of which can serve different purposes and be suitable for different settings. These six types can be paired into three categories:

1. process and result accountability mechanisms
2. internal and external accountability mechanisms
3. vertical and horizontal accountability mechanisms

4.3.1. Process and result accountability mechanisms

Accountability mechanisms can hold lead bodies accountable for the process used in allocating inputs and performing tasks and/or the quality of results achieved (output-outcome-impact accountability). The accountability system for human rights planning requires both types of accountability in order to increase reliability, transparency, and effectiveness, though with different weight depending on tasks, context, and timeline. Whereas process accountability is more suitable to control accomplishment of the assigned tasks especially where the result is not totally under control, the result accountability gives space for innovative ideas for achieving better outcomes during the implementation phase which is key to the implementation of the NHRAP in certain situations in particular 'complicated' and 'complex' situations (in Cynefin model's terminology). Hence, a balance should be made between control and innovation while setting tasks, lead bodies, and performance

[48] Common approaches for the evaluation and implementation in complex situations include, among others: developmental evaluation; systems-and-complexity-based interactive design; rapid assessment; rapid feedback; emergent evaluation; real-time evaluation; ongoing environmental scanning and outcomes monitoring; reflective practice; participatory action research; network analysis; and systems change mapping (Patton, *Developmental Evaluation: Applying Complexity Concepts to Enhance Innovation and Use*, note 41, at 46).

[49] See Melvin J Dubnick and H George Frederickson, 'Introduction' in M J Dubnick and H G Frederickson (eds), *Accountable Governance: Problems and Promises* (1st edn, Routledge 2011) xvii.

indicators.[50] To do so, as Patil and others argue, four empowering factors should be taken into account when designing a NHRAP: (1) task role fit (meaning); (2) competence; (3) self-determination; and (4) impact. Task role fit refers to the perceived fit between lead bodies' self-concepts and their assigned tasks.[51] Competence is concerned with the lead body's ability to perform tasks which is key to the accomplishment of activities.[52] Self-determination, which involves a degree of discretion to adjust interventions to the context (and changing patterns in 'complex situations'), can play an important role in advancing innovative ideas and intrinsically-motivated performance during implementation. These all pertain to the desired impact.

4.3.2. Internal and external accountability mechanisms

Internal accountability refers to accountability among those who are involved in planning whereas external accountability (labelled as 'social accountability', 'direct accountability', or 'stakeholder accountability') is concerned with holding lead bodies accountable to those who are affected. A key challenge of the implementation phase is to create tracking mechanisms to determine whether progress is being made and adjust the plan accordingly. This requires effective internal and external communication. To enhance co-ordination, effectiveness, transparency, and the sense of ownership, it is essential that those who are involved in implementing the plan stay informed about the process. An effective and systematic communication can create synergies and allow for open and creative discussion, feedback, and revision of the ongoing implementation work. There is likewise a need for an effective, free, clear, and interacting communication with those affected by the plan relating to the changes and obstacles in place. This can not only raise public awareness of human rights planning but also enhance transparency and legitimacy of the plan among the target population. These communications can be useful to the extent that they are carried out at regular intervals systematically.

4.3.3. Vertical and horizontal accountability mechanisms

If a NHRAP is developed through networking in a way that various stakeholders can have the opportunity to become directly or indirectly involved in the process of planning and implementation, then, the horizontal form of accountability would be the predominant form of accountability, though a network cannot be devoid of the vertical form of accountability.[53] Internal accountability can take different forms

[50] See Shefali V Patil, Ferdinand Vieider, and Philip E Tetlock, 'Process versus Outcome Accountability' in M Bovens, R E Goodin, and T Schillemans (eds), *The Oxford Handbook of Public Accountability* (1st edn, Oxford University Press 2014).

[51] See Sebastiaan Rothmann and Lukondo Hamukang'andu, 'Callings, Work Role Fit, Psychological Meaningfulness and Work Engagement among Teachers in Zambia' (2013) 33(2) South African Journal of Education.

[52] See Patil, Vieider, and Tetlock, 'Process versus Outcome Accountability', note 50, at 80.

[53] Erik Hans Klijn and Joop F M Koppenjan, 'Accountable Networks' in M Bovens, R E Goodin, and T Schillemans (eds), *The Oxford Handbook of Public Accountability* (1st edn, Oxford University Press 2014) Chapter 15, at 248.

such as accountability of lead bodies to each other (horizontal accountability), to their mother organization (vertical accountability), and to the network co-ordinator (if planning is advanced through networking).

Learning is an essential part of the accountability system in human rights planning. As Damgaard and Lewis mention, a forward-looking notion of accountability implies formulating new solutions for inadequate performance or unexpected results.[54] There is a broad range of tools, methods, and techniques such as social auditing, reporting, media strategy, which can be used to set up an accountability system.[55] The type of mechanism used depends on the type of task, level of lead bodies, timing, etc. Although there is a need for a comprehensive system of accountability covering all lead bodies and all phases of planning, enough attention should be paid to the possibility of the overload of accountability demands which can undermine efficiency and effectiveness of planning.[56] This is what Koppell refers to as 'multiple accountabilities disorder'.[57] Moreover, accountability mechanisms should be clear enough to prevent the problem of many hands especially in collaborative projects. Likewise, the assessment criteria should not be contested setting out conflicting expectation for performing bodies.[58]

5. Assessment Phase

An essential element of any planning including a NHRAP is an ongoing formative assessment of its performance during the implementation (monitoring) and an overall summative assessment of the results achieved at completion (evaluation). They can strengthen planning by highlighting progress, exposing obstacles, and allowing the plan to learn and adjust its design to changing situations. However, as the findings of the cross-case analysis of NHRAPs in Chapter 5 indicate, most of the existing NHRAPs are not accompanied by any effective monitoring or evaluation mechanism. For an effective human rights planning, in this section, I would suggest a seven-feature model of assessment. These features include:

1. theory-driven assessment
2. systems-based assessment (systemism)
3. top-down bottom-up assessment
4. internally and externally driven assessment

[54] Bodil Damgaard and Jenny M Lewis, 'Accountability and Citizen Participation' in M Bovens, R E Goodin, and T Schillemans (eds), *The Oxford Handbook of Public Accountability* (1st edn, Oxford University Press 2014) Chapter 16, at 266.

[55] See Alnoor Ebrahim, 'Accountability in Practice: Mechanisms for NGOs' (2003) 31(5) World Development 813–29.

[56] Arie Halachmi, 'Accountability Overloads' in M Bovens, R E Goodin, and T Schillemans (eds), *The Oxford Handbook of Public Accountability* (1st edn, Oxford University Press 2014) Chapter 34, at 560.

[57] Jonathan G Koppell, 'Pathologies of Accountability: ICANN and the Challenge of "Multiple Accountabilities Disorder"' (2005) 65(1) Public Administration Review 94–109.

[58] See Thomas Schillemans and Mark Bovens, 'The Challenge of Multiple Accountability: Does Redundancy Lead to Overload?' in M Dubnick and H Frederickson (eds), *Accountable Governance: Problems and Promises* (1st edn, Routledge 2011).

5. mixed methods assessment
6. Fuzzy logic-based assessment
7. measurement equivalence

These features will be discussed respectively here.

5.1. Theory-driven assessment

The use of planning theory, both general and special, to inform the design and content of assessment is relevant almost to all types of planning including human rights action planning. In the context of assessment, planning theory can serve at least five purposes. First, reference to planning theory clarifies the scope of monitoring and evaluation. Drawing on the general theory of human rights planning, for instance, the scope of assessment should be broad including all the rights set forth in the core human rights treaties (at the minimum) and the fourfold obligation of respect, protect, promote, and fulfil.

Second, planning theory can be used as a frame of reference against which indicators can be selected or index(es) can be constructed. As Green says, 'without such recourse to theory, the process of selecting indicators can be rather like plucking straws out of the air'.[59] A thorough theoretical analysis of the empirical evidence collected in a baseline study can serve to identify output-outcome-impact indicators in a logical framework including a range of potential outputs-outcomes-impacts as a basis for making a selection of those indicators to be most relevant. Furthermore, as Green states, 'a theoretical framework allows these indicators to be ordered in relation to an anticipated time sequence-effectively constructing a proximal-distal chain of events'.[60]

Third, substantive and analytical theories of planning can provide criteria to weigh indicators and also to ascertain the extent to which the plan's objectives have been attained. They can also help to assess priority setting through planning.

Fourth, it is worth emphasizing that recourse to theory in identifying indicators need not be restricted to the content of human rights planning or the result achieved. The argument applies equally to the process. In this instance, by providing criteria, the procedural theory of planning allows the various stages in the process to be recognized and indictors appropriate to each stage to be selected. This includes criteria for the identification and selection of process indicators in order to monitor and evaluate the process of planning as a whole and the process of delivering each task individually. According to the procedural theory of human rights planning, the process of developing, implementing, and assessing NHRAPs should be participatory, accountable, empowering, and non-discriminatory. Equal weights can be used for process indicators as all four principles are equally important.

[59] Jackie Green, 'The Role of Theory in Evidence-based Health Promotion Practice' (2000) 15(2) Health Education Research 125–29 <https://academic.oup.com/her/article/15/2/125/550414/The-role-of-theory-in-evidence-based-health> accessed 23 December 2017.

[60] ibid.

Fifth, realistic assessment requires theoretical insights about contextual factors and mechanisms by which interventions achieve their effects in different domains of society. As mentioned before, here 'context' is used in two senses: (1) 'general context' at the high level of abstract discussed in the contextual theory of human rights planning (as part of the general theory of planning) in Chapter 1; and (2) 'spatio-temporal context' which must be dealt with in special theories of planning for the country or region in question.

5.2. Systems-based assessment

A systems approach can contribute to a more comprehensive and in depth assessment. As remarked before, assessment, both monitoring and evaluation, can be set up based on the logical model of 'output-outcome-impact' linking tasks to objectives and goals. The model, which is based on a cause and effect relationship, assumes that the plan is an instrument of change from activities to objectives and goals. Through a systems thinking lens, the cause and effect relationship is not often linear and in one direction, but instead causality is often circular with effect feeding back to influence the causes and sometimes causes affecting each other. Circular causality is indeed in line with the principle of interrelatedness of human rights according to which human rights are interdependent and often reinforce each other. Related to this, also, systemism is based on a dynamic causality meaning that causal dependencies are not always static and can be changed over time, that is to say, causality is seen as an on-going process, not a one-time event. Systems Dynamics (SD) in particular can help planners to present causal loop diagrams with negative and positive feedbacks.[61] Likewise, interventions in each system should be assessed with respect to its environment. System and environment have often the capacity to mutually influence each other.[62] For assessment, it is not enough to look only into results (ie outputs, outcomes, and impacts) in an isolated manner, without taking the contextual factors into account. Results should be assessed with respect to the context within which human rights problems are embedded.

5.3. Top-down bottom-up assessment

The top-down bottom-up approach needs to be taken in all phases of human rights planning, including the assessment phase. A comprehensive assessment should be informed by both expert knowledge of human rights standards and scientific and technical understanding of different causal mechanisms which are at work (from

[61] See Kimberly A Fredericks, Michael Deegan, and Joanne G Carman, 'Using System Dynamics as an Evaluation Tool Experience From a Demonstration Program' (2008) 29(3) American Journal of Evaluation 251–67.

[62] Richard Hummelbrunner and ÖAR Regionalberatung, 'A System Approach to Evaluation: Applications of Systems theory and Systems thinking in Evaluations', Paper prepared for the 4th EES Conference, 12–14 October 2000, Lausanne.

the top-down) and detailed local knowledge of human rights issues, local factors, strengths, vulnerabilities, etc (from the bottom-up). Using a method that integrates both sources of knowledge can enhance the validity and reliability of the assessment and facilitate adjustment during monitoring. The top-down approach alone is criticized for ignoring the local contexts in which each plan is implemented, which in turn can produce significant differences in the outcomes and impacts of NHRAPs in different locations.[63] A plan cannot be effectively implemented and comprehensively assessed unless supported by the social will of those people among whom it is going to be implemented. Due to its exclusionary and unrepresentative nature, top-down planning is often unsustainable and locally unacceptable. An effective involvement of local people and communities in the monitoring and evaluation of plan is critical in enhancing social will. Technical expert knowledge needs to be completed by crucially relevant local realities, skills, perspectives, and inputs from the bottom-up. It is an essential feature of human rights planning that those who are affected by planning should be able to participate in developing the plan but also in monitoring and evaluating its success or failure. Their participation can bring to light human rights issues of concern to the general public, in particular vulnerable groups that may not necessarily feature prominently on the agenda of an exclusively top-down assessment.

5.4. Internally and externally driven assessment

Internally-driven and externally-driven assessments can complement each other. Internally driven-assessments, initiated and conducted by those who are involved in developing and implementing a NHRAP, can provide first-hand detailed feedback which can nurture the adjustment process.[64] However, internally-driven assessments may run the risk of being biased. Often those who are involved in planning tend to have a favourable impression of the plan and that is why relying exclusively on internally-driven assessment may undermine the credibility of the process.

Externally-driven assessments, conducted by those outside the plan, can provide an independent (free from potential bias) feedback, though this is not perhaps as detailed as an internally-driven one.[65] It is especially important to include a systematic, constant, and consistent assessment of regional and international human rights

[63] Julia L Smith, 'A Critical Appreciation of the "Bottom-up" Approach to Sustainable Water Management: Embracing Complexity Rather Than Desirability' (2008) 13:4 Local Environment 353–66; see Nathan P Kettle, Kirstin Dow, Seth Tuler, Thomas Webler, Jessica Whitehead, and Karly M Miller, 'Integrating Scientific and Local Knowledge to Inform Risk-based Management Approaches for Climate Adaptation' (2014) 4–5 Climate Risk Management 17–31; Piyapong Boossabong, 'Policy Analysis in Thailand: Comparing the Roles of Expert and Local Knowledge' (2017) 19:2 Journal of Comparative Policy Analysis: Research and Practice 173–83.

[64] Richard M Grinnell, Peter A Gabor, and Yvonne A Unrau, *Program Evaluation for Social Workers: Foundations of Evidence-Based Practice for Social Workers* (6th edn, Oxford University Press 2012).

[65] See ibid; Yvonne A Unrau, Peter A Gabor, and Richard M Grinnell, JR, *Evaluation in Social Work: The Art and Science of Practice* (4th edn, Oxford University Press 2007) at 32.

bodies, particularly the views of the UN treaty bodies, reports of special rapporteurs, the Human Rights Council's Universal Periodic Review's recommendations, and any relevant International Labour Organisation reports. It is always likely that external evaluators offer new and possibly innovative inputs to planning. The presence of both external and internal evaluation can enhance transparency, legitimacy, and accountability.

5.5. Mixed methods assessment

Assessments are conducted to address a range of questions as to design, process, implementation, outputs, outcomes, and impacts. The value of an assessment is measured in the strength of the methods used and reliability and validity of the data collected. Most traditional evaluation designs rely either on quantitative or qualitative methods for the assessment of plans. Despite significant progress, each method by itself is often limited in its ability to address some important aspects of planning. Instead of focusing on any of these two methods, a mixed methods assessment combines the advantages of both qualitative and quantitative methods. As Bamberger and others state:

> Mixed method approaches combine quantitative approaches that permit estimates of magnitude and distribution of effects, generalization and tests of statistical differences with qualitative approaches that permit in-depth description, analysis of processes and patterns of social interaction. These integrated approaches provide the flexibility to fill in gaps in the available information, to use triangulation to strengthen the validity of estimates, and to provide different perspectives on complex, multi-dimensional phenomena. When working under real-world constraints, a well-designed mixed-methods approach can use the available time and resources to maximize the range and validity of information.[66]

Different types of mixed methods designs have been suggested in the literature.[67] John Creswell classified the most important of these into two sets: sequential designs and concurrent designs. The former includes sequential explanatory design, sequential exploratory design, and sequential transformative design, and the latter encompasses concurrent triangulation design, concurrent embedded design, and concurrent transformative design.[68] Depending on the types of interventions, time-budget, planning theory, and resources available, planners can choose a suitable design for evaluating the plan.[69]

[66] Michael Bamberger, Vijayendra Rao, and Michael Woolcock, 'Using Mixed Methods in Monitoring and Evaluation Experiences from International Development' (2010) Policy Research Working Paper 5245.

[67] See eg Abbas Tashakkori and Charles Teddlie, *Handbook of Mixed Methods in Social and Behavioral Research* (1st edn, Sage 2003).

[68] For details see John W Creswell, *Research Design: Qualitative, Quantitative, and Mixed Methods Approaches* (3rd edn, Sage 2009) Chapter 10.

[69] See ibid; Steven Miller and Marcel Fredericks, 'Mixed-Methods and Evaluation Research: Trends and Issues' (2006) 16(4) Qualitative Health Research 567–79.

5.6. Fuzzy logic-based assessment

Although fuzzy logic-based evaluation has been widely used across different disciplines, the current system of evaluation of human rights performance in general and NHRAPs in particular is primarily based on binary logic which is restricted to two values: true (1.00) or false (0.00). A binary logic-based assessment seeks to address questions as to whether plans are successful or unsuccessful, whether plans are designed correctly or incorrectly, and whether a lead body has performed its tasks successfully or unsuccessfully. Similarly, as discussed in Chapter 4, at the international level, a binary logic-based question is whether the state is in compliance with the obligation to adopt a NHRAP or in non-compliance. This two-valued logic is not often compatible with the real world. The reality is that a plan can be to some degree successful and to some degree unsuccessful. A lead body may have performed its tasks to some degree successfully and to some degree unsuccessfully. The degree of compliance is relative and takes account of the diverse situations of countries, which are obligated to achieve full realization progressively, to the maximum of available resources. A state may be to some degree in compliance with its obligation and to some degree in non-compliance. Given resource constraints, the performance of states with regard to the progressive realization of human rights cannot be judged solely on the enjoyment of rights (result indicators). Some relatively new indexes such as the Social and Economic Rights Fulfillment Index (SERF Index) have sought to capture the diverse situation of each country in terms of available resources.[70] Despite significant progress, however, most human rights indexes, if not all, are still constructed solely based on binary logic.

Instead of relying on binary logic, I would suggest using fuzzy-logic which is a multi-valued logic allowing intermediate values to be defined between conventional evaluations like compliance/incompliance, successful/unsuccessful, effective/ineffective, true/false, yes/no, high/low, etc. In addition to being either fully successful (1.00) or fully unsuccessful (0.00), an outcome might take a range of values between 0.00 and 1.00, that is, a fuzzy logic-based assessment can capture the fact that a plan may be partially (say for instance 0.40) successful and partially (for instance 0.60) unsuccessful at the same time.

As remarked before in Chapter 4, in a fuzzy-based assessment, concepts are defined as sets (and not as variables). A fuzzy set scales degree of membership (eg, membership in the set of successful plans) in the interval between 0.00 (full exclusion from a set) to 1.00 (full inclusion in a set).[71] How can we measure the degree of membership of each NHRAP in a set, for example, the set of effective or successful NHRAPs? What would a plan with a high fuzzy membership function value eg 0.75 in this set (more in than out, but not fully in) be like? What constitutes full

[70] See Sakiko Fukuda-Parr, Terra Lawson-Remer, and Susan Randolph, *Fulfilling Social and Economic Rights* (1st edn, Oxford University Press 2015); Sakiko Fukuda-Parr, Terra Lawson-Remer, and Susan Randolph, 'An Index of Economic and Social Rights Fulfillment: Concept and Methodology' (2009) 8 Journal of Human Rights 195–221.

[71] Charles C Ragin, 'Fuzzy Sets: Calibration Versus Measurement', <http://www.u.arizona.edu/~cragin/fsQCA/download/Calibration.pdf> accessed 12 January 2018.

membership? What constitutes full non-membership? How would this plan differ from a plan with 0.95 membership?[72]

To answer these questions, fuzzy sets should be calibrated based on theoretical knowledge and/or expert knowledge. A fuzzy-set calibration of action planning permits us to not only compare plans and performances quantitatively with a meaningful zero (difference of degree) but also measure qualitative differences among them (difference of kind). A calibrated scale of human rights action planning can be utilized by UN human rights bodies, governments, human rights NGOs, practitioners, and human rights institutions for the measurement of the degree of membership (between 0.00 and 1.00) of each NHRAP in qualitatively different sets of, for instance, 'fully successful/effective plans', 'mostly successful/effective plans', 'slightly successful/effective plans', 'mostly unsuccessful/ineffective plans' and 'fully unsuccessful/ineffective plans'.

5.7. Measurement equivalence

Equivalence of measurement across cultures is a prerequisite for any assessment.[73] When collecting data to monitor or evaluate the performance of planning for different social groups, planners and evaluators commonly assume measurement invariance in their underlying scaling methods. However, sometimes the same indicator may measure different things in different social groups or cultural settings. Meaningful assessment of same interventions across different cultural groups require equivalent measurements of relevant constructs. This is especially true for assessment of subjective attributes such as values, feelings, attitudes, opinions, or behaviours.[74] As Carol Ing argues, when planning in cross-cultural settings, evaluators must be culturally competent and have the skills to adapt the technical processes of assessment so that they are appropriate for the setting.[75]

Monitoring and evaluation would not be meaningful if there is any measurement variance across different groups of right holders. Necessary skills in cross-cultural communications are required to ensure equivalence of measurement. Different approaches such as latent variable models, Test Theory, Confirmatory Factor Analysis (CFA), Observed Variable Methods, and Item Response Theory (IRT) can be used for exploring measurement invariance.[76]

[72] Charles C Ragin, *Redesigning Social Inquiry: Fuzzy Sets and Beyond* (1st edn, University of Chicago Press 2008).

[73] See Sebastian Jilke, Nicolai Petrovsky, Bart Meuleman, and Oliver James, 'Measurement equivalence in replications of experiments: when and why it matters and guidance on how to determine equivalence' (2017) 19:9 Public Management Review 1293–310; Dario Spini, 'Measurement Equivalence of 10 Value Types from the Schwartz Value Survey Across 21 Countries', Journal of Cross-Cultural Psychology, May 2003.

[74] See Eldad Davidov, Bart Meuleman, Jan Cieciuch, Peter Schmidt, and Jaak Billiet, 'Measurement Equivalence in Cross-National Research' (2014) 40 Annual Review of Sociology 55–75.

[75] Carol Ing, 'Culturally Appropriate Evaluations' in Y A Unrau, P A Gabor, R M Grinnell (eds), *Evaluation in Social Work: The Art and Science of Practice* (4th edn, Oxford University Press 2007) at 418.

[76] See Gordon W Cheung and Roger B Rensvold, 'Evaluating Goodness-of-Fit Indexes for Testing Measurement Invariance' (2002) 9(2) Structural Equation Modeling: A Multidisciplinary Journal; Rex B Kline, *Principles and Practice of Structural Equation Modeling* (4th edn, Guilford Press 2015).

Taken together, for a NHRAP to be effective, it needs to be based on a model of planning which is multi-level, top-down bottom-up, participatory, evidence-based, and theory-laden. A NHRAP, if properly designed and implemented, through an informed and continued demand by and meaningful participation of all the stakeholders, committed to working with a vibrant civil society and independent National Human Rights Institution in a transparent and accountable way, supported by adequate resources and political will of those who are in power, can pave the way for human rights-based development. Otherwise, adopting a NHRAP for the sake of doing would be more like window dressing rather than an effective roadmap to development.

Bibliography

Abashidze A, 'The Process of Strengthening the Human Rights Treaty Body System' (2014) 5 Czech Yearbook of International Law 3–18

Abbott K and Snidal D, 'The governance triangle: Regulatory standards institutions and the shadow of the state' in K W Abbott and D Snidal (eds), *The Politics of Global Regulation* (1st edn, Princeton University Press 2009) 44–88

Abbott KW and Hale T, Orchestrating Global Solution Networks: A Guide for Organizational Entrepreneurs (4 April 2014)

Abbott KW, Genschel P, Snidal D, and Zangl B, 'Orchestration: Global Governance Through Intermediaries' in K Abbott, P Genschel, D Snidal, and B Zangl (eds), *International Organizations as Orchestrators* (1st edn, Cambridge University Press 2015) 3–36

Acemoglu D, Ticchi D, and Vindigni A, 'Emergence and Persistence of Inefficient States' (2011) 9(2) Journal of the European Economic Association 177–208

Action Plan for the Implementation of the Human Rights Roadmap (HRRM) For Somalia 2015–2016 <http://www.ohchr.org/EN/Issues/PlansActions/Pages/PlansofActionIndex.aspx> accessed 9 December 2017

Action Plan of the Government of Georgia on the Protection of Human Rights 2014–2016 <https://www.coe.int/t/commissioner/source/NAP/Georgia-National-Action-Plan-on-Human-Rights.pdf> accessed 28 December 2017

Action Plan of the Government of the Federal Republic of Germany on the Implementation of United Nations Security Council Resolution 1325 on Women, Peace and Security for the Period 2017–2020 <http://peacewomen.org/sites/default/files/170111_Aktionsplan_1325.pdf> accessed 25 January 2018

Adams SJ, 'Projecting the Next Decade in Safety Management: A Delphi Technique Study' (2001) 46(10) Professional Safety 26–29

African Human Rights Reports, Communication 241/2001, Sixteenth Annual Activity Report (2003) Annex VII 96.

Airey v Ireland App no 6289/73 (1981) 3 EHRR 305

Alexander E, *Evaluation in Planning: Evolution and Prospects. Contributions in Honour of Nathaniel Lichfield* (1st edn, Ashgate 2006)

Alexander JC, *The Civil Sphere* (1st edn, Oxford University Press 2006)

Alizadeh H, 'A Proposal for How to Realize Human Rights at the National and Regional Level: A Three-Pillar Strategy' (2011) 33(3) Human Rights Quarterly 826–55

Alkire S, 'Needs and Capabilities' (2005) 80(57) Royal Institute of Philosophy Supplement 229

Alkire S and Black R, 'A Practical Reasoning Theory of Development Ethics: Furthering the Capabilities Approach' (1997) 9:2 Journal of International Development 236

Alkire S, *Valuing Freedoms. Sen's Capability Approach and Poverty Reduction* (1st edn, Oxford University Press 2002)

Allmendinger P, *Planning Theory* (2nd edn, Palgrave Macmillan 2009)

Alston P, 'The Populist Challenge to Human Rights' (2017) 9 Journal of Human Rights Practice 1–15

Alston P, United Nations Special Rapporteur on extreme poverty and human rights, Statement on Visit to the USA, release on 15 December 2017 <http://www.ohchr.org/EN/NewsEvents/Pages/DisplayNews.aspx?NewsID=22533> accessed 2 January 2018

Alston P, United Nations Special Rapporteur on Extreme Poverty and Human Rights, End-of-mission statement on China, 23 August 2016 <http://www.ohchr.org/en/NewsEvents/Pages/DisplayNews.aspx?NewsID=20402&LangID=E> accessed 28 January 2018

Alston P, 'The Contribution of the Agency to the Realization of Social and Economic Rights' in Philip Alston and Olivier De Schutter (eds), *Monitoring Fundamental Rights in the EU: The Contribution of the Fundamental Rights Agency* (1st edn, Hart Publishing 2005) 159–89

Alston P, 'The Historical Origins of "General Comments" in Human Rights Law' in Laurence Boisson De Chazournes and Vera Gowlland-Debbas (eds), *The International Legal System in Quest of Equity and Universality* (1st edn, Brill 2001) 763–76

Alston P, 'Beyond "Them" and "Us": Putting Treaty Body Reform into Perspective' in P Alston and J Crawford (eds), *The Future of UN Human Rights Treaty Monitoring* (1st edn, Cambridge University Press 2000) 501–25

Alston P, *The United Nations and Human Rights: A Critical Appraisal* (1st edn, Clarendon Press 1992)

Alston P, 'Out of the Abyss: The Challenges Confronting the New UN Committee on Economic, Social and Cultural Rights' (1987) 9 Human Rights Quarterly 332–81

Alston P and Quinn G, 'The Nature and Scope of States Parties' Obligations under the International Covenant on Economic, Social and Cultural Rights' (1987) 9(2) Human Rights Quarterly 156–85

Alvaredo F, Atkinson A, Piketty T, and Saez E, The World Top Incomes Database <http://wid.world> accessed 3 October 2017

And GS and Heskin A, 'Foundations for a Radical Concept of Planning' (1973) 39(2) Journal of the American Institute of Planners 106–14

Anderson I, 'Mutual Obligation, Shared Responsibility Agreements and Indigenous Health Strategy' (2006) 3(10) Australia and New Zealand Health Policy <http://www.publish.csiro.au/hp/pdf/HP060310> accessed 21 January 2018

Arambulo K, *Strengthening the Supervision of the International Covenant on Economic, Social and Cultural Rights: Theoretical and Procedural Aspects* (1st edn, Intersentia-Hart 1999)

Arato J, 'Corporations as Lawmakers' (2015) 56(2) Harvard International Law Journal

Archer R, 'The Strengths of Difference Traditions: What Can be Gained and What Might be Lost by Combining Rights and Development?' (2006) 3(4) SUR International Journal of Human Rights 80

Arfi B, 'Fuzzy Decision Making in Politics: A Linguistic Fuzzy-Set Approach' (2005) 13 Political Analysis 23–56

Arneson RJ, 'Equality and Equal Opportunity for Welfare' (1989) 56 Philosophical Studies 77–93

Arnstein S, 'A Ladder of Citizen Participation' (1969) 35(4) Journal of American Planning 216–24

Assessment Report on the Implementation of the National Human Rights Action Plan, (2004–2008 and 2011–2014) <https://rm.coe.int/1680597a50> accessed 23 December 2017

Atkinson A and Piketty T, *Top Incomes over the Twentieth Century: A Contrast between Europeans and English-Speaking Countries* (Oxford University Press 2007)

Australia's National Human Rights Action Plan (2012) <http://www.ohchr.org/Documents/Issues/NHRA/NHRPAustralia2012.pdf> accessed 25 September 2013

Australian Bureau of Statistics, Personal Safety Survey Australia, Catalogue No 4906.0 (2006), <http://www.ausstats.abs.gov.au/ausstats/subscriber.nsf/0/056A404DAA576AE6CA2571D00080E985/$File/49060_2005%20%28reissue%29.pdf> accessed 12 July 2015

Australian study tour report: Visit of the UN Special Rapporteur on Violence against Women, 2012 <https://www.humanrights.gov.au/publications/australian-study-tour-report-visit-un-special-rapporteur-violence-against-women> accessed 12 July 2015

Baderin M A and McCorquodale R, 'The International Covenant on Economic, Social and Cultural Rights: Forty Years of Development' in M A Baderin and R MacCorquodale (eds), *Economic, Social and Cultural Rights in Action* (1st edn, Oxford University Press 2007) 3–27

Baird N, 'The Universal Periodic Review: building a bridge between the Pacific and Geneva?' in H Charlesworth and E Larking (eds), *Human Rights and the Universal Periodic Review* (1st edn, Cambridge University Press 2015) 187–212

Balakrishnan B, Heintz J, and Elson D, *Rethinking Economic Policy for Social Justice: The Radical Potential of Human Rights* (1st edn, Routledge 2016)

Balakrishnan R, 'Taxation and Economic and Social Rights in the US' in R Balakrishnan and D S Elson (eds), *Economic Policy and Human Rights: Holding Governments to Account* (1st edn, Zed Books Ltd 2011) 153–75

Balakrishnan R, Elson D, Heintz J, and Lusiani N, 'Maximum Available Resources & Human Rights: Analytical Report' (2011) Center for Women's Global Leadership Rutgers, The State University of New Jersey

Bamberger M, Rao V, Woolcock M, 'Using Mixed Methods in Monitoring and Evaluation Experiences from International Development' (2010) Policy Research Working Paper 5245

Barker B, 'Protecting, Promoting and Fulfilling Human Rights in Australia: A National Human Rights Action', A paper prepared for the Australian Human Rights Commission (January 2011)

Bassiouni M C, 'A Critical Introduction Assessment of the UN Human Rights Mechanisms' in M Cherif Bassiouni and W A Schabas (eds), *New Challenges for the UN Human Rights Machinery* (1st edn, Intersentia 2011) 1–15

Bayefsky A F, *The UN Human Rights Treaty System: Universality at the Crossroads* (1st edn, Martinus Nijhof 2001)

Beetham D, 'The Right to Development and Its Corresponding Obligations' in Bard A Andreassen and Stephen P Marks (eds), *Development as a Human Rights: Legal, Political and Economic Dimensions* (2nd edn, Intersenita 2010) 79–95

Bernaz N, 'Continuing Evolution of UN Treaty Bodies System' in N Rodley and S Scott (eds), *Routledge Handbook of International Human Rights Law* (1st edn, Routledge 2014) 707–25

Besley T and Persson T, 'State Capacity, Conflict, and Development' (2010) 78 Econometrica 1–34. <doi:10.3982/ECTA8073> accessed 11 January 2013

Biermann F, Pattberg P, Asselt H, and Zelli F, 'The Fragmentation of Global Governance Architectures: A Framework for Analysis' (2009) 9 Global Environmental Politics 14–40

Bilchitz D, 'The Necessity for a Business and Human Rights Treaty' (2016) 1(2) Business and Human Rights Journal 203–27

Birdsall N, Income Distribution: Effects on Growth and Development, 2007 <https://www.cgdev.org/files/13505_file_Income_Distribution_Birdsall.pdf> accessed 10 May 2012

Blake C, 'Normative Instruments in International Human Rights Law: Locating the General Comment', Center for Human Rights and Global Justice Working Paper Number 17, 2008

Boesen K and Sano H, 'The Implications and Value Added of a Human Rights-Based Approach' in Bård A Andreassen and S Marks (eds), *Development as a Human Right: Legal, Political, and Economic Dimensions* (1st edn, Intersentia 2010) 45–69

Bolivia. National Plan of Action for the Promotion and Protection of Human Rights in the Medium and Long Term (1999) <http://www.ohchr.org/EN/Issues/PlansActions/Pages/PlansofActionIndex.aspx> accessed 12 January 2013

Boossabong P, 'Policy Analysis in Thailand: Comparing the Roles of Expert and Local Knowledge' (2017) 19(2) Journal of Comparative Policy Analysis: Research and Practice 173–83

Boulesbaa A, 'The Nature of the Obligations Incurred by States under Article 2 of the UN Convention Against Torture' (1990) 12(1) Human Rights Quarterly 53–93, 80

Brazil, National Action Plan for Human Rights (1996) <http://www.ohchr.org/EN/Issues/PlansActions/Pages/PlansofActionIndex.aspx> accessed 2 November 2016

Brown A, 'New Human Rights Action Plan a Step Forward for Rights but Needs Stronger Accountability Measures', 18 December 2012 <http://www.humanrightsactionplan.org.au/nhrap-blogs/new-national-human-rights-action-plan-a-modest-success> accessed 25 December 2014

Brownlie I, The Human Right to Development: Study prepared for the Commonwealth Secretariat (Human Rights Unit occasional paper) (Commonwealth Secretariat 1989)

Buckley W F, *Sociology and Modern Systems Theory* (1st edn, Prentice Hall 1967)

Bulto TS, 'Africa's engagement with the Universal Periodic Review: Commitment or Capitulation?' in H Charlesworth and E Larking (eds), *Human Rights and the Universal Periodic Review* (1st edn, Cambridge University Press 2015) 235–55

Bunge M, *Political Philosophy: Fact, Fiction, and Vision* (1st edn, Transaction 2009)

Bunge M, *Chasing Reality: Strife over Realism* (1st edn, University of Toronto Press 2006)

Bunge M, 'How Does It Work?: The Search for Explanatory Mechanisms' (2004) 34 Philosophy of the Social Sciences 182, 190–91

Bunge M, *Treatise on Basic Philosophy- Ethics: The Good and The Right* (1st edn, Springer 1989)

Bunge M, 'A Systems Concept of Society: Beyond Individualism and Holism' (1979) 10 Theory and Decision 13–30

Bunge M, 'Treatise on Basic Philosophy' Vol 4, *A World of Systems* (1st edn, Springer 1979)

Bunn I, 'The Right to Development: Implications for International Economic Law' (2000) 15(6) American University International Law Review 1425–67.

Çalı B, 'Specialized rules of treaty interpretation: Human Rights' in D B Hollis (ed), *The Oxford Guide to Treaties* (1st edn, Oxford University Press 2012) 525–50

Campbell TD, 'The Rights of the Minor' in P Alston, S Parker, and J A Seymour (eds), *Children, Rights, and the Law* (1st edn, Oxford University Press 1992) 1–23

Carey G and McLoughlin P, 'The Powerful Pull of Policy Targeting: Examining Residualisation in Australia' (2016) 26(2) Critical Public Health 147–58 <http://dx.doi.org/10.1080/09581596.2014.973018> accessed 6 May 2017

Carter I, 'Is the Capability Approach Paternalistic?' (2014) 30 Economics and Philosophy 75–98

CAT, Concluding Observations: Australia, CAT/C/ AUS/CO/3, 22 May 2008

CAT, Concluding Observations: Iceland, CAT/C/ISL/CO/3, 8 July 2008, Fortieth session, Geneva, 28 April–16 May 2008

CAT, Concluding Observations: Indonesia, CAT/C/IDN/CO/2, 2 July 2008

CAT, Concluding Observations: Kazakhstan, CAT/C/KAZ/CO/2, 12 December 2008

CAT, Concluding Observations: Sweden, CAT/C/SWE/CO/5, 4 June 2008

CAT, Concluding Observations: Zambia, CAT/C/ZMB/CO/2, 26 May 2008

CAT, Conclusions and Recommendations: Costa Rica, CAT/C/CRI/CO/2, 7 July 2008

CDC (November 2008), 'Behind International Rankings of Infant Mortality: How the United States Compares with Europe'

CEDAW, Concluding Observations on the combined sixth and seventh periodic reports of Cyprus adopted by the Committee at its fifty fourth session (11 February–1 March 2013) CEDAW/C/CYP/CO/6-7, 1 March 2013

CEDAW, Concluding Observations on the seventh periodic report of Greece adopted by the Committee at its fifty fourth session (11 February–1 March 2013) CEDAW/C/GRC/CO/7, 1 March 2013

CEDAW, Concluding Observations on the third to fourth periodic report of Turkmenistan adopted by the Committee at its fifty-third session (1–19 October 2012) CEDAW/C/TKM/CO/3-4, 24 October 2012

CEDAW, Concluding Observations: Brazil, CEDAW/C/BRA/CO/7, 23 February 2012

CEDAW, Concluding Observations: Egypt, CEDAW/C/EGY/CO/7, 5 February 2010

CEDAW, Concluding Observations: Finland, CEDAW/C/FIN/CO/6, 15 July 2008

CEDAW, Concluding Observations: Iceland, CEDAW/C/ICE/CO/6, 18 July 2008

CEDAW, Concluding Observations: Indonesia, CEDAW/C/IDN/CO/5, 10 August 2007

CEDAW, Concluding Observations: Nepal, CEDAW/C/NPL/CO/4-5, 29 July 2011

CEDAW, Concluding Observations: New Zealand, CEDAW/C/NZL/CO/6, 10 August 2007

CEDAW, Concluding Observations: Romania, CEDAW/C/ROU/CO/7-8, 24 July 2017

CEDAW, Concluding Observations: Russian Federation, CEDAW/C/USR/CO/7, 16 August 2010

CEDAW, Concluding Observations: Serbia, CEDAW/C/SRB/CO/2-3, 25 July 2013

CEDAW, Concluding Observations: Slovakia, CEDAW/C/SVK/CO/4, 30 June–18 July 2008,

CEDAW, Concluding Observations: Sweden, CEDAW/C/SWE/CO/7, 8 April 2008

CEDAW, Concluding Observations: Tanzania, CEDAW/C/TZA/CO/6, 16 July 2008

CEDAW, Concluding Observations: Turkmenistan CEDAW/C/TKM/CO/3-4, 10 August 2012

CEDAW, General Recommendation No 30 on Women in Conflict Prevention, Conflict and Post-conflict Situations, CEDAW/C/GC/30, 1 November 2013

CEDAW, General Recommendation No 34, on the rights of rural women, CEDAW/C/GC/34, para 54(c), 4 March 2016

CERD, Committee on the Elimination of Racial Discrimination to hold eighty-fourth session in Geneva from 3 to 21 February 2014, CERD/C/CHE/CO/7-9, 21 February 2014

CERD, Concluding Observations of the Committee on the Elimination of Racial Discrimination New Zealand, CERD/C/NZL/CO/18-20, 1 March 2013

CERD, Concluding Observations: Italy, CERD/C/ITA/CO/15, 16 May 2008

CERD, Concluding Observations: Belgium, CERD/C/BEL/CO/15, 11 April 2008, Seventy-second session

CERD, Concluding Observations: Fiji, CERD/C/FJI/CO/17, 16 May 2008

CERD, Concluding Observations: Germany, CERD/C/DEU/CO/18, 21 August 2008

CERD, Concluding Observations: Indonesia, CERD/C/IDN/CO/3, 15 August 2007

CERD, Concluding Observations: Moldova, CERD/C/MDA/CO/7, 16 May 2008

CERD, Concluding Observations: Republic of Moldova, CERD/C/MDA/CO/8-9, 10 March 2011

CERD, Concluding Observations: Russian Federation, CERD/C/RUS/CO/20-22, 17 April 2013

CERD, Concluding Observations: United States of America, CERD/C/USA/CO/7-9, 25 September 2014

CERD, Concluding Observations: United States of America, CERD/C/USA/CO/6, 8 May 2008

CESCE, Consideration of Reports Submitted by States Parties under Articles 16 and 17 of the Covenant, Twenty-sixth (extraordinary) session, 13–31 August 2001, E/C.12/1/Add.67, 2001

CESCR, 'Report on the forty-sixth and forty-seventh session'(2–20 May 2011, 14 November–2 December 2011), UN Doc E/2012/22, E/C.12/2011/3 (23 March 2012)

CESCR, 'Report on the forty-fourth and forty-fifth sessions' (May 2010, 1–19 November 2010, E/2011/22)

CESCR, 'Report on the forty-second and forty-third sessions' (4–22 May 2009, 2–20 November 2009) UN Doc E/2010/22, E/C.12/2009/3 (30 April 2010)

CESCR, 'Report on the thirty-sixth and thirty-seventh sessions' UN Doc E/2007/22, E/C.12/2006/1 (1 October 2007)

CESCR, 'Report on the thirty-fourth and thirty-fifth sessions' UN Doc E/2006/22 06/06/2006 (6 June 2006)

CESCR, 'Report on the thirty-fourth and thirty-fifth sessions' UN Doc E/2006/22, E/C.12/2005/5 (16 March 2005)

CESCR, 'Report on the thirty-second and thirty-third sessions' UN Doc E/2005/22, E/C.12/2004/9 (16 March 2005)

CESCR, 'Report on the thirtieth and thirty-first sessions' (5–23 May 2003, 10–28 November 2003), UN Doc E/2004/22, E/C.12/2003/14 (8 March 2004)

CESCR, 'Report on the twentieth and twenty-first sessions' UN Doc. E/2000/22, E/C.12/1999/11 (18 May 2000)

CESCR, Concluding Observations: Albania, E/C.12/ALB/CO/1 (24 November 2006)

CESCR, Concluding Observations: Argentina, E/2000/22 (8 December 1999)

CESCR, Concluding Observations: Cyprus, E/C.12/CYP/CO/6 (28 October 2016)

CESCR, Concluding Observations: Jordan, E/2001/22 (31 December 2000)

CESCR, Concluding Observations: Kazakhstan, UN Doc E/C.12/KAZ/CO/1 (21 May 2010)

CESCR, Concluding Observations: Kazakhstan, E/C.12/KAZ/CO/1 (21 May 2010)

CESCR, Concluding Observations: Netherlands E/C.12/NLD/CO/6 (6 July 2017)

CESCR, Concluding Observations: Pakistan, E/C.12/PAK/CO/1 (20 July 2017)

CESCR, Concluding Observations: Sri Lanka, E/C.12/LKA/CO/5 (4 August 2017)

CESCR, Consideration of reports submitted by States parties under Articles 16 and 17 of the Covenant, Frothy Sixth Session, UN Doc. E/C.12/RUS/CO/5 (20 May 2011)

CESCR, Consideration of reports submitted by States parties under articles 16 and 17 of the Covenant

CESCR, General Comment No 1, Reporting by states parties, 13th Sess, UN Doc E/1989/22 (27 July 1981)

CESCR, General Comment No. 11: Plans of Action for Primary Education (Art 14 of the Covenant) E/1992/23 (10 May 1999)

CESCR, General Comment No. 14: The Right to the Highest Attainable Standard of Health (Art 12 of the Covenant), E/C.12/2000/4 (11 August 2000)

CESCR, General Comment No 15: The Right to Water (Arts 11 and 12 of the Covenant), E/C.12/2002/11 (20 January 2003)

CESCR, General Comment No 18: The Right to Work (Art 6 of the Covenant), E/C.12/GC/18 (6 February 2006)
CESCR, General Comment No 19: The right to social security (Art 9 of the Covenant), E/C.12/GC/19 (4 February 2008)
CESCR, General Comment No 20: Non-discrimination in economic, social and cultural rights (Art 2, para 2, of the International Covenant on Economic, Social and Cultural Rights), E/C.12/GC/20 (2 July 2009)
CESCR, General Comment No 22 (2016) on the right to sexual and reproductive health (article 12 of the International Covenant on Economic, Social and Cultural Rights) E/C.12/GC/22
CESCR, General Comment No 24 (2017) on State obligations under the International Covenant on Economic, Social and Cultural Rights in the context of business activities, E/C.12/GC/24 (10 August 2017)
CESCR, General Comment No 13: The Right to Education (Art. 13 of the Covenant) 21st Sess, UN Doc E/C.12/1999/10 (8 December 1999)
CESCR, General Comment No 12, The Right to Adequate Food (Art.11), 20th Sess, Para 21, UN Doc E/C.12/1999/5 (12 May 1999)
CESCR, General Comment No 7 The Right to Adequate Housing (Art.11.1): Forced Evictions, E/1998/22 (20 May 1997)
CESCR, General Comment No 5, Persons with Disabilities, E/1995/22 (9 December 1994)
CESCR, General Comment No 4, The Right to Adequate Housing (Art.11(1)): Forced Evictions, 6th Sess, UN Doc E/1992/23 (13 December 1991)
CESCR, General Comment No 3: The Nature of States Parties' Obligations (Art 2, para 1, of the Covenant), E/1991/23 (14 December 1990)
CESCR, Report on the forty-fourth and forty-fifth sessions, UN Doc E/2011/22 (3 May 2011)
CESCR, Report on the forty-second and forty-third sessions, UN Doc E/2010/22, E/C.12/2009/3 (30 April 2010)
CESCR, Report on the fortieth and forty-first sessions, UN Doc E/2009/22, E/C.12/2008/3 (1 April 2009)
CESCR, Report on the thirtieth and thirty-first sessions, UN Doc E/2004/22, E/C.12/2003/14 (8 March 2004)
CESCR, Report on the twenty-eighth and twenty-ninth sessions, UN Doc E/2003/22, E/C.12/2002/13 (21 July 2008)
CESCR, Report on the twenty-fifth, twenty-sixth and twenty-seventh sessions, UN Doc E/2002/22, E/C.12/2001/17 (6 June 2002)
CESCR, Report on the twenty-fifth, twenty-sixth and twenty-seventh sessions, E/2002/22, E/C.12/2001/17 (6 June 2002)
CESCR, Report on the twenty-second, twenty-third and twenty-fourth sessions, E/2001/22; E/C.12/2000/21 (7 June 2001)
Chadwick G F, *A Systems View of Planning: Towards A Theory of the Urban and Regional Planning Process* (1st edn, Pergamon Press 1971)
Chalabi A, 'Australia's National Human Rights Action Plans: Traditional or Modern Model of Planning?' (2016) 20(7) The International Journal of Human Rights 993–1017
Chalabi A, 'Law as A System of Rights: A Critical Perspectives' (2013) 15(2) Human Rights Review 117–38
Chalabi A, 'National Human Rights Action Plans: A Roadmap to Development' (2014) 28(8) The Journal of Development in Practice 989–1002

Chalabi A, 'The Problem-Oriented Approach to Improving National Human Rights Action Plans' (2015) 7(2) Journal of Human Rights Practice 272–98, 1 July

Chambers S and Kopstein J, 'Civil Society and the State' in J S Dryzek, B Honig, and A Phillips (eds), *The Oxford Handbook of Political Theory* (1st edn, Oxford University Press 2008) 362–81

Chapman A and Russell S, *Core Obligations: Building a Framework for Economic, Social and Cultural Rights* (1st edn, Intersentia 2002)

Chapman A R, 'Towards an Understanding of the Right to Enjoy the Benefits of Scientific Progress and Its Applications' (2009) 8:1 Journal of Human Rights 1–36

Charlesworth H and Chinkin C, *The Boundaries of International Law: A Feminist Analysis* (1st edn, Manchester University Press 2000)

Checkland P, *Systems Thinking, Systems Practice* (1st edn, John Wiley & Sons 1994)

Checkland P and Poulter J, 'Soft systems methodology' in M Reynolds and S Holwell (eds), *Systems Approaches to Managing Change: A Practical Guide* (1st edn, Springer 2010) 191–243

Cheung G and Rensvold R, 'Evaluating Goodness-of-Fit Indexes for Testing Measurement Invariance' (2002) 9(2) Structural Equation Modeling: A Multidisciplinary Journal

China- National Human Rights Action Plan of China (2009–2010) <https://www.law.hku.hk/ccpl/research/NationalHumanRightsActionPlan_ChinaV1.1.pdf> accessed 17 January 2018

China- National Human Rights Action Plan of China (2009–2010) <http://www.ohchr.org/EN/Issues/PlansActions/Pages/PlansofActionIndex.aspx> accessed 5 December 2017

China- National Human Rights Action Plan of China (2012–2015) <http://news.xinhuanet.com/english/china/2012-06/11/c_131645029.htm.> accessed 23 January 2016

China- National Human Rights Action Plan of China (2016–2020) <http://english.gov.cn/archive/publications/2016/09/29/content_281475454482622.htm> accessed 9 January 2018

China's Five-Year Plans are a series of social and economic development initiatives. available at <http://en.ndrc.gov.cn/newsrelease/201612/P020161207645765233498.pdf> accessed 2 December 2017

Clapham A, 'The Use of International Human Rights Law by Civil Society Organizations' in N Rodley and S Sheeran (eds), *Routledge Handbook of International Human Rights* Law (1st edn, Routledge 2014) 153–69

Clark D , The Capability Approach: Its Development, Critiques and Recent Advances, GPRG-WPS-032, Global Poverty Research Group, 2005

Clark D, *Visions of Development: A Study of Human Values* (1st edn, Edward Elgar 2002)

CMW, Concluding Observations of the Committee on the Protection of the Rights of All Migrant Workers and Members of Their Families, CMW/C/ALB/CO/1, 10 December 2010

CMW, Concluding Observations of the Committee on the Protection of the Rights of All Migrant Workers and Members of Their Families, CMW/C/LKA/CO/1, 14 December 2009

Cole WM, 'Human Rights as Myth and Ceremony? Reevaluating the Effectiveness of Human Rights Treaties, 1981 to 2007' (2012) 117(4) American Journal of Sociology 1131–71.

Committee on Enforced Disappearances, Report of the Committee on Enforced Disappearances on Its Twelfth Session, Geneva 6–17 March 2017, Twelfth session,

Committee on Enforced Disappearances, Report of the Committee on Enforced Disappearances on Its Eleventh Session, Geneva 3–14 October 2016, Twelfth session

Committee on the Rights of Persons with Disabilities, Seventh session Geneva, 16–20 April 2012 Implementation of the Convention on the Rights of Persons with Disabilities, CRPD/C/ARG/Q/1, 16 May 2012

Connolly N and Kaisershot M, 'Corporate Power and Human Rights' (2015) 19(6) The International Journal of Human Rights 663–72 <DOI:10.1080/13642987.2015.1074458> accessed 21 January 2017

Conte A, 'Democratic and Civil Rights' in Alex Conte and Richard Burchill (eds) *Defining Civil and Political Rights* (2nd edn, Ashgate 2009) 43–85

Cornwall A and Gaventa J, 'From Users and Choosers to Makers and Shapers: Repositioning Participation in Social Policy' (2000) 31 IDS Bulletin 50–62

Cornwall A and Nyamu-Musembi C, 'Putting the "Rights-Based Approach" to Development into Perspective' (2004) 25(8) Third World Quarterly 1415

Council of Europe, Conclusions of a Workshop on Developing and Implementing National Action Plans for Human Rights, Strasbourg, 27–28 March 2014

Council of the European Union, EU Strategic Framework and Action Plan on Human Rights and Democracy, Luxembourg, 25 June 2012, 11855/12

Council panel on anti-corruption (2013) <http://www.ohchr.org/EN/Issues/Development/GoodGovernance/Pages/AntiCorruptionPanel.aspx> accessed 20 January 2018

Craven M, *The International Covenant on Economic, Social and Cultural Rights: A Perspective on its Development* (1st edn, Clarendon Press 1998)

Crawford S and Ali S, Situational Analysis of FGM/C Stakeholders and Interventions in Somalia, 2015, Health and Education advice and resource team, UNICEF and UNFPA

CRC, 'Guidelines for the participation of partners (NGOs and individual experts) in the pre-sessional working group of the Committee on the Rights of the Child' (CRC/C/90, Annex VIII)

CRC, Concluding Observations: United Kingdom of Great Britain and Northern Ireland. CRC/C/GBR/CO/4, 20 October 2008

CRC, Concluding Observations: Afghanistan, CRC/C/AFG/CO/1, 4 February 2011

CRC, Concluding Observations: Afghanistan, CRC/C/AFG/CO/1, 8 April 2011

CRC, Concluding Observations: Belarus, CRC/C/OPSC/BLR/CO/1, 8 April 2011

CRC, Concluding Observations: Brazil, 3 November 2004, CRC/C/15/Add.241

CRC, Concluding Observations: Cambodia, CRC/C/KHM/CO/2-3, 3 August 2011

CRC, Concluding Observations: Egypt, CRC/C/EGY/CO/3-4, 20 June 2011

CRC, Concluding Observations: Egypt, CRC/C/OPSC/EGY/1, 20 June 2011

CRC, Concluding Observations: Germany, CRC/C/15/Add.226, 26 February 2004

CRC, Concluding Observations: Greece, CRC/C/GRC/CO/2-3, 13 August 2012

CRC, Concluding Observations: Italy, CRC/C/ITA/CO/3-4, 31 October 2011

CRC, Concluding Observations: Japan, CRC/C/OPSC/JPN/CO/1, 22 June 2010

CRC, Concluding Observations: Japan, CRC/C/JPN/CO/3, 20 June 2010

CRC, Concluding Observations: Kazakhstan, CRC/C/KAZ/CO/3, 8 June 2007

CRC, Concluding Observations, Nepal, CRC/C/OPSC/NPL/CO/1, 18 July 2012

CRC, Concluding Observations: New Zealand, CRC/C/NZL/3-4, 19 January 2011

CRC, Concluding Observations: Nigeria, CRC/C/NGA/CO/3-4, 21 June 2010

CRC, Concluding Observations: Panama, CRC/C/PAN/CO/3-4, 21 December 2011

CRC, Concluding Observations: Republic of Moldova, CRC/C/MDA/CO/3, 20 February 2009

CRC, Concluding Observations: Russian Federation, CRC/C/RUS/CO/3, 23 November 2005

CRC, Concluding Observations: Singapore, CRC/C/SGP/CO/2-3, 4 May 2011

CRC, Concluding Observations: Sweden, CRC/C/SWE/CO/4, 26 June 2009

CRC, Concluding Observations: Turkey, CRC/C/TUR/CO/2-3, 20 July 2012

CRC, Concluding Observations: Ukraine, CRC/C/OPAC/UKR/CO/1, 21 April 2011

CRC, Concluding Observations: Ukraine, CRC/C/UKR/CO/3-4, 21 April 2011

Creswell J, *Research Design: Qualitative, Quantitative, and Mixed Methods Approaches* (3rd edn, Sage 2009)

Crocker D, (1995), 'Functioning and Capability: The Foundation of Senís and Nussbaumís Development Ethic, part II' in M Nussbaum and J Glover (eds), *Women, Culture and Development* (Oxford: Clarendon Press 1995) 153–98

CRPD, Concluding Observations: Paraguay, CRPD/C/PRY/1, 28 June 2011

CRPD, Concluding Observations: Peru, CRPD/C/PER/CO/1, 16–20 April 2012

CRPD, Concluding Observations: Spain, CRPD/C/ESP/CO/1, 19 October 2011

CRPD, Implementation of the Convention on the Rights of Persons with Disabilities: Hong Kong–China, CRPD/C/CHN-HKG/1, 11 February 2011

Csermely P, *Weak Links: Stabilizers of Complex Systems from Proteins to Social* Networks (1st edn, Springer 2006)

Cypher J and Diestz J, *The Process of Economic Development* (3rd edn, Routledge 2009)

Damgaard B and Lewis J, 'Accountability and Citizen Participation' in M Bovens, R E Goodin, and T Schillemans (eds), *The Oxford Handbook of Public Accountability* (1st edn, Oxford University Press 2014) 258–72

Danish toolkit on business and human rights, 2014 <https://www.humanrights.dk/business/tools/national-action-plans-business-human-rights> accessed 16 May 2017

Daruwalla N, Chakravarty S, Chatterji S, More N, Alcock G, Hawkes S, and Osrin D, 'Violence Against Women with Disability in Mumbai, India: A Qualitative Study', SAGE Open, July–September (2013) Sage Open 1

Davidoff P, 'Advocacy and Pluralism in Planning' (1965) 31(4) Journal of the American Institute of Planners 331–38

Davidov E, Meuleman B, Cieciuch J, Schmidt P, and Billiet J, 'Measurement Equivalence in Cross-National Research' (2014) 40 Annual Review of Sociology 55–75

Davidson, S. 'Spinning the Wheel of Empowerment' (1998) Planning, Vol 1262

De Schutter O, 'Towards a New Treaty on Business and Human Rights' (2016) 1 Business and Human Rights Journal 41–67

Dedeurwaerdere T, (2005) 'The Contribution of Network Governance to Sustainable Development' <http://www.iddri.org/Evenements/Seminaires-reguliers/s13_dedeurwaerdere.pdf> accessed 9 March 2016;

Delva S and Bilchitz D, *Building a Treaty on Business and Human Rights* (1st edn, Cambridge University Press 2017)

Deneulin S, 'Ideas Related to Human Development' in S Deneulin (ed), *An Introduction to the Human Development and Capability Approach Freedom and Agency* (1st edn, Earthscan 2009) 49–71

Denmark's Action Plan on Implementation of Security Council Resolution 1325 on Women and Peace and Security <http://peacewomen.org/nap-denmark> accessed 25 May 2016

Desai M, 'Poverty and Capability: Towards an Empirically Implementable Measure' in Meghnad Desai (ed), *Poverty, Famine and Economic Development* (1st edn, Edward Elgar 1995) 185–204

Doyal L and Gough I, *A Theory of Human Need* (1st edn, Palgrave 1991)

Dubnick M J and Frederickson H G, 'Introduction: The Promises of Accountability Research' in M J Dubnick and H G Frederickson (eds), *Accountable Governance: Problems and Promises* (1st edn, Routledge 2011) xi–xxx

Dutch Ministry of the Interior and Kingdom Relations, National Action Plan on Human Rights: The protection and promotion of human rights within the Netherlands, February 2014

Dutch National Action Plan on Resolution 1325: Taking a stand for women, peace and security (2007) <http://peacewomen.org/sites/default/files/dutch_nationalactionplan_december2007.pdf> accessed 8 September 2015

Dworkin R, 'What is Equality? Part 1: Equality of Welfare' (1981) 10 Philosophy and Public Affairs 185–246

Easterly W, 'Inequality Does Cause Underdevelopment: Insights From a New Instrument' (2007) 84(2) Journal of Development Economics 755–76

Ebrahim A, 'Accountability in Practice: Mechanisms for NGOs' (2003) 31(5) World Development 813–29

ECtHR *Loiziou v Turkey* (1995) 20 EHRR 99, 102

Ecuador. National Human Rights Program (1998) <http://www.ohchr.org/EN/Issues/PlansActions/Pages/PlansofActionIndex.aspx> accessed 5 December 2017

Edwards M, *Civil Society* (2nd edn, Polity Press 2009)

Eekelaar J, 'The Emergence of Children's Rights' (1986) 6(2) Oxford Journal of Legal Studies 161–82

Egan S, 'Strengthening the United Nations Human Rights Treaty Body System' (2013) 13(2) Human Rights Law Review 209–43

Eide A, 'Group accommodation and the Challenges of Education: Multicultural or Intercultural – or a Combination of the Two?' in Jonas Grimheden and Rolf Ring (eds), *Human Rights Law: From Dissemination to Application: Essays in Honour of Göran Melander* (1st edn, Martinus Nijhoff Publishers 2006) 3–25

Elder-Vass D, 'Collective Intentionality and Causal Powers' (2015) 1(2) Journal of Social Ontology 251–69

Elder-Vass D, *The Causal Power of Social Structures* (1st edn, Cambridge University Press 2010)

Ellis B, 'Powers and Dispositions' in R Groff (ed), *Revitalizing Causality: Realism About Causality in Philosophy and Social Sciences* (1st edn, Routledge 2008) 76–92

Elster J, *Sour Grapes: Studies in the Subversion of Rationality* (1st edn, Cambridge University Press 1983)

End-of-mission statement on China, 23 August 2016 <http://www.ohchr.org/en/NewsEvents/Pages/DisplayNews.aspx?NewsID=20402&LangID=E> accessed 14 November 2017

Ethiopia's water and sanitation crisis, <https://water.org/our-impact/ethiopia/> accessed 27 December 2017

Etzioni A, 'The Responsive Community: A Communitarian Perspective' (1996) 61(1) American Sociological Review 1–11

European Parliament, Directorate-General for External Policies Policy Department, The Role of Regional Human Rights Mechanisms, 2010

Evans P, *Embedded Autonomy States and Industrial Transformation* (1st edn, Princeton University Press 1995)

Falleti T G and Mahoney J, 'The comparative sequential method' in J Mahoney and K Thelen (eds), *Advances in Comparative-Historical Analysis* (1st edn, Cambridge University Press 2015) 211–39

Fawcett P and Daugbjerg C, 'Explaining Governance Outcomes: Epistemology, Network Governance and Policy Network' (2012) 10 Political Studies Review 195–207

Feeney P, 'Business and Human Rights: The Struggle for Accountability in the UN and the Future Direction of the Advocacy Agenda' (2009) V 6, N 11, Dec, 161–75

Feldman D, *Civil Liberties and Human Rights in England and Wales* (2nd edn, Oxford University Press 2002)

Finland National Action Plan on Fundamental and Human Rights 2012–2013 <http://www.ohchr.org/EN/Issues/PlansActions/Pages/PlansofActionIndex.aspx> accessed 1 June 2015

Finland, Ministry of the Employment and the Economy, National Action Plan for the implementation of the UN Guiding Principles on Business and Human Rights (2014)

Finnis J, *Natural Law and Natural Rights* (1st edn, Clarendon Press 1980)

Finnish National Action Plan for the Implementation of the UN Guiding Principles on Business and Human Rights (2014) <http://www.ohchr.org/EN/Issues/Business/Pages/NationalActionPlans.aspx> accessed 9 October 2016

Fischer F, 'Beyond empiricism: policy analysis as deliberative practice' in Hajer MA and Wagenaar H (eds), *Deliberative Policy Analysis. Understanding Governance in the Network Society* (Cambridge University Press 2003) 209–27

Fiske J, 'For Cultural Interpretation: A Study of the Culture of Homelessness' (1991) 8(4) Critical Studies in Mass Communication 455–74

Floyd R, 'Why We Need Needs-Based Justifications of Human Rights' (2011) 7 JIPT 1

Ford J, Business and Human Rights: Emerging Challenges to Consensus and Coherence, International Law Programme, February 2015, <https://www.chathamhouse.org/sites/files/chathamhouse/field/field_document/20150226BusinessHumanRightsFord.pdf> accessed September 2016

Formisano MP, *Empowering the Poor: Through Human Rights Litigation* (1st edn, UNESCO 2012)

Fortin J, *Children's Rights and the Developing Law* (1st edn, Cambridge University Press 1998)

Fredericks KA, Deegan M, Carman JG, 'Using System Dynamics as an Evaluation Tool Experience From a Demonstration Program' (2008) 29(3) American Journal of Evaluation 251–67

Fredman S, *Human Rights Transformed: Positive Rights and Positive Duties* (1st edn, Oxford University Press 2008)

Fredman S, 'Human Rights Transformed: Positive Duties and Positive Rights' (2006) 38 Oxford Legal Studies Research Paper

Freeman M, 'Universalism of Human Rights and Cultural Relativism' in S Sheeran and N Rodley (eds), *Routledge Handbook of International Human Rights Law* (1st edn, Routledge 2013) 49–63

Friedmann J, *Insurgencies: Essays in Planning Theory* (1st edn, Routledge 2011)

Friedmann J, 'Planning Cultures in Transition' in B Sanyal (ed), *Comparative Planning Cultures* (1st edn, Routledge 2005) 29–45

Friedmann J, *Empowerment: The Politics of Alternative Development* (1st edn, Blackwell 1992)

Friedmann J, *Planning in the Public Domain: From Knowledge to Action* (1st edn, Princeton University Press 1987)

Friedmann J and Huxley M, 'Transactive Planning and Life Space' (1985) 3(3) Urban Policy and Research

Friedmann J, *Retracking America: A Theory of Transactive Planning* (1st edn, Anchor Press 1973)

Fukuda-Parr S, 'The Metrics of Human Rights: Complementarities of the Human Development and Capabilities Approach' (2011) 12:1 Journal of Human Development and Capabilities 73

Fukuda-Parr S, Lawson-Remer T, and Randolph S, *Fulfilling Social and Economic Rights*, (1st edn, Oxford University Press 2015)

Fukuda-Parr S, Lawson-Remer T, and Randolph S, 'An Index of Economic and Social Rights Fulfillment: Concept and Methodology' (2009) 8 Journal of Human Rights 195–221

Gallagher A, 'Making Human Rights Treaty Obligations a Reality: Working with New Actors and Partners' in P Alston and J Crawford (eds), *The Future of UN Human Rights Treaty Monitoring* (1st edn, Cambridge University Press 2000) 201–28

Gasper D, Human Rights, Human Needs, Human Development, Human Security: Relationships between four International 'Human' Discourses (2007), <www2.warwick.ac.uk/fac/soc/garnet/workingpapers/2007.pdf> accessed 12 January 2014

Gasper D, 'Is Sen's Capability Approach an Adequate Basis for Considering Human Development?'(2002) 14(4) Review of Political Economy 435–61

Gasper D, 'Sen's Capability Approach and Nussbaum's Capabilities Ethic' (1997) 9(2) Journal of International Development 281–302

Gaventa J, 'Finding the Spaces for Change: A Power Analysis' (2006) 37(6) IDS Bulletin

Gaventa J and Cornwall A, 'Challenging the Boundaries of the Possible: Participation, Knowledge and Power' (2006) 37 IDS Bulletin 122–28 <doi:10.1111/j.1759-5436.2006.tb00329.x> accessed 7 April 2013

General Assembly, Resolution 48/141, A/RES/48/141, 20 December 1993

Genschel P and Zangl B, *Transformations of the State: From Monopolist to Manager of Political Authority* (1st edn, Univ, Sonderforschungsbereich 2008)

Gerring J, *Social Science Methodology: A Unified Framework* (2nd edn, Cambridge University Press 2012)

Global Justice 2016 report <http://www.globaljustice.org.uk/news/2016/sep/12/10-biggest-corporations-make-more-money-most-countries-world-combined> accessed 21 December 2017

Gould R, 'Why do networks matter? Rationalist and structuralist interpretations' in M Diani and D McAdam (eds), *Social Movements and Networks: Relational Approaches to Collective Action* (1st edn, Oxford University Press 2003) 233–57

Granovetter M, 'The Strength of Weak Ties' (1973) 78(6) American Journal of Sociology 1360–80

Graventa J, 'Towards Participatory Local Governance: Assessing the Transformative Possibilities' in S Hickey and G Mohan (eds), *Participation: from Tyranny to Transformation: Exploring New Approaches to Participation in Development* (1st edn, Zed Books 2004) 25–41

Green J, 'The Role of Theory in Evidence-based Health Promotion Practice' (2000) 15(2) Health Education Research 125–29

Green R A, The Delphi Technique in Educational Research (2014) SAGE Open, April–June 1–8

Grinnell R M, Gabor P A, Unrau Y, *Program Evaluation for Social Workers: Foundations of Evidence-Based Practice for Social Workers* (6th edn, Oxford University Press 2012)

Grover A, Report of the Special Rapporteur on the right of everyone to the enjoyment of the highest attainable standard of physical and mental health: Mission to Australia, UN Doc A/HRC/14/30/Add.4 (2010) 21–24

Gudykunst W B, Ting-Toomey S, and Chua E, *Culture and Interpersonal Communication* (1st edn, Sage Publications 1988)

Gudykunst W D, 'Anxiety/Uncertainty Management (AUM) Theory: Current Status' in R L Wiseman (ed), *International and Intercultural Communication Annual, Vol 19. Intercultural Communication Theory*, 8–58 (1st edn, Sage Publications 1995) 8–58

Guirdham M, *Communicating Across Cultures at Work* (3rd edn, Palgrave 2011) at 49–50

Gumru B and Fritz J, 'Women, Peace and Security: An Analysis of the National Action Plans Developed in Response to UN Security Council Resolution 1325' (2009) 4(2) Societies Without Borders 209–25

Hafner-Burton E, Tsutsui K, and Meyer J, 'International Human Rights Law and the Politics of Legitimation: Repressive States and Human Rights Treaties' (2008) 23 International Sociology 115–27

Hafner-Burton E, 'Human Rights in a Globalizing World: The Paradox of Empty Promises' (2005) 110(5) American Journal of Sociology (AJS) 1373–411

Halachmi A, 'Accountability Overloads' in M Bovens, R E Goodin, and T Schillemans (eds), *The Oxford Handbook of Public Accountability* (1st edn, Oxford University Press 2014) 560–74

Hamilton L A, *The Political Philosophy of Needs* (1st edn, Cambridge University Press 2003)

Hamm B, 'A Human Rights Approach to Development' (2001) 23:4 Human Rights Quarterly 1005

Hammarberg T, Council of Europe Commissioner for Human Rights, Recommendation of the Commissioner for Human Rights on Systematic Work for Implementing Human Rights at the National Level, Strasbourg, 18 February 2009

Hanson J K and Sigman R, 'Leviathan's Latent Dimensions: Measuring State Capacity for Comparative Political Research' (September 2013). APSA. <https://papers.ssrn.com/sol3/papers.cfm?abstract_id=1899933> accessed 14 March 2017

Hardoon D, Ayele S, and Fuentes-Nieva R, An Economy for the 1%: How privilege and power in the economy drive extreme inequality and how this can be stopped, Oxfam International Report,18 January 2016

Hardoon D and Slater J (2015), Inequality and the end to extreme poverty, Oxfam

Harris D, 'The International Covenant on Civil and Political Rights and the United Kingdom' in D Harris and S Joseph (eds), *The International Covenant on Civil and Political Rights and United Kingdom Law* (1st edn, Oxford University Press 1995) 1–60

Hart R, 'Children's participation: from tokenism to citizenship' (1992), Essay for UNICEF, Innocenti Essay No 4, UNICEF International Child Development Centre

Hart R, 'Children's Participation: From Tokenism to Citizenship' (1992) Essay for UNICEF, Innocenti Essay No 4

Hartley C, 2012. Your voice is required <http://www.humanrightsactionplan.org.au/nhrap-blogs/your-voice-is-required-participate-in-the-development-of-the-national-human-rights-action-plan> accessed 9 March 2013

Hausman D, McPherson M, and Satz D, *Economic Analysis, Moral Philosophy, and Public Policy* (3rd edn, Cambridge University Press 2016)

Hayek F, *The Road to Serfdom* (1st edn, George Routledge & Sons 1944)

Héritier A, 'New modes of governance in Europe: policy-making without legislating?' in Adrienne Windhoff-Héritier (ed), *Common Goods: Reinventing European and International Governance* (1st edn, Rowman & Littlefield Publishers 2002) 185–206,

Hertting N and Vedung E, 'Purposes and Criteria in Network Governance Evaluation: How Far Does Standard Evaluation Vocabulary Take Us?' (2012) 18(1) Evaluation 27–46

Hettne B, *Development Theory and the Three Worlds: Towards an International Political Economy of Development* (2nd edn, Longman 1995)

Hickey S and Mohan G, 'Towards Participation as Transformation: Critical Themes and Challenges' in S Hickey and G Mohan (eds), *Participation: from Tyranny to Transformation: Exploring New Approaches to Participation in Development* (1st edn, Zed Books 2004) 3–24

Hirst v United Kingdom (No 2), Application No 74025/01 (2005)

Hoch C, 'Pragmatism, Planning, and Power' (1984) 4(2) Journal of Planning Education and Research 86–95

Hofkirchner W, ' "Mechanisms" at Work in Information Society' in MS Archer (ed), *Generative Mechanisms Transforming the Social Order* (1st edn, Springer 2015) 95–112

Hofstede G, *Culture's Consequences: International Differences in Work-related Values* (1st edn, Sage 1980)

Hoy C and Sumner A, 'Gasoline, Guns, and Giveaways: Is There New Capacity for Redistribution to End Three Quarters of Global Poverty?' (2016) Center for Global Development Working Paper 433

HRC Res 6/20, 28 September 2007, A/HRC/6/20; HRC Res 12/15, 1 October 2009, A/HRC/12/15.

HRC, Ninetieth session 9–27 July 2007, Concluding Observations of the Human Rights Committee, CCPR/C/SDN/CO/3, 29 August 2007

Hsu C and Sandford B, 'The Delphi Technique: Making Sense Of Consensus, Practical Assessment' (2007) 12(1) Res Eval

Hudson B, Galloway T, and Kaufman J, 'Comparison of Current Planning Theories: Counterparts and Contradictions' (1979) 45(4) Journal of the American Planning Association

Human Rights Committee, 'Report of the Human Rights Committee Seventy-ninth session' (20 October–7 November 2003) Eightieth session (15 March–2 April 2004) Eighty-first session (5–30 July 2004), UN Doc A/59/40 (Vol I)

Human Rights Committee, Focused reports based on replies to lists of issues prior to reporting (LOIPR): Implementation of the new optional reporting procedure (LOIPR procedure) Ninety-ninth session, CCPR/C/99/4 Geneva, 12–30 July 2010

Human Rights Committee, General Comment No 3, Article 2 Implementation at the national level (Thirteenth session, 1981), Compilation of General Comments and General Recommendations Adopted by Human Rights Treaty Bodies, UN Doc HRI/GEN/1/Rev.6 at 125 (2003)

Human Rights Committee, General Comment No 35 (Article 9: Liberty and security of person) 16 December 2014, CCPR/C/GC/35

Human Rights Council, 'Elaboration of an International Legally Binding Instrument on Transnational Corporations and Other Business Enterprises with Respect to Human Rights', A/HRC Res 26/9 (26 June 2014)

Human Rights Council, Implementation of General Assembly Resolution 60/251 of 15 March 2006 Entitled 'Human Rights Council', Report of the Special Rapporteur on contemporary forms of racism, racial discrimination, xenophobia and related intolerance, Doudou Diène, Addendum, Mission to the Russian Federation, A/HRC/4/19/Add.3, 30 May 2007

Human Rights Law Resource Centre. 2011. Making rights real: A National Human Rights Action Plan for Australia, Submission to the Attorney-General's Department on the development of a National Human Rights Action Plan, February 2011

Human Rights Watch (2011), Promises Unfulfilled: An Assessment of China's National Human Rights Action Plan

Hummelbrunner R and Regionalberatung O, A System Approach to Evaluation: Applications of Systems theory and Systems thinking in Evaluations, Paper prepared for the 4th EES Conference, 12–14 October 2000, Lausanne

Huppé G, Creech H, and Knoblauch D, 'The Frontiers of Networked Governance' (2012) The International Institute for Sustainable Development

Ibhawoh B, 'The Right to Development: The Politics and Polemics of Power and Resistance' (2011) 33 Human Rights Quarterly 76–104

ICAR and European Coalition for Corporate Justice, 'Assessments of Existing National Action Plans (NAPs) on Business and Human Rights' (2014) <http://accountabilityroundtable.org/wp-content/uploads/2014/10/ICAR-ECCJ-Assessments-of-Existing-NAPs.pdf> accessed 14 August 2015

Ife J, *Human Rights from Below: Achieving Rights Through Community Development* (1st edn, Cambridge University Press 2009)

Indonesia- National Plans of Action for the Promotion and Protection of Human Rights (1998–2003) <http://www.ohchr.org/EN/Issues/PlansActions/Pages/PlansofActionIndex.aspx> accessed 23 February 2014

Ing C, 'Culturally Appropriate Evaluations' in Y A Unrau, P A Gabor, R M Grinnell (eds), *Evaluation in Social Work: The Art and Science of Practice* (4th edn, Oxford University Press 2007) 417–36

International Commission of Jurists (ICJ), 'Maastricht Guidelines on Violations of Economic, Social and Cultural Rights', 26 January 1997

International Covenant on Economic, Social and Cultural Rights, 16 December 1966, S Treaty Doc No 95-19, (1967) 6 ILM 360, 993 UNTS 3, art 14

Iraq-The Iraqi National Human Rights Action Plan (2011) <http://www.ohchr.org/EN/Issues/PlansActions/Pages/PlansofActionIndex.aspx> accessed 1 December 2017

Ireland's National Plan on Business and Human Rights (2017–2020) <http://www.ohchr.org/EN/Issues/Business/Pages/NationalActionPlans.aspx> accessed 1 February 2018

Ireland's second National Action Plan on Women, Peace and Security 2015–2018 <http://peacewomen.org/sites/default/files/Revised%20NAP%20Ireland%20(2015-2018).pdf> accessed 25 January 2018

Isett K, Mergel I, Leroux K, Mischen P, and Rethemeyer K, 'Networks in Public Administration Scholarship: Understanding Where We are and Where We Need to Go' (2011) 21 (Suppl 1) Journal of Public Administration Research and Theory 157–73

Isett K R and Provan K G, 'The Evolution of Interorganizational Network Relationships Over Time: Does Sector Matter?' (2005) 15 Journal of Public Administration Research and Theory 149–65

ISHR, China | UN expert says respect for human rights and civil society essential to development and poverty alleviation <https://www.ishr.ch/news/china-un-expert-says-respect-human-rights-and-civil-society-essential-development-and-poverty> 14 November 2017

Italian National Action Plan on Business and Human Rights (2016–2021) <http://www.cidu.esteri.it/resource/2016/12/49117_f_NAPBHRENGFINALEDEC152017.pdf> accessed 25 January 2018

Jackson M C, *Systems Thinking: Creative Holism for Managers* (1st edn, John Wiley & Sons 2003)

Jackson R, 'Regime Security' in A Collins (ed), *Contemporary Security Studies* (4th edn, Oxford University Press 2016) 185–201

Jassen T A, 'Monosemy vs Polysemy' in H Cuyckens, R Dirven, and J R Taylor (eds), *Cognitive Approaches to Lexical Semantics* (1st edn, Mouton de Gruyter 2003) 93–121

Jilke S, Petrovsky N, Meuleman B, and James O, 'Measurement Equivalence in Replications of Experiments: When and Why it Matters and Guidance on How to Determine Equivalence' (2017) 19:9 Public Management Review 1293–310

Jolly R, 'Employment, Basic Needs and Human Development: Elements for a New International Paradigm in Response to Crisis' (2010) 11:1 Journal of Human Development and Capabilities 11

Jones P and Long G, 'Universalism, Relativism and Difference' in D Moellendorf and H Widdows (eds), *The Routledge Handbook of Global Ethics* (1st edn, Routledge 2014) 82–94

Joseph S and Fletcher A, 2012. Castan Centre For Human Rights Law: National Human Rights Action Plan: Draft Baseline Study

Kapucu N and Wart MV, 'The Evolving Role of the Public Sector in Managing Catastrophic Disasters: Lessons Learned' (2006) 38 Administration and Society 279–308

Kashyap A, 'Laws Hurting Bangladesh Women Linger on the Books' (2012) <http://womensenews.org/story/law/121221/laws-hurting-bangladesh-women-linger-the-books> accessed 9 January 2013

Keith L C, 'Constitutional Provisions for Individual Human Rights (1976–1996): Are They More than Mere "Window Dressing?"' (2002) 55 Political Research Quarterly 111–43

Keller H and Ulfstein G, 'Introduction' in Helen Keller and Geir Ulfstein (eds), *UN Human Rights Treaty Bodies: Law and Legitimacy* (1st edn, Cambridge University Press 2012) 1–15

Kenis P and Provan KG, 'The Control of Public Networks' (2006) 9 International Public Management Journal 227–47

Kettle N P, Dow K, Tuler S, Webler T, Whitehead J, Miller K M, 'Integrating Scientific and Local Knowledge to Inform Risk-based Management Approaches for Climate Adaptation' (2014) 4–5 Climate Risk Management 17–31

Kilduff M and Tsai W, *Social Networks and Organizations* (1st edn, Sage Press 2003)

Klijn E and Skelcher C, 'Democracy and Governance Networks: Compatible or Not?' (2007) 85(3) Public Administration 587–608

Klijn E and Koppenjan J, 'Accountable Networks' in M Bovens, R E Goodin, and T Schillemans (eds), *The Oxford Handbook of Public Accountability* (1st edn, Oxford University Press 2014) 242–58

Kline R B, *Principles and Practice of Structural Equation Modeling* (4th edn, Guilford Press 2015)

Kluckhohn F and Strodtbeck F, *Variations in Value Orientations* (1st edn, Evanston, IL: Row, Peterson 1961)

Koppell J G, 'Pathologies of Accountability: ICANN and the Challenge of "Multiple Accountabilities Disorder"' (2005) 65(1) Public Administration Review 94–109

Koppenjan J and Klijn E, *Managing Uncertainties in Networks: A Network Approach to Problem Solving and Decision Making* (1st edn, Routledge 2004)

Koskenniemi M and Leino P, 'Fragmentation of International Law? Postmodern Anxieties' (2002) 15 Leiden Journal of International Law 553–79

Kramer M, *Rights, Wrongs and Responsibilities* (1st edn, Palgrave 2001)

Kramer M, 'Some Doubts about Alternatives to the Interest Theory' (2013) 123 Ethics 245–63

Kramer M, Simmonds N, and Steiner H, *A Debate Over Rights* (1st edn, Oxford 1998)

Kurt v Turkey, Application No 24276/94 [1998] ECHR 44 (25 May 1998)

Latvia. National Programmes for the Protection and Promotion of Human Rights (1995) <http://www.ohchr.org/EN/Issues/PlansActions/Pages/PlansofActionIndex.aspx> accessed 01 December 2017

Law D and Versteeg M, 'The Evolution and Ideology of Global Constitutionalism' (2011) 99(5) California Law Review 1163–174

Layton R, *Order and Anarchy: Civil Society, Social Disorder and War* (1st edn, Cambridge University Press 2006)

Lazer D, 'Global and Domestic Governance: Modes of Interdependence in Regulatory Policymaking' (2006) 12(4) European Law Journal 455–68.

legislationline.org/documents/id/16659> accessed 21 February 2014

Lemmi A and Betti G, *Fuzzy Set Approach to Multidimensional Poverty Measurement* (1st edn, Springer 2006)

Li Q, 'Indirect Membership Function Assignment Based on Ordinal Regression' (2016) 43(3) J Appl Stat 441–60

Li RS, 'Alternative Routes to State Breakdown: Toward an Integrated Model of Territorial Disintegration' (2002) 20(1) Sociological Theory 1–23

Lindblom C, *The Intelligence of Democracy* (1st edn, Free Press 1965)

Lindblom C, 'The Science of "Muddling Through"' (1959) 19 Public Administration Review 79–88

Lithuania. National Programmes for the Protection and Promotion of Human Rights (2002) <http://www.ohchr.org/EN/Issues/PlansActions/Pages/PlansofActionIndex.aspx> accessed 17 March 2015

M'Baye K, 'Le Droit du Développement comme un Droit de l'Homme' (1972) 5 Revue des Droits de l'Homme 503

MacCormick N, 'Rights in legislation' in A Kavanagh and J Oberdiek (eds), *Arguing About Law* (1st edn, Routledge 2009) 321–35

MacCormick N, 'Children's Rights: A Test-Case for Theories of Rights' in C Nino (ed), *Rights* (1st edn, New York University Press 1992) 75–86

MacCormick N, *Legal Right and Social Democracy* (1st edn, Oxford University Press 1982)

MacCormick N, 'Rights in legislation' in P Hacker and J Raz (eds), *Law, Morality and Society: Essays in Honour of HLA Hart* (1st edn, Oxford University Press 1977) 189–209

Mackled-Garcia S and Cali B, *The Legalization of Human Rights: Multidisciplinary Perspectiv es on Human Rights and Human Rights Law* (1st edn, Routledge 2006)

Maggetti M and Gilardi F, 'Network Governance and the Domestic Adoption of Soft Rules' (2014) 21:9 Journal of European Public Policy 1293–310

Mahoney J, 'What is a concept? Two definitions and their research implications' (2010) Mimeo, North Western University, Evanston, IL, 7

Makaratzis v Greece Application No 50385/99 (2004)

Malawi. National Plan of Action in the Field of Human Rights (1995–1996) <http://www.ohchr.org/EN/Issues/PlansActions/Pages/PlansofActionIndex.aspx> accessed 7 May 2015

Mann M, *The Sources of Social Power: The Rise of Classes and Nation States 1760–1914,* volume 2 (1st edn, Cambridge University Press 1993)

Mann M, 'The Autonomous Power of the State: its Origins, Mechanisms, and Results' in J A Hall (ed), *States in History* (1st edn, Blackwell 1986) 109–36

Mann M, 'The Autonomous Power of the State: Its Origins, Mechanisms and Results' (1984) 25 Arch Eur Sociol 185–213

Marks SP, 'Human Rights and Development' in Sarah Joseph and Adam MacBeth (eds), *Research Handbook on International Human Rights Law* (1st edn, Edward Elgar Publishing 2010) 167–96

Marks SP, 'The Human Right to Development: Between Rhetoric and Reality' (2004) 17 Harvard Human Rights Journal 139

Marks S P, 'Obstacles to the Right to Development' (2003) 5:2–3 Harvard Human Rights Journals 2

Marrakech Statement on Strengthening the Relationship Between NHRIs and the Human Rights Treaty Body System, Marrakech, 9–10 June 2010

Marslev K and Sano H, 'The Economy of Human Rights: Exploring Potential Linkages between Human Rights and Economic Development' (2016) No 2, Matters of Concern, Human Rights Research Papers

Max-Neef M A, *Human Scale Development: Conception, Application and Further Reflections* (1st edn, Zed Books 1991)

McInerney-Lankford S, 'Human Rights and Development: a Comment on Challenges and Opportunities from a Legal Perspective' (2009) 1:1 Journal of Human Rights Practice 51

McKay A and Vizard P, 'Rights and Economic Growth: Inevitable Conflict or "Common Ground"?' (2005) Overseas Development Institute

McLaughlin J A and Jordan G B, 'Using Logic Models' in J S Wholey, H P Hatry, and K E Newcomer (eds), *Handbook of Practical Programme Evaluation* (2nd edn, Jossey-Bass 2004) 62–88

Mechlem K, 'Treaty Bodies and the Interpretation of Human Rights' (2009) 42 Vanderbilt Journal of Transnational Law 905

Melnychenko v Ukraine Application No 17707/02 (2004)

Mexico. National Program to Promote and Strengthen Human Rights (1998) <http://www.ohchr.org/EN/Issues/PlansActions/Pages/PlansofActionIndex.aspx> accessed 23 February 2014

Meyer J W and Rowan B, 'Institutionalized Organizations: Formal Structure as Myth and Ceremony' (1977) 83 Journal of Sociology 340–63

Meyerson M, 'Building the Middle-Range Bridge for Comprehensive Planning' (1956) 22(2) Journal of the American Institute of Planners 58 <http://www.tandfonline.com/doi/abs/10.1080/01944365608979224> accessed 23 August 2015

Milić T, International Convention for the Protection of All Persons from Enforced Disappearance, Vol LXII, br 1, str 37–64 Izvorni naučni rad Februar 2010

Miller D, *National Responsibility and Global Justice* (1st edn, Oxford University Press 2007)

Miller S and Fredericks M, 'Mixed-Methods and Evaluation Research: Trends and Issues' (2006) 16(4) Qualitative Health Research 567–79

Ministry of Constitutional and Legal Affairs, United Republic of Tanzania National Human Rights Action Plan 2013–2017 <http://www.ohchr.org/Documents/Issues/Education/Training/actions-plans/Excerpts/Tanzania_en%202013-2017.pdf> accessed 10 December 2017

Ministry of Human Rights, Government of Pakistan, Action Plan for Human Rights 2016 <http://www.mohr.gov.pk/userfiles/APBL.pdf> accessed 21 January 2018

Mission Statement of OHCHR (2000) <http://www.ohchr.org/EN/AboutUs/Pages/MissionStatement.aspx> accessed 12 May 2017

Mongolia- National Human Rights Action Programme of Mongolia (2003) <http://www.ohchr.org/EN/Issues/PlansActions/Pages/PlansofActionIndex.aspx> accessed 3 March 2012

Morgan J and Sun W, 'Corporations, Taxation and Responsibility: Practical and Onto-Analytical Issues for Morphogensis and Eudaimonia—*A posse ad esse*?' in M S Archer (ed), *Morphogenesis and Human Flourishing* (1st edn, Springer 2017) 185–211

Morijn J, 'Reforming United Nations Human Rights Treaty Monitoring Reform' (2011) 58:3 Neth Int'l L Rev 295

Mowbray A, *The Development of Positive Obligations under the European Convention on Human Rights by the European Court of Human Rights* (1st edn, Hart Publishing 2004)

Mumford S, 'Powers, Dispositions, Properties, or a Causal Realist Manifesto' in R Groff (ed), *Revitalizing Causality: Realism about Causality in Philosophy and Social Sciences* (1st edn, Routledge 2008) 139–51

Murray K, 'Do not disturb: "Vulnerable Populations" in Federal Government Policy Discourse' (2004) 13:1 Canadian Journal of Urban Research 50

Mutua M, 'Standard Setting in Human Rights: Critique and Prognosis' (2007) 29 Human Rights Quarterly 547–630

Nepal, Office of the Prime Minister and Council of Ministers Singh Durbar, National Human Rights Action Plan (2004) <http://www.ohchr.org/Documents/Issues/NHRA/Nepal_NHRAP.pdf> accessed 28 January 2018

Neurath O, 'Alternatives to Market Competition: Review of F. Hayek, The Road to Serfdom' (1945) The London Quarterly of World Affairs 121–22

Newman J, Constructing Accountability: Network Governance and Managerial Agency (2004) 19 Public Policy and Administration 17–33

Nickel J and Reidy D, 'Relativism, Self-determination and Human Rights' in D Chatterjee (ed), *Democracy in a Global World: Human Rights and Political Participation in the 21st Century* (1st edn, Rowman & Littlefield 2008) 91–109

Nickel J W, *Making Sense of Human Rights* (2nd edn, Blackwell 2007)

Nigeria- National Action Plan for the Promotion and Protection of Human Rights in Nigeria (2009–2013) <http://www.ohchr.org/EN/Issues/PlansActions/Pages/PlansofActionIndex.aspx> accessed 1 December 2017

North D, *Structure and Change in Economic History* (1st edn, Norton 1981)

Norway- The Norwegian Government's Action Plan for the Implementation of UN Security Council Resolution 1325 (2000) on Women, Peace, and Security <http://peacewomen.org/sites/default/files/norway-nationalactionplan_march2006.pdf> accessed 2 January 2015

Nowak M, *UN Covenant on Civil and Political Rights* (2nd edn, Engel 2005)

Nussbaum M, *Creating Capabilities: The Human Development Approach* (1st edn, Harvard University Press 2011)

Nussbaum M, 'In Defense of Universal Values' in C Wainryb, J Smetana and E Turiel (eds), *Social Inequalities, and Social Justice* (1st edn, Lawrence Erlbaum Associates (LEA) 2008) 209–34

Nussbaum M, *Frontiers of Justice: Disability, Nationality, Species Membership* (1st edn, Harvard University Press 2006)

Nussbaum M, 'Capabilities as Fundamental Entitlement: Sen and Social Justice' (2003) 9(2–3) Feminist Economics 33–59

Nussbaum M, *Sex and Social Justice* (1st edn, Oxford University Press 2000)

Nussbaum M, *Women and Human Development: The Capabilities Approach* (1st edn, Cambridge University Press 2000)

Nussbaum M, *Cultivating Humanity: A Classical Defense of Reform in Liberal Education* (1st edn, Harvard University Press 1997)

O'Brien C, Mehra A, Blackwell S, and Poulsen- Hansen C, 'National Action Plans: Current Status and Future Prospects for a New Business and Human Rights Governance Tool' (2016) 1 Business and Human Rights Journal 117–26

O'Flaherty M, 'The United Nations Human Rights Treaty Bodies as Diplomatic Actors' in M O'Flaherty, Z Kędzia, A Müller and G Ulrich (eds), *Human Rights Diplomacy: Contemporary Perspectives* (1st edn, Brill 2011) 155–71

O'Flaherty M, 'Reform of the UN Human Rights Treaty Body System: Locating the Dublin Statement' (2010) 10(2) Human Rights Law Review 319–35, 322

O'Flaherty M, 'Towards Integration of United Nations Human Rights Treaty Body Recommendations: The Rights-Based Approach Model' in M A Baderin and R MacCorquodale (eds), *Economic, Social and Cultural Rights in Action* (1st edn, Oxford University Press 2007) 27–45

O'Flaherty M, 'The Concluding Observations of United Nations Human Rights Treaty Bodies' (2006) 6(1) Human Rights Law Review 27–52

O'Flaherty M and O'Brien C, 'Reform of UN Human Rights Treaty Monitoring Bodies: A Critique of the Concept Paper on the High Commissioner's Proposal for a Unified Standing Treaty Body' (2007) 7:1 Human Rights Law Review 141–72

O'Neill W and Bye V, (2002) 'From High Principles to Operational Practice: Strengthening OHCHR Capacity to Support UN Country Teams to Integrate Human Rights in Development Programming'. Geneva, Consultancy report to the Office of the High Commissioner for Human Rights OHCHR

Oberman K, 'Immigration as a Human Right' in S Fine and L Ypi (eds), *Migration in Political Theory: The Ethics of Movement and Membership* (1st edn, Oxford University Press 2016) 32–57

Öcalan v Turkey Application No 46221/99 (2005)

OECD (Organization for Economic Cooperation and Development). 2009b. OECD Factbook 2009 <www.oecd.org> accessed 23 March 2011

Offe C, 'Civil Society and Social Order: Demarcating and Combining Market, State and Community' (2000) 41(1) European Journal of Sociology 71–94

Optional Protocol to the Convention on the Rights of the Child on the Involvement of Children in Armed Conflict, 12 February 2002, A/RES/54/263, Article 6

Ostry J, Berg A, and Tsangarides C, 2014, Redistribution, Inequality, and Growth, <https://www.imf.org/external/pubs/ft/sdn/2014/sdn1402.pdf> accessed 14 March 2016

Oxfam 2017 report released 16 January 2017 <https://www.oxfam.org.uk/media-centre/press-releases/2017/01/eight-people-own-same-wealth-as-half-the-world> accessed 29 January 2017

Oxfam 2018 report released 22 January 2018 <https://www.oxfam.org/en/pressroom/pressreleases/2018-01-22/richest-1-percent-bagged-82-percent-wealth-created-last-year> accessed 26 January 2018

Pal A, *Planning from the Bottom Up: Democratic Decentralization in Action* (1st edn, IOS Press BV 2008)

Papadopoulos F and Tsakloglou P, 'Social Exclusion in the EU: A Capability-based Approach' in F Comim, M Qizilbash, and S Alkire (eds), *The Capability Approach: Concepts, Measures and Applications* (1st edn, Cambridge University Press 2008) 268–309

Paris C, 'Introduction' in C Paris (ed), *Critical Readings in Planning Theory* (Pergamon Press 1982) 13–27

Patil S, Vieider F, and Tetlock P, 'Process versus Outcome Accountability' in M Bovens, R E Goodin, and T Schillemans (eds), *The Oxford Handbook of Public Accountability* (1st edn, Oxford University Press 2014) 69–90

Patton M Q, *Developmental Evaluation: Applying Complexity Concepts to Enhance Innovation and Use* (1st edn, The Guilford Press 2011)

Pauwelyn J, Wessel R, and Wouters J, 'The Stagnation of International Law', Working Paper No 97, Leuven Centre for Global Governance Studies, October 2012, Social Science Research Network <http://ssrn.com/abstract=2271862> accessed 23 April 2015

Pedone J and Kloster A, 'New Proposals for Human Rights Treaty Body Reform' (2012) 22 Journal of Transnational Law & Policy 29

Peet R and Hartwick E, *Theories of Development: Concepts, Arguments, Alternatives* (2nd edn, The Guilford Press 2009)

Pegram T, 'Regulatory Stewardship and Intermediation: Lessons from Human Rights Governance', The ANNALS of the American Academy of Political and Social Science, Vol 670, No 1, March 2017, 225–44.

Pellet A, 'The Function of the Right to Development: A Right to Self- Realization' (1984) 3 Third World Legal Studies, Article 9 <http://scholar.valpo.edu/twls/vol3/iss1/9> accessed 20 January 2012

Pholi K, Black D, and Richards C, 'Is "Close the Gap" a Useful Approach to Improving the Health and Wellbeing of Indigenous Australians?' (2009) 9:2 Australian Review of Public Affairs 1

Piketty T, *Capital in the Twenty-First Century* (1st edn, Harvard University Press 2014)

Piketty T and Atkinson A B, *Top Incomes: A Global Perspective* (1st edn, Oxford University Press 2010)

Pillay N, United Nations High Commissioner for Human Rights, Strengthening the United Nations human rights treaty body system A report by the United Nations High Commissioner for Human Rights, June 2012

Pillay N, United Nations High Commissioner for Human Rights, Dublin Statement, 19 December 2009

Pirson M, and Turnbull S, 'Toward a More Humanistic Governance Model: Network Governance Structures' (2011) 99 Journal of Business Ethics 101–14

Polish National Action Plan for the Implementation of the United Nations Guiding Principles on Business and Human Rights (2017–2020) <http://www.ohchr.org/Documents/Issues/Business/NationalPlans/PolandNationalPland_BHR.pdf> accessed 1 February 2018

Posner E, 'A Human Welfare, "Not Human Rights"' (2008) 108(7) Columbia Law Review 1758–801

Post-2015 Development Agenda: Guidelines for Country Dialogue, United Nation Development Group, June 2012

Powell W W, White D R, Koput K W, and Owen-Smith J, 'Network Dynamics and Field Evolution: The Growth of Interorganizational Collaboration in the Life Sciences' (2005) 110 American Journal of Sociology 1132–205

Provan K G, and Kenis P, 'Modes of Network Governance: Structure, Management, and Effectiveness' (2007) 18 JPART 229–52

Przeworski A, Alvarez M E, Cheibub J A, and Limongi F, *Democracy and Development: Political Institutions and Well-being in the World, 1950–1990* (1st edn, Cambridge University Press 2000)

Putnam R, *Bowling Alone: The Collapse and Revival of American Community* (1st edn, Simon & Schuster Paperbacks 2000)

Qizilbash M, 'Capabilities, Well-being and Human Development: A Survey' (1996) 33(2) Journal of Development Studies 143–62

Quaranta M, Concept Structures and Fuzzy Set Theory: A Proposal for Concept Formation and Operationalization, COMPASSS Working Paper 2010-62 <http://www.compasss.org/wpseries/Quaranta2010.pdf> accessed 18 September 2016

Ragin C, Fuzzy Sets: Calibration Versus Measurement, <http://www.u.arizona.edu/~cragin/fsQCA/download/Calibration.pdf> accessed 12 January 2018

Ragin C, *Redesigning Social Inquiry: Fuzzy Sets and Beyond* (1st edn, University of Chicago Press 2008)

Ragin C, *Fuzzy-Set Social Science* (1st edn, University of Chicago Press 2000)

Ranis G, Stewart F, and Ramirez A, 'Economic Growth and Human Development' (2000) 28(2) World Development 197–219

Rawls J, 'Social Unity and Primary Goods' in A Sen and B Williams (eds), *Utilitarianism and Beyond* (1st edn, Cambridge University Press 1982) 159–87

Raz J, *The Morality of Freedom* (1st edn, Oxford University Press 1986)

Reade E, *British Town and Country Planning* (Open University Press 1987)

Realizing Human Rights Through Government Budget, OHCHR, 2017, HR/PUB/17/3

Reif L C, 'The UN Guiding Principles on Business and Human Rights and Networked Governance: Improving the Role of Human Rights Ombudsman Institutions as National Remedies' (2017) 17:4 Human Rights Law Review 603

Reinicke WH and Deng FM, The United Nations, Networks, and the Future of Global Governance, IDRC 2000

Report of the Human Rights Committee, UN Doc A/59/40 (Vol I) sec76(10)

Republic of Chile, National Plan of Action for the Implementation of the UN Security Council Resolution No 1325/2000 (2009) <http://peacewomen.org/sites/default/files/chile_nap_2009_english.pdf> accessed 24 September 2017

Republic of Rwanda, National Action Plan 2009-2012, The United Nations Security Council Resolution 1325/2000 on Women, Peace and Security (2009) <http://peacewomen.org/sites/default/files/rwandan_national_action_plan_1325.pdf> accessed 21 January 2015

Republic of Turkey Prime Ministry: General Directorate on the Status of Women. National Action Plan: Gender Equality (2008–2013) <http://www.huksam.hacettepe.edu.tr/English/Files/NAP_GE.pdf> accessed 25 March 2016

Rhodes R, *Understanding Governance: Policy Networks, Governance, Reflexivity, and Accountability* (1st edn, Open University Press 1997)

Robeyns I, 'Capabilitarianism' (2016) 17:3 Journal of Human Development and Capabilities 397–414

Robeyns I, 'Sen's Capability Approach and Gender inequality: Selecting relevant Capabilities' (2003) 9(2–3) Feminist Economist 61

Rodley N, 'The United Nations Human Rights Council, Its Special Procedures, and Its Relationship with the Treaty Bodies: Complementarity or Competition?' in Kevin Boyle (ed), *New Institutions for Human Rights Protection* (1st edn, Oxford University Press 2009) 49–73

Rogers PJ, Petrosino A, Huebner T, and Hacsi T, 'Program Theory Evaluation: Practice, Promise, and Problems' (2000) 87 New Directions for Evaluation 5–13 <10.1002/ev.1177> accessed 25 January 2012

Rose-Ackerman S, *International Handbook on the Economics of Corruption* (1st edn, Edward Elgar 2006)

Rose-Ackerman S, *From Elections to Democracy Building Accountable Government in Hungary and Poland* (1st edn, Cambridge University Press 2005)

Rose-Ackerman S, *Corruption and Government: Causes, Consequences, and Reform* (1st edn, Cambridge University Press 1999)

Rothmann S and Hamukang'andu L, 'Callings, Work Role Fit, Psychological Meaningfulness and Work Engagement Among Teachers in Zambia' (2013) 33(2) South African Journal of Education 1

Ruggi J G, 'Global Governance and "New Governance Theory": Lessons from Business and Human Rights' (2014) 20(1) Global Governance: A Review of Multilateralism and International Organizations: January–March 2014, 5–17

Ruggie J G, Third United Nations Forum on Business & Human Rights Closing Plenary Remarks, Geneva, 3 December 2014 <http://www.ohchr.org/Documents/Issues/Business/ForumSession3/Submissions/JohnRuggie_SR_SG_BHR.pdf> accessed 24 December 2016

Ruggie J G, *Just Business: Multinational Corporations and Human* Rights (1st edn, W W Norton & Company 2013)

Salomon M E and Arnott C, 'Better Development Decision-making: Applying International Human Rights Law to Neoclassical Economics' (2014) 32(1) Nordic Journal of Human Rights 44–74

Sandercock L, *Towards Cosmopolis: Planning for Multicultural Cities* (1st edn, Wiley and Sons 1998)

Sayer A, *Methods in Social Science: A Realist Approach* (2nd edn, Routledge 2010)

Scanlon T, 'Preference and Urgency' (1975) 72 Journal of Philosophy 655–69

Schaber P, 'Human Rights and Basic Needs' in M Albers, T Hoffmann, and J Reinhardt (eds), *Human Rights and Human Nature* (1st edn, Springer 2014) 109–21

Schillemans T and Bovens M, 'The Challenge of Multiple Accountability: Does Redundancy Lead to Overload?' in M Dubnick and H Frederickson (eds), *Accountable Governance: Problems and Promises* (1st edn, Routledge 2011) 3–21

Schneider C and Wagemann C, *Set-Theoretic Methods for the Social Sciences: A Guide to Qualitative Comparative Analysis* (1st edn, Cambridge University Press 2012)

Schonwandt W, *Planning in Crisis? Theoretical Orientations for Architecture and Planning* (1st edn, Ashgate 2008)

Schwartz SH and Bilsky W, 'Toward a Theory of the Universal Content and Structure of Values: Extensions and Cross-Cultural Replications' (1990) 58(5) Journal of Personality and Social Psychology 878–91

Scotland's National Action Plan for Human Rights (SNAP) 2013–2017 <http://www.snaprights.info> accessed 8 October 2017

Searle J, *Making the Social World: The Structure of Human Civilization* (1st edn, Oxford University Press 2010)

Sen A, *Development as Freedom* (1st edn, Oxford University Press 1999)

Sen A, *Resources, Values and Development* (1st edn, Blackwell 1984)

Sengupta A, 'On the Theory and Practice of the Right to Development' (2002) 24:4 Human Rights Quarterly 837

Sengupta A, 'Fifth Report of the Independent Expert on the Right to Development', Submitted in Accordance with Commission Resolution 2002b/69 (UN Doc E/CN.4/2002/WG.18/6 and Add 1)

Sepulveda M, *The Nature of the Obligation under the International Covenant on Economic, Social and Cultural Rights* (1st edn, Intersentia 2003)

Seymour D and Pincus J, 'Human Rights and Economics: The Conceptual Basis for Their Complementarity' (2008) 26(4) Development Policy Review 387–405

Shields K, 'Ethical Trade Networks as a Catalyst for Corporate Compliance with Human Rights' in M Fenwick, S Van Uytsel, and S Wrbka (eds), *Networked Governance, Transnational Business and the Law* (1st edn, Springer 2014) 127–45

Shue H, *Basic Rights: Substance, Affluence, and US Foreign Policy* (1st edn, Princeton University Press 1980)

Sierra Leone- The Sierra Leone National Action Plan for the Sierra Leone National Action Plan for the Full Implementation of United Nations Security Council Resolutions 1325 (2000) and 1820 (2008) <http://peacewomen.org/sites/default/files/sierra_leone_nap.pdf> accessed 2 March 2016

Simmie J, *Planning at the Crossroads* (1st edn, Routledge 1993)

Sinha M K, 'Development at the Crossroads-Is Right to Development a Human Right' (2002) 42:4 Indian Journal of International Law 512

Skogly S, 'Extraterioriality: Universal Human Rights Without Universal Obligations?' in S Joseph and A McBeth (eds), *Research Handbook on International Human Rights Law* (1st edn, Edward Elgar Publishing 2010) 71–97

Skogstad G, 'Legitimacy and/or Policy Effectiveness?: Network Governance and GMO Regulation in the European Union' (2003) 10:3 Journal of European Public Policy 321–38

Smith J, 'A Critical Appreciation of the "Bottom-up" Approach to Sustainable Water Management: Embracing Complexity Rather Than Desirability' (2008) 13:4 Local Environment 353–66

Smithson M and Verkuilen J, *Fuzzy Set Theory: Application in Social Sciences* (1st edn, Sage Publications 2006)

Soja E, 'Planning in/for Postmodernity' in G Benko and U Strohmayer (eds), *Space and Social Theory: Interpreting Modernity and Postmodernity* (1st edn, Wiley 1997) 236–49

Sørensen E, 'Introduction Governance Network Research: Towards a Second Generation' in E Sørensen and J Torfing (eds), *Theories of Democratic Network Governance* (Houndmills: Palgrave 2007) 1–21

Sørensen E, 'Democratic Theory and Network Governance' (2002) 24(4) Administrative Theory and Praxis 693–721.

Sørensen E and Torfing J, 'Making Governance Networks Effective and Democratic through Metagovernance' (2009) 87(2) Public Administration 234–58.

South Africa. National Action Plan for the Protection and Promotion of Human Rights (1998) <http://www.ohchr.org/EN/Issues/PlansActions/Pages/PlansofActionIndex.aspx> accessed 9 May 2013

Spini D, Measurement Equivalence of 10 Value Types from the Schwartz Value Survey Across 21 Countries, Journal of Cross-Cultural Psychology, May 2003

Ssenyonjo M, 'Reflections on State Obligations With Respect to Economic, Social and Cultural Rights in International Human Rights Law' (2011) 15(6) The International Journal of Human Rights 969

Ssenyonjo M, 'Economic, Social and Cultural rights: An Examination of State Obligations' in S Joseph and A McBeth (eds), *Research Handbook on International Human Rights Law* (1st edn, Edward Elgar Publishing 2010) 36–71

Starmer K, 'Positive Obligations Under the Convention' in J Jowell and J Cooper (eds), *Understanding Human Rights Principles* (Oxford, Hart Publishing 2001) 139–59

Steets J, *Accountability in Public Policy Partnerships* (1st edn, Palgrave Macmillan 2010)

Steets J, 'Networks: Engaging Governance? The Case of Transparency International', Paper presented at the United Nations Interregional Workshop on 'Engaged Governance', Colombo, Sri Lanka, 9–11 December 2003

Steger M B, *Globalisation: A Very Short Introduction* (2nd edn, Oxford University Press 2008)

Steiner H J, 'International Protection of Human Rights' in M D Evans (ed), *International Law* (1st edn, Oxford University Press 2003) 784–814

Steiner H J, 'Individual Claims in a World of Massive Violations: What Role for the Human Rights Committee' in P Alston and J Crawford (eds), *The Future of UN Human Rights Treaty Monitoring* (1st edn, Cambridge University Press 2000) 15–53

Steptoe A, Shankar A, Demakakos P, and Wardle J, 'Social Isolation, Loneliness, and All-Cause Mortality in Older Men and Women' (2013) 110(15) PANS 5797–801

Stewart F, 'Basic Needs Approach' in David Alexander Clark (ed), *The Elgar Companion to Development Studies* (1st edn, Edward Elgar 2006) 14–19

Stewart F, *Planning to Meet Basic Needs* (1st edn, Palgrave Macmillan 1985)

Streeten P, Burki S, ul Haq M, Hicks N, and Stewart F, *First Things First: Meeting Basic Human Needs in Developing Countries* (1st edn, Oxford 1981)

Subedi S P, *The Effectiveness of the UN Human Rights System: Reform and the Judicialisation of Human Rights* (1st edn, Routledge 2017)

Susanti B, 'Constitution and Human Rights Provisions in Indonesia: An Unfinished Task in the Transitional Process' (2001) Paper presented at the Conference on 'Constitution and Human Rights in a Global Age: An Asia-Pacific History', Canberra, 30 November–3 December 2001.

Swaine A, 'Globalising Women, Peace and Security: Trends in National Action Plans' in S Aroussi (ed), *Rethinking National Action Plans on Women, Peace and Security, NATO Science for Peace and Security Series* (1st edn, IOS Publishing 2017) 7–29

Sweden. National Action Plan for Human Rights (2006–2009) <http://www.ohchr.org/EN/Issues/PlansActions/Pages/PlansofActionIndex.aspx> accessed 17 March 2015

Szreter S and Woolcock M, 'Health by Association? Social Capital, Social Theory, and the Political Economy of Public Health' (2004) 33(4) International Journal of Epidemiology 1, 650–67

Sztompka P, *Sociological Dilemmas: Toward a Dialectic Paradigm* (1st edn, Academic Press 1979)

Talbott W, *Human Rights and Human Well-being* (1st edn, Oxford University Press 2010)

Talbott W, *Which Rights Should Be Universal?* (1st edn, Oxford University Press 2005)

Tanzania. National Action Plan for Human Rights (2013–2017) <http://www.ohchr.org/EN/Issues/PlansActions/Pages/PlansofActionIndex.aspx> accessed 28 December 2017

Tashakkori A and Teddlie C, *Handbook of Mixed Methods in Social and Behavioral Research,* (1st edn, Sage 2003)

Tasioulas J, 'The Moral Reality of Human Rights' in T Pogge (ed), *Freedom from Poverty as a Human Right: Who Owes What to the Very Poor?* (1st edn, Oxford University Press 2007)

The Concept Paper on the High Commissioner's Proposal for a Unified Standing Treaty Body, 14 March 2006, HRI/MC/2006/2

The Federal Democratic Republic of Ethiopia, National Human Rights Action Plan 2013–2015 <http://www.ohchr.org/Documents/Issues/Education/Training/actions-plans/Excerpts/NHRAP%20Ethiopia%20Draft%20213-2015.pdf.pdf> 2 January 2018

The Federal Government of Somalia, Ministry of Women and Human Rights Development, Action Plan for the Implementation of the Human Rights Roadmap (HRRM) For Somalia 2015–2016 <http://www.ohchr.org/Documents/Issues/NHRA/Somalia_en.pdf> accessed 20 December 2017

The ILO (2014) Brief on the Protocol to the Forced Labour Convention, 1930 <http://www.ilo.org/global/topics/forced-labour/publications/WCMS_321414/lang--en/index.htm> accessed 9 November 2016

The New Zealand Action Plan for Human Rights (2005–2010) <http://www.ohchr.org/Documents/Issues/NHRA/New_Zealand.pdf> accessed 12 January 2018

The Parliamentary Human Rights Committee, The National Action Plan for Human Rights in Lebenon 2014–2019 <http://www.ohchr.org/Documents/Issues/NHRA/Lebanon_en.pdf> accessed 25 January 2018

The UN Committee on Economic, Social and Cultural Rights, 'An Evaluation of the Obligation to Take Steps to the 'Maximum of Available Resources' Under an Optional Protocol to the Covenant', Thirty-eighth session, 10 May 2007, E/C.12/2007/1

Thiem A and Dusa A, *Qualitative Comparative Analysis with R* (1st edn, Springer 2013)

Thomas MJ, 'The Procedural Planning Theory of A. Faludi' in C Paris (ed), *Critical Readings in Planning Theory* (1st edn, Pergamon Press 1982) 13–27

Tilley J, 'Cultural Relativism' (2000) 22(2) Human Rights Quarterly 501–47

Timmermans S and Tavory I, 'Theory Construction in Qualitative Research: From Grounded Theory to Abductive Analysis' (2012) 30(3) Sociological Theory 167–86

Ting-Toomey S, *Communicating Across Cultures* (1st edn, Guilford Press 1999)

Tistounet E, 'The Problem of Overlapping Among Different Treaty Bodies,' in P Alston and J Crawford (eds), *The Future of UN Human Rights Treaty Monitoring* (1st edn, Cambridge University Press 2000) 383–403

Tobin J, 'Justifying Children's Rights' (2013) 21(3) International Journal of Children's Rights 395–441

Tomuschat C, *Human Rights Between Idealism and Realism* (1st edn, Oxford University Press 2003)

Triandis H, 'Individualism-Collectivism and Personality' (2001) 69(6) Journal of Personality 907

Triandis H, *Individualism and Collectivism: New Directions in Social Psychology* (Westview Press 1995)

Trubek D, 'The Rule of Law in Development Assistance: Past, Present and Future' in D M Trubek and A Santos (eds), *The New Law and Economic Development A Critical Appraisal* (1st edn, Cambridge University Press 2006) 74–95

Trubek D and Mosher J, 'New Governance, Employment Policy, and the European Social Model' in J Zeitlin and D M Trubek (eds), *Governing Work and Welfare in a New Economy: European and American Experiments* (1st edn, Oxford University Press 2003) 33–58

Trubeck D, Cottell P, and Nance M, 'Soft Law, Hard Law and the EU Integration' in G de Búrca and J Scott (eds), *Law and New Governance in the EU and the US* (1st edn, Hart Publishing 2006) 65–79

Trubek D and Trubek L, 'Hard and Soft Law in the Construction of Social Europe: The Role of the Open Method of Co-ordination' (2005) 11(3) European Law Journal 343–64

Twomey P, 'Human Rights-based Approaches to Development: Towards Accountability' in M A Badering and R MaCorquodale (eds), *Economic, Social and Cultural Rights in Action* (1st edn, Oxford University Press 2007) 45–71

Uganda- The Republic of Uganda, The Uganda Action Plan on UN Security Council Resolutions 1325 and 1820 and the Goma Declaration (2008) <http://peacewomen.org/sites/default/files/uganda_nationalactionplan_december2008.pdf> accessed 12 September 2017

UN Commission on Human Rights, Report of the Special Rapporteur on violence against women, its causes and consequences, Yakin Erturk: Mission to the Russian Federation. E/CN.4/2006/61/Add.2.

UN Development Programme (UNDP). 2003. A Desk Study of National Human Rights Action Plans

UN General Assembly Second Optional Protocol to the International Covenant on Civil and Political Rights 15 December 1989, A/RES/44/128, article 7

UN General Assembly, 'International Convention on the Protection of the Rights of All Migrant Workers and Members of their Families', 18 December 1990, A/RES/45/158, art 3(3)

UN General Assembly, 'Optional Protocol to the Convention against Torture and other Cruel, Inhuman or Degrading Treatment or Punishment', 22 June 2006, A/RES/57/199

UN General Assembly, 'Second Optional Protocol to the International Covenant on Civil and Political Rights, Aiming at the Abolition of the Death Penalty', 15 December 1989, A/RES/44/128

UN General Assembly, Convention Against Torture and Other Cruel, Inhuman or Degrading Treatment or Punishment, 10 December 1984, United Nations, Treaty Series, vol 1465

UN General Assembly, Convention on the Elimination of All Forms of Discrimination Against Women, 18 December 1979, United Nations Treaty Series, vol 1249, 13

UN General Assembly, Convention on the Rights of the Child, 20 November 1989, United Nations, Treaty Series, vol 1577, 3 Art4

UN General Assembly, International Convention for the Protection of All Persons from Enforced Disappearance, 20 December 2006

UN General Assembly, International Covenant on Civil and Political Rights, 16 December 1966, United Nations, Treaty Series, vol 999, 171

UN General Assembly, Promotion and Protection of All Human Rights, Civil, Political, Economic, Social and Cultural Rights including The Right to Development Report of the Special Rapporteur on torture and other cruel inhuman or degrading treatment or punishment, Manfred Nowak, Mission to Indonesia, A/HRC/7/3/Add.7, 10 March 2008

UN General Assembly, Vienna Declaration and Programme of Action, 12 July 1993, A/CONF.157/23

UN Human Rights Council, No Real Will to Account: Shortcomings in Sri Lanka's National Plan of Action to Implement the Recommendations of the LLRC. A/HRC/21/NGO/72. 5 September 2012

UNDG Human Rights Working Group, 2003 The Human Rights Based Approach to Development Cooperation Towards a Common Understanding Among UN Agencies

UNDP, Human Development Report, 'Human Rights and Development' (2000) <http://hdr.undp.org/en> accessed 24 July 2009

UNESCO, Regional Overview: Sub-Saharan Africa <https://en.unesco.org/gem-report/sites/gem-report/files/157229E.pdf> accessed 28 January 2018

UNGA, International Convention on the Elimination of All Forms of Racial Discrimination, 21 December 1965, United Nations, Treaty Series, vol 660, 195

UNHRC, Report of the Human Rights Committee Seventy-ninth session (20 October–7 November 2003) Eightieth session (15 March–2 April 2004) Eighty-first session (5–30 July 2004) UN Doc A/59/40 (Vol I)

UNICEF, Report on Female Genital Mutilation <https://www.unicef.org/protection/files/00-FMGC_infographiclow-res.pdf> accessed 20 December 2017

United Kingdom, Good Business: Implementing the UN Guiding Principles on Business and Human Rights

United Nations Declaration on Human Rights Education and Training, GA Res (adopted by the Human Rights Council) UN Doc A/HRC/RES/16/1 (8 April 2011)

United Nations Development Programme, Development Effectiveness–Spotlight on performance: Why Some Countries Do Better Than Others, 2003

United Nations Human Development Report (Oxford University Press 1990) <http://hdr.undp.org/sites/default/files/reports/219/hdr_1990_en_complete_nostats.pdf> accessed 9 February 2014

United Nations Human Rights Council, 26/9 Elaboration of an international legally binding instrument on transnational corporations and other business enterprises with respect to human rights, Twenty-sixth session, 26 June 2014 A/HRC/RES/26/9

United Nations Human Rights Council, Report of the Working Group on the Universal Periodic Review: Australia, 24 March 2011, A/HRC/17/10

United Nations Human Rights Council, Special Representative of the Secretary-General, John Ruggie, Guiding Principles on Business and Human Rights: implementing the United Nations 'Protect, Respect and Remedy' framework, annexed to the Human Rights Council report A/HRC/17/31, 2011

United Nations Security Council, Resolution 1325 Adopted at its 4213th meeting, 31 October 2000 S/RES/1325

United Nations Security Council, Resolution 1889 Adopted at its 6196th meeting, on 5 October 2009 S/RES/1889

United Nations Security Council, Resolution 2122 Adopted at its 7044th meeting, 18 October 2013 S/RES/2122

United Nations Security Council, Resolution 2242 Adopted at its 7533rd meeting, 13 October 2015 S/RES/2242

United Nations Security Council, S/PRST/2016/9 (15 June 2016)

United Nations Security Council, S/PRST/2014/21 (28 October 2014)

United Nations Security Council, S/PRST/2012/23 (31 October 2012)

United Nations Security Council, S/PRST/2011/20 (28 October 2011)

United Nations Security Council, S/PRST/2010/22 (26 October 2010)

United Nations Security Council, S/PRST/2007/40 (24 October 2007)

United Nations Security Council, S/PRST/2007/5 (7 March 2007)

United Nations Security Council, S/PRST/2006/42 (26 October 2006)

United Nations Security Council, S/PRST/2005/52 (27 October 2005)

United Nations Security Council, S/PRST/2004/40 (28 October 2004)

United Nations Security Council, S/PRST/2002/32 (31 October 2002)

United States Census Bureau 2017 <https://www.census.gov/data/tables/time-series/demo/income-poverty/historical-poverty-thresholds.html> accessed 10 January 2018

UNOHCHR, Handbook on National Human Rights Plans of Action, 29 August 2002 <http://www.ohchr.org/Documents/Publications/training10en.pdf> accessed 24 January 2018

UNOHCHR, Consultation on treaty body strengthening with UN entities and specialized agencies, 28 November 2011

UNOHCHR, Strengthening the United Nations Human Rights Treaty Body System: A report by the United Nations High Commissioner for Human Rights, Navanethem Pillay, 26 June 2012, A/66/860 <http:// www2.ohchr.org/english/bodies/ HRTD/> accessed 29 October 2016

Unrau YA, Gabor PA, and Grinnell RM, *Evaluation in Social Work: The Art and Science of Practice* (4th edn, Oxford University Press 2007)

Uvin P, *Human Rights and Development* (1st edn, Kumarian Press 2004)

Vaghri Z, Arkadas A, Kruse S, and Hertzman C, 'CRC General Comment 7 Indicators Framework: A Tool for Monitoring the Implementation of Child Rights in Early Childhood' (2011) 10(2) Journal of Human Rights

VeneKlansen L and Miller V, *A New Weave of People, Power and Politics: The Action Guide for Advocacy and Citizen Participation* (2nd edn, World Neighbors 2007)

Verkuilen J, 'Assigning Membership in a Fuzzy Set Analysis' (2005) 33(4) Sociol Methods Res 462–96

Visser J, 'Neither convergence nor frozen paths: bounded learning, international diffusion of reforms, and the open method of coordination' in M Heidenreich and J Zeitlin (eds),

Changing European Employment and Welfare Regimes: The Influence of the Open Method of Coordination on National Reforms (1st edn, Routledge 2009) 37–61

Vizard P, *Poverty and Human Rights: Sen's Capability Perspective Explored* (1st edn, Oxford University Press 2006)

Vizard P, Fukuda-Parr S, and Elson D, 'Introduction: The Capability Approach and Human Rights' (2011) 12(1) Journal of Human Development and Capabilities

Vries P, *State, Economy and the Great Divergence: Great Britain and China, 1680s–1850s* (1st edn, Bloomsbury Publishing 2015)

Wakefield M, 'The International Human Rights Treaty System: Impact at the Domestic and International Levels' (2014) 21:1 Human Rights Brief 32–36

Weiss L, 'Infrastructural Power, Economic Transformation, and Globalization' in John A. Hall & R. Schroeder (eds), *An Anatomy of Power: The Social Theory of Michael Mann* (1st edn, Cambridge University Press 2006) 167–87

WHO/UNICEF Joint Monitoring Programme (JMP) Report 2017 (update) <http://www.unwater.org/new-publication-whounicef-joint-monitoring-programme-2017-report/> accessed 12 June 2017

Wholey J S, 'Exploratory Evalustion' in J S Wholey, H P Hatry, and K E Newcomer (eds), *Handbook of Practical Programme Evaluation* (3rd edn, Jossey-Bass 2010) 81–100

Wiggins D, *Needs, Values and Truth: Essays in the Philosophy of Values* (1st edn, Oxford University Press 1998)

Wiggins D, 'Needs, Need, Needing' (1987) 13 Journal of Medical Ethics 62–68

Wilikilagi V, What is Network Governance and its Implications for Public Policy Formulation? (23 October 2009) <http://dx.doi.org/10.2139/ssrn.1494757> accessed 23 April 2016

Williams B and Hummelbrunner R, *Systems Concepts in Action: A Practitioner's Toolkit* (1st edn, Stanford University Press 2011)

Woshinsky O H, *Explaining Politics Culture, Institutions, and Political Behavior* (1st edn, Routledge 2008)

D J Elazar, *American Federalism: A View from the States* (3rd edn, Longman Higher Education 1984)

Wright E O and Rogers J, *American Society: How It Really Works* (2nd edn, W W Norton & Company 2010)

Young I, *Justice and the Politics of Difference* (1st edn, Princeton University Press 1990)

Young K, 'The Minimum Core of Economic and Social Rights: A Concept in Search of Content' (2008) 33 Yale International Law Journal 113–75

Zadeh L A, 'Fuzzy Logic' (1988) 21(4) Computer 83

Zadeh L A, 'The Concept of a Linguistic Variable and its Application to Approximate Reasoning-I' (1975) 8 Information Sciences 199–249

Zagorski P W, *Comparative Politics: Constituity and Breakdown in the Contemporary World* (1st edn, Routledge 2009)

Zamria N and Abdullah L, 'A New Linguistic Variable in Interval Type-2 Fuzzy Entropy Weight of a Decision Making Method' (2013) 24 Procedia Computer Science 42–53

Zerk J, Corporate liability for gross human rights abuses: Towards a fairer and more effective system of domestic law remedies, A report prepared for the Office of the UN High Commissioner for Human Rights (OHCHR, February 2014)

Zimmermann H, *Fuzzy Set Theory and Its Applications* (4th edn, Springer 2001)

Index

The manufacturer's authorised representative in the EU for product safety is Oxford University Press España S.A. of el Parque Empresarial San Fernando de Henares, Avenida de Castilla, 2 – 28830 Madrid (www.oup.es/en or product.safety@oup.com). OUP España S.A. also acts as importer into Spain of products made by the manufacturer.

www.ingramcontent.com/pod-product-compliance
Lightning Source LLC
LaVergne TN
LVHW011754200926
848484LV00003B/700
* 9 7 8 0 1 9 8 8 2 2 8 4 4 *